Controlling Laughter

Controlling Laughter

POLITICAL HUMOR IN THE LATE
ROMAN REPUBLIC

Anthony Corbeill

PRINCETON UNIVERSITY PRESS

PRINCETON, NEW JERSEY

Library of Congress Cataloging-in-Publication Data

Corbeill, Anthony, 1960–
Controlling laughter : political humor in the late Roman
Republic / Anthony Corbeill.
p.   cm.
Includes bibliographical references and index.
ISBN 0-691-02739-0 (CL : alk. paper)
1. Rome—Politics and government—Humor.   2. Political
oratory—Rome.   3. Political ethics—Rome.   4. Politics and
culture—Rome.   5. Wit and humor—Social aspects.   I. Title.
DG82.C67   1996 320.937—dc20   96-868

This book has been composed in Bembo

Printed in the United States of America by Princeton Academic Press
1   3   5   7   9   10   8   6   4   2

To my parents

―――――――――――――

CONTENTS

ACKNOWLEDGMENTS

THIS BOOK began as a dissertation written for the Department of Classics at the University of California, Berkeley, under the direction of William S. Anderson, Erich Gruen, and Thomas Habinek. While at Berkeley I also benefited from discussions with Andrew Kelly, Annie Thrower, and Florence Verducci. Financial support for the final year of thesis writing was provided by a Charlotte W. Newcombe Dissertation Fellowship (Woodrow Wilson Foundation); occasional lunches and a stimulating exchange of ideas were supplied during that same year by a fellowship from the Townsend Center for the Humanities at Berkeley. I would like to thank both institutions for their generosity and support.

After completing my dissertation, a fellowship from the American Philological Association, sponsored jointly by the National Endowment for the Humanities and the Packard Foundation, introduced me to the rigors of philology as practiced at the *Thesaurus linguae Latinae* in Munich. Cornelis van Leijenhorst, my editor and friend in Germany, provided a special source of encouragement and expertise. I can only hope to have brought back with me to America at least a small portion of what I learned from my colleagues at the Thesaurus.

Back in the United States, the Graduate Research Fund at the University of Kansas provided generous financial support for revisions and additions made during the summers of 1992 and 1993. While I was preparing the manuscript for publication the following friends and colleagues read and commented at different stages on various parts: Anastasios Daskalopoulos, Judith Hallett, Peter Holliday, Karl Kirchwey, L. R. Lind, Stanley Lombardo, Andrew Riggsby, and Marilyn Skinner. I appreciate the time and suggestions of all and extend a separate thanks to Linda Montgomery for relief and to Craig Voorhees for hours worth of challenges. Two anonymous readers for the press also provided helpful suggestions. Final revisions of the manuscript were made during part of a nine-month stay at the American Academy in Rome in 1994/95, where I had the incomparable privilege of holding a Rome Prize funded by the National Endowment for the Humanities. My time in Rome benefited especially from conversations with, and encouragement from, Malcolm Bell III, John Clarke, and Nicholas Horsfall.

Four final expressions of gratitude: to Amy Richlin, for improving much of this book—if it is not better, that is because I have obstinately and perhaps unwisely stood by my own ideas; to Erich Gruen, a model as both a scholar and a teacher, who somehow seems always to have time for his students even after they are long gone; to Arthur Riss, who was present from the moment the idea for this project appeared in a Berkeley cafe through all the painful steps of writing and revision; and to Babette Crowder, for special support.

ABBREVIATIONS

Abbreviations for ancient authors can be found at the beginning of the "Works Cited" section.

CIL	*Corpus inscriptionum Latinarum.*
Foerster	R. Foerster, *Scriptores physiognomonici*, 2 vols. (Leipzig 1893).
Forcellini	A. Forcellini, *Totius latinitatis lexicon*, revised by V. De Vit, 6 vols. (Prati 1858–75).
FPL	C. Buechner, *Fragmenta poetarum Latinorum* (Leipzig 1982).
HRR	H. Peter, *Historicorum romanorum reliquiae* (Stuttgart 1967).
Kühner-Stegmann	R. Kühner, *Ausführliche Grammatik der lateinischen Sprache*, revised by C. Stegmann (Munich 1912–14).
LCL	Loeb Classical Library series of Greek and Roman authors.
LSJ	H. G. Liddell, R. Scott, and H. S. Jones, eds., *A Greek-English Lexicon* (Oxford 1968).
OCT	Oxford Classical Texts series of Greek and Roman authors.
OLD	P. G. W. Glare, ed., *Oxford Latin Dictionary* (Oxford 1982).
ORF	H. Malcovati, *Oratorum romanorum fragmenta liberae rei publicae* (Turin 1976).
PGM	K. Preisendanz, *Papyri Graecae Magicae: Die griechischen Zauberpapyri*, 2 vols. (Leipzig 1928–31).
RE	A. Pauly and G. Wissowa, eds., *Real-Encyclopädie der classischen Altertumswissenschaft* (Stuttgart 1894–).
SB	D. R. Shackleton Bailey, *Cicero's Letters to Atticus*, 7 vols. (Cambridge 1965–70); *Cicero, Epistulae ad Familiares*, 2 vols. (Cambridge 1977); *Cicero, Epistulae ad Quintum fratrem et M. Brutum* (Cambridge 1980).
Stangl	T. Stangl, *Ciceronis orationum scholiastae* (Leipzig 1912).
TLL	*Thesaurus linguae Latinae* (Leipzig 1900–).

Controlling Laughter

INTRODUCTION

> *Brian:* You've got to think for yourself! You are all
>   individuals.
> *Crowd:* Yes, we are all individuals!
> *Brian:* You are all different!
> *Crowd:* Yes, we are all different!
> *Voice from crowd:* I'm not.
>   —From Monty Python's *Life of Brian*

CICERO would not have gotten this joke; or at least he wouldn't have laughed. Pointedly absurd to a modern audience, the exchange manipulates a potential paradox inherent in any society that values individual expression. The more a community prizes individuality, the greater a role the concept of individuality plays in defining that community's goals. Yet when the expression of this ideal is taken to its extreme—that is, when group values become merely the sum of the contrasting values of the individual members—communality, of necessity, becomes difficult to locate. Individuality endangers the group, which must contain some common points of agreement to ensure cohesion. In the epigraph above, the voice from the crowd creates the outcast, paradoxically damning the speaker through the public affirmation of one of modern society's most fundamental values.

Cicero—as an orator shaping public discourse, as a politician developing public policy, as a thinker transmitting political and moral ideas—had an important stake in the relationship between individual and state. At a pivotal point in his treatise *On Moral Duties*, he asserts that "there should be one objective for all persons: that the interests of each individual and of the community as a whole be the same" (*unum debet esse omnibus propositum, ut eadem sit utilitas unius cuiusque et universorum; Off.* 3.26). Cicero's formulation initially strikes the modern reader as humanitarian, as a recognition of individual worth. But as the Monty Python skit illustrates so well, individuality is a culture-bound concept, and if community and individual are to share the same interests, the goals of at least one side must be compromised. In Cicero's subsequent discussion, it becomes clear that it is the *individual's* task to conform to the wishes of

the state. Monty Python's mockery of groupthink would have been lost
on Cicero; for he argues that it is only through the suppression of personal desire that individual and communal needs can merge. A tyrant's
murder is justifiable, for example, because he has put his own desires
before those of the community (*Off.* 3.29–32). Cicero does not explain
how to evaluate other, less extreme instances of individuality. There remains unanswered the question of how the individual citizen must be
defined in relation to other members of society and to the community at
large.

One can hardly expect prescriptive works such as *On Moral Duties* to
have much influence on the reality of the forum. But the converse is not
true: Cicero's philosophical notions do not arise in a political vacuum. To
examine the actual processes operating to define the Roman self, it is best
to turn to another Cicero, Cicero as orator. In the political discourse of
the late Republic, Romans define their civic status in part negatively.
Women, of course, play no significant role; indeed, in chapter 4 I discuss
how the conception of maleness and Romanness are inextricably linked.[1]
Among men, rhetoric as taught and practiced further defines the narrow
body of persons who constitute the elite: by demonstrating that an opponent behaves contrary to the well-being of the state, the orator can isolate
that opponent as an individual who has no place in society. In this book I
concentrate in particular on how political denigration is effected through
humorous invective. Laughter, even in an apparently innocent form, has
long been recognized by theorists as having "an unavowed intention to
humiliate, and consequently to correct our neighbor, if not in his will, at
least in his deed."[2] By removing the word "unavowed" from this formulation one finds an apt description of public humor in the late Roman
Republic. *Ad hominem* attacks characterize the bulk of political humor
during this period. A cursory reading of any of Cicero's invective texts—
the *Verrines* or *Philippics*, for example—leads one to suspect that humor
in Rome serves as a mechanism for public humiliation. An examination
of the only extant treatise on oratorical humor from the period—Caesar
Strabo's discussion in the second book of Cicero's *On the Orator*—
confirms that suspicion. By far the majority of political jokes from the
late Republic operate according to the principles Freud would later as-
cribe to the "tendentious" joke: "By making our enemy small, inferior,
despicable or comic, we achieve in a roundabout way the enjoyment of

---

[1] Hallett 1984: 4–8 surveys the limited legal and civic rights of women in Roman public
life. Following de Beauvoir's *The Second Sex*, Hallett 1989b explores the ways in which
Roman women were socially defined largely by reference to Roman men and speculates
that Roman women themselves consented to this mode of definition. Richlin 1992b offers
an analysis of "the maleness of Roman public speech" (1323).

[2] Bergson 148.

overcoming him—to which the third person, who has made no efforts, bears witness by his laughter."[3] The orator conspires with his audience to exclude the third person, the political opponent.

I shall argue throughout this book that aggressive humor exercises real powers of persuasion over a late Republican audience and that, as a cultural product, this humor also helped shape the ethical standards current during the politically convulsive period of the late Republic.[4] I stand firmly opposed to the two conventional scholarly explanations for the proliferation of abusive language in Roman oratory. The first asserts that public invective—filled with extravagant lies and unwarranted attacks—was unconstrained by what we would consider strictures of propriety.[5] There survives no evidence to back such a claim. In fact, one wonders whether a public sphere of activity can ever remain unaffected by forces within its own culture. The second common explanation contends that Roman invective represents an artifice borrowed wholesale from Greek tradition and that consequently an orator's audience was not expected to believe the charges it heard publicly advanced.[6] Such a theory can hardly be maintained, for it presupposes a Roman audience making legal and political decisions according to a system of beliefs to which it at best only partially subscribes. On the contrary, I wish to argue that the topics exploited in the political invective of this period participate in specific biases already present in Roman society. The persuasive power of humor lies not merely in the speaker's ability to relax and entertain the audience (*captatio benevolentiae*). Rather, within each instance of abuse reside values and preconceptions that are essential to the way a Roman of the late Republic defined himself in relation to his community.

Invective at Rome works within a wide political context, beyond the level of individuals. The phenomenon of exclusion observed by Freud can be applied to an entire community, for Roman humorous abuse cre-

---

[3] Freud 103.

[4] The first comprehensive attempt to locate humor as a prevalent force throughout Roman literature and culture is that of Saint-Denis, whose survey covers prose and poetry from Plautus to Hadrian. Other studies have focused on humor as a rhetorical device (Brugnola; Haury 1955) or as a means of understanding Cicero's personal psychology (Hands; Manzo). More recent works have examined Ciceronian invective in light of parallel literary phenomena in other genres, such as comedy and satire (Geffcken; Richlin 1992a). No one, however, has studied Roman humorous invective strictly within its social and political context.

[5] This argument is best represented by Syme 1939, especially chap. 11, "Political Catchwords": "In the allegation of disgusting immorality, degrading pursuits and ignoble origin the Roman politician knew no compunction or limit" (149).

[6] Jerome 50–65; R. Austin 52; Nisbet 1961: 192–96. Nisbet's discussion contains an interesting analysis of the literary precedents to Roman invective. I do not object so much to his own findings as to how subsequent scholars of invective cite them as proof of Roman oratory's lack of concern for "truth."

ates social norms by exposing the violators of those norms. Rome's humor of aggression caters to, in Cicero's words, "the interests of each individual and of the community as a whole" by simultaneously creating and enforcing the community's ethical values. Jokes become a means of ordering social realities. The process resembles the interaction between individual and society posited by recent "labeling" theories of social deviance: "social groups create deviance by making the rules whose infraction constitutes deviance, and by applying these rules to particular people and labeling them as outsiders. . . . The deviant is one to whom that label has successfully been applied; deviant behavior is behavior that people so label."[7] At Rome, deviant behavior is behavior that public speakers so define in their invective. As they label deviance through political humor, the positive values of society—the "proper" way to look and behave—become reinforced by contrast. In creating and maintaining the ideal society envisioned in *On Moral Duties*, Cicero's Rome does have access to a disciplinary mechanism: laughter.

In one of his *Moral Epistles*, Seneca discusses the importance of maxims (*praecepta*) for an ethical education. Taut, epigrammatic axioms appeal naturally to the human emotions, he argues, and hence ably facilitate the soul's pursuit of knowledge.[8] The preeminence of the maxim can be located in the more general aspects of Roman education as well, for the moralizing *sententia* played a central role in the tendency to instruct through exemplary tales (*exempla*). One recalls the idealized tradition propagated by the elder Cato, according to which children received moral instruction by listening to elders sing of the virtuous deeds of their ancestors.[9] Tales such as these were to form the basis of Roman education in the Republic and early Empire.[10] As a result, teaching through examples come to be portrayed as distinctly Roman, and threats to this tradition provoked Cicero's laments over the corruption foreign influences have wrought on the old Roman wit.[11] Given the value placed on *praecepta* and *exempla* in Roman education, it should come as little surprise that the three prominent shapers of Latin prose style and hence of Roman thought—Cato the elder, Julius Caesar, and Cicero—all relied on collections of other people's jokes and *sententiae* in their training as public

---

[7] Becker 9, as quoted in Schur 7.

[8] Sen. *Epist.* 94; see especially section 28: "maxims touch our very emotions, and are effective since nature is exercising its own force" (*adfectus ipsos ⟨praecepta⟩ tangunt et natura vim suam exercente proficiunt*); section 47: "maxims check and banish our emotions as if through force of law" (*praecepta, quae adfectus nostros velut edicto coercent et ablegant*).

[9] Cic. *Brut.* 75; *Tusc.* 1.3, 4.3; *De orat.* 3.197; Varro at Nonius pp. 77–78 (Mercerus); Hor. *Carm.* 4.15.29–32; Val. Max. 2.1.10.

[10] Maslakov contains the most recent thorough discussion. See also Marrou 234–36, 252–53; Quint. *Inst.* 12.2.30.

[11] As most clearly expressed in *Fam.* 9.15.2 (SB 196); cf. *Fam.* 7.5.3 (SB 26), *Brut.* 172; Hor. *Sat.* 1.7.32.

figures.[12] Nor is it surprising that the witticisms and maxims of these three men should also have been collected and circulated during or soon after their lifetimes.[13] I shall conclude this book by considering the sinister implications of one such collection. Julius Caesar, at the close of the civil war, sent spies to write down all the jokes that Cicero may have uttered throughout the course of his day, both in public and in private. Cicero's humor had clearly found a rapt audience—at least in the person of Caesar, who, after seizing the republic, wished also to control laughter, a means of communal expression not readily vanquished by arms. One can only wonder if similar motives of censorship drove Augustus to prohibit the dissemination of Caesar's own collection of jokes.[14] For, as I mentioned above and shall argue in detail below, the modes of humor prominent in late Republican political discourse do not provide space for a preeminent individual.

The writings of Cicero constitute, by necessity, the basis of this study. Yet this necessity is a welcome one, for not only was Cicero the most popular orator of his day and among the foremost practitioners of wit, but those speeches that have survived represent (not accidentally) his most successful efforts.[15] Even during the orator's lifetime it seems that his invective and humor were regarded both in the courts and at school as models for imitation.[16] And since, as Cicero himself says, "the aim of

[12] Cato's *apophthegmata*: Cic. *Off.* 1.104, *De orat.* 2.271; the collection most likely contained Greek maxims (cf. Plut. *Cat. Ma.* 2.4), but it is disputed whether Cato included any jokes of his own (Rossi 177–79, following Jordan cvi, argues against this notion, but her objections seem adequately met by Astin 188). Julius Caesar's *dicta collectanea*: Suet. *Iul.* 56.7, most likely to be identified at least in part with the collection referred to at Cic. *Fam.* 9.16.4 (SB 190); this assemblage, like Cato's, seems to have emphasized the maxims of others. Cicero: *De orat.* 2.216–90 adequately attests to the importance Cicero attached to humor as a persuasive tool; for his source material, see Rabbie 200–204.

[13] Cato: Jordan cites 67 distinct examples (cv–cvi, 97–111). Caesar: see Peter 853. At least three collections by his contemporaries seem to be attested for Cicero: one by P. Volumnius Eutrapelus (*Fam.* 7.32 = SB 113), a second by C. Trebonius (*Fam.* 15.21.2 = SB 207), and a third by his freedman Tiro (or perhaps someone else) in three books (Quint. *Inst.* 6.3.5; Schol. Bob. p. 140, 16–17 [Stangl]; Macr. *Sat.* 2.1.12); see also Quint. *Inst.* 8.6.73, Macr. *Sat.* 2.1.13.

[14] See Suet. *Iul.* 56.7, where Augustus also is said to have suppressed two of Caesar's youthful writings, a work in praise of Hercules and a tragedy *Oedipus*, presumably to preserve his adoptive father's literary reputation. Yet the *princeps* apparently did not reveal his motives—the letter forbidding publication was "short and sweet" (*brevem admodum ac simplicem*).

[15] See Crawford 3–16; Vasaly 8–10 argues for accepting the extant speeches as "documents of persuasion."

[16] Cic. *Ad Q. fr.* 3.1.11. Cf. also Cicero's own testimony at *Planc.* 35; on this same occasion his opponent Laterensis had tried to anticipate Cicero's jokes (85). Not everyone appreciated Cicero's wit, either among his contemporaries (Cic. *Phil.* 2.39; Plut. *Cic.* 27.1, 50.5 [with Leeman 216–17]) or among later critics (e.g., Sen. *Contr.* 7.3.9; Quint. *Inst.* 6.3.2–5, 12.10.12; Tac. *Dial.* 23.1; Plut. *Mor.* 803c, *Cic.* 5.6).

oratory is to win the approval of one's audience" (*effectus eloquentiae est audientium approbatio*; *Tusc.* 2.3), his success virtually ensures that the humorous appeals found in these oratorical texts articulate values and presuppositions present in the majority of his Roman audience.

I divide my initial discussion of political humor according to topics of abuse. These topics include the mockery of physical appearance (chapter 1); of names (chapter 2); of the mouth (chapter 3); and of association with feasting and effeminacy (chapter 4). These were the categories I found suggested most often by the surviving material. My analysis of each separate category begins, when possible, with examples of witticisms that Cicero identifies as humorous and effective in his discussion of humor in book 2 of *On the Orator*. By this empirical method, I am able to separate those areas that the Romans distinguished as constituting a subject of humor from those that merely provided matter for simple degradation (if indeed such a category as the latter even exists).[17] I also include in my analysis witticisms culled from the wider range of political discourse. Here I rely primarily on jokes found in oratory, but I also include, where applicable, jokes that survive in imperial authors and seem to date to the late Republic.[18] Passages from other Republican authors are also frequently cited to support or qualify my arguments.

My analysis of each specific object of abuse involves two distinct steps. First, I assess evidence outside of political discourse—from prayer ritual to philosophical treatises to physiognomic texts—in an attempt to locate independently the biases in Roman society that enabled the orator's jokes to persuade his hearers. My second step is to explore how the public speaker uses the medium of humor to articulate these predispositions into commonly acknowledged values. For example, when Cicero ridicules his opponent Vatinius for facial swellings, he appeals to a potential bias in Roman society to equate physical appearance with moral character, a tendency one finds confirmed in contemporary philosophical speculation. Through the course of the oration against Vatinius, Cicero exploits this cultural prejudice until it becomes a construct that his audience is compelled to acknowledge. It then becomes a moot point whether or not Vatinius can be shown to be in fact culpable of the fault Cicero constructs with his rhetoric. In other words, I do not wish to claim that

---

[17] In my belief that the most vigorous and moralistic denunciation gave pleasure to an audience and even aroused laughter I follow the observation of Frye 224: "It is an established datum for literature that we like hearing people cursed and are bored with hearing them praised, and almost any denunciation, if vigorous enough, is followed by a reader with a kind of pleasure that soon breaks into a smile."

[18] The most important sources for late Republican humor outside of Cicero are the collections preserved in Quint. *Inst.* 6.3, Plutarch's *Lives* (especially *Cic.* 25–27), and Macr. *Sat.* 2.1–7, 7.3.

Cicero's audience, if asked, would necessarily attribute Vatinius' despicable character to his physical appearance. For Vatinius' facial sores act not so much as a clear window to internal character as a text that Cicero interprets for his hearers. Cicero offers a reading of Vatinius' appearance for which contemporary cultural prejudices provide corroborative evidence. Vatinius' immoral character depends just as much on Cicero's ability to articulate for his audience its own bias against physical deformities as it depends on the actual appearance of Vatinius himself.

In each of the categories I discuss, the teller of the joke isolates his opponent by portraying him as an individual, as someone who stands at odds with acceptable Roman notions of the role of the self in society. Within every community, Nietzsche has claimed, objects of truth arise from social conformity, and human beings shape for themselves the categories of good and evil.[19] Roman society lacked the model of a single all-moral deity according to which ethical standards could be formed and enforced. As a result, the community had to collaborate in the labeling of deviance in order to define its own moral codes. In manipulating the beliefs of his Roman audience, Cicero was not blind to the role humor could play in this process of communal self-definition. At one point in *On the Orator*, he has Caesar Strabo remark that "no type of joke is such that stern and serious principles may not be drawn from the same source" (*nullum genus est ioci quo non ex eodem severa et gravia sumantur; De orat.* 2.251). Political humor, no less than serious political discussion, both creates and enforces a community's norms.

Chapter 1 treats the mockery of physical peculiarities. The first two portions of this chapter discuss the ethical biases underlying Roman invective. I then analyze Cicero's rhetorical treatises to explain how the mockery of physical deformities represents a socially acceptable means for the public castigation of an opponent. In this section I examine in particular passages from Cicero's philosophical and rhetorical works in order to distinguish between Greek and Roman views of personal responsibility for physical appearance. There emerges from this analysis a recognition that the Romans tended to view physical peculiarities as marking a deviation from humanity's natural state and, moreover, that the deformed individual is responsible for any physical peculiarity he bears. A deformity signals a moral fault and hence its bearer represents a potential threat to

---

[19] E.g., Nietzsche 151: "Fortunately I learned in good time to divorce the theological prejudice from the moral and no longer to seek the origin of evil *behind* the world. A certain amount of historical and philological training, together with a native fastidiousness in matters of psychology, before long transformed this problem into another, to wit, 'Under what conditions did man construct the value judgments of *good* and *evil*?'" (original emphases).

society. I conclude the chapter with a critical reading of passages from the speeches *On Behalf of Quintus Roscius* and *Against Vatinius*. In these two orations, Cicero exploits his audience's bias that a person's physical appearance can reveal moral character. Fannius and Vatinius are constructed as villains for whom external signs reveal internal corruption.

The mockery of physical peculiarities leads naturally into an analysis of the Roman cognomen, or surname. Varro "the knock-kneed," "squinty-eyed" Strabo, and "warty" Verrucosus all attest to the odd fascination the Romans had with labeling individuals according to their physical deformities. My second chapter explores the strong rhetorical force that the mockery of these surnames and other names possessed in the late Republic. I begin by outlining the peculiar nature of the Roman cognomen during this period: although commonly pejorative in meaning, the names are largely confined at Rome to members of the political elite. To explain this anomaly, I suggest that these names were used in earlier stages of the Republic to check families that were growing in size and importance. Support for this contention is sought in an analysis of the supernatural associations names carried in archaic and later Rome. In religious, military, and medical language, names and naming afford a speaker both contact with and power over supernatural elements. This power, conceived of as inherent in the word, informs the many puns on names that occur in political debate. The chapter closes with a selection from this material. Orators frequently mock names to reveal a character flaw in an opponent or to demonstrate why a person has failed to conform to the expectations raised by his name. The orator makes an appellation into a label that directs the Roman audience to read the moral contents of an individual in a particular way.

The next two chapters examine the Roman belief that, just as physical peculiarities could indicate character, so too certain affectations and acquired physical traits provide evidence for moral depravity. In chapter 3 I analyze jokes that center on the immoral behavior of the mouth (*os impurum*). In Roman invective, the mouth represented an area particularly charged with negative connotations. Various activities of the mouth—excessive eating and drinking, oral sex—are represented as performing a dual function: they both effect certain types of evil and, in so doing, transform the mouth into a sign of corruption visible to the properly discerning viewer. The exploitation of an opponent's mouth receives particular attention in Cicero's orations *Against Verres* (2.3) and *On Behalf of His Home*. After a close reading of these two works, I conclude by suggesting that this "morality of orality" does more than exclude from society those labeled corrupt. Emphasis on the mouth also allows members of the political elite to legislate the facial expression of the "proper" Roman.

Chapter 4 begins by focusing on the conventional signs to which an orator could appeal in order to implicate his opponent in the immoderate feast. As constructed by Roman rhetoric, the illicit banquet conjures up a bewildering variety of improper activities. To succeed in identifying an adversary as a participant in these banquets is to label him as one who neglects the proper functions of a Roman citizen. I concentrate especially upon how signs of the feast intersect with signs for effeminacy. The orator had access to a specific set of external indicators that he could exploit to demonstrate his adversary's lapse from proper male behavior. The strangely androgynous figure of the effeminate male appealed to Roman fears of the potentially unstable nature of masculinity. I conclude the chapter with Cicero's portrayal of Lucius Calpurnius Piso Caesoninus. The figure of Piso challenged those Roman representations of self that I discuss in my first four chapters. In physical appearance, name, and mannerisms, he seemed the model Roman; yet Cicero's attack on Piso shows how this exception does not undermine but rather supports the principles of humorous invective. Piso, he claims, has adopted commonly recognized signs of the proper Roman citizen in order to pervert them for his own insidious ends.

In chapter 5 I historicize my findings by linking the isolating tendencies of Roman humor to political events of the late Republic. The preceding chapters establish Cicero as the primary exponent of a traditional Roman wit. Yet alternatives existed to the ethical modes constructed by Cicero's witticisms. The military leaders Gnaeus Pompeius and Julius Caesar wield a brand of humor that tends to valorize the individual at the expense of traditional state structures. The clash of the differing modes of humor practiced by Cicero and each of these individuals results in attempts to censor Cicero's public employment of witticisms. In particular, a letter of Cicero demonstrates that Caesar as dictator recognized in the orator's humor a potential threat to the stability of his rule and that, as a result, he took steps to control Cicero's freedom of expression. In the final segment of this "Political History of Wit," I discuss the prominent role humor played in the final days of Cicero—and of the Republic.

Although the categories I treat in these chapters may strike a modern reader as peculiar and even immoral, I hope to demonstrate that they do constitute a clear and consistent code. A system of values underlies them, but the values belong to an elite that is small and powerful and that wishes to remain so. Other types of jokes that I shall not be discussing, such as the mockery of low-class birth and of non-Roman origins, also support an elite ideology. In these instances, the mechanisms for excluding persons from political power are more obvious. It is well documented how the urban aristocracy, through both legislation and more

covert means, continually maneuvered to stabilize social and political categories of birth and geographical origin.[20] The witticisms discussed in
the following chapters, however, do not have a clearly discernible correlation to social class and political power. Rather, the political abuse I
analyze—and the responsive laughter that continually endorses the content of that abuse—shapes an ideology of the body that Romans are able
to accept as objective reality.[21] In the following chapters, I show how a
trial audience laughs approvingly at the public mockery of a man's physique (chapter 1), how comic texts reaffirm aristocratic strictures concerning proper sexual behavior (chapter 4), and how a political rally de-
volves into public rebuke of a major political figure's personal life
(chapter 5).

Through the mockery of a deviant physique, name, appearance, or
gesture, the public speaker helps mark, and the public audience helps
reinforce, the bodily form and movement that are improper for the elite.
In so doing, the elite defines its boundaries and excludes those who vio-
late these socially constructed norms. And it would appear that the particular ideology promoted at Rome is peculiar to the capital city itself.
Our sources indicate that orators from the municipalities generally avoid
using any type of humor when speaking in Rome. This avoidance seems
to have two causes: in part, Roman humor has its own flavor, and so is
not readily accessible to a nonurbanite.[22] But more significant, I would
claim, is the fact that the humor traditionally employed in Rome's forum
originated in an elite "education"—and I use the word in the broadest
sense—to which municipal orators could not easily claim access.[23]

We hear diverse voices from the early Empire bewailing the decline of
moral standards, a lament that often links the loss of morality with a
lapse from the rhetorical standards maintained during the glory days of

[20] See Wiseman 1–5 (trials for corruption used to circumvent popular electoral legislation), 77–89 (social and legal stigma attached to lower-class occupations); Salmon 118–21
(political rivalries determining which Italians are admitted to citizenship); David 1983: 318–
22 (biases faced by newly arrived municipals in Rome); Vasaly 191–205 (Cicero's representation of non-Romans in his speeches *On Behalf of Fonteius*, *On Behalf of Scaurus*, and *On
Behalf of Flaccus*).

[21] I follow here Althusser's notion of ideology: "The ideological 'level' . . . represents an
objective reality: . . . that is, a reality independent of the subjectivity of the individuals who
are subject to it, even whilst it concerns these individuals themselves" (23).

[22] Cicero remarks in the *Brutus* on the "particular flavor" (*nescio quo sapore vernaculo*) of
native Roman humor (170–72). The elusiveness of taste at Rome is further attested by the
difficulty modern scholars have had in determining what precisely constitutes *urbanitas* (see
Ramage and the bibliography he cites).

[23] David 1983: 318–22 compiles evidence for this claim. Cicero, of course, provides a
notable exception. Part of his success in overcoming these obstacles surely lay in his self-
portrayal as a staunch defender of the status quo. Edwards 17 discusses the tendency of
Romans from the municipalities to maintain the sternest moral profile.

the Republic.[24] If one understands the role played by political invective in the late Republic, it becomes clear why the Romans linked morality and oratory. Invective reaffirmed publicly what was right and proper for the true, elite Roman. Morality, then, did not simply depend on oratory for its expression. It was through oratory that the Roman moral codes found constant confirmation.

[24] See Williams 1978: 6–51; Edwards 137–72.

Chapter 1

PHYSICAL PECULIARITIES

The skin, after all, is extremely *personal*, is it not? The
temptation is to believe that the ills and the poisons of
the mind or the personality have somehow or other
erupted straight out on to the skin. "Unclean!
Unclean!" you shout, ringing the bell, warning us to
keep off, to keep clear. The leper in the Bible, yes?
But that is nonsense, you know.
Do you know? Well—one part of you does, I'm sure.
—D. Potter, *The Singing Detective* 56

*sit . . . inscriptum in fronte unius cuiusque quid de re
publica sentiat.*

(Let it be inscribed on each individual's forehead what
that person thinks about the republic.)
—Cicero, *First Speech against Catiline* 32

THE DICHOTOMY of "nature" and "culture" has long oriented discussions
about the origins of ethical behavior. This division represents a conflict
over the extent to which human action is determined either by natural
causes or by socially constructed norms. From its ancient Greek formulation of *phusis* versus *nomos* ("nature" vs. "custom"), the opposition finds
its modern expression in the notions of essentialism and constructionism.
As in most dichotomies, however, the distinctions between the two
halves are more formal than real. Few so-called essentialists would say
that they believe social context exerts no influence on human behavior.
Similarly, it would be difficult (although perhaps less so) to find a con-
structionist who would be willing to deny that there exist among human
beings certain constants that are not culture specific.[1] In this book I adopt
an approach clearly sympathetic with constructionism. At least since
Nietzsche it has been commonly argued that ethical systems consist not
of stable entities but of socially constructed notions that the changing
needs of society are constantly shaping. My object then is to explore how

[1] Geertz offers an entertaining assessment of the issue; see also Boswell 1990. Fuss (esp.
1–21) analyzes the interdependence of the two concepts, arguing that "essentialism is *essential* to social constructionism" (1, original emphasis).

the dominant, elite culture at Rome during the period of the late Republic created and reinforced its own concept of "Romanness" through the use of public invective. I shall begin in this first chapter with a phenomenon common in humorous abuse, one often noted but seldom confronted by later admirers of Roman oratory: the public mockery of physical peculiarities. It would seem easy to cite this mode of humor as simply another example of constructed notions of the physical self: for example, that the Romans had valorized Greek aesthetics of form and proportion to such an extent that violation of these strictures became a permissible subject of abuse. Yet labeling this practice as simply cruel or unenlightened would be misguided. The Romans certainly recognized in this case a distinction between nature and custom, between natural law and human practice. It was, in fact, precisely this dichotomy that they attempt to mediate in their discussion of physical appearance.

Natura—"nature"—was a slippery term. In a public context, it could denote the character peculiar to an individual, a character that determines one's actions ("that's in his nature"). According to this conception of nature, human behavior is not fixed. Hence any person's inborn qualities, when represented in the courtroom, could vary from positive to negative, depending on whether a speaker wished to attach praise or blame to his subject. In the closing sentences of his defense of Sextus Roscius, for example, Cicero asserts how he and his audience are "*naturally* very gentle" (*natura mitissimi*; *S. Rosc.* 154); a passage from a speech against Verres, in contrast, finds the word *natura* bearing responsibility for continual wrongdoing ("this *natura*, which has committed so great a crime"—*ea natura quae tantum facinus commiserit*; *Verr.* 2.1.40).[2] In public depictions of personal responsibility, *natura* is fickle and capricious, its activities ranging from humanitarian sympathy to wicked crime.

When occurring in a philosophical and moral context, however, *natura* usually denotes a divine agent. This version of nature as fixed and constant creates standards of appearance and behavior—"for what is *natura* other than god and divine reason?"[3] As a result of nature's preeminence, there arises the common practice of appealing to nature to make moral distinctions. Any deviation from the rules of nature is "unnatural" in the strictest sense of the word. From a moral standpoint, then, the Roman conception of physical appearance can be viewed as very much a conscious construction, predicated on the desire to fuse natural law and cultural practice. Nature, endowed by philosophers with complete perfection, becomes the touchstone for determining deviance. In the case of the

[2] For other appeals to the positive actions of *natura*, see, e.g., *Clu.* 200, *Sull.* 73, *Lig.* 38; for *natura* denoting a morally corrupt character, *Clu.* 46, *Sull.* 71, *Pis.* 27.

[3] Sen. *Ben.* 4.7.1: *quid enim aliud est natura quam deus et divina ratio?* Cf. Cic. *Leg.* 1.26–30 and Kenter on *Leg.* 1.16.

Roman practice against physical peculiarities, therefore, one can recognize the workings of a "constructed essentialism." To justify the attendant ethical construct—that physical appearance provided indications of moral character—appeals were made to essentializing notions of the theoretical perfection of nature. A naturally beautiful physique bespoke a morally sound interior. This fusion of nature and custom, of physical beauty and ethical norms, provides a necessary foundation for rhetorical invective. For the existence of a human community, as constructed by public figures at Rome, depended on the identification of soul with body, on the ability to recognize the workings of nature in the very face of the citizen.

THE NATURE OF ROMAN ORATORICAL INVECTIVE

Before I examine the particular case of the mockery of physical peculiarities, it will be useful to outline how speakers at Rome defined for themselves the basic character of humorous invective. There is no question that the audience's admiration of a clever turn of phrase or of a particularly witty comeback constituted a part of the orator's success. I shall not, however, be concerned with the strictly rhetorical aspect of these moves, maneuvers to which rhetoricians and scholars have directed their attention from Greek antiquity to the present.[4] Rather, I shall concentrate on the assumptions that the extant texts never explicitly address, the unstated biases to which invective makes its appeal and by which it is justified. Even those attacks that seem most cruel and unprovoked find their origin in the ethical considerations that a skillful speaker was able to compel his Roman audience to recognize.

The modern reader of Roman oratory cannot fail to be struck by both the omnipresence and caustic character of Roman invective. In his rhetorical treatises, Cicero does not equivocate in recommending attacks on character. In *On the Orator*, the abuse of an opponent ranks equally with the favorable representation of a speaker and his client:

> valet igitur multum ad vincendum probari mores et instituta et facta et vitam eorum, qui agent causas, et eorum, pro quibus, et item improbari adversariorum. (*De orat.* 2.182)

> In persuading successfully, it is very important that the character, principles, actions, and way of life be approved of both those who will plead the case as

---

[4] The most important ancient discussions are in Aristotle's *Rhetoric* 2, Cicero's *On the Orator* 2, and Quintilian's *Institutes* 6. M. Grant provides a convenient overview of these treatises. For Cicero in particular, see Haury 1955.

well as those on behalf of whom [the case will be spoken], and that likewise [the corresponding traits] of one's opponents be exposed to disapproval.

To point up the faults of the opposition constitutes legitimate oratorical practice. The principle applies here to speakers for both defense and prosecution (*De orat.* 2.183). In his speech on behalf of Murena, Cicero concentrates specifically upon how the opposing prosecutor has attacked Murena's character. In referring to the earlier speech of this prosecutor, Cicero provides general remarks on the application of personal invective (*reprehensio vitae*):

> quae gravissima debebat esse ita fuit infirma et levis ut illos lex magis quaedam accusatoria quam vera male dicendi facultas de vita L. Murenae dicere aliquid coegerit. (*Mur.* 11)

> That which ought to have been the weightiest [part of the charge] was so weak and slight that it was a kind of "rule of the prosecution" (*lex accusatoria*) rather than any real opportunity for slandering that compelled them to say anything at all about Lucius Murena's life.

Cicero claims that his client Murena stands free from blame and so he attributes any abuse on the prosecution's part to a kind of pro forma exercise. Yet even if one allows for hyperbole here, the force of the word *lex* ("rule") attests to the frequency and, presumably, efficacy of such tactics. In fact, nowhere in his writings on oratory does Cicero question the relevance an *ad hominem* attack might have to the case at hand.[5]

Part of the accuser's skill depends upon his ability to expose the faults of a defendant without slipping into slander. In a context similar to that of the passage cited above, Cicero finds himself in his speech *On Behalf of Caelius* having to refute the accusations of the young prosecutor Atratinus. His remarks show that the Romans observed limitations on how far one could go in reproaching another person's way of life:

> sed aliud est male dicere, aliud accusare. accusatio crimen desiderat, rem ut definiat, hominem notet, argumento probet, teste confirmet; maledictio autem nihil habet propositi praeter contumeliam; quae si petulantius iactatur, convicium, si facetius, urbanitas nominatur. (*Cael.* 6)

> But it's one thing to slander, another to accuse. Accusation needs a charge so that it may define the matter at hand, censure the person [accused] (*hominem notet*), make a demonstration through a proof, and confirm through witnesses. Slander on the other hand has no agenda other than insulting

---

[5] Stroh 252–53.

language, which, if bandied about rather recklessly, is called abuse, if rather
wittily, clever elegance.

Few commentators on this passage fail to note that the facts of Caelius'
case compel Cicero to condemn here what he himself often practices
elsewhere.[6] But the distinction Cicero describes between slander and a
proper accusation has not been entirely fabricated for the occasion. The
passages I have cited from *On the Orator* and *On Behalf of Murena*, as well
as the many examples from the speeches that I shall quote below, all
confirm that at least some types of abusive language were expected and
even encouraged on the part of counsels for both the prosecution and
defense. And in fact Cicero's remarks here do not exclude the possibility
of a vehement attack on character. As defined in this passage, a legitimate
accusation (*accusatio*) includes censure of the accused. The phrase *ut . . .
hominem notet* ("to censure the person accused") derives from the reproof
employed by a magistrate, especially a censor, against citizens leading an
illicit lifestyle.[7] Such a formulation provides the orator with a legitimate
pretext to reproach an opponent's character vigorously. Hence Cicero's
definition of an accusation here makes ample allowance for *contumelia*—
what one might term "abusive language." Only one precondition exists:
a charge to justify the abuse (*accusatio crimen desiderat*).[8] To understand the
circumstances informing Roman invective, therefore, it is necessary to
concentrate on what constitutes a legitimate charge. It is here, and not
simply in the language of abuse, where justification for invective is
located.

On those occasions when Cicero chose to take on a role less familiar to
himself—that of accuser—he appears on first inspection to have ignored
any standards of discretion. Harsh invective flourishes in the speeches
against Verres, Piso, Vatinius, and Marcus Antonius. In the vivid conclusion of his scathing invective *Against Piso*, Cicero describes the effects the
speech has had on his opponent. Properly employed, invective disables
its target, marking him as unfit for human society.

---

[6] R. Austin ad loc.: "Cicero's audience when he delivered the speech *In Pisonem* a year
later might justifiably have reminded him of his present remarks."

In *On Behalf of Murena*, Cicero makes a distinction similar to the one cited from *On
Behalf of Caelius*: "if one attacks truthfully, it is the slander (*maledictum*) of a forceful accuser;
but if [one attacks] falsely, [this is the slander] of a slandering slinger of abuse" (*maledictum
est, si vere obicitur, vehementis accusatoris; sin falso, maledici conviciatoris*; *Mur.* 13).

[7] For the phrase *aliquem notare* in reference to the censors, see *Clu.* 119, 130; *Sest.* 101;
Mil. 31. For passages outside of Cicero, see Forcellini, s.v. *noto* II 3, 4.

[8] *Contumelia* is a practice accessible to the orator elsewhere. Quintilian includes among
his four classes of jokes the *contumeliosum genus*; cf. also *De orat.* 2.222, where Crassus deems
his opponent Brutus "worthy of *contumelia*."

numquam ego sanguinem expetivi tuum: numquam illud extremum, quod posset esse improbis et probis commune supplicium legis ac iudicii; sed abiectum, contemptum, despectum a ceteris, a te ipso desperatum et relictum, circumspectantem omnia, quidquid increpuisset, pertimiscentem, diffidentem tuis rebus, sine voce, sine libertate, sine auctoritate, sine ulla specie consulari, horrentem, trementem, adulantem omnes, videre te volui; vidi. (*Pis.* 99)

For my part, I never sought to draw your blood: I never sought the ultimate punishment of the law and courtroom, a punishment which can be shared by the good and evil alike; instead I wanted to see you spurned, rejected, and scorned by everyone else while forsaken and abandoned by yourself; I wanted to see you looking around at everything, starting at the slightest noise, having no confidence in your own resources as you lack voice, freedom, authority, and any resemblance to one of consular rank; shivering, trembling, fawning upon all others, that is how I wanted to see you; and this is what I have seen.

Despite its scornful character, this passage reveals that Roman invective has what I would call an ethical basis. The orator reserves his contempt for the evil citizen; invective provides a kind of supplement to normal legal proceedings. The language of *Against Piso* does more than expose Piso's criminality, however. It makes Piso the object of all Rome's contempt, a man deprived of the attributes proper to a free Roman citizen, a man who virtually becomes a fearful and shivering beast. Invective maintains the distinction between what is proper for a Roman citizen and what is not. Such use of language as an extralegal means of enforcing moral codes can be compared to the archaic Roman practice of *flagitium* (or *flagitatio*), in which socially unacceptable—but not strictly illegal—acts were exposed to public defamation.[9] When effectively employed, this form of public exposure could destroy the social position of a citizen.[10] Despite apparent legislation to curtail the employment of *flagitium*, the practice proved so effective that, as references in Republican authors indicate, some forms survived to Cicero's day.[11] Both oratorical invective and *flagitium* arise from similar motivations: to regulate types of social behavior that stand outside the purview of formal legislation. Through-

---

[9] Usener, conveniently summarized in Kelly 1966: 21–23. The effectiveness of these verbal censures may ultimately derive from an archaic notion that curses can inflict direct physical harm—indeed, a comparison of the *Against Piso* passage cited in the text with Archilochus frag. 79a (Diehl) seems to indicate a common lineage; cf. Elliott 3–48, who discusses curse literature among the Greeks, Arabs, and Irish.

[10] Fraenkel 1925: 198.

[11] Usener 18–28; cf. Fraenkel 1961.

out this book I shall be exploring how the aggressive tendencies of Roman humor play a crucial role in effecting moral denigration and, thereby, in maintaining ethical and social distinctions.

If the Romans used invective as an extralegal means of enforcing social codes, how then do conceptions of the body tie in with these discursive practices? Roman rhetorical treatises, the distillation of what was taught to the aspiring orator, provide the first step toward understanding the relationship between natural law and oratorical practice.

PHYSICAL PECULIARITIES: *ON THE ORATOR* AND ROMAN REALITIES

In the year 55 BCE, political circumstances provided Cicero with the opportunity of composing a new rhetorical work to supersede the handbook of his youth, *On Rhetorical Invention (De inventione)*. He intended his new work to go beyond the almost slavish adherence to Hellenistic precedents that typified both this earlier treatise—a work he may never even have wanted published[12]—and similar works such as *Rhetorica ad Herennium*. *On the Orator (De oratore)*, a dialogue in three books, was to convey Cicero's own mature understanding of the importance of oratory in the Roman world. The author's ideal orator finds a model less in Aristotle's *Rhetoric* than in Plato's philosopher-king: "no one can be an orator equipped with every praiseworthy attainment unless he has first acquired a knowledge of all important affairs and skills" (*nemo poterit esse omni laude cumulatus orator, nisi erit omnium rerum magnarum atque artium scientiam consecutus*; *De orat.* 1.20). In keeping with the Roman conception of the dialogue, Cicero posits as its chief interlocutors the three greatest orators of the previous generation: Lucius Licinius Crassus and Marcus Antonius, between whom Cicero was unable to decide who possessed greater eloquence (*Brut.* 143, 186), and Julius Caesar Strabo, a speaker whose reputation was exceeded only by these two more experienced orators (*Brut.* 207). Cicero attributes to these men an authority in rhetorical matters that surpasses even the most learned Greek teachers (*De orat.* 1.23). The author, the subject, and the interlocutors of Cicero's dialogue *On the Orator* all promise a work that will be the consummate expression of the Roman orator's role in his society.

It is Caesar Strabo to whom Cicero assigns the task of discussing the role of wit in Roman oratory. He reluctantly agrees: "But I do think that a man who is the slightest bit charming can discourse more wittily on any other topic than wit itself" (*ego vero . . . omni de re facetius puto posse ab homine non inurbano, quam de ipsis facetiis disputari*; *De orat.* 2.217). The

---

[12] If, as seems likely, Cicero's words in the preface to *On the Orator* refer to *On Rhetorical Invention (De orat.* 1.5). See also *De orat.* 1.23, 2.117 (Antonius speaking); Quint. *Inst.* 3.5.15.

topic of wit does not in itself represent a novelty; humor had long been employed by orators and prescribed by handbooks as a means of obtaining the favor of an audience and of thereby satisfying the traditional threefold injunction that oratory should not only persuade and instruct (*movere, docere*) but also entertain (*delectare*).[13] Yet Strabo's lengthy discussion, covering more than thirty pages in our modern texts, contains two important innovations over previous treatises on rhetorical wit. First, Strabo stresses the applicability of his remarks to everyday speech:

> et hercule omnia haec, quae a me de facetiis disputantur, non maiora forensium actionum quam omnium sermonum condimenta sunt. (*De orat.* 2.271)

> And in fact all these things I am arguing about wit give no more spice to cases conducted in the forum than to all types of daily conversation.

This remark suggests that Strabo's discourse will provide insight into the nature of Roman humor as commonly practiced among aristocrats during the late Republic. It thus comes as a surprise to contemporary readers when Strabo's discussion offers its second innovation to previous treatises on rhetorical wit: he includes among the acceptable subjects of humor the mockery of an individual for his physical deformities.[14]

---

[13] The extant works of Aristotle do not contain a complete discussion of the rhetorical use of wit, but he clearly implies its importance in the orator's manipulation of *ethos* and *pathos*; see M. Grant 24–32.

I use with caution the words "novelty" and "innovation" in the subsequent discussion; M. Grant 71 points out that Cicero never cites a source for his discussion at *On the Orator* 2.216–40 and that any sources may well be lost. The two points I consider innovations, however—the application of humor to everyday speech and the liberty to abuse any physical deformity—occur neither in the relevant works that precede nor in those that follow *On the Orator* (e.g., Plut. *Mor.* 612c–748d and Macrobius' *Saturnalia*). Cicero appears to stand outside the tradition on these two points.

Quellenforschung is of especially dubious value here. Arndt (esp. 25–40) has traced Strabo's discussion back to a lost Peripatetic work (perhaps Demetrius Phalereus' *On Laughter*), which derives from a lost work of Theophrastus, which is in turn indebted to Aristotle, primarily the lost second book of *Poetics*. Yet even Arndt cannot find precedents for the two passages I discuss below in the text (*De orat.* 2.239, 271). At one point in his discussion he concedes, despite his own efforts to the contrary, that "no one will be so stupid as to deny that a very funny man [i.e., Cicero] added something of his own" (*nemo erit tam stultus ut neget virum facetissimum quicquam de suo adiecisse*; 36).

[14] Commentators often cite at this point Aristotle's ostensibly parallel statement in *Poetics* that "the laughable is a species of the ugly"—τοῦ αἰσχροῦ ἐστι τὸ γελοῖον μόριον (5.1449a32–34; cf. Plato *Phil.* 48–50, *Rep.* 5.452d–e). But as the surrounding context makes clear, Aristotle is thinking here primarily of *morally* base actions and actors (μίμησις φαυλοτέρων), and not physical ugliness (the same can be said for the Plato passages cited). Although it is true that the only example the philosopher gives of this category of the laughable is a grotesque comic mask (τὸ γελοῖον πρόσωπον αἰσχρόν τι καὶ διεστραμμένον ἄνευ ὀδύνης; *Poetics* 5.1449a34–37), one cannot infer from this that Aristotle would condone the mockery of physical deformities in the same way Cicero does. In the *Poetics* exam-

Context heightens the surprise. Strabo has just been outlining the limitations of rhetorical humor (*quatenus autem sint ridicula tractanda oratori*; *De
orat.* 2.237): a speaker should not mock either popular personages, serious criminals, or victims of excessively bad luck.[15] One would expect
this last group of persons, namely, those who have suffered great misfortune, to include the physically deformed. But Strabo continues; he ap-
pends a fourth category, one that does not, as do these previous three areas,
provide for a restriction but rather describes an allowable space for wit.
The description of this new category is itself expressed with a wordplay:[16]

est etiam deformitatis et corporis vitiorum satis bella materies ad iocandum.
(*De orat.* 2.239)

The deformity and faults of the body also provide some quite "pretty" material for jokes.

A cursory examination of the poetry of Catullus or of the Ciceronian
corpus—including not only the orations but also his correspondence and
even the philosophical works—provides sufficient examples of the
mockery of physical deformities to indicate that such remarks pervaded
the humorous discourse of the upper classes at Rome.[17] The mockery
itself may not surprise the modern reader—consider the political carica-
tures that appear daily alongside newspaper editorials. Yet the directness
with which Strabo introduces this new category, following as it does a
careful delineation of how the orator should avoid mocking the unfortunate, indicates that the Romans could conceive of bodily deformities as a
category separate from accidents of nature.

Ciceronian scholarship of the previous two centuries has taken two
basic approaches to the problem of jokes on physical deformities: an ex-

---

ple, the wearer does not bear personal responsibility for the ugliness of his mask and so the
laughter arising from its appearance is directed not at the person but at the mask itself; cf.
Janko 209, who discusses the "new detail" added by the *Tractatus Coislinianus* to Aristotelian
theory: ὁ σκώπτων ἐλέγχειν θέλει ἁμαρτήματα τῆς ψυχῆς καὶ τοῦ σώματος ("The joker
aims to expose faults of mind and body"; [5] VIII = Janko 36–37). This important Aristotelian distinction between what aspects of one's appearance an individual is and is not
accountable for—a distinction not recognized by Strabo in his discussion of wit—will be
referred to again below.

15 Cf. *Orat.* 88; Quint. *Inst.* 6.3.31. I follow Rabbie ad loc. in his interpretation of *caritati
hominum.*

16 Pack, assuming that "physical blemishes surely fall under the head of misfortunes"
(407), concludes that Cicero here draws on another source without recognizing that *De orat.*
2.239 "contradicts the preceding." My discussion rescues Cicero in this case from the frequently unjustified accusation of being a mere copyist.

17 I do not discuss directly those poems of Catullus that contain mockery of physical
deformities. For a short but insightful analysis of some of these poems using the line of
argument I employ below, see Cèbe 1967: 174–78.

pression of simple and direct disapproval—which ranges from regret to contempt, depending upon the degree of admiration felt for the orator— or an attempt to redeem Cicero by pointing to his inability to escape from a strong, Hellenic rhetorical tradition. These two alternatives represent roughly a chronological division between scholars of the nineteenth and early twentieth centuries and those of approximately the past fifty years. A brief survey of their opinions will help situate my own approach toward this mode of invective.

In their edition of Cicero's correspondence, Tyrrell and Purser display the normal nineteenth-century reaction when they attribute the widespread abuse of Vatinius' physical deformities to "the lack of refinement of the age," a time when such remarks "were considered not merely allowable, but even witty" (5:xcv). Another prominent Ciceronian, who produced the only complete English commentary on Cicero's speeches, refers to the abuse levied on Vatinius' facial sores as "Cicero's disgraceful practice."[18] Other editors attempt greater objectivity, but clearly they too find it difficult to avoid reprimanding Cicero for this type of abuse. The same passage concerning Vatinius is referred to elsewhere as "an allusion in the bad taste, by which Cicero's jokes were sometimes characterized."[19] To another scholar, Cicero's remarks on the exploitation of physical deformities at *On the Orator* 2.239 "show how widely his canons of good taste differed from those now universally recognized"; yet even this apparently balanced judgment betrays notions of ethical progress with those final three words, "now universally recognized."[20] This list could easily grow—making fun of another person's warts was hardly an acceptable public practice among classicists of one hundred years ago. Accordingly, nineteenth-century commentators duly observe the phenomenon, voice their disapproval, and then pass on.

The next age produced apologists. In the conclusion to his book on Cicero's use of humor and irony, a French scholar expresses what earlier critics of the orator had only implied: the harshness of Cicero's wit can be attributed to his ignorance of the Christian concept of charity. Nevertheless, the scholar maintains, this fact should not allow us "to criticize a witty man for having lived too early."[21] Most other recent critics who excuse Cicero's abuse of physical peculiarities display less of a Christian ethical bias. Roman orators, their argument goes, did not have bad taste; they simply followed earlier models too faithfully (as Romans do). Nisbet best represents this trend when he asserts that "Roman invective

---

[18] Long 3:566 (on *Sest.* 135).

[19] Holden ad loc.

[20] Wilkins ad loc.

[21] Haury 1955: 279 ("à damner un homme d'esprit pour avoir vécu trop tôt").

shows more regard for literary convention than for historical truth."[22]
He bases his conclusion on parallels from Greek modes of invective. Austin takes a similar tack: "lurid personalities were a feature of Roman public life, and were often neither intended seriously nor taken so."[23] Nisbet and Austin properly recognize the literary character of the mockery of physical deformities—it is unquestionably a common feature of the genre of public oratory—and their view has been adopted by most subsequent scholars of Cicero. Yet a literary explanation ignores Strabo's assertion that all his comments on wit apply equally well to everyday speech (*De orat.* 2.271). More significantly, attributing harsh invective simply to generic convention places Roman oratory in a cultural vacuum. The immoral pagans of earlier scholarship have become a group of Greeklings, bound by a tradition of invective that is not native and that somehow has the power to persuade an audience that, it is supposed, does not take such abuse seriously.

Roman invective exhibits clear generic elements; yet the mockery of physical peculiarities does not represent simply a literary phenomenon. Invective produced tangible effects in the political sphere. A recent study of litigation in the late Republic outlines the importance of avoiding disgrace (*infamia*) during this period and examines how rhetorical invective —which includes, of course, the mockery of physical deformities—helps effect such disgrace through the lowering of an opponent's personal reputation (*existimatio*). There is no evidence for believing that the space of the Roman court provided any type of legal "privilege" for its speakers. In fact, as seems intuitively more likely, public language could do real damage:

> The objection might be raised here that insults uttered in court may have somehow not counted as "real" insults, . . . that perhaps they were not taken too seriously and so were no real danger to one's *existimatio*. But the sources would in fact entirely invalidate such a suggestion; there is no doubt whatever that court abuse was indeed felt as an attack on *existimatio*.[24]

Public insults, the study concludes, fulfill an important function: the Romans tolerated harsh invective since they recognized in it a means of inhibiting excessive litigation. The potential threat of having one's way of life displayed publicly caused the Roman, it is argued, to avoid instigating legal matters that were not absolutely essential. These arguments for why invective continued to be employed are persuasive. Yet they do not account for the origin of this license, this readiness to raise

[22] Nisbet 1961: 193.
[23] R. Austin 52.
[24] Kelly 1976: 101–2.

issues that appear irrelevant, if not morally objectionable, to a modern reader.

Evidence survives regarding the status of physical peculiarities in civic life. As early as the fifth century BCE, the Twelve Tables prescribed death for any child born with a deformity (Cic. *Leg.* 3.19; cf. Sen. *Dial.* 3.15.2). Scattered references also indicate that bodily defects prevented an individual from holding political and sacred office in the late Republic. A physical fault could prevent one from becoming a priest (DH 2.21.3, Sen. *Contr.* 4.2; cf. *ORF* 9.1.14–16, Plut. *Mor.* 281c), Vestal (Gell. 1.12.3; Fronto p. 149 = Loeb 2.73 [Haines]), and, at least under Augustus, even a senator (Dio 54.26.8–9); in particular, blindness, not surprisingly, prevented one from petitioning for a magistracy (Ulp. *Dig.* 3.1.1.5, Iust. *Cod.* 10.32[31].8). For other disabilities and offices in this period, however, there are only tentative allusions. Thus in a letter to his friend Atticus, Cicero describes a tribune's political activity with the strange juxtaposition "the lame man, under good auspices, promulgated the law" (*bono auspicio claudus homo promulgavit*).[25] Dionysius of Halicarnassus preserves legislation from the period of the kings and the early Republic that may have been in force in the first century BCE.[26] It must be left open to what extent a physically abnormal individual encountered legal obstacles to a political career. Indeed, it is not even possible to define precisely what constituted a physical abnormality. The texts cited above are of little help, as they describe the "disabled" only in the vaguest terms: "deformed," "weak," "monstrous," "unwhole" (*deformis, debilis, monstrosus, non integer*). Nor does extant political invective provide more precise criteria. As one would expect, the public speaker was interested in proving the moral deviance of his opponent, not in prescribing a set of beauty standards.

Yet in Strabo's treatment of jokes on physical peculiarities, there are recognizable limits to this type of witticism. As will become clear, however, this respect for decorum does not stem from the sort of ethical considerations that inform the rhetorical works of the Greeks. In those treatises written before Cicero's *On the Orator*, the extent of an individual's personal responsibility is the key to determining whether or not he

---

[25] *Att.* 1.16.13 (SB 16). Cicero probably intends the juxtaposition to be, at least in part, humorously ironic. There may also be a pun on the fact that the law being proposed by the lame tribune deals with *ambitus* (a legal term that encompasses electoral bribery but literally means "walking about").

[26] DH 2.21.3, 5.25.3 (cf. Appian *Reg.* 1 frag. 10), and 9.13.4. I owe most references in this paragraph to Mommsen 1887–88 1:493–94. Cic. *Att.* 2.9.2 (SB 29) may provide further evidence. Here Vatinius is described as covering his swellings (*struma*) with an augur's robe. The bitterness of the remark would be sharpened if Cicero regarded Vatinius' possible position as augur as something abnormal (if not illegal).

may be rebuked for physical appearance. According to the Aristotelian tradition, for example, a speaker may not hold an opponent responsible for the social position into which he has been born, since personal characteristics such as this arise by chance. But one may attach moral blame to an opponent's poor physical health if it results from lack of exercise.[27] The Romans treated the condemnation of physical disadvantages quite differently. According to *On the Orator*, they employed such criticism looking not to a distinction between fate and individual agency but to rhetorical utility, a utility that, as will be shown, has its own ethical basis. A Roman located the responsibility for any deformity, regardless of its origin, solely in the person who bore that deformity. In the Roman realm of the physical, accidents never happen.

Strabo delineates the parameters to jokes on physical defects as follows:

> est etiam deformitatis et corporis vitiorum satis bella materies ad iocandum; sed quaerimus idem, quod in ceteris rebus maxime quaerendum est, quatenus; in quo non modo illud praecipitur, ne quid insulse, sed etiam, si quid perridicule possis, vitandum est oratori utrumque, ne aut scurrilis iocus sit aut mimicus. (*De orat.* 2.239)

> The deformity and faults of the body also provide some quite "pretty" material for jokes. But we ask the same thing that must be especially asked in relation to the rest of our concerns: to what extent? In response, it is taught not only that one not [act] without charm, but also, if one is able [to make] a very funny point, the orator must avoid a joke that resembles that of either an idle wit (*scurrilis*) or an actor in a mime (*mimicus*).

---

[27] My example is taken from [Arist.] *Rh. Al.* 1426a3–10; cf. also 1440b16–23 and Arist. *Rhet.* 1.9.33. *On Rhetorical Invention* and *Rhetorica ad Herennium*, the two Roman rhetorical treatises most directly influenced by Hellenistic models, do not use this dichotomy in their discussion of the rhetorical use of physical peculiarities. Instead they borrow the alternative tripartite system, by which one attributes an individual's faults to one of three categories ("external phenomena, body, or spirit"; *Rhet. Her.* 3.10, *Inv.* 2.177). For a full list of the use of this three-part division in both Greek and Roman writers see Caplan's edition of the *Rhetorica ad Herennium* (174 n. a).

Aristotle allows a speaker in a speech of praise or blame to refer to bodily attributes arising by chance, but only when those physical attributes of the subject are numerous and prominent; even then, such characteristics can only be employed as points providing secondary proof of character; cf. *Rhet.* 1.9.32–33: τὰ συμπτώματα καὶ τὰ ἀπὸ τύχης ὡς ἐν προαιρέσει ληπτέον. ἂν γὰρ πολλὰ καὶ ὅμοια προφέρηται, σημεῖον ἀρετῆς εἶναι δόξει καὶ προαιρέσεως. . . . τὸ δ' ἐγκώμιον τῶν ἔργων ἐστίν, τὰ δὲ κύκλῳ εἰς πίστιν ("one must assume that accidents and strokes of good fortune are due to moral purpose; for if a number of similar examples can be adduced, they will be thought to be signs of virtue and moral purpose. . . . But encomium deals with achievements—all attendant circumstances conduce to persuasion" [Freese trans.]).

Strabo clarifies through his subsequent discussion what he means by the joke of the idle wit and mime actor: the witticisms of the *mimicus* depend upon *res*, "an anecdote accompanied by gestures," and the witticisms of the *scurra* depend upon *dictum*, "the verbal form of expression."[28] In employing jokes deriving from *res*, one must avoid the excessive gesturing that typifies "the indecent movement of mime actors" (*mimorum . . . et ethologorum . . . sicut obscenitas*; *De orat.* 2.242).[29] But it is Strabo's subsequent discussion of the humor dependent upon verbal expression that is of interest here, for this half of his dichotomy encompasses most of the extant humor involving physical deformities. In fact, when Strabo describes the allowable parameters of jokes arising from verbal expression, his two principal examples center on the mockery of bodily defects.

Strabo introduces the subject of verbal humor (*in dicto*) as follows:

> in dicto autem ridiculum est id, quod verbi aut sententiae quodam acumine movetur; sed ut in illo superiore genere vel narrationis vel imitationis vitanda est mimorum et ethologorum similitudo, sic in hoc scurrilis oratori dicacitas magno opere fugienda est. . . . hoc, opinor, primum, ne, quotienscumque potuerit dictum dici, necesse habeamus dicere. (*De orat.* 2.244)

> As for wit deriving from the form of expression (*in dicto*),[30] laughter arises from a kind of sharpness of a word or phrase; but, just as in the type of narration or mimicry that we discussed above one must avoid seeming like a silent actor in a farce, so too in this type the speaker must take great care to shun the humor befitting an idle wit (*scurrilis*). . . . I think the most important point is this: we should not feel compelled to make a joke (*dictum*) whenever there is an opportunity for a joke to be made.

In the deployment of wit deriving from wordplay, Strabo cautions the orator to avoid expressions that may cause personal embarrassment. It is significant that he does not mention that the speaker should have any concerns about offending the target of his humor.

To illustrate his ideal of an effective witticism, Strabo relates two occa-

---

[28] This dichotomy between *res* and *dictum* corresponds to the earlier division Strabo makes between *cavillatio* and *dicacitas* (*De orat.* 2.218). M. Grant's discussion of Cicero's divisions is flawed (108–11); for corrections, see Herter 725–26 and especially Rabbie 177–83.

[29] The *ethologoi* are mentioned in classical Latin only in this passage (*De orat.* 2.242, 244) and in a dedicatory inscription (*CIL* 6.10129). It is not clear how they differed—if at all—from a normal actor in a mime (*mimus*).

[30] My cumbersome rendering of *dictum* attempts to convey in a single phrase both its literal ("a thing spoken") and extended ("a witticism") meaning. In the late Republic the plural form *dicta* was commonly used for the fuller expression *facete dicta* ("things said wittily"), as Cicero himself remarks in a letter to Cornelius Nepos (Cic. *Epist. fr.* 2.1 = Macr. *Sat.* 2.1.14).

sions on which a speaker did not use enough forethought in mocking an opponent's physique. I shall now quote at length a pair of Strabo's examples, together with his own explanatory remarks:

> pusillus testis processit. "licet" inquit "rogare?" Philippus. tum quaesitor properans "modo breviter." hic ille "non accusabis: perpusillum rogabo." ridicule. sed sedebat iudex L. Aurifex brevior ipse quam testis etiam: omnis est risus in iudicem conversus; visum est totum scurrile ridiculum. [A] *ergo haec, quae cadere possunt in quos nolis, quamvis sint bella, sunt tamen ipso genere scurrilia*; ut iste, qui se volt dicacem et mehercule est, Appius, sed non numquam in hoc vitium scurrile delabitur. "cenabo" inquit "apud te," huic lusco familiari meo, C. Sextio; "uni enim locum esse video." est hoc scurrile, et [B] *quod sine causa lacessivit* et [C] tamen *id dixit, quod in omnis luscos conveniret*; ea, quia meditata putantur esse, minus ridentur. (*De orat.* 2.245–46; my emphases)

> A very short witness stepped forward. "May I question him?" Philippus asked. The judge, being in a hurry, replied, "Only briefly." Whereupon [Philippus remarked], "You won't find fault with me; he won't be long (*perpusillum rogabo*)." A funny joke; but a juror attending on the case was Lucius Aurifex, [who was] himself even shorter than the witness. Everyone directed their laughter toward this juror; the whole affair seemed a joke fit for an idle wit (*scurrilis*). [A] *So those [remarks] which could fall upon unwanted targets—no matter how fine the remarks may be—still befit an idle wit* (scurra) *by their very nature*; it's like that Appius who wants to be clever (and, in fact, is), but who occasionally slips into this fault of scurrility. He said to my friend, Gaius Sextius, who only has one eye, "I'll have dinner at your place—I see you've got room for one more." This befits an idle wit, both [B] *because he harassed Sextius without provocation* and, after all, [C] *he said what could apply to all one-eyed men*; these [types of remarks], because they are thought to be premeditated, excite laughter less.[31]

Strabo clearly disapproves of these two jokes. The objections he raises against them fall into the three categories I have labeled [A], [B], and [C]. All three objections concern matters of rhetorical utility. The witticism, first of all, [A] must not apply personally to an individual important to the case (other than the opponent, of course). Philippus' joke provides a negative exemplum of this prescription, since he alienated one of the very

---

[31] On the importance of humor seeming spontaneous see *Orat.* 89. Similarly, speakers valued most the witty rejoinder (wit *in respondendo*); see *De orat.* 2.230, 236.

Strabo goes on to express his admiration for Sextius' reply, *"manus lava et cena"* ("Get your hands clean and then eat"), both because it arose *ex tempore* and because it had rhetorical point (2.247). The reference, as Wilkins says ad loc., is "doubtless . . . to his love for 'filthy lucre.'" Macr. *Sat.* 7.3.15 and Plut. *Mor.* 614d–615c preserve a similar joke about a person's hands.

people he needed to convince: a juror. Second, [B] the witticism must
not be without a rhetorical purpose (*sine causa*);[32] and finally [C], it must
not be (or at least seem) premeditated. These last two strictures constitute
the only objections Strabo raises against the joke about Sextius' monocularity. Strabo, in other words, offers no ethical objections of a Judaeo-
Christian nature: that is, he expresses no concern over attacking an opponent unjustly or offending the sensibilities of a member of his audience. It
is of further interest that he phrases all three points negatively. In other
words, his points restrict; they do not prescribe. Apart from these three
restrictions—not attacking a potential supporter and not using gratuitous
or prepared jokes—the orator appears to have free rein in his abuse of
physical traits.[33]

Such a conclusion may warrant no surprise. A rhetorical handbook
would be expected to concern itself only with rhetorical considerations
when outlining speaking strategies. Yet one would also expect Strabo to
mention any possible ethical objections on the part of a speaker's auditors
that could hinder his success in winning their favor. Instead Strabo gives
absolutely no indication that a joke concerning a physical trait should be
avoided because a member of the audience may take offense merely on a
principle of ethics. The Philippus example, in fact, proves the opposite:
far from commiserating with the juror Aurifex, those in attendance (who
presumably include the other members of the jury) direct their laughter
toward him. Therein lay Philippus' failure: in addition to losing the favor
of Aurifex, he caused attention to be diverted from his own interrogation. What is more, with the proviso "it doesn't matter how fine [inop-
portune jokes] may be" (*quamvis sint bella*), Strabo implies that Philippus'
witticism would have been perfectly appropriate under other conditions,

---

[32] The phrase *sine causa* ("without cause") expresses the antithesis to the ideal goal Strabo
later assigns to humor: "that we [i.e., the speaker] might achieve some gain" (*ut proficiamus
aliquid*; *De orat.* 2.247). This purpose clause provides an explanation for an earlier *cum causa*,
translated by Rabbie ad loc. as "zu einem (bestimmten) Zweck" ("for a specific goal"). The
phrase *sine causa* also contains the related idea that the most effective humor arises *in respondendo* (see previous note).

[33] I do not claim that other restrictions may not arise under particular circumstances. As
one would expect, fear of vengeance can also be a restriction. In my final chapter I discuss in
detail how Julius Caesar wields this type of censorship. The mockery of blindness—or, as
here, monocularity—traditionally provided writers on *decorum* with an example of uncouth
behavior (e.g., Aristotle *EN* 3.5.1114a24–27; Persius 1.128). Cicero here clearly seems to
be drawing from this tradition, which attributes blindness to fate and not to personal responsibility (Aristotle *EN* 3.5.1114a26–27). He does not, however, isolate blindness *per se*
as an exceptionable target for mockery. For another example of Cicero's simultaneous in-
debtedness to, and freedom from, his tradition, see n. 13 above.

Orat. 88 offers a one-sentence version of *De orat.* 2.237–46: *illud admonemus tamen, ridiculo
sic usurum oratorem, ut nec nimis frequenti, ne scurrile sit, nec subobsceno, ne mimicum, nec petu-
lanti, ne improbum, nec in calamitatem, ne inhumanum, nec in facinus, ne odi locum risus occupet,
neque aut sua persona aut iudicum aut tempore alienum; haec enim ad illud indecorum referuntur.*

namely, when he did not need to persuade a short person. A barb directed against a physical peculiarity, then, can be employed provided that the speaker gives proper consideration to rhetorical efficacy. Once again, Cicero's treatise reverses earlier Greek views on humor. Whereas Strabo stresses the joke and its efficacy in disabling a target, the Hellenic treatises consider the victim's position, emphasizing repeatedly that the speaker should avoid seriously damaging another's reputation.[34]

On the Orator, Cicero's most substantial rhetorical treatise, makes it clear that the humorous abuse of physical peculiarities does not arise simply out of a Roman proclivity for admitting any type of language in the courtroom. The discourse of Strabo does prescribe restrictions to this practice in terms of rhetorical utility—but most of these would have become obvious upon reflection. Yet despite Strabo's emphasis on rhetorical efficacy, a system of values that is distinctly Roman does inform the practice. I have mentioned how the Greeks divided responsibility for physical defects into two areas, those aspects for which an individual bore direct responsibility and those for which he did not. The Romans, in contrast, often ignored such a distinction. An explanation for why the Romans blur this dichotomy can be found in the philosophical works of Cicero.

Physical Peculiarities: *On the Laws*

Nature taught human beings alone how to walk upright, Cicero says in the first book of *On the Laws* (*De legibus*), and to gaze toward the heavens in recollection of their former home. Cicero closes this progressivist account of human evolution by emphasizing the natural correspondence between a person's external and internal nature:

> tum [natura] speciem ita formavit oris, ut in ea penitus reconditos mores effingeret; nam et oculi nimis arguti, quem ad modum animo affecti simus, loquuntur, et is, qui appellatur vultus, qui nullo in animante esse praeter hominem potest, indicat mores, cuius vim Graeci norunt, nomen omnino non habent. (*Leg.* 1.27)

> Then [nature] shaped the facial features (*speciem oris*) in such a way that it represented in them the character hidden deep within. For the eyes tell with great clarity how we have been affected in our spirit, and that which is called our countenance (*vultus*)—and which is able to exist in no living thing other

---

[34] Cf. especially Aristotle *EN* 4.8.1128a, on propriety in wit; Aristotle applies these views to rhetoric at *Rhet.* 2.2.12, 2.3.12, 2.4.13, and 2.12.16 and to comedy at *Poetics* 5.1449a32–33. M. Grant passim treats this Greek attitude toward humor; see especially her observation that Plato, Aristotle, and Plutarch limit their humor "to foibles rather than serious faults" (37).

than human beings—reveals our character. The Greeks recognized its purport [i.e., the connotations contained in the Latin word *vultus*], but have no
word for it at all.

The visage as the mirror of the soul: Cicero uses the word *vultus* here to
refer not to a temporary expression but to a permanent expression, or set
of expressions, predetermined by the physical makeup of the face (*species
oris*)—those features that one art historian has termed "physiognomic
constancy."[35] As Cicero indicates with the phrase "the Greeks recognized
its purport" (*vim Graeci norunt*), a similar belief in the power of the face to
reflect one's essential nature runs throughout ancient Greek thought. Beginning with Homer's Thersites in *Iliad* 2—for whom the adjective
aischistos describes both physical and moral ugliness—the Greeks tended
"to regard physical appearance as a correlate of moral worth, and to re-
late both to social class."[36] From the time of Pythagoras on, this belief
informs the many treatises on physiognomics, a science whose subjects
include the study of the relationship between physical appearance and
inner character or states of mind. This science and the system of beliefs
from which it arose provide the foundation for Aristotle's justification of
slavery in *Politics* and exert an inevitable influence on late Hellenistic rhetorical treatises.[37] In Rome, one of the earliest extant inscriptions praises
a man "whose appearance equaled his virtue" (*quoius forma virtutei par-*

[35] Gombrich 106 (cf. *De orat.* 1.127, "those things which we cannot feign: the face, the
expression, the voice" [*ea quae nobis non possumus fingere, facies, vultus, sonus*]; *Fin.* 5.47). The
belief that an individual possesses—or should possess—a permanent and unalterable set of
expressions seems to lie behind *Pis.* 1: Piso's danger to the state rests in his ability to change
various features of his face.

Kenter ad loc. cites *Orat.* 60 and *De orat.* 3.221–22 as parallels for this passage from *On
the Laws*. Although both passages do contain the phrase "the expression is the mirror of the
soul" (*imago est animi vultus*), they refer to the ways in which an orator should manipulate
his expression (*vultus*) and eye movement (*oculi*) to convey his emotions, not to how a set of
features specific to the *vultus* reflects its bearer's *mores*. For *vultus* outside of a philosophical
context signifying not just a temporary facial expression but rather a kind of permanent
attitude, see the audience aside at Plaut. *Aul.* 717: *tibi credere certum est; nam esse bonum ex
voltu cognosco* ("I certainly trust you, for I recognize from your *vultus* that you are a good
man").

[36] Thalmann 15; see also Kirk 139.

[37] Aristotle *Pol.* 1.2.14: βούλεται μὲν οὖν ἡ φύσις . . . τὰ σώματα διαφέροντα ποιεῖν
τὰ τῶν ἐλευθέρων καὶ τῶν δούλων ("the intention of nature therefore is . . . to make the
bodies of free men and of slaves different"; Rackham 1944 trans.). This difference, Aristotle
goes on to say, reflects relative differences in the soul; see further the discussion by Magli
87–88 of Aristotle's *De anima*.

Evans 1969 surveys the influence of physiognomical principles on ancient literature.
Gleason 1991 analyzes their bearing on the Second Sophistic. For details of the relation
between the physiognomical and rhetorical treatises see Evans 1935: 45–51. I know of no
similar treatment of physiognomical treatises and Roman oratory during the Republic.

isuma fuit; CIL 1².7). The equation of internal and external states of being, therefore, had numerous precedents before Cicero.[38]

Yet Cicero felt himself to be more than simply heir to a tradition. In the above passage from *On the Laws*, he implies that the Greeks place less importance than do the Romans on how the countenance reveals *mores*—for although they recognize its significance, Cicero notes that the Greeks do not even have a word corresponding to the Latin *vultus*. The passage contains a rare exception to the conceit about the poverty of the Latin language frequently employed by Roman philosphers frustrated at trying to express complex philosophical notions in their native tongue.[39] Yet perhaps the putative absence of a Greek term corresponding to *vultus* does not so much indicate an oversight on the part of the Greeks as provide evidence that they did not wholly accept the implications lying behind the word *vultus*. Indeed, it has recently been argued that for public speakers in fifth- and fourth-century Athens, nature (*phusis*) did not describe a force that regulated social behavior but one that reflected an individual's "unnegotiable bent."[40] As an expression of the character peculiar and specific to each person, nature as conceived by the Greeks did not serve as an inflexible enforcer; instead, it could be represented as fickle and disorganized. This clearly was not the case for the *natura* envisaged by Cicero in *On the Laws*, where nature figures as an omnipotent and external determinant of physical appearance. Just as Strabo's verdict on the abuse of physical defects seems to reflect a Roman innovation in rhetorical technique, so too the philosophical precept Cicero offers here signals a changed perception of the relationship between body and character.

When this statement is considered within the larger context of *On the Laws*, it becomes clear that Cicero must establish the relationship between physical exterior and moral interior in order to prove his more

[38] For the widespread nature of this belief throughout antiquity, see the discussions and bibliographies in Tarrant 198; Woodman 166–67. The belief also informs Suetonius' conception that physical appearance portends character (Plass 79). Origen reveals that this bias continued in early Christianity: "the gentle precision of God's mercy ensures that each body was adjusted to the peculiar needs of its soul down to the finest details" (in P. Brown 165–66); with Augustine one begins to see the sympathetic treatment I have been labeling "Judaeo-Christian" (e.g., *City of God* 22.19). Even in the late nineteenth and early twentieth centuries, Cesare Lombroso, the founder of criminal anthropology, seems to have grounded his theories of the "born criminal" in the scientific tradition of physiognomy (Schrader, esp. 63–65).

There existed in antiquity, of course, exceptions to this tendency. Lucretius 5.1110–12 describes the valorization of beauty as an element of primitive and outdated belief; cf. Sall. *Cat.* 10.5–6.

[39] For full references to the use and range of this conceit throughout Roman literature, see Pease's notes in 1955 1:143–45 and 1963: 368. Pease observes that on occasion the Greeks too expressed dissatisfaction with their language.

[40] Winkler 64–70; quotation is from 65.

general claim, that justice among mortals derives directly from the workings of *natura* (*Leg.* 1.18–34). For Cicero, the equation of moral and
physical appearance in a human being provides evidence that nature is
inherently just; for if human beings were endowed by nature with the
ability to use their appearance as a means of deception, it would then be
impossible to trust nature in any of its capacities. The concept of natural
law depends upon nature itself—including its inhabitants—being
decipherable.

Immediately following his remarks on the human countenance, Cicero
seeks to demonstrate that if human beings had retained their natural state,
then all persons would desire the same (natural) law. This original state,
he seems to think, requires that all persons had once resembled one another. We have deviated from this uniformity on account of wicked
ways. Cicero formulates the deviation in the following elliptical manner:

> quodsi depravatio consuetudinum, si opinionum vanitas non imbecillitatem
> animorum torqueret et flecteret quocumque coepisset, sui nemo ipse tam
> similis esset quam omnes essent omnium. (*Leg.* 1.29)

> Nay, if bad habits and false beliefs did not twist the weaker minds and turn
> them in whatever direction they are inclined, no one would be so like his
> own self as all men would be like others. (Keyes trans.)[41]

Without evil, then, individuality would be nonexistent. That is the law.
Cicero's language here, describing the twisting and turning from an
imagined ideal (*depravatio, torqueret, flecteret*), commonly recurs in the invective against physical peculiarities. The depraved soul, twisting from
the straight path of nature, is portrayed as the property of the "unnatural"
Roman—the nonelite member of society who possesses "bad habits and
false beliefs." Hence those without access to what have been chosen as
proper beliefs and opinions are caught in a double bind: if their behavior
or appearance betrays them as other—not only as un-Roman but as
unnatural—the cause must be "weakness of mind" (*imbecillitas an-
imorum*), a weakness that will only further aggravate their continual deviance from the established norms of society. This ideological representation of the relation between human society and nature can, in the hands
of a powerful speaker, become a means of ordering and controlling
broader political, economic, and social realities.[42]

---

[41] For this curious passage I adopt the translation and interpretation of C. Keyes 1928,
the Loeb editor, who remarks ad loc.: "Apparently a paradox, designed to enforce a fundamental truth with emphasis. It seems merely to mean 'men would all be exactly alike.'"

[42] See Althusser, esp. 24: "Ideological *representations* concern nature and society, the very
world in which men live; they concern the life of men, their relation to nature, to society, to
the social order, to other men and to their activities, including economic and political practice" (original emphasis).

Cicero refuses to speculate how his hypothetical "universal similarity" (*similitudo omnium*) would express itself in terms of physique. In other contexts he also seems unwilling to confront the issue. In his treatise *On the Nature of the Gods* (*De natura deorum*), the interlocutor Cotta, a speaker for Stoicism, argues against an anthropomorphic conception of the gods. Cotta objects that since the gods are perfect, and perfection must represent a single, unchanging state of being, then the gods would all have to appear exactly alike if they had human traits. Any deviation would constitute a blemish. This could of course not be the case, Cotta asserts without argumentation. So here too one encounters a conception of natural physical perfection, a perfection whose characteristics are never made explicit.

However, on imperfection Cicero is more forthcoming. The first passage I cited from *On the Laws*, where nature plays a role in shaping the human countenance (1.27), is relevant here. Wicked people, who carry the marks of evil in their facial features (*speciem oris*), have grown apart and have thus become distinguishable from an imagined original uniformity of beauty. A physical peculiarity, therefore, marks an individual. Individuality, when understood as deviation from the natural norm (*depravatio consuetudinum*), betrays an evil nature. External and internal ugliness produce and reflect each other.

A third passage from Cicero's philosophical works supports the contention that to a Roman, a physical peculiarity provides visible evidence of moral deviance. In *On the Limits of Good and Evil* (*De finibus*), the interlocutor Piso argues that human beings desire to be physically whole and beautiful and that this desire arises from an innate longing (*natura*; 5.46–47). In his rebuttal, the respondent Cicero does not take Piso to task for this remark. One can now understand why: Piso's observation accords with the model of human development outlined by Cicero himself in *On the Laws*. A person's longing to be beautiful reflects the desire to return to an original state. This belief finds further support in the basic Latin vocabulary for beauty and ugliness. Behind these designations often stands the idea of a beautiful norm from which deviation has occurred; consider, for example, the pairs *formosus* : *deformis* ("shapely" : "unshapely") or *rectus* : *pravus* ("straight" : "crooked").[43] It is surely no coincidence that the words denoting moral character also refer to an implied norm of perfection and balance: *aequus* : *iniquus* ("levelness" describing "just" behavior; cf. *pravus*, *perversus*: depravity as behavior that literally de-viates).

The humor deriving from an opponent's physical appearance now stands in a new light. Strabo's advocacy of the mockery of physical pecu-

---

[43] Monteil 249.

liarities is predicated upon a philosophical understanding of natural justice: deviance from normal human physique can signify a moral failing
hidden deep within (*penitus reconditos mores*). In public invective, the orator's task is to point out this deviance, thereby reinforcing the inherent
justice of social and political stratification. The proper Roman can read
injustice on the face of the "outlaw." A physical peculiarity damns its
bearer for individuality.

Physical Peculiarities and Political Rhetoric

Physical peculiarities individualize; but what threat does a deformed individual embody? A passage from one of Cicero's earliest writings, *On
Rhetorical Invention* (*De inventione*), provides the final link between an idealized conception of primal man (*On the Laws, On the Limits of Good and
Evil*) and the application of the body to political rhetoric (*On the Orator*).
In the first book of *On Rhetorical Invention*, Cicero observes how the orator may use to equal effect both the positive and negative physical features of his subject. He includes among the allowable objects of abuse
those who have been misshapen by nature (*ab natura . . . deformis*; *Inv.*
1.35). In the second book, Cicero again treats the subject of personal
characteristics. He discusses how the orator may use attributes either to
support or to call into question a proof:

> ex persona autem coniectura capietur, si eae res quae personis attributae sunt
> diligenter considerabuntur. . . . omnia enim *haec*, vir an mulier, huius an
> illius civitatis sit, quibus sit maioribus, quibus consanguineis, qua aetate,
> quo animo, *quo corpore, quae naturae sunt attributa*, ad aliquam coniecturam
> faciendam pertinebunt. (*Inv.* 2.28–29; my emphases)

> In addition, an inference will be made from one's person, if those qualities
> that have been attributed to persons will be carefully considered. . . . For
> *these things that have been attributed to nature*—i.e., whether [one's subject] is a
> man or woman, from our state or another, who are his ancestors and blood
> relatives, how old he is, *what type of* spirit and *physique he has*—all these
> things will be relevant in making an inference.

The young Cicero ascribes the origin of bodily attributes to a single
source, *natura*. In contrast, the Greek treatises, as we have seen, posit two
sources for these attributes: either accident or personal responsibility. By
the time of *On Rhetorical Invention*, an individual has primary responsibility for *any* physical fault, regardless of its origin.[44] In discussing the

---

[44] I do not necessarily credit Cicero with this innovation. The general consensus among
scholars holds that *On Rhetorical Invention* contains very few original ideas and consists
largely of Cicero's notes, compiled when he was still a student (see n. 12 above). G. Ken-

mockery of physical deformities as formulated in *On the Orator* book 2, I noted that Strabo did not include the physically deformed among those who have been oppressed by exceptionally bad luck (*De orat.* 2.239), a failure that puzzles a modern reader. An understanding of the Roman conception of physical appearance explains the apparent contradiction: the Romans preferred to conceive of a physical peculiarity as arising not out of chance but out of an evil character. Cicero firmly maintains this conflation of physique and spirit throughout his public career.

Thirty years later, the period of 46/45 BCE finds Cicero once again writing a treatise on rhetoric. Almost a decade has passed since the composition of *On the Orator*, the work that, as I have already remarked, expresses most fully Cicero's conception of the ideal Roman orator. In his new rhetorical treatise, *On the Classification of Oratory* (*De partitione oratoria*), Cicero reformulates the equation of external and internal appearance. While enumerating the order of subjects one should treat in a speech of praise or blame (*Part.* 70), the orator advises beginning with the subject's family and then proceeding to his fortune and means. Cicero continues:

> postea de corporis bonis [erit dicendum], in quibus quidem quae virtutem maxime significat facillime forma laudatur. (*Part.* 74)

> Afterward [one should speak] of physical advantages, and among these beauty is most easily praised as it indicates virtue most clearly.

The context—"everything connected with virtue should definitely be praised and everything connected with faults should be blamed" (*omnia . . . sunt profecto laudanda quae coniuncta cum virtute sunt, et quae cum vitiis vituperanda*; *Part.* 71)—leaves no doubt that the converse of the passage cited also holds true; that is, lack of physical beauty reflects a corresponding deficiency in virtue. This sentiment recalls Cicero's primal man in *On the Laws*. In their original state, human beings possessed uniformity of virtue and appearance, and evil brought about deviance from this ideal state (*Leg.* 1.29). Moral deviance in turn created an ugly exterior. From the early treatise *On Rhetorical Invention* to the later *On the Classification of Oratory*, from the nascent stages of his oratorical career to the intense

---

nedy, after a detailed discussion of the relationship between *On Rhetorical Invention* and *Rhetorica ad Herennium*, concludes that both works stem from the house of the orator Crassus (126–38). Although such a precise conclusion seems risky, Kennedy's arguments suggest that Cicero's comments in *On Rhetorical Invention* on the rhetorical use of the body reflect a Roman source. In any event, even if the source were Greek, the willingness of the Romans to accept such a practice indicates their recognition of its potential effectiveness for a Roman audience.

period of literary activity that preceded his death, Cicero remains convinced of the advantage a speaker might gain from an opponent's physical peculiarities. Provided that one interprets it properly—in the best circumstances, with the help of a Cicero—the human body provides access to a person's inner nature. Exposing the faults of the body strengthens one's case on the side of what is good and natural.

As might be expected, an opposing aesthetic is acknowledged in Cicero's ethical and philosophical treatises, but even here only rarely. The infrequency with which moral and physical beauty are dissociated in these works attests further to how inextricably bodies and behavior could be linked in the Roman mind. On two occasions Cicero cites Socrates as an example of an ugly man being able to transcend physical appearance. Yet Socrates provides simply a noble exception to the recognized norm. The Greek philosopher could overcome his natural disabilities, Cicero argues, only through the earnest pursuit of truth—"with will, effort, and training" (*in voluntate studio disciplina*; *Fat.* 10–11; cf. *Tusc.* 4.80). The average intellect, it is clearly implied, would not be so fortunate. Among Cicero's political enemies, the impressive physical appearance of Lucius Calpurnius Piso posed a particular problem. The noble exterior of Piso should by all accounts presage a morally upright interior. I discuss in detail at the close of chapter 4 the ways in which Cicero resolves this dilemma: Cicero asserts that Piso is especially evil because he attempts through his attractive exterior to conceal from the citizens of Rome his base internal character.

The most effective means of highlighting an opponent's deformities lies, as Caesar Strabo saw, in their mockery before an audience. The public exposure of a person's physical deviance isolates him as an individual and enables the speaker to unite with the spectators in a joint chorus of derisive laughter. In the remainder of this chapter I shall concentrate on how the public speaker at Rome manipulates the bias against physical peculiarities. The texts I have chosen to examine show the orator encouraging the presuppositions of his hearers and thereby helping them to shape their own critical reaction to the individual being attacked.

A passage from *On the Orator* provides a rare glimpse of an audience's reaction to a joke on a physical peculiarity. Strabo recounts an example of humorous irony from a public debate in the nineties BCE:

invertuntur autem verba, ut, Crassus apud M. Perpernam iudicem pro Aculeone cum diceret, aderat contra Aculeonem Gratidiano L. Aelius Lamia, deformis, ut nostis; qui cum interpellaret odiose, "audiamus" inquit "pulchellum puerum" Crassus; cum esset adrisum, "non potui mihi" inquit Lamia "formam ipse fingere, ingenium potui;" tum hic "audiamus" inquit "disertum!" multo etiam adrisum est vehementius. (*De orat.* 2.262)

Words also are used in irony, like the time when Crassus spoke on behalf of Aculeo before the judge Marcus Perperna. The opposing counsel representing Gratidianus was Lucius Aelius Lamia, a disfigured man, as you all know. Since this Lamia kept interrupting him in an offensive manner, Crassus remarked, "Let's hear the pretty little boy"; when there was a peal of approving laughter Lamia replied, "I wasn't responsible for molding my beauty, but I was for my talent." At this Crassus responded, "Let's hear the skillful speaker!" He was met with a much stronger burst of approving laughter.[45]

A few preliminary remarks are needed to appreciate this exchange fully. Lamia has some type of deformity—we don't know exactly what. One can infer from Cicero's text only that the nature of the deformity made him far from beautiful (*pulcher*) and that presumably it would have been visible to anyone in his presence. But note how Strabo introduces Lamia's defect: "a disfigured man, as you all know" (*deformis, ut nostis*). The phrase teases by its very conciseness. From the point of view of the interlocutors, this aside by Strabo would have been gratuitous; after all, the other personage in the anecdote, Crassus, belongs to their number and the participants reveal elsewhere in the dialogue a close knowledge of one another's judicial experience. Strabo need not inform them (as of course the phrase *ut nostis* itself concedes) that Lamia is disfigured. Rather, the aside provides Cicero's *readers* with the information necessary to understand the witticism that follows and so creates a group bond between his own reading audience and the spectators in the anecdote. From the beginning, Lamia stands apart.

Cicero's one-word description of Lamia as "disfigured" reaffirms my earlier conclusion regarding the Roman attitude toward the responsibility an individual has for his physical deformities. Cicero's failure here to specify Lamia's deformity demonstrates that the precise nature of an opponent's disability should not concern the orator. A physical defect of *any* kind provides sufficient proof of responsibility. The type of deformity does not seem to matter so much as what its existence can reveal about an individual's character and his relationship with nature.

The exchange itself can now be analyzed. Strabo intends to provide an example of irony (*inversio verborum*), and Crassus' initial remark meets this expectation: he refers to Lamia as a "pretty little boy" (*pulchellus puer*). This alliterative grouping involves a double insult. In chapter 4 I discuss the ways in which "boy" (*puer*) marks Lamia as the submissive partner in a male-male sexual relationship.[46] The diminutive *pulchellus*

---

[45] I borrow the rendering of *invertuntur* ("to use in irony") from Wilkins ad loc.; for *adridere* in its usual sense of "to laugh *in approval*," see *TLL* 2:637.27–41.

[46] Richlin 1992a: 33–44 discusses the erotic ideal of the *puer* as revealed in the literature of the period.

("pretty little"), however, is the key to this joke, since it directly answers Lamia's own comment on his physical appearance (*formam*). And as the audience's laughter shows, the remark has achieved its intended effect. So far nothing strikes the modern reader as peculiar; an equivalent response to such a joke on the part of a modern audience may be considered cruel but certainly not unusual.

Lamia then attempts to confront Crassus and the laughter with reason. He may not be held responsible for his physical characteristics, he maintains, but only for his intellectual attainments. Lamia recognizes that Crassus' remark depended upon the expectation that an unsightly person would be rude. Crassus' second response echoes his initial use of irony: "let's hear the skillful speaker" (*audiamus disertum*). Yet this is not a simple repetition. If Crassus' statement were merely a variation on his first jibe, it would be difficult to explain why Strabo stresses its substantially greater effect on the audience—Crassus "met with a much stronger burst of approving laughter" (*multo . . . adrisum est vehementius*). In commenting on this passage, Wilkins infers that the humor in Crassus' remark relies on the fact that "doubtless Lamia . . . was a very poor speaker." By this logic, however, Crassus seems to introduce a fault entirely separate from Lamia's physical appearance. This would run contrary to Cicero's usual practice in the humor section of On the Orator book 2, in which he provides his reader with all the information necessary to understand a witticism. Strabo would have referred in advance to Lamia's lack of eloquence if such a fact were relevant. Yet Strabo only emphasizes that Lamia is *deformis*.

Crassus has pretended to yield to Lamia's argument that he bears no responsibility for his appearance, but by incongruously applying the adjective "eloquent" (*disertus*) to one with a physical deformity—or, more specifically, to a disfigured person having the ability to shape his own *ingenium*, his own intellectual capabilities—Crassus prompts the Roman audience to an even stronger degree of laughter. The humor arising from Crassus' initial ironic reference to Lamia as a "pretty little boy" (*pulchellus puer*) is increased by the unlikely juxtaposition of a speaker being both *disertus* and *deformis*, eloquent and yet ugly.[47]

Strabo relates another joke on physical peculiarities that won great ap-

---

[47] The remark from the crowd concerning Calvus' eloquence that Catullus finds so witty—"*Di magni, salaputtium disertum!*" ("Great gods! An eloquent *salaputtium!*"; Catull. 53.5)—may derive at least some of its force from the similar incongruity of a short man— i.e., a man with a physical peculiarity—having a forceful and effective speaking style. (We know from Sen. *Contr.* 7.4.7 that the word *salaputtium*, a *hapax legomenon*, refers to Calvus' small stature; any interpretation beyond this requires educated guesswork. Whether the word also served as a slang for "penis," which would certainly give a humorous picture, is still open to question: see Adams 65.)

proval from the Roman spectators. It involves the public humiliation of
an opponent by means of a visual comparison. The witticism is one of
Strabo's own:

> valde autem ridentur etiam imagines, quae fere in deformitatem aut in ali-
> quod vitium corporis ducuntur cum similitudine turpioris: ut meum illud in
> Helvium Manciam "iam ostendam cuius modi sis," cum ille "ostende,
> quaeso;" demonstravi digito pictum Gallum in Mariano scuto Cimbrico sub
> Novis distortum, eiecta lingua, buccis fluentibus; risus est commotus; nihil
> tam Manciae simile visum est. (*De orat.* 2.266; cf. Quint. *Inst.* 6.3.38, Plin.
> *Nat.* 35.25)

> Representations are also very humorous. They are usually directed at a de-
> formity or at some bodily fault, which is compared to something uglier. For
> example, there's that [joke] I directed at Helvius Mancia [when I remarked],
> "Now I'll show what kind of person you are." When Mancia [replied],
> "Please do," I pointed with my finger to a Gaul that was painted on one of
> Marius' Cimbrian shields [hanging] near the New Shops. [The Gaul was]
> distorted, with his tongue hanging out and flabby cheeks. This stirred up
> laughter; nothing seemed so much like Mancia.

The humor depends upon the ambiguity of the phrase "I'll show what
kind of person you are" (*ostendam cuius modi sis*). Mancia, expecting
Strabo will launch an attack on his character, defiantly challenges his
opponent to proceed. Strabo, playing on a concrete interpretation of *cuius
modi sis*—"what you *look* like"—instead points to a sign hanging nearby
that bears the caricature of a Gallic savage.[48] Through his external resemblance to the Gaul, Mancia becomes the foreigner's moral equivalent: his
physical appearance labels him as an outcast. The positive crowd reaction
shows that Strabo has succeeded in revealing "what kind of person" his
opponent is: "nothing seemed so much like Mancia" (*nihil tam Manciae
simile visum est*). The wit of Strabo's attack derives, as I have said, from
his interpreting the phrase *cuius modi sis* in a way his audience did not
expect. Yet the joke's rhetorical power resides in the Roman predisposition toward associating physical appearance with moral character. "What
you look like" and "what kind of person you are" can be rendered as
equivalents not only in the Latin language (*cuius modi sis*) but in the Latin
worldview as well.

Strabo attempted to convince his hearers of Mancia's unsavory character by appealing to a pictorial caricature. Hyperbolic representations similar to that on the shopkeeper's sign would have been familiar to a Roman
audience from nonpolitical contexts. Equally familiar would have been

---

[48] Perl argues convincingly that Strabo (or Cicero?) errs here, and that the figure on the
shield represents not a Gaul but a Gorgon. However, this does not affect my conclusions.

the interpretation of these representations. The masks worn by actors on the comic stage, for example, depict the marginalized figures of society as physically other, thus rendering them more susceptible to mockery. Slaves, moneylenders, pimps, and parasites were readily recognizable from their distorted features. Masks with gaping mouths, vicious teeth, bald heads, and distorted noses characterize the evil and absurd to the spectator at the theater.[49] This equation of exterior and interior in the dramatic setting influenced everyday linguistic usage. The Latin word for mask, *persona*, came to denote the personality of the character behind the mask and thus, by extension, was commonly applied to any individual's moral temperament.[50] In other words, whether in a dramatic or a political context, the *persona* did not serve as concealment but as a visual cue to the person beneath.

Fascination with the grotesque was to peak under the early Empire, as freak shows displaced traditional theatrical performances. Even the courts of emperors became populated with anatomically peculiar human beings.[51] Moralizing texts of the period conflate this obsession over physical peculiarities with a contemporaneous decline in rhetoric. At one point in his treatise on the rhetorical education of children, the first-century CE writer Quintilian discusses how it is sometimes valuable for students to read faulty and corrupt rhetoric. These inferior texts, the rhetorician claims, can provide a helpful counterexample of the style toward which the aspiring orator should aim. The subject stimulates Quintilian to critique the oratory of his day which, he laments, has rejected "natural" forms of expression (*secundum naturam*):

> illa vero, quae utcumque deflexa sunt, tamquam exquisitiora miramur non aliter quam distortis et quocumque modo prodigiosis corporibus apud quosdam maius est pretium quam iis, quae nihil ex communis habitus bonis perdiderunt. (Quint. *Inst.* 2.5.11)

> And yet the more abnormal the [rhetorical elements] are, the more we marvel, as if they were more precious. This is no different from those people who consider bodies that have somehow become twisted and unnatural as more valuable than those which have lost none of the qualities people commonly share.

People share a recognizable physique, one that, if morality were secure, would be desirable for all properly discerning persons. This conflation of

---

[49] Bieber 147–56, 247–48 argues, with many illustrations, that Roman masks exaggerate grotesque features to a greater extent than their Greek models.

[50] See Garton 11–12. Dozens of examples of this extended use of *persona* occur in Cicero's writings; see most conveniently *OLD*, s.v. 4; Merguet, s.v.

[51] Barton 86–90, 168, to which I owe the following reference to Quint. *Inst.* 2.5.11.

moral breakdown with the collapse of Ciceronian rhetorical standards is
not peculiar to the rhetorician Quintilian. Numerous texts from the first
century CE see the deterioration of oratorical style not only as symptom-
atic of moral decay but often as being one of the causes of this decay.[52]
Seneca encapsulates the position with characteristic brevity in his discussion of how the improper speaking style of Augustus' advisor Maecenas
matches his effeminate behavior: "our way of speaking mirrors our way
of life" (*Epist.* 114.1).

In all these discussions of oratorical decline, Cicero looms as the standard from which contemporary speakers have degenerated. For as we
have seen, in Cicero's rhetoric the beauty of the physical form and a trust
in nature coincide. This equation, as Quintilian attests, has as its necessary complement a certain purity of expression.[53] The deformed Lamia
clearly demonstrates how a lack in any one of these areas implies a lack in
another: the ironic references to his ugliness (*pulchellus puer*) and lack of
eloquence (*disertus*) both evoked complicit peals of laughter. The superior
Roman citizen speaks well and has an attractive physique. The combination provides proof that nature has not erred.

Jokes employed outside the courts, the senate house, and public gather-
ings provide further indications of the popular attitude toward physical
appearance. Although teasingly few, these apparently everyday jokes
further indicate that the abuse found in late Republican rhetoric would
not have been considered unusual by a contemporary audience. As was
the case in court with the unfortunate Lucius Lamia, deformities also
prompted witticisms in daily life. On one occasion a dinner guest of the
great painter Lucius Mallius remarked on the inconsistency of Mallius'
creative genius: although he produced beautiful paintings, his children
were exceptionally ugly (*deforme*). Mallius replied: "I procreate at night, I
create in light" (*"tenebris enim fingo," inquit, "luce pingo"*: Macr. *Sat.*
2.2.10; other jokes on ugliness occur at Cic. *Scaur.* 6; Cic. *Att.* 1.13.2 =
SB 13, 12.11 = SB 249; Plut. *Cic.* 27.4 [cf. *Mor.* 205c]). Examples of the
mockery of small stature indicate that our short juror Aurifex would not
have walked the streets unassailed (Macr. *Sat.* 2.3.3, 4; perhaps Quint.
Inst. 6.3.67). Two remaining categories of jokes that seem to have had
currency outside public life provide a convenient segue into the final section of this chapter: loss of hair and bodily swellings. Both insufficiency
and excess invite laughter. Julius Caesar, as he marched triumphantly
through the city streets after defeating the Gauls, was chided by his soldiers as "the bald-headed adulterer" (*moechum calvum*, Suet. *Iul.* 51; for

[52] The appropriate texts are assembled and discussed by Williams 1978: 6–51; see also
Edwards 137–72.
[53] David 1983: 315 discusses the ways in which orators from the municipalities were
discriminated against on account of their means of expression.

more jokes on baldness see Cic. *De orat.* 2.250, *Att.* 14.2.3 = SB 356; cf.
Tusc. 3.62). The playwright Publilius Syrus, happening upon a hydro-
cephalic slave lying in the sun, explained to his companion that the boy
was "boiling water" (*aquam calefacit,* Macr. *Sat.* 2.7.6; funny swellings are
also mentioned at Suet. *Gramm.* 9.3, *Rhet.* 29.1; Macr. *Sat.* 2.3.5; Quint.
Inst. 6.3.77 [cf. Macr. *Sat.* 2.6.4]). All these instances of abuse do more
than entertain: they strengthen the already present bias concerning the
moral significance of a physical failing. The men who laughed at these
jokes and preserved them for posterity are the same men who listened to
Cicero as he took control of their laughter and molded it into the recognized definition of the proper citizen of Rome.

FANNIUS AND VATINIUS: CICERO TEACHES HIS AUDIENCE TO READ

Cicero's defense of Quintus Roscius, one of his earliest extant orations,
reveals the same strategies for the treatment of physical peculiarities that
his early rhetorical handbook, *On Rhetorical Invention*, prescribed. Cicero
wishes to demonstrate that his client, the famous actor Quintus Roscius,
could not have defrauded the accusing party, Gaius Fannius. Proof lies in
Fannius' physical appearance:

> oro atque obsecro vos, qui nostis, vitam inter se utriusque conferte. qui non
> nostis, faciem utriusque considerate. nonne ipsum caput et supercilia illa
> penitus abrasa olere malitiam et clamitare calliditatem videntur? nonne ab
> imis unguibus usque ad verticem summum (si quam coniecturam affert
> hominibus tacita corporis figura) ex fraude, fallaciis, mendaciis constare
> totus videtur? qui idcirco capite et superciliis semper est rasis, ne ullum
> pilum viri boni habere dicatur. (*Q. Rosc.* 20)

> I beg and beseech those of you who know them to compare their way of life.
> As for those of you who do not know them, ponder each of their faces.
> Surely Fannius' (*illa*) very head and eyebrows, so closely shaven, seem to
> stink of evil and proclaim his shrewd nature. Surely [this man] (if physical
> appearance does in fact allow one to make inferences even though it cannot
> speak) from the tips of his toenails to the very top of his head, is entirely
> made up of fraud, deceit, and lies. Here's why he's always got his head and
> eyebrows close-cropped: he's afraid somebody will say he's got a single hair
> of a good man.

Cicero caps his comparison between Fannius' physical exterior and spiritual interior with a verbal play, a technique common in the examples of
wit already cited from *On the Orator*. The closing witticism rests on an
allusion to the idiom *aliquid pili habere,* "to have a hair's worth"—that is,
to possess a negligible amount of some quality. Fannius, in his state of

depilation, cannot even be considered worth a hair of anything, much less the hair of a good man. This play on the double meaning of *pilus*, "hair" or "shred," made conspicuous by a favored rhythmic clausula, underscores the absurdity of the nearly hairless Fannius by supplying an even more absurd motive for his self-depilation. Cicero makes Fannius' inner corruption apparent to all by equating the man's outward appearance with the very idiom that describes his evil nature—"without a single hair of a good man." The audience can now truly "read" Fannius' appearance. The capping witticism transforms him into a verbalized expression of his own internal character.

We shall never know how humorous Cicero's audience would have found this wordplay—did his reputation as the funniest man in Rome rest on witticisms such as this? Fortunately for my purposes, more significant than the joke itself are the premises informing it. The orator makes clear to his audience the ethical bias from which his remarks will stem: if they do not already realize the decadence of Fannius' lifestyle when compared to Roscius', this will become apparent from a comparison of their facial features (*qui [vitam utriusque] non nostis, faciem utriusque considerate*). A scholar of this century who has studied Cicero's humor accuses the young orator here of the "exaggeration of an imagination that is still too contrived."[54] Such an accusation, however, ignores the fact that Fannius stands before everyone's eyes as this description proceeds. Cicero relies upon the accuracy of his words just as much as their art in achieving the full effect of this humiliation. For Cicero's remarks do not reflect the excesses of an artful imagination but rather recognize the predispositions of his audience.

Despite what he says, however, Cicero does not limit his portrait to Fannius' face and mysterious predilection for short head and facial hair; rather, he hints at how Fannius' entire physique indicates his foul nature.[55] In this way, he extrapolates on the beliefs given in *On the Laws*, as he moves beyond the countenance (*vultus*) to point out the corrupt nature of Fannius' entire physical and moral being. A similar movement from describing the particular aspects of a face to criticizing the entire body

[54] Haury 1955: 101 ("on critiquera sans doute ce que le traducteur appelle l' 'exagération d'une imagination encore trop artificielle'"). The "traducteur" is J. Bayet, *Littérature latine* (Paris 1934) 191–92.

[55] Cicero's remarks here closely resemble Scipio Aemilianus' attack on the *homo delicatus* Publius Sulpicius Galus (Gell. 6.12.5 = *ORF* 21.17). In that instance, however, Galus plucks hair on not only his face but his thighs. I shall discuss further the force of Aemilianus' statements in chapter 4. For now I simply note that whereas Aemilianus uses his remarks to attribute to Galus a single, private fault (that he is a *cinaedus*), Cicero here uses Fannius' lack of hair as an indicator of faults more directly connected to public concerns (*olere malitiam et clamitare. . . . ex fraude fallaciis mendaciis constare totus videtur*).

and its associated character occurs in Cicero's portrait of Vatinius, which I shall discuss below.

Before leaving the passage from *On Behalf of Quintus Roscius*, however, I would like to note how Cicero facilitates this transition from the traits for which Fannius bears direct responsibility—namely his "close-cropped head and eyebrows" (*ipsum caput et supercilia illa penitus abrasa*)—to those with which he has been endowed by nature—that is, his physique "from the tips of his toenails to the very top of his head" (*ab imis unguibus usque ad verticem summum*). Cicero provides a link through the aside "if physical appearance does in fact allow men to make inferences even though it cannot speak" (*si quam coniecturam affert hominibus tacita corporis figura*). The phrase recalls the statement from *On Rhetorical Invention* that personal attributes are relevant for making inferences about character (*Inv.* 2.29). This parenthetical expression in the oration does not, as may seem at first glance, represent Cicero's apology for admitting this kind of evidence in his speech. Rather, the incomplete conditional conveys to his audience a reminder of the connection between the physical and spiritual. Two factors strongly favor such a reading. The first is grammatical: the indicative *affert* in the protasis (hence my translation "does in fact allow") indicates that Cicero's trust in nature represents a *fact* about internal and external correspondence and not simply an hypothesis. Second and more significantly, it is highly unlikely that Cicero would interrupt his carefully prepared climax (*constare totus videtur*) with a point that would undercut the course of his entire argument up to that moment. Hence Cicero's parenthesis provides valuable evidence for how a Roman audience would have received the aside. Rather than causing them to doubt the premise of the orator's whole narrative (as, one would expect, such an offhand "if" clause would lead a modern audience to do), the remark instead recalls to their attention their own already existing understanding of the connotations behind an individual's physical peculiarities. One look informs the astute observer that Fannius cannot be believed. By pointing explicitly to the preconceived notions of his audience, Cicero ensures that his description will attain its intended and anticipated effect: the identification of his opponent as an evil character who must not be trusted.

Fannius should be thankful for the relatively gentle treatment he received from the young Cicero. By the time of the speech against Vatinius twenty years later, Cicero has developed a disarmingly direct technique for exposing an opponent's physical peculiarities. The orator no longer contents himself with the single compact portrait one finds in *On Behalf of Quintus Roscius*. Instead, Vatinius' deformities constitute a recurrent motif that grows steadily throughout the oration.

Publius Vatinius' various physical deformities—including facial swellings and a severe case of gout—reached legendary proportions beyond the sphere of rhetorical invective.[56] The *strumae* that received such close attention from his enemies are described by the medical writer Celsus as "glandular swellings of pus and blood" that take an unusually long time to heal (5.28.7; leaving this pleasant image in the reader's mind, I shall simply refer to them as "swellings"). A notorious demagogue, Vatinius spent a lifetime deflecting the abuse aimed at these defects. One of the final recorded events of his life represents the culmination of this abuse. As governor of Illyria in 43 BCE, Vatinius attempted to keep Brutus out of Dyrrachium despite the counterdemands of his own soldiers. Velleius explains the soldiers' refusal to cooperate:

> et Brutus cuilibet ducum praeferendus videretur et Vatinius nulli homini non esset postferendus, in quo deformitas corporis cum turpitudine certabat ingeni, adeo ut animus eius dignissimo domicilio inclusus videretur. (Vell. 2.69.3)

> They thought both that Brutus was to be preferred to any other leader and that there was no one whom they wouldn't prefer over Vatinius, in whom physical deformity carried on such a struggle with foulness of character that his soul seemed trapped in a most fitting residence.

Dio's account ascribes similar motives to the army.[57] Since the two historians do not doubt the plausibility of the soldiers' motivations, their texts most likely reveal their audience's acceptance of the correlation between the physical and spiritual. That Velleius and Dio could even suggest that such motives underlie the soldiers' desertion attests to the power inherent in the equation of external ugliness and internal corruption.

Seneca describes Vatinius as "a man born for both laughter and scorn"

---

[56] In addition to the references discussed below in the text, cf. *RE* 8A.1:515–16 (H. Gundel).

[57] Dio 47.21.6: "For his soldiers revolted, angry at him and despising his disease" (οἱ γὰρ στρατιῶται ἀχθόμενοί τε αὐτῷ καὶ προσκαταφρονήσαντες αὐτοῦ διὰ νόσον μετέστησαν). I understand Dio's "disease" to be equivalent to Velleius' *deformitas*, although Gundel 516 (see previous note) expresses uncertainty as to which *deformitas* Velleius refers. It seems most likely, however, that Velleius has in mind here (or the soldiers do) the famous *struma(e)* that loom so large in the speech *Against Vatinius*. Celsus (5.28.7) records that *strumae* leave scars and tend to recur throughout one's lifetime, regardless of whether one treats them with surgery (*ferrum*) or salves (*medicamenta*). Hence it is quite likely that Vatinius would have had scars (if not recurrent swellings) that would have been visible to all. In addition, I suspect that the only other certain affliction of Vatinius, his gout (*podagra*), would not be referred to as a *deformitas*, although I suppose this is not impossible. Cicero (*Phil.* 10.13) and Appian (*BC* 4.75) say that Vatinius willingly surrendered Dyrrachium to Brutus. Their accounts are not necessarily incompatible with those of Velleius and Dio.

(*hominem natum et ad risum et ad odium*; *Dial*. 2.17.3). This characterization suggests that the episode at Dyrrachium does not represent an isolated instance of Vatinius' appearance being used publicly against him. Seneca chose to mention Vatinius in his essay *On the Constancy of the Philosopher* to illustrate a type of strength in the face of adversity: one who mocks himself will avoid being mocked. The philosopher admires Vatinius' response to his many attackers:

> in pedes suos ipse plurima dicebat et in fauces concisas. sic inimicorum, quos plures habebat quam morbos, et in primis Ciceronis urbanitatem effugit. si hoc potuit ille duritia oris, qui assiduis conviciis pudere dedidicerat, cur is non possit qui studiis liberalibus et sapientiae cultu ad aliquem profectum pervenerit? (Sen. *Dial*. 2.17.3)

> He would voluntarily make many remarks about his feet and scarred throat. In this way he escaped the wit of his enemies—of which he possessed a greater number than of diseases—and especially Cicero's. If he was able [to accomplish this] through brazenness (*duritia oris*), a man who had learned how not to feel shame before constant abuse, why shouldn't one who has reached an advanced state through liberal studies and the pursuit of philosophy be able to [do the same]?

Only one anecdote survives in which Vatinius practices the kind of self-deprecation in the face of abuse Seneca describes here. Unfortunately, the joke does not directly concern his physical appearance and, in addition, lies concealed within yet another joke directed against him. It appears that Vatinius' unpopularity had become so great that, during a set of games that he had sponsored, the people in attendance pelted him with stones. Presumably in the spirit of genial self-effacement that Seneca admires, Vatinius succeeded in having the aediles pass an edict allowing the spectators at his games to throw only fruit. This witty gesture did not, however, quell the abuse. During this same period, someone happened to ask the legal expert Cascellius whether a pinecone (*nux pinea*) qualified as a fruit. Cascellius replied, "if you're going to throw it at Vatinius, it's a fruit" (*"si in Vatinium missurus es, pomum est"*; Macr. *Sat*. 2.6.1).

Seneca interprets such actions on Vatinius' part as exemplifying the Stoic resolve of a human being secure in the possession of virtue: the wounded politician does not lash out but turns the other cheek, even mocking himself.[58] An understanding of jokes on physical deformities provides an explanation more in keeping with late Republican values.

---

[58] Sen. *Dial*. 2.16.1–3. Richlin 1992a: 103, 284 cites many other examples from Seneca and elsewhere of how "a man in public life has to be able to bear insults with equanimity." Vatinius, however, is certainly unique in the sheer volume of abuse he received for his physical appearance.

Contrary to Seneca's view, Vatinius does not act out the role of a self-effacing Stoic. Rather, his actions represent a tactic, however imperfect, for self-preservation. One need only recall the Lamia/Crassus exchange from *On the Orator* book 2: to confront humor directed towards one's defects was to invite even harsher laughter. Vatinius fought fire with its fuel. Only by subscribing to the popular belief that caused the legendary scorn against him did he have any chance of fending off that scorn.

Cicero's own attacks on Vatinius were of far more serious import than the legal definition of the pinecone. The earliest datable jab at Vatinius occurred during Cicero's praetorship in 66 BCE:

> ἐπεὶ δὲ Οὐατίνιος, ἀνὴρ ἔχων τι τραχὺ καὶ πρὸς τοὺς ἄρχοντας ὀλίγωρον ἐν ταῖς συνηγορίαις, χοιράδων δὲ τὸν τράχηλον περίπλεως, ἠτεῖτό τι καταστὰς παρὰ τοῦ Κικέρωνος, καὶ μὴ διδόντος, ἀλλὰ βουλευομένου πολὺν χρόνον, εἶπεν ὡς οὐκ ἂν αὐτὸς διστάσειε περὶ τούτου στρατηγῶν, ἐπιστραφεὶς ὁ Κικέρων, "Ἀλλ' ἐγώ," εἶπεν, "οὐκ ἔχω τηλικοῦτον τράχηλον." (Plut. *Cic.* 9.3)

> Vatinius was a man who had a somewhat rough and contemptuous attitude toward the officials presiding over the courts. He also had a neck covered with swellings. One time, in the court of [the praetor] Cicero, he made a request that Cicero did not grant immediately, but pondered over for a long time. Whereupon Vatinius said that he himself would not waver (διστάσειε) about this if he were in charge. Cicero, turning to him, replied, "But I don't have a neck like yours."

The interpretation of Cicero's reply is controversial. Some scholars believe that Plutarch's διστάσειε represents an original form of the Latin verb *nutare* ("to nod" or "waver"). Through a careless rendering, it is argued, Plutarch has destroyed an original pun on the literal meaning of *nutare* on Cicero's part.[59] On this interpretation, Cicero mocks Vatinius for his swollen neck, which, he ironically pretends, gives the illusion of strength and so, by metaphorical extension, reveals an unwavering attitude.

An understanding of the Roman attitude toward physical peculiarities offers an alternative explanation that both redeems Plutarch and provides a more complex and effective joke. At Rome, a large or thick neck could negatively connote defiance in the face of legitimate authority.[60] Three

---

[59] Erbse 190–91, following Sickinger 66–67. For the metaphorical use of *nutare*, Erbse cites *Nat. deor.* 1.120 and *Fin.* 2.6.

[60] Cic. *Verr.* 2.3.135; Sen. *Contr.* 3.praef.16, where Seneca describes himself after making an outrageous joke as one "who has such a thick neck" (*qui tam crassas cervices haberem*). Cf. Persius 1.98, in which the phrase *laxa cervice* ("with a slack neck") accompanies the adjective *tenerum* ("tender").

separate considerations demand that one interpret Plutarch's "But I don't have a neck like yours" ("Ἀλλ' ἐγὼ οὐκ ἔχω τηλικοῦτον τράχηλον") along these lines, that is, as referring to Vatinius' contumacy. First, Plutarch's introductory description of Vatinius as "a man who had a somewhat rough and contemptuous attitude toward the officials presiding over the courts" (ἀνὴρ ἔχων τι τραχὺ καὶ πρὸς τοὺς ἄρχοντας ὀλίγωρον ἐν ταῖς συνηγορίαις) then provides information necessary for Cicero's subsequent witticism. If the intended pun is on the notion of nodding (*nutare*), however, this introductory description has little point. Indeed, it may not be accidental—and may in fact reflect Plutarch's Roman source—that this description of Vatinius' obstinate character immediately precedes the grammatically parallel clause describing his physical qualities: "he also had a neck covered with swellings" (χοιράδων δὲ τὸν τράχηλον περίπλεως [ἔχων]). Second, my proposed interpretation makes it unnecessary to suppose that Plutarch has here misunderstood and so mistranslated his source; in fact, Plutarch may even be attempting to preserve Cicero's pun through the similar-sounding words τραχύ ("harsh") and τράχηλον ("neck"). Third and most significantly, Cicero's witticism then possesses the same structure as his later jokes against the unfortunate Vatinius and accords with the findings of this chapter: the use of humor in describing an opponent's physical faults can provide the Roman with a means of revealing a negative internal trait. Vatinius' bold behavior before the praetor Cicero could have been predicted by his physical appearance.

Ten years after his praetorship, in the *Interrogatio in Vatinium* of 56 BCE, Cicero questions Vatinius as the chief witness in a charge of violence (*de vi*) that has been brought against Publius Sestius. Ostensibly the orator intends to impugn the former tribune's testimony. As the extant speech shows, however, Cicero also takes the opportunity to malign Vatinius' character in matters that seem unrelated to the charges brought against Sestius.[61] This abuse encompasses the entire range of the subject's life and includes references to Vatinius' physical defects. As the speech progresses, these physical peculiarities gradually assume an independent existence until they have metamorphosed into a visible extension of Vatinius' corruption.

Cicero begins his interrogation by questioning its necessity: Vatinius' way of life makes him too trivial a witness for his charges to be treated seriously and too suspect a one for his testimony to be believed (*Vat.* 1). The orator can make these statements on account of the popular hatred of

---

[61] Only sections 1–3 and 40–41 treat the charges directly. On the extent to which *Against Vatinius* represents an original speech or a version substantially revised for publication, see Pocock's commentary 4–5, 134–45 (= appendix I).

his subject, a hatred later attested by Seneca and Velleius.[62] Cicero portrays this hatred as felt strongly by his entire audience: "although because of your crime against me I should surpass all in my hatred of you, I am nevertheless exceeded by nearly everyone" (*in quo [odio tui] etsi omnis propter tuum in me scelus superare debeo, tamen ab omnibus paene vincor*; *Vat.* 1). This simultaneous reminder and verification of Vatinius' unpopularity facilitates Cicero's final step in separating his victim from all else present. Vatinius becomes a true outcast—"no one deems him worthy of meeting, of approaching, of a vote, of citizenship, even of the light of day" (*quem nemo congressu, nemo aditu, nemo suffragio, nemo civitate, nemo luce dignum putet*; *Vat.* 2). Each successive phrase makes Vatinius less of a member of his immediate community, less a citizen, until finally he does not even deserve to live. In the opening address to Vatinius, Cicero has isolated his subject and shown how his unpopularity makes him unfit for human society. Vatinius' unpopularity, Cicero will argue, stems in part from those physical defects that cause him to stand out as an individual.

After having quickly dispensed with some matters pertaining to the Sestius case (*Vat.* 2–3), Cicero returns emphatically to Vatinius' personality: "you are by nature excessively violent and headstrong" (*nimium es vehemens feroxque natura*; *Vat.* 4). This violent nature has not lain hidden, however; Cicero proceeds to inform his audience how he was able to foresee it on an earlier occasion. The orator's language stresses his foreknowledge through the use of four different verbs in the course of one short sentence: "as soon as I saw you, before you started speaking, . . . I felt and foresaw" (*simul ac te aspexi, prius quam loqui coepisti*, . . . *sensi atque providi*; *Vat.* 4). On this earlier occasion Vatinius' personal appearance presaged his potential for doing harm:

> repente enim te tamquam serpens e latibulis oculis eminentibus, inflato collo, tumidis cervicibus intulisti. (*Vat.* 4)

> For suddenly you came on like a serpent from its lair—eyes jutting out, throat swollen, neck bulging.

Vatinius metamorphoses into a snake poised to strike Cicero.[63] As in his portrait of Fannius, the orator describes a combination of Vatinius' per-

---

[62] Hatred of Vatinius, which I won't pretend to attribute entirely to his looks, is well attested; in addition to the passages cited, see Catull. 14.3, 52; *ORF* 165.26 (Calvus). Cicero also gets much mileage out of the related jokes on Vatinius' claim to be a *popularis*, which include the particularly cruel remarks on Vatinius' (reported) death (Quint. *Inst.* 6.3.68, 84).

[63] See Pocock 78–80 and 134–45 (appendix I), for the specific occasion Cicero here describes and its relation to the prosecution of Sestius. The passage cited continues with *ut mihi renovatus ille tuus in to*. . . and then trails off into a lacuna (Peterson in the OCT estimates a gap of approximately forty lines). Pocock provides in his appendix I (especially at

manent and temporary appearance: the inflated neck and throat allude to his notorious facial swellings, whereas the protruding eyes seem to derive from the excitement of the moment.[64] Such a description serves two ends. First, the grotesque portrait of Vatinius' features *temporarily* roused to excitement anticipates the final state of despair the orator wishes to reduce him to before ending his interrogation. I quoted at the beginning of this chapter Cicero using similar tactics in his invective against Piso, in which powerful language reduces Piso to a timid and quivering beast (cf. *Vat.* 1: *vexatum potius quam despectum vellem dimittere*—"I preferred to send [you] off harassed rather than hated"). Second, the allusion to Vatinius' *permanent* deformities demonstrates Cicero's ability to anticipate Vatinius' violent reaction from his appearance. Swollen like an angry serpent, he is bound to act the way he does. Cicero's listeners should now, in turn, have no problem interpreting Vatinius' physique as a reflection of his internal turpitude.

In a later passage of the speech, Vatinius' swollen countenance again betrays an emotional reaction. Cicero, having occasion to compare his own political career with that of Vatinius, asks the former tribune to tell him whose actions have reaped more benefits for the state. He continues:

> cum mihi hoc responderis, aut ita impudenter ut manus a te homines vix abstinere possint, aut ita dolenter ut aliquando ista quae sunt inflata rumpantur, tum memoriter respondeto ad ea quae te de te ipso rogaro. (*Vat.* 10)

> When you have answered this either with such impudence that people will scarcely be able to keep their hands off you or with such distress that those

---

137–38) an attractive reconstruction of what Vatinius' counterattack, now lost in the lacuna, may have included.

The *Rhetorica ad Herennium* gives as an example of "simile for the sake of abuse" a description of a snake that resembles Cicero's simile here (*Rhet. Her.* 4.62). The *ad Herennium* comparison, however, relies solely upon similarities of temperament, not physique. This variation may indicate further ways in which Hellenistic treatises differ from Roman practice in the treatment of physical peculiarities.

[64] There may be another reference to Vatinius having a visible eye problem at *Vat.* 25, which would account for the ironic use of *credo* in that passage: "[you wished to check] Lucius Domitius, whose dignity and splendor, I hear, dazzled the eyes of Vatinius" (*L. Domitium, cuius dignitas et splendor praestringebat, credo, oculos Vatini ⟨opprimere voluisti⟩*). No other evidence exists, however, for Vatinius having an eye problem—Pocock 79 argues against one possibility—and attributing the reference here at *Vat.* 25 (if there is any) to temporary excitement would fit the context, where Cicero lists a number of prominent citizens whom Vatinius wished to do away with in his co-conspiracy with Vettius.

One scholiast recognizes the references to Vatinius' physical deformities at *Vat.* 10 (Schol. Bob. p. 145, 13 [Stangl]); cf. his remarks on *Sest.* 135 (p. 141, 10–12 [Stangl]). Other specific references to Vatinius' neck or *strumae* include Plut. *Cic.* 9.3, 26.3; Cic. *Att.* 2.9.2.

puffed up things of yours (*ista . . . inflata*) will eventually burst, then respond accurately to what I'll ask you about yourself.

Vatinius' facial swellings are clearly alluded to through the deictic pronoun *ista* ("those things of yours") and the adjective *inflata* ("puffed up," which recalls the "puffed up neck" described at *Vat.* 4—*inflato collo, tumidis cervicibus*). Cicero puns on the literal meaning of *inflata* ("puffed up") and *rumpere* ("to burst"): literally, they refer to the visible swellings on Vatinius' face; metaphorically, they can describe a person's reaction to excessive distress—he "bursts with emotion."[65] The rhetorical handbooks advise the defendant to display intense grief and distress as a ploy to win the audience's sympathy.[66] The humor behind Cicero's mockery lies in the difficulty Vatinius' physique presents in allowing him to display such grief—if he were to attempt to do so, his already swollen countenance would not endure the strain. As a result, just as Fannius embodied the expression of "not having the single hair of a good man," so too would Vatinius literalize the expression "bursting with grief."[67]

As Cicero reaches the speech's close, he recalls his opening themes, through which he represented Vatinius as unfit for human society (*Vat.* 1–2).[68] Since the intervening portions of the speech marshaled evidence for Vatinius' unsociability, Cicero can now use even more vehemence and specificity in his concluding remarks. The long period at section 39 begins with Cicero describing how Julius Caesar rejected Vatinius, a former ally. Caesar does not, as it turns out, stand alone in his judgment:

[65] *Inflo*: see Petronius 74.13, where Trimalchio says of the weeping Fortunata, "she blows herself up like a frog" (*inflat se tamquam rana*). For *rumpere* and its compounds in Cicero, see *Vat.* 16; *Dom.* 99 (concerning Clodius); *Ad Q. fr.* 3.7(9).1 (SB 27). For other puns on "bursting" from emotion see Plaut. *Bacch.* 603, *Cas.* 325–26. Juvenal calls overly bombastic orators "cheeks" (*buccae*, 11.34; cf. the scholiast's explanation ad loc. [Wessner]: "they just blow up their cheeks and say nothing").

[66] E.g., [Arist.] *Rh. Al.* 1445a; Cic. *Inv.* 1.109; *Rhet. Her.* 2.50.

[67] A dictum preserved by Plutarch depends upon a similar relationship between Vatinius' appearance and his attempts at rhetorical deception: αὐτὸν δὲ τὸν Βατίνιον ἔχοντα χοιράδας ἐν τῷ τραχήλῳ καὶ λέγοντα δίκην οἰδοῦντα ῥήτορα προσεῖπεν (*Cic.* 26.2)—"Vatinius himself had swellings on his neck, and once when he was pleading a case Cicero called him a *tumid* orator" (Perrin trans. and emphasis). An anecdote preserved at Quint. *Inst.* 6.3.60, however, paints a picture of Vatinius as a more direct and less deceptive character in the courtroom.

Gundel (see n. 56 above) understands Vatinius' neck swellings as distinct from his *strumae*; but cf. Celsus' testimony that *strumae* "usually occur on the neck" (*nascuntur maxime in cervice*; 5.28.7). I see no good reason to doubt that Plutarch is translating *struma* by χοιράς both in this passage and at *Cic.* 9.3.

[68] I take *Vat.* 39 to be the formal *peroratio*; the final two sections, 40–41, revert to concluding questions on specific aspects of Sestius' case, a concern that is not, in spite of the title *interrogatio*, an aspect of the speech itself (see n. 61 above).

si te vicini, si adfines, si tribules ita oderunt ut repulsam tuam triumphum suum duxerint, si nemo aspicit quin ingemescat, nemo mentionem facit quin exsecretur, si vitant, fugiunt, audire de te nolunt, cum viderunt, tamquam auspicium malum detestantur, si cognati respuunt, tribules exsecrantur, vicini metuunt, adfines erubescunt . . . (*Vat.* 39)

If your neighbors, in-laws, and fellow-tribesmen hate you so much that they considered your defeat their triumph, if no one looks at you without groaning, no one mentions you without cursing, if they avoid you, flee from you, don't want to hear about you, [and], when they have seen you, they curse you like some bad omen, if relatives reject you, fellow tribesmen curse you, neighbors fear you, in-laws feel ashamed . . .

Through his public invective, Cicero becomes the society's moral spokesperson, inveighing against the outrage Vatinius embodies.[69] The list above presents a specific facet of Vatinius' despicable nature: his unpopularity with men at every rank of state and relation to him. The cumulative technique used recalls passages from other speeches in which Cicero represents all of Roman society as hostile to his opponent.[70] Yet the isolation of Vatinius differs from these other occasions in one important respect. The enumeration concludes by isolating the motif that I have been tracing throughout the speech—Vatinius' physical appearance:[71]

[si] strumae denique ab ore improbo demigrarunt et aliis iam se locis conlocarunt, . . . quid est quam ob rem praeturam potius exoptes quam mortem? (*Vat.* 39)

[if], finally, your swellings have moved away from the wicked area around your mouth and have already located themselves in other parts, . . . what reason could you have for preferring the praetorship to death?

Cicero figures his invective as the extension of an outcry from the entire community. As the vocabulary of this passage seems to indicate (*exsecretur, detestantur*), those near Vatinius have had recourse not simply to public defamation of him but even to rites that involved curses and magical spells. And yet it is not only society that refuses to have any contact

[69] Elliott 285–92, following Jane Harrison, discusses the notion that the two commonest means of maintaining social stability—prayer and legal codes—ultimately derive from curse practice. Political invective should be added to this list.

[70] E.g., *Catil.* 1.17; *Dom.* 48; *Pis.* 99.

[71] In his otherwise thorough analysis of how Cicero makes Vatinius into a political outcast in this speech, Albini fails to mention this portion of section 39. He does not see the relevance of Vatinius' deformities in the creation of this picture of a social monster (see esp. 181–82).

with Vatinius; his own body parts recoil from further contagion. In the earlier portions of the speech, the swellings (*strumae*) covering Vatinius' face constituted a signifier by which Cicero and his audience could read internal character. By the speech's close, Vatinius' internal evil has now escaped through his "wicked mouth" (*os improbum*). As a result, even his facial swellings—the outward representations of that evil—cannot endure its presence as they flee the source from which the evil emanates. In chapter 3 I shall examine why Cicero chooses the mouth as his symbol of wickedness and perversity. For now, I simply observe the effect the orator produces here. Vatinius, Cicero's paradigm for the correlation between physical and spiritual ugliness, has transcended even this basic concept. His evil interior refuses to be content with mere external representation; in struggling to emerge in full force, it leaves the body that is its container. Vatinius has become a Pandora's box.

The invective against Vatinius ends; Vatinius has not escaped. The trial that provided the occasion for this interrogation also produced Cicero's defense speech on behalf of Sestius. Near the end of this oration, Cicero turns to criticize the way Vatinius both condemned elite politicians (*optimates*) and voiced disapproval of Cicero's deeds while consul (*Sest.* 132–35). The orator alludes ironically to Vatinius' famous looks: among his hired thugs, Vatinius stands out as the most beautiful (*ipse pulcherrimus*; *Sest.* 134). The audience recalls Vatinius' unpopularity, for Cicero's humorous rhetoric has made it inseparable from Vatinius' appearance. Cicero has set the stage for exploiting the association once again. Vatinius has ignored not only Cicero's own laws, the orator maintains, but also other consular legislation—even that of Caesar, his supposed friend. The orator then recalls the words of Albinovanus, Sestius' prosecutor: he dared to encourage the judges to be stern at last and provide a remedy (*medicina*) for the republic (*Sest.* 135). This medical imagery appeals to Cicero, who borrows it from the opposing counsel in order to turn it back on the chief witness:

> non ea est medicina, cum sanae parti corporis scalpellum adhibetur atque integrae, carnificina est ista et crudelitas: ei medentur rei publicae qui exsecant pestem aliquam tamquam strumam civitatis. (*Sest.* 135)

> It's not a remedy when someone applies a lancet to a healthy and whole part of the body—it's butchery and cruelty on your part.[72] The ones who cure the republic are those who cut out a sore as if it were a pustular swelling (*struma*) in the state.

---

[72] I interpret *ista* with Holden ad loc.: "sc. id quod vos, iudices, accusator cohortatus est de Sestio."

The allusion would be unmistakable for the audience. References to Vatinius as a "pustular swelling" (*struma*) were not restricted to Cicero's correspondence with Atticus (*Att.* 2.9.2 = SB 29). One scholiast, writing centuries after the speech's delivery, recognizes the implications: "this applies to Vatinius himself, who reportedly had a face covered with swellings and a body covered with blemishes" (*pertinet . . . ad ipsum Vatinium, qui traditur fuisse strumosa facie et maculoso corpore*; Schol. Bob. p. 141, 10– 12 [Stangl]). Catullus too parodies this distinguishing characteristic when he encapsulates the relationship between Vatinius and one of his henchmen in the single phrase "that swelling Nonius" (*struma Nonius*; Catull. 52.2)—Nonius is an ugly appendage living off its carrier, just like Vatinius' other growths.[73] But here in his speech for Sestius Cicero exploits the established associations of these swellings in order to achieve a new effect. Instead of the swellings fleeing from Vatinius' evil, as occurred at the close of *Against Vatinius*, the opposite metamorphosis now takes place. Vatinius himself becomes a parasitic growth, one that plagues the state. More than an outcast, Vatinius is perceived as a clinging, scrofulous swelling. Such a condition requires obvious and immediate treatment: radical surgery.

We are fortunate in this case not to have to resort to guessing whether Cicero's attack constituted part of a successful defense. The orator tells his brother Quintus that Sestius was acquitted by a unanimous vote and that he himself concluded his attack on Vatinius "to the applause of gods and men" (*dis hominibusque plaudentibus*). As for Vatinius' temperament after the trial: "What do you think? The impudent and audacious man, [feeling] very distraught and crushed, went away" (*quid quaeris? homo petulans et audax valde perturbatus debilitatusque discessit*; Ad Q. fr. 2.4.1 = SB 8).

PHYSICAL PECULIARITIES AS SIGNS

Cicero's treatment of his opponents Fannius and Vatinius confirms what I have argued throughout this chapter. In Roman society of the late Republic, a physical peculiarity indicated otherness, becoming a mark that

[73] This attractive interpretation (from Pocock 129) explains the otherwise oddly coincidental occurrence of *struma* and *Vatinius* in consecutive lines (Catull. 52.2–3; I do not think that *Struma* is Nonius' cognomen, as Cornish and Forcellini construe it, apparently through a misreading of Plin. *Nat.* 37.81). Catullus had himself witnessed his friend Calvus' speech against Vatinius (Catull. 53—cf. 14.3; other poems attesting to this friendship include 50 and 96; testimonia and fragments of Calvus' speech are in *ORF* pp. 492–98). The poet was not one to overlook another's physical deformities (see n. 17 above). It is hard to believe he would have passed over Vatinius, who provided such excellent material on this score, in composing poem 52.

distinguished the person affected from his peers. Cicero, relying on the notion that nature does not deceive and that hence all creations of nature present human viewers with legible and interpretable signs, manipulated this contemporary bias in his speeches in order to isolate and expel opponents he found undesirable. In the cases of Fannius and Vatinius, the orator focuses upon a specific feature of an opponent to elicit his audience's assent to particular claims: that the man standing before them has a flawed character and that external appearance affords access to that character. Cicero elaborates physical "faults"—Fannius' short hair and Vatinius' swellings—until these characteristics find expression in the entire physique and character of the subject. Fannius becomes the embodiment of fraud and deceit; Vatinius metamorphoses into a parasitic growth. Both threaten society at large. The orator employs the abuse of bodily peculiarities to conciliate the audience to his point of view. But the means do not simply involve laughter; they also involve an implicit agreement about the connotations conveyed by an individual's physical peculiarities.

Chapter 2

NAMES AND COGNOMINA

> And if I have a son, I think I'm gonna name him . . .
> BILL! or GEORGE! anything but SUE!
> —Johnny Cash, "A Boy Named Sue"

In his *Third Philippic* against Marcus Antonius, Cicero invokes the name of his opponent's father-in-law, Marcus Fulvius Bambalio ("The Stutterer").[1] The man's odd third name provides proof of his ignoble character:

> nihil illo contemptius qui propter haesitantiam linguae stuporemque cordis cognomen ex contumelia traxerat. (*Phil.* 3.16)

> Nothing is more contemptible than that man, who had received his name (*cognomen*) in abuse for the clinging nature of his tongue and the dullness of his soul.

Cicero links Fulvius' cognomen to traits that are both physical (*haesitantia linguae*) and mental (*stupor cordis*). The designation *Bambalio* directly describes the disability of stammering speech, and this physical blemish in turn reflects internal moral failings. This technique of abuse and the biases underlying it are familiar from the previous chapter. The *Third Philippic*, however, reveals a new dimension in the abuse of an opponent's physical peculiarities. Cicero has exploited the etymology of a name; the cognomen *Bambalio* allows him to conjure Fulvius' disability for the audience. Once the faults inherent in the name have been exposed to view, the orator uses the name's connotations to justify his judgment of Fulvius' character.

---

[1] Bambalio also appears in the alleged speech of Cicero at Dio 45.47.4 (where he receives infamy "on account of his surname") and at *Phil.* 2.90—"we would have the peace, which arose on account of a hostage, that well-born boy, the grandson of Marcus Bambalio" (*pacem haberemus, quae erat facta per obsidem puerum nobilem, M. Bambalionis nepotem*)—where the mere sound of his name in juxtaposition to *nobilem* appears to be a source for humor (appropriately so, considering *Bambalio* applies onomatopoetically to the physical defect it describes: cf. Hesych., s.v. βαμβαλύζειν; LSJ, s.v. βαμβαίνω). For an awareness of onomatopoetic etymologies among the Romans, see Varro *Ling.* 5.75.

In the wider context of the *Phil.* 3 passage cited in the text, Cicero unfavorably contrasts Bambalio with Marcus Atius Balbus. Cicero conveniently overlooks the fact that *Balbus* also means "stammering," a meaning of which he is well aware in other contexts (see n. 90).

Bambalio's fate highlights a phenomenon of Roman naming practice that has yet to receive satisfactory explanation. In the late Roman Republic, all free Roman males had at least two names: a *nomen*, the name that marked a person's family or *gens* (Marcus *Antonius*), and a *praenomen*, a name used to distinguish among siblings and more or less equivalent to our own first or given name (*Marcus* Antonius). When a male belonged to a family that had held an important magistracy in Rome, however, he often possessed a *cognomen*, an additional name or, occasionally, names, that set him off from other classes of persons in the city—plebeians, women, freedmen, and slaves. The cognomen, then, would seem to be a mark of honor, a badge of distinction. Yet when the cognomina that survive from the period are examined, the distinction becomes a dubious one: in almost half the cases, the cognomen describes, as with the bumbling *Bambalio*, a peculiarity of the body, mind, or both.[2] And within this particular class, the name with much greater frequency refers to these physical and mental traits pejoratively:[3] one readily recalls figures such as Strabo "the Cross-eyed," "Warty" Verrucosus, and "Stupid" Brutus. In chapter 1, we saw one man ridiculed before his peers because of his small stature and another constructed as an overwhelming threat to political stability because of his unsightly pustules. It should come as little surprise, then, to learn that the pejorative cognomen also receives attention in political oratory as a symbol of otherness. The cognomen acted as signifier, marking character in much the same way as did Vatinius' facial sores. An additional name both elevated and isolated.

THE NATURE OF THE ROMAN COGNOMEN

The adoption and application of this odd third name raises provocative questions for an analysis of Roman political humor. On the one hand, the custom owes nothing to Greek influence, the source all too often sought by scholars when attempting to explain Roman attitudes.[4] On the other

---

[2] The exact figure is 44 percent (Kajanto 131). The next two largest categories are geographical (13.6 percent) and praenominal (9 percent). Kajanto conjectures from the diachronic dispersion of name groups that the "cognomina recording traits of character came in use much later than the cognomina recording physical peculiarities" (67).

[3] Kajanto 63–67. It would be misleading to give a percentage here since so many of these names are susceptible to conflicting interpretations.

It is possible, in fact, to make the already comparatively short list of positive cognomina even shorter. See Marx on Lucilius 24 (*Pulcher*); Varro *Ling.* 7.97 (*Scaevola* denotes a phallic amulet); Plin. *Nat.* 33.133 (the original *Crassus Dives* was a bankrupt); Plut. *Cor.* 11.3 (*Diadematus* and *Celer* were originally given in mockery); Schulze 503 n. 3 (*Maximus* means "Eldest"); Alföldi, esp. 717 (names deriving from professions), 721 (*Poplicola*). Badian has convincingly demonstrated that *Catus* was not an actual cognomen in the late Republic and has suggested that the same may be true of *Sapiens* (6–12).

[4] Cf. especially Süss 245–60, who is followed by Nisbet 1961 (esp. 192–97).

The discussion of May 1–13 goes a long way toward correcting this view. Through a

hand, these nicknames arose from an array of different situations over the course of at least three centuries, thereby involving politicians and their audience from different periods of the Republic. An analysis of the cognomen, then, provides a rare opportunity for assessing Roman cultural practice, since this naming system seems to have originated among the Romans and its employment involved a large number of citizens.

The origins of the cognomen are obscure.[5] A few certain facts can, however, be gleaned from observation. The earliest record of a contemporary cognomen—that of Lucius Cornelius Scipio Barbatus ("bearded")—dates back to 298 BCE (*CIL* 6.1284/5 = Dessau 1), but the traditional lists of magistrates (*fasti*) register their presence from as far back as the fifth century.[6] In the Republican period these names possess three characteristics of particular interest. First, they were applied almost exclusively among males of the senatorial class, with the practice not becoming widespread among plebs or women until the Augustan age.[7] Second, cognomina of the nobility were usually passed on to all male descendants, whereas the few examples attested for freedmen and lower-class free persons were, so far as our sources tell us, not hereditary.[8] These two features of the cognomen seem to demonstrate that the permanent acquisition of a third name served to distinguish individuals among the political aristocracy. The likelihood of this inference increases upon consideration of the third and most peculiar characteristic of the Republican cognomen, which I have noted above: names with negative or pejorative connotations enjoyed the widest popularity.[9] This Roman tendency runs contrary to previous Indo-European naming practice, according to

---

consideration of Rome's "sociopolitical and . . . judicial climate" (10), May attempts to reconcile the differences between Aristotelian theory and Ciceronian practice.

[5] The most concise discussion is by A. Mau (*RE* 4:225–30). In English, Balsdon 1979: 146–60 offers an entertaining survey. The "three names" of the Romans baffled ancient commentators as well; see Plut. *Marius* 1; Pausanias 7.7.8; Courtney on Juvenal 5.127.

[6] Kajanto 19. My ensuing discussion owes much of its background material to Kajanto's work, which consists primarily of a compendium and taxonomy of all extant Latin cognomina (excluding fictional names from poetry) up until approximately 600 CE.

Book 1 of Livy includes cognomina from as far back as Rome's regal period, with the Tarquinii Priscus and Superbus; Ogilvie 145 suggests reasons for doubting the authenticity of these nicknames. Ogilvie does not, however, question the authenticity of the legend surrounding the cognomen *Brutus* (ad 1.56.7); cf. *contra* Broughton 1:xii, and Kajanto's remark that the story of Brutus' naming is "naturally worthless" (69).

[7] Kajanto 19, 132.

[8] Thylander 100.

[9] Kajanto 132, who approximates that 24 percent of cognomina from the late Republic have clear pejorative connotations, as opposed to 4 percent in his total sample from all periods (I would put the late Republican percentage much higher; see n. 3 above). Quintilian also attests to this tendency when he says that the best type of pun on a name occurs "if one refers to something rather lowly and insignificant; those [Romans] of old used to make jokes of this sort when they said that Lentulus was a 'Spinther' and Scipio a 'Serapio'"

which names connoting reproach did not occur; rather there predomi-
nated "appellations suggesting divine favor and good will, or descriptive
of . . . conceptions of ideal men and women."[10] At Athens could be
found men who were "the People's Strength" (*Demosthenes*) or "Zeus-
born" (*Diogenes*), while on the streets of Rome walked "Bowlegs"
(*Varus*) and "Fathead" (*Capito*). It also appears that the practice does not
derive from the Etruscans, as most scholars once believed.[11] Hence, the
cognomen seems to represent a distinctly Latin naming system that, in
Rome at least, serves to distinguish the political elite from the lower
classes by the strange practice of applying opprobrious sobriquets to the
politically most powerful families.

Abuse, in other words, marked privilege. Yet it is unlikely that this
abuse parallels the hazing commonly found in modern, elite male institutions, where enduring abuse from peers constitutes a condition of mem-
bership. Roman invective is not the equivalent of prep-school bonding.
Names at Rome derive from a different phenomenon, but one equally
well-attested in other cultures: names as a means of social control.
Among the Iroquois, for example, an inherited name was "replete with
expectations about the behavior of any person so named"; as a result,
names offered the entire community insight into the character of each
member of the group.[12] Similarly, in Roman politics names are openly
available signifiers, labels used to mark publicly the characteristics of an
individual and his ancestry—for better or for worse.

THE ROMAN COGNOMEN AND ARISTOCRATIC COMPETITION

Scholars who discuss the origins of the Latin cognomen generally agree
that the name arose out of a native Italic spirit of "gibe and criticism."[13]
The majority of cognomina are observed to describe uncomplimentary
traits or characteristics, and these features still invited derisive laughter in

---

(*si . . . ad aliquid inferius leviusque referatur; quae iam veteres illi iocabantur qui Lentulum "Spin-
therem" et Scipionem "Serapionem" esse dixerunt*; *Inst.* 6.3.57). *Spinther* was allegedly the name
of a slave (cf. *spintria*, a male prostitute, from Greek *sphigktēs*), *Serapio* of an actor (Plin.
Nat. 7.54; Val. Max. 9.14.3–4).

[10] Chase 106; using as his database all cognomina from Livy and *CIL* 1, Chase concludes
that "with regard to their signification alone, hardly a single name from our lists of cognomina could be derived from the original [Indo-European] system" (116).

[11] Kajanto 19–20; Alföldi 710–11.

[12] For the general belief that names imply character, see the cross-cultural study of naming practices in Alford 74–78; for the quotation on the Iriquois, see Alford 4.

[13] Chase 116. See also Paoli 273–74; McCartney 343; Kajanto 63–64. These authors
agree with ancient sources that attest to occasions when cognomina were given in mockery,
e.g., Plin. *Nat.* 7.54 (Spinther), 8.213 (Hybrida); Val. Max. 9.14.3–4 (Serapio); Plut. *Cor.*
11 (Diadematus, Celer).

Cicero's time. Yet no scholar has, as far as I have discovered, considered the repercussions of this onomastic phenomenon.[14] It seems odd that a naming practice that originates as a type of mockery was, in the Republican period, restricted primarily to the aristocracy (*nobiles*); moreover, for those who possessed such a name, the cognomen appears to have constituted an important part of a Roman male's political definition. For beginning from the time of Sulla, the cognomen tends to replace the tribal designation on laws and senatorial decrees.[15]

One possible explanation for the practice of pejorative naming is that the cognomen originally served an apotropaic function: if one names a son *Verrucosus* ("full of warts"), then the child will avoid divine enmity and will thereby not grow up to develop warts, or some even worse affliction. A recent cross-cultural study of naming practices in sixty contemporary societies has shown that a belief in apotropaic naming underlies all surviving instances of derogatory names.[16] However, two significant objections prevent one from applying this hypothesis to the Roman cognomen. First, I find no traces in the ancient evidence of a belief in the apotropaic naming of children; on the contrary, numerous texts presuppose that the cognomen describes its original bearer literally.[17] Second, and more concretely, a new cognomen appears to have been bestowed at the earliest in young adulthood and was not, as is normally the case with apotropaic names, given to a child.[18]

Before I advance my own theory regarding the origin of the cognomen, it will be helpful to review the generally accepted reconstruction of the name's development as a social and political designation. Mommsen advanced two explanations of why the cognomen originally arose as a

---

[14] The findings of Chase 108 that the Roman deviation from the Indo-European naming system is due to a "fundamental abhorrence of the Latin language for long compounds" explains only the letter, and not the spirit, of the change. Kajanto, who devotes an entire monograph to the Latin cognomina, is surprisingly silent on the question of their origin; cf. the reviews of Jones 208 and B. Rawson 154.

Plutarch suggests that the Romans adopted names describing bodily misfortune in order that such disabilities would not be considered disgraceful (*Cor.* 11; he is not referring in this passage to the notion of apotropaic naming). This explanation is unsatisfactory on two counts. First, it does not account for other types of pejorative names. Second, as I demonstrated in chapter 1, the Romans did in fact judge physical peculiarities quite harshly.

[15] Mommsen 1864: 62–63. As early as 122 BCE, in the *lex Acilia* (*CIL* 1².2.583), cognomina are used to identify future jurors.

[16] Alford 63–64. The practice was still current in thirteen of the sixty societies surveyed.

[17] In addition to the passages cited throughout this chapter that testify to a cognomen's literal application, one can compare Plutarch's assessment at *Marius* 1.1–5.

Apotropaic naming occurs in many cultures. For example, in Amoy, a district of China, names such as "Stupid Dog" and "Swine Piss" were still regularly given at the turn of this century to avoid the jealousy of the gods; see de Groot 6:1128–34.

[18] Mommsen 1864: 43–44.

supplement to the nomen and praenomen. First, he conjectures that a third name was necessary to distinguish between respective families when a given family unit (*gens*) had grown too large—the determinant of size being, he suggests, the amount of room in the clan's burial plot.[19] This theory has gained general acceptance even though no extant evidence supports it. Its virtue rests in its ability to explain why a new cognomen seems to have been applied only in adulthood, a practice at variance with the conditions under which the nomen and praenomen were bestowed.[20] Second, Mommsen points to the social and political advantage the *nobiles* saw in distinguishing their own names from those belonging to other portions of the population; this would have been an especially important desideratum since a freedman normally adopted his master's nomen and praenomen. In such cases, then, the cognomen would constitute the only onomastic feature unique to the aristocrat.[21] Both Mommsen's points seem plausible and mutually reconcilable. They do not, however, explain why particular cognomina, especially pejorative cognomina, were chosen.

Beginning from around the time of Sulla, the cognomen seems to occur with more frequency on public documents.[22] It is uncertain whether or not this move was accompanied by any sort of legal enactment.[23] Although the cognomen does not regularly appear in official inscriptions earlier, it does surface in unofficial sources, such as the epitaph of Lucius Cornelius Scipio Barbatus of 298 BCE (cited above). As for the choice of each particular name, it has always been assumed that the cognomen

[19] Ibid. 49.

[20] Ibid. 43–44.

[21] Ibid. 59–60. Erich Gruen has pointed out to me that Mommsen's second contention has little force in explaining the cognomen's *origin*, since the Romans did not own slaves in great numbers before the third, or even the second, century. Mommsen's theory may, however, help explain why the cognomen eventually became officially recognized at the beginning of the first century.

I do not consider the phenomenon of the aristocratic cognomen to be equivalent to the practice of freed slaves retaining their slave name as surname, especially since these names seem, during the late Republic, to be easily recognizable as slave names (A. Mau, *RE* 4:228.6–12). For a list of people in the late Republic who bore cognomina but did not belong to the *nobiles*, see Treggiari 7 n. 1.

[22] Mommsen 1864: 47, followed by Balsdon 1979: 150, Badian 6; Schulze 503–4 reserves judgment. Admittedly, the scarcity of documents before the Sullan period prevents any certainty on this issue. But Chase 132 proves that cognomina have been around at some level of usage for a long time, since 10–40 percent of praenomina seem to derive from an original cognomen.

[23] Badian 6 thinks "actual enactment" is "more likely." Mommsen 1864: 59 gives no opinion but does believe that an official decree sometime around 100 BCE enabled a plebeian *nobilis* to adopt a cognomen, thereby making plebeian and patrician names formally indistinguishable.

given to a new branch of the family was selected by a free decision within the *gens*.[24] Yet this assumption, a plausible one a priori, rests on little evidence and, again, does not explain why the majority of cognomina describe their bearers pejoratively.

As a way of providing a historical context for my discussion of name puns in the late Republic, I would like to offer a tentative explanation for the development of the pejorative cognomen at Rome. The following suggestions apply only to the situation in the capital during the last two centuries of the Republic. It is clear that a variety of factors influenced the Latin cognomina in general, and I am certain one explanation cannot account for the many different kinds of cognomina preserved from throughout Italy and the provinces.[25] Yet the exclusive features of the name at Rome, coexisting with abusive meanings, suggest that here the cognomen did more than simply signify.

In the second century BCE, political competition prevailed among the prominent families in Rome. The combination of high infant mortality rates and low life expectancy—in a period of constant warfare—ensured that a great part of a family's strength depended upon its ability to reproduce.[26] It follows, then, that a large family threatened equilibrium within the oligarchy. It is within such a historical situation that I envision the cognomen receiving its impetus: the application of a pejorative name— presumably describing a characteristic of its original owner—provided a label by which political progress was felt to be hindered. The derisive spirit informing the meaning of most cognomina represents not the expression of jovial humor, therefore, but the competitive spirit of the Roman *nobiles*. These names, I suggest, acquired their importance as a result of aristocratic competition, whereby a family unit that had become too large—and, consequently, too threatening—was labeled with a descrip-

---

[24] Mommsen 1864: 49. The only evidence he cites for this claim is Suet. *Tib.* 1.1–2: "The patrician *gens* of the Claudii . . . rejected by consensus the praenomen *Lucius*. . . . Moreover, it took up also *Nero* among its cognomina" (*patricia gens Claudia . . . Luci praenomen consensu repudiavit. . . . inter cognomina autem et Neronis assumpsit*). In this passage, however, one need not understand *consensu* with *assumpsit*. In any event, the particular case of the cognomen *Nero* could easily represent an exception to the rule since, as Suetonius himself tells us (*Tib.* 1.2), *Nero* is not a Latin word and does not have pejorative connotations (it means "strong" in the Sabine dialect).

[25] Schulze 504 discusses the many complexities of the early history of the cognomen— e.g., Etruscan influence, manumission, victory names, Celtic roots—and concludes that a single explanation of origins is irrecoverable, if not entirely misguided.

[26] Hopkins 70–74 estimates that in the last two centuries of the Republic one-third of all families would have had one son and one-third no son surviving to age forty; in less than one-third of the families would there be two or more sons surviving to forty, who thus might be expected to acquire cognomina. The entire second chapter of Hopkins's book ("Political Succession in the Late Republic," cowritten with G. Burton) is relevant here.

tive appellation that exposed its bearers to the scorn of peers and humili-
ated them before the Roman populace. As I shall argue throughout this
chapter, names could be highly meaningful when properly exploited.
Often, I assume, the cognomen applied would have already had some
currency, for example as a nickname acquired on campaign or as a result
of legal battles. A social apparatus then emerged to maintain this practice.
Perhaps the apparatus arose from a legal enactment; references in our
texts suggest that the senate could regulate the names allowed to Roman
citizens.[27] Alternatively, and more likely, the practice represented an in-
formal agreement among the *nobiles*, the implementation of which varied
according to the political situation; a passage from Plutarch's *Life of Cicero* that I shall discuss below describes one way in which pejorative names
could have been bestowed. Such a scenario would also explain the creation of positive cognomina during this period such as *Pius* or *Maximus*.[28] Those names that seem to pertain to agriculture, such as *Cicero*
("chickpea") or *Scrofa* ("sow"), most likely found their origin in the rural
communities of Italy, where there exists a difference in kind from those
cognomina held by the urban aristocracy.[29] Most of the interlocutors in
Varro's treatise *On Agriculture*, for example, bear cognomina relating to
farming and rural life.[30] The pejorative cognomen, it seems, had special
prominence in the capital.

Admittedly, this theory has its own problems. I can find no concrete
example of a negative name effectively hindering a family's political advancement. Yet Cicero's rhetorical practice certainly indicates that depre-
catory names had the potential for such employment. In fact, modern
studies of name giving and social labeling have clearly demonstrated that
a label can have a profound psychological effect on the person receiving
the designation, as well as on others' evaluation of that person.[31] Finally,

[27] In addition to the decree of 240 BCE mentioned below in the text, I have found the
following examples: Antonii prohibited from using the praenomen *Marcus* (30 BCE: Plut.
Cic. 49.6; Dio 51.19.3); cognomen *Drusus* taken from Scribonii (16 CE: Tac. *Ann.* 2.32.2);
Cn. Piso forced to change praenomen (20 CE: Tac. *Ann.* 3.17.8).

[28] See, however, n. 3 above.

[29] Mommsen 1864: 55–56 notes that *municipes* who were only freedmen could have cognomina in the late Republic (cf. A. Mau, *RE* 4.226.25–29).

[30] In addition to the names listed below in n. 97, Varro includes among his interlocutors
his father-in-law Gaius Fundanius (from *fundus*, "farm"), as well as a Gaius Agrarius and
Publius Agrasius (cf. *ager*, "field"), and Gaius Licinius Stolo ("plant shoot;" see the anecdote at *Rust.* 1.2.9). Pliny believed that the earliest cognomina derived from agriculture
(*Nat.* 18.10).

[31] "The deviant is one to whom that label has successfully been applied" (Becker 9, cited
in Schur 7). For examples, see Alford 62–63 (the Ashanti in Ghana) and Marcus 75, who
surveys how contemporary psychologists and educators have shown that names "can help
or hinder the development of a good self-image, friendships, and even affect success in
school and on the job."

this hypothesis is able to explain many of the peculiarities surrounding the cognomen. In spite of the problems my theory raises, I have come across no better solution in the scholarly literature.

The theory I am proposing also provides an interesting context for a senatorial decree from, apparently, 240 BCE: "in the consulship of Marcus Claudius and Titus Sempronius, the Romans decreed that only the eldest son could share his father's cognomen" (ἐπὶ Μάρκου Κλαυδίου καὶ Τίτου Σεμπρωνίου ὑπάτων μόνῳ τῆς τοῦ πατρὸς ἐπωνυμίας τῷ πρεσβυτέρῳ τῶν παίδων μετέχειν Ῥωμαῖοι παρεκελεύσαντο).[32] The facts demonstrate that this decree must refer to a special type of cognomen (ἐπωνυμία), one bestowed in honor of military success—and accompanied by some type of official sanction—such as *Asiaticus* or *Macedonicus*.[33] No such restrictions on inheritance applied to pejorative cognomina. The exceptional nature of victory names may be attributed, then, to a recognition of the privileged status of these honorific titles: since cognomina denoting military success did not hinder a family's political fortunes, limitations had to be placed on how many heirs could accept such a name.

An incident from the early first century BCE provides our only evidence for how the application of cognomina may originally have operated. Plutarch describes the occasion upon which Publius Cornelius Lentulus Sura acquired his second cognomen. The anecdote supports my theory that some cognomina were designed to advertise negative characteristics of the person named:

λέγεται δὲ καὶ τὴν ἐπίκλησιν αὐτῷ γενέσθαι τὸν Σούραν ἐξ αἰτίας τοιαύτης. ἐν τοῖς κατὰ Σύλλαν χρόνοις ταμιεύων συχνὰ τῶν δημοσίων χρημάτων ἀπώλεσε καὶ διέφθειρεν. ἀγανακτοῦντος δὲ τοῦ Σύλλα καὶ λόγον ἀπαιτοῦντος ἐν τῇ συγκλήτῳ, προελθὼν ὀλιγώρως πάνυ καὶ καταφρονητικῶς λόγον μὲν οὐκ ἔφη διδόναι, παρέχειν δὲ τὴν κνήμην, ὥσπερ εἰώθεισαν οἱ παῖδες ὅταν ἐν τῷ σφαιρίζειν ἁμάρτωσιν. ἐκ τούτου Σούρας παρωνομάσθη· σούραν γὰρ οἱ Ῥωμαῖοι τὴν κνήμην λέγουσι. (Plut. *Cic.* 17.2–3)

[32] Dio frag. 44 (Bekker). The consulship referred to is apparently that of *Gaius* Claudius and *Marcus* Sempronius in 240 BCE; see Mommsen 1864: 53 n. 82, whose discussion here and at 1887–88 3:213 I follow in the text.

[33] Mommsen 1864: 52–53.

There is evidence that this decree was still in effect in the late Republic. According to Dio 43.44.2–3, when the senate decreed that Julius Caesar might adopt the title *imperator* as part of his name (cf. Suet. *Iul.* 76.1, who anachronistically calls it a *praenomen*), it was necessary to add that his descendants too could bear the name. The "excessive flattery" (τοσαύτη ὑπερβολή) that Dio denounces in this latter grant may include the fact that the senate allowed more than one heir to receive the honorific name. Syme 1979: 365–66 doubts Dio's reliability.

It's said that he received the nickname Sura for the following reason. As quaestor in the time of Sulla, he lost and squandered a great amount of public money. After Sulla angrily summoned him to give an account in the senate, Lentulus came forward with great coolness and contempt, saying that he had no account to give, but that he offers his calf, just as children are accustomed to do when they make an error in a ball game. For this reason he was given the name Sura, *sura* being the Roman word for the calf of the leg.

There seems to be no reason to doubt the authenticity of this episode, which occurred soon after Sura's quaestorship in 81 BCE.[34] Lentulus receives the name *Sura* as an apt way of designating the haughty contempt he displayed before his peers in the senate. The appellation preserves for public consideration an instance when Lentulus attempted to place himself in a privileged position among his peers in the aristocracy, as one no longer liable for crimes committed while quaestor. The name stuck. Plutarch does not mention any official move to ensure that Publius and his heirs should be known from this point on as "Legs" Lentulus; we can only suppose that usage—including mockery—caused this nickname to be preserved.

Suetonius records a second example from the late Republic in which a cognomen seems clearly intended to provide its bearer with a continual source of reproach. During the civil wars, Julius Caesar kept in his camp a Cornelius "who had the cognomen 'Salvito' to mark his shameful way of life" (*cui ad opprobium vitae Salvitoni cognomen erat*).[35] The name *Salvito* provided a pejorative label that an outsider was expected to read and interpret accordingly. Cornelius apparently did not have the power to change his nickname—communal pressure again seems to be operating to ensure that he keeps his label. These passages from Plutarch and Suetonius present cognomina that were clearly intended to designate, and were construed as designating, negative traits of their bearers.

The theory I am proposing about the function of the cognomen as a tool for political stability need not replace Mommsen's theory that the cognomen served a utilitarian purpose by distinguishing among families

[34] Broughton 2:76. A Sura from the Bruttian *gens* was legate from 93 to 86 BCE (Broughton 2:15). The circumstances of his naming are unknown, but the difference in *gens* would lead one to expect that its occasion was entirely unconnected with the event narrated here by Plutarch.

Although this incident occurred at a special time—namely, under the dictatorship of Sulla—nevertheless the fact that the name *Sura* stuck would indicate that factors beyond the authority of a dictator were in operation here.

[35] Suet. *Iul*. 59. Pliny calls him *Salvitto* (*Nat*. 7.54, 35.8) and says he was named after an actor in a mime. Plut. *Caes*. 52.2 and Dio 42.58.1 give the name as *Salutio* without mentioning what the name means. Billows discusses this man's relationship to the famous Scipios.

within the upper class and by marking the *nobiles* as separate from other segments of the population. Comparative parallels support the dual existence of what a naming system may have intended and what eventually developed separately out of that system. A recent study of nicknaming in Andalusian culture has shown how a nicknaming practice originally adopted simply to distinguish among family members with the same surname eventually evolved into a means of creating social distinctions.[36] This naming practice in contemporary Spain and my theory of Roman naming exhibit remarkable similarities. The Andalusian nicknames— which feature such unflattering sobriquets as "Joey Shits-on-the-floor" and "Tony Big-twat"—are originally applied as a result of a prominent trait of the bearer or because of a single socially embarrassing situation. Eventually, however, the name comes to be construed by the community as "actually the aural equivalent of the person."[37] Andalusian practice also recognizes the connection for which I have argued in the case of Rome, where a son inherits from his father a moral character as well as a name: the Spanish names can be passed down from generation to generation and yet still connote serious reproach—even when the original motivation for the name's bestowal has been forgotten.[38] Moreover, those Andalusian names that are semantically neutral or ambiguous often provoke the greatest embarrassment and anger in their holders.[39] The anthropologist conducting this study concludes that the ultimate function of these names resides in "punishing deviance through the fiercest form of destructive mockery."[40] By applying embarrassing labels that allude to antisocial acts, the community attempts to discourage such acts. The names keep everyone continually aware of a neighbor's potential for deviant behavior. One important difference between Andalusian and Roman naming should be noted, however. In the Andalusian case, pejorative nicknames are only uttered when their owners are not present; in Roman society, as we shall see in examples from oratory, public speakers repeatedly present an opponent's name to the community to indicate his potential for transgressing social boundaries.[41] Despite these differences,

[36] Gilmore, esp. chap. 5, "Nicknames" (77–95). He discusses the development of the naming practice particularly at 80–81.

[37] Ibid. 91.

[38] Ibid. 82.

[39] Ibid. 81–84.

[40] Ibid. 91. Another parallel exists among the Zinacantecos of Mexico, whose inheritable nicknames largely constitute humorous epithets used to "ridicule anyone whose appearance or behavior deviates from norms" (Collier and Bricker 291). As in the Andalusian example, however, these names are used only in reference and never for direct address.

[41] The difference between Roman and Spanish practice is significant in this respect. In Andalusia, to utter a nickname in the presence of the referent was considered the gravest insult, and often resulted in physical violence and even murder (Gilmore 77, 86–87).

however, in both cultures a society applies names to regulate individual behavior. The type of checks-and-balance system that I envision for the Roman cognomen can be inferred from this modern example once the Andalusian model has been transferred into an explicitly political realm.

One can also find a parallel from within Roman society for the theory I am proposing concerning the rise of cognomina. The *carmina triumphalia* —the songs sung by triumphing soldiers—often contain direct abuse of the victorious general at the very moment when he is enjoying the highlight of a Roman military career. Much as a prominent *nobilis* receives an opprobrious name to hinder his political success, so too the triumphing general, at the celebration of his greatest glory, is exposed to taunts about everything from baldness to the murder of his own brother.[42] In a similar vein, the general is accompanied in the triumphal chariot by a public slave who repeatedly whispers a reminder that, in spite of his successes, he remains a human being.[43] To preserve stability among the Roman aristocracy, taunts and warnings are given to those who threaten to become too prominent. The pejorative cognomen represented a similar check. Further support for my claim that the cognomen could be employed as a form of social control lies in the mechanics of the naming process in Republican Rome. An examination of the overall importance of a name provides a better appreciation of the context within which political figures such as Cicero could use name puns as a means of rhetorical persuasion. In Republican Rome names could *denote*, in the strongest sense of this verb. That is, names could be elicited not simply as empty signifiers but as labels that provide direct access to internal content.

THE POWER OF A NAME

The form of public prayer attests to the power and importance of words and wording in Republican Rome. Prayers consisted of set formulae that a priest or magistrate had to read (or repeat) without the slightest variation from his prescribed text.[44] In fact, the Romans considered the form of the prayer so sacred that they adhered to its precise wording even when the text was no longer completely intelligible.[45] In his grammatical

---

[42] For baldness, see Suet. *Iul.* 51; for the *carmen triumphale* referring to the murder of brothers, see n. 95 below. I discuss the *carmina triumphalia* preserved at Suet. *Iul.* 49, 80, and Dio 43.20.2 in my chapter 5 (for a full selection see *FPL*). Richlin 1992a: 10 with n. 9 puts these songs in the context of other events "promoting license and reversed values" (10). Barton 107–44 discusses how "[e]xcessive differentiation of status . . . creates the intense desire on the part of the dependent to degrade the patron" (143).

[43] Tertullian preserves the slave's words as *"respice post te! hominem te memento!"* ("Look behind you! Remember that you are a human being!"—*Apol.* 33.4; cf. Dio 6.21 = Zonaras 7.21).

[44] Plin. *Nat.* 28.11; cf. Wissowa 394, 397 (esp. n. 7).

[45] Wissowa 37.

treatise on the Latin language (*De lingua Latina*), the antiquarian Varro gives an example of this type of set formula (*quibusdam conceptis verbis*). In explaining how an augur delimits his field of vision for observing bird signs, Varro cites the following archaic prayer:[46]

> tem⟨pla⟩ tescaque me ita sunto, quoad ego ea *rite* lingua nuncupavero.
>
> Olla *ver⟨a⟩* arbos quirquir est, quam me sentio dixisse, templum tescumque *me* esto in sinistrum.
>
> Olla *ver⟨a⟩* arbos quirquir est, qu*am* me sentio dixisse, te⟨m⟩plum tescumque *me* esto ⟨in⟩ dextrum.
>
> Inter ea conregione conspicione cortumione, utique ea ⟨rit⟩e *dixisse* me sensi. (Varro *Ling.* 7.8)

> Temples and wild lands be mine in this manner, up to where I have named (*nuncupavero*) them with my tongue in proper fashion.
>
> Of whatever kind that truthful tree is, which I consider that I have mentioned, temple and wild land be mine to that point on the left.
>
> Of whatever kind that truthful tree is, which I consider that I have mentioned, temple and wild land be mine to that point on the right.
>
> Between these points, temples and wild lands be mine for direction, for viewing, and for interpreting, and just as I have felt assured that I have mentioned them in proper fashion. (Kent trans.)

In this prayer, language alters physical reality by creating boundaries between the secular and the sacred. By affixing a name to an area (*nuncupare* derives from *nomen capere*, "to take a name"), the augur defines its parameters. The verb *nuncupare* performs a similar delineating function in a passage from the Twelve Tables, where oral naming ensures the legality of a business transaction.[47] In the legal realm as well, to pronounce the name of an object or person created a bond between namer and named. The converse also held true: the main priest of Jupiter, the *flamen dialis*, maintained his purity by avoiding contact with dogs and goats, an avoidance that even included the very mention of the words "dog" or "goat."[48] In Roman religious practice before the time of Cicero there

[46] Serv. *Aen.* 1.466 and Varro *Ling.* 6.53 indicate that the prayer comes from the college of augurs. Linderski (esp. 2256–96) offers a thorough discussion of its religious context.

[47] "When [someone] enters into a debt or makes a sale, let it be binding in accordance as he has pronounced with his tongue" (*cum nexum faciet mancipiumque, uti lingua nuncupassit, ita ius esto*: Fest. p. 173 [Mueller]; I translate *lingua* as an ablative in light of Cic. *Off.* 3.65). When the word is not simply used as an ornate synonym of *nominare* (Cic. *De orat.* 3.153; Quint. *Inst.* 8.3.27), the commonest uses of *nuncupare* and its noun *nuncupatio* in our extant texts refer to the making of vows to a deity (*vota*) and to the instituting of heirs. I assume that a formal naming process underlay each practice: in wills, the *heredes* were named in *nuncupatio* (Iust. *Dig.* 28.5.1; Paul. *Dig.* 28.5.59); in vows, the gods affected were named (cf. Liv. 8.9.8).

[48] Plut. *Mor.* 290a. Rose 114 explains that naming "is a kind of touching, for the name is part of the thing."

existed the strictest respect for words and for the particular designation of items.[49]

A belief in the power of the word extends, as one would expect, into the realm of proper names. The correct naming of the gods in prayer provides the clearest example. When addressing a particular deity, it was deemed essential to include the epithet of the god appropriate to the prayer's specific goal. Comprehensiveness in the matter was ensured by appending to the direct address of the god some such formula as "or with whatever name you want to be addressed."[50] If the deity appropriate to a given prayer were unknown, the petitioner tried to approximate a direct address by employing a sweeping formula—"and all the remaining gods and goddesses as well."[51] A similar need to know a god's "true name" (τὸ ὄνομα ἀληθίνον) has numerous parallels in contemporary magical papyri and is considered essential to a spell's success.[52] The same emphasis on proper knowledge would seem to underlie the mysterious military practice of the "calling out" (evocatio), by which a commander summons forth an enemy city's tutelary divinities before completing a siege: the success of the evocation is contingent upon the commander knowing how properly to address by name the foreign gods. For this reason, the Romans were themselves careful to keep secret the name of Rome's own tutelary deity.[53] In medicine, Roman doctors practiced incantations that in their phrasing bear striking resemblance to an evocatio. Marcellus preserves the following formula:

exi, si hodie nata, si ante nata, si hodie creata, si ante creata,
hanc pestem, hanc pestilentiam, hunc dolorem,
hunc tumorem, hunc ruborem, has toles, has tosillas,
hunc panum, has panuclas, hanc strumam, hanc strumellam,
hac religione evoco educo excanto de istis membris medullis.

(Marcell. *Med.* 15.11)

Be gone, whether born today or earlier, whether created today or earlier: with this formula I call out, lead out, and sing out

[49] Latte 62–63 relates this reliance on the word in religion to the overall political and social structure of the Romans.

[50] E.g., *sive quo alio nomine te appellari volueris* (Serv. *Aen.* 2.351); Appel 75–79 gives other examples.

[51] E.g., *di deaeque omnes*; cf. Wissowa 38.

[52] *PGM* 8.41, 13.621, passim; cf. the discussion of this material in Graf 1991. Hirzel 17–24 provides examples from early Greek literature and Bächtold-Stäubli 6:956–59 supplies, with bibliography, parallels from non-Western societies.

[53] Macr. *Sat.* 3.9; Plin. *Nat.* 28.18; complete references are collected by Basanoff. Cf. Dumézil 1970: 424–27 and Stanley, who argues that the mystery name is the palindromic *amor*. Frazer 3:387–91 offers comparative examples from other cultures; for early China, see de Groot 6:1125–28.

from the limbs and marrow of this person here
this disease, plague, pain, polyp, redness, goiters, tonsils, inflammation,
growths, tumor, and swelling.

Just as the Roman priest attempts to address every applicable deity and
the military commander must know the proper way to summon the enemy gods, ancient doctors took care to mention every possible disease
afflicting the patient. In religious, military, and medical practice, then,
names and naming perform a function beyond human communication.
Properly employed, they can provide the Romans contact with supernatural elements.

This care for proper modes of address is meant to ensure a correct
response from the *numen*, or divine spirit, of the deity. It seems hardly a
coincidence, then, that our earliest extant occurrences of the word *numen*
are found in paronomasia with *nomen*.[54] The pun points up what one
scholar has called the "ritualistic equivalence of the words."[55] The name
(*nomen*) plays a crucial role in obtaining the favor of a divine power (*numen*). Popular etymology reflects this connection between a name and an
object's inner essence. According to Varro, the word *nomen* stems from
the verb *nosco* ("to recognize"): *res NOVAE in usum quom additae erant,
quibus ea⟨s⟩ NOVISSENT, NOMINA ponebant* ("when NEW things had
come into use, they added NAMES by which they might KNOW
them").[56] A knowledge of the proper names of the gods, then, showed
that the petitioner had authority to address the deity.[57] Thus the knowledge of how properly to name the deity ensured the acquisition of divine
favor.

As one would expect, the names of human beings operate along principles similar to those of the gods. In the magical papyri surviving from
this period, an effective spell will normally include the name of the person at whom the incantation is directed.[58] The same practice applies to
the charms found on curse tablets and in Latin literature.[59] In the medical
incantations preserved in his *Natural History*, Pliny regularly prescribes
including the name of the patient.[60] In the Roman world, those who

[54] Accius 646, 691 (Ribbeck).

[55] Lind 249 (cf. Wagenvoort 78) summarizes previous arguments about the role of the
numen in Roman thought.

[56] Varro *Ling.* 6.60; cf. Isid. *Orig.* 1.7.1.

[57] Graf 1991 discusses the role of *voces magicae* in ancient incantations. These words,
which seem gibberish to us, were understood to be secret names of the gods, the privileged
possession of a skilled magician. For the practitioner of magic, such names "take the place
of, and serve as, the credentials, an ample display of knowledge" (192).

[58] *PGM* 5.311, 7.521, passim.

[59] Curse tablets: Audollent xlix–l; cf. *CIL* 11.4639 (1st c. CE). Roman literature: e.g.,
Verg. *Ecl.* 8.68; Ov. *Am.* 3.7.29; Tac. *Ann.* 2.30.2, 2.69.5.

[60] E.g., Plin. *Nat.* 21.143, 176; cf. *RE* 1:89.19–27 (E. Riess). For comparative parallels
and bibliography see Bächtold-Stäubli 6:960–61.

appealed to the supernatural elements recognized the significance a name possessed for the efficacy of their actions.

A passage from Cicero's treatise on divination brings us to late Republican conceptions of naming and expands further the areas into which Roman belief in the power of names might reach. After discussing the set phrases the earlier Romans had employed for good omen, Cicero continues as follows:

> itemque in lustranda colonia ab eo qui eam deduceret, et cum imperator exercitum, censor populum lustraret, bonis nominibus qui hostias ducerent eligebantur. quod idem in dilectu consules observant, ut primus miles fiat bono nomine. (*Div.* 1.102)

> Similarly, in the ceremonial purification (*lustro*) of a colony by its founder, and when a general reviewed his army and a censor the people, the men who led the sacrificial victims were chosen according to their auspicious names (*bonis nominibus*). The consuls observe the same practice in military levies, so that the first soldier chosen has a good name (*bono nomine*).

Proper procedure in religious ritual entails using names of good omen. And within the spheres Cicero mentions in this treatise—the establishment of colonies, the census, the military review—other texts reveal that a concern for auspicious names extended beyond lustration ceremonies. For example, the Romans changed the name of a colony when its original appellation contained a potentially bad omen; hence, Maleventum became Beneventum, Epidamnus Dyrrachium, and Egesta Segesta.[61] By a similar kind of sympathetic magic, the Romans named their spirits of the dead *Manes*, "the good ones" (*TLL* 8:293.35–41). Once again, the Roman invests names with the potential for affecting reality.

The belief in names of good omen seems to survive especially among the Roman soldiers. Men with auspicious names participated in ritual activities not only during the late Republic, as Cicero mentions. Tacitus too records that the rebuilding of the Capitolium after the civil wars of 69 CE included a ceremony in which soldiers with "favorable-sounding names" participated (*fausta nomina*; *Hist.* 4.53.2). Livy mentions an instance of how names of good omen were considered important in the field. In an address to some rebellious troops, Scipio Africanus derided his soldiers for not recognizing the inauspicious significance of their instigator's name, the Umbrian Atrius, "a leader who even has a name of ill omen" (*Atrium Umbrum . . . nominis etiam abominandi ducem*; 28.28.4). The ill omen presumably derives from the resemblance between the

---

[61] Maleventum ("bad arrival"): Plin. *Nat.* 3.105. Epidamnus ("for a loss"—ἐπὶ *damnum*): Plin. *Nat.* 3.145; cf. Plaut. *Men.* 263–64. Egesta (cf. *egere*, "to be in need"): Fest. p. 340 (Mueller).

name *Atrius* and the Latin word *ater*, "black," a resemblance felt in the Umbrian dialect as well—there is perhaps also a pun on *umbra*, "shadow." Cicero also appeals to the "omen of a name" (*omen nominis*) in two of his orations (*Verr.* 2.2.18–19, *Scaur.* 30). Names of good omen, then, supplied at the very least a sense of security both inside and outside the Roman community, and an unseemly name could portend bad fortune.

A contemporary scholar of language offers intriguing insight into the semantic value a Roman of the Republic may have attached to a name. In his treatise *On the Latin Language*, Varro describes a certain group of adjectives as "those words that are just like cognomina" (*ea verba quae erant proinde ac cognomina*; *Ling.* 8.17). This assessment of the grammatical category of cognomina is reasonably accurate—the adjectival type of name comprises an "enormous majority" of the extant examples.[62] But it is the way in which Varro frames his analogy that is particularly striking. Varro clearly conceived of cognomina not only as grammatically equivalent to adjectives, but as operating upon the same semantic principles: that is, both types of words describe the qualities of the thing—or person—to which they are attached. Moreover his phrasing seems to indicate that Varro believed cognomina to have preceded adjectives in the development of the Latin language.[63] If this is true, he perceived of names as being among the earliest constituents of vocabulary. As labels, then, cognomina would not lack semantic value. They would reveal to an observer important features of the person so named.

Names and naming played a prominent role in the early religious and social practices of the Roman community.[64] From early times, names and naming seem to have possessed significance in determining the workings of the divine. To the Romans, appellatives contained the potential for affecting external reality. But every name necessarily presupposes a referent, and hence must also reflect inward, toward its signified. When applied to human beings in particular, the name, like a physical

---

[62] Kajanto 20.

[63] Varro does, for example, seem to believe that abstract nouns existed before their corresponding adjectives (*Ling.* 8.15) and, similarly, that words for concepts preceded words relating to the application of those concepts (e.g., the phrase *ars medicina* existed before *medicus*: *Ling.* 5.93; cf. 5.129). He also willingly allows one word to have two equally viable etymologies (e.g., *Ling.* 6.13: *Feralia* derives from *inferi* and *ferre*; cf. the remarks of Ahl 22–25).

[64] I shall pass over the vast subject of the significant name in Roman (and Greek) literature. Most recent discussions treat the phenomenon not simply as a literary device but as reflecting cultural biases in the writer's audience. For an extensive bibliography, see Hijmans, particularly nn. 9 (on Greek literature; for Homer, add the recent work by Peradotto, especially chap. 4), 10 (on Latin literature; Hijmans asserts here, without discussion, that "the attitude to names underlying [the puns in Cicero and in fiction] is much the same").

peculiarity, provides external evidence for internal traits. Could Gaius Annius "the Ass" (*Asellus*) or Tiberius Minucius "the Pansy" (*Molliculus*) be considered anything but internally flawed? This bias—that the name of a human being allowed access to that person's moral character—informs the public attacks orators employed against an opponent's name.

NAMES AS INDICATORS OF CHARACTER

In late Republican oratory, the abuse of names, a practice not confined to Cicero, occurs with remarkable frequency. Yet by the first century of the Empire, the rhetorician Quintilian advises discretion in the practice: only names with positive connotations provide suitable proof of character (*Inst.* 5.10.30; cf. 6.3.53, 55). More recent scholars echo Quintilian's censure and attribute the mockery of names to the outrageous liberties a Roman orator allowed himself in the pursuit of an argument.[65] In light of my discussion of the importance attached to names in other aspects of Roman society, I would like to propose a different understanding of this mode of invective. The power of the word, I suggest, simultaneously reflected and contributed to the Roman's bias toward believing in a label's literal denotation. This bias in regard to a name's "meaning," like that regarding physical peculiarities, legitimated the verbal evidence a political figure could deploy in indicating to his audience an opponent's true character. Cicero's opponent Bambalio, with whom I began this chapter, need not open his mouth for his character to be revealed. His name speaks for him.

Cicero's own rhetorical advice offers a suggestive contrast to Quintilian's reserve. In his early treatise *On Rhetorical Invention*, Cicero discusses how the orator may discredit his opponent through reference to negative attributes (*Inv.* 1.34–36). In the previous chapter I cited the portion of this passage in which Cicero mentions peculiarities of the body. Heading this list of potentially negative evidence is a person's name:

> ex persona autem coniectura capietur, si eae res quae personis attributae sunt diligenter considerabuntur. . . . nam et de nomine nonnunquam aliquid suspicionis nascitur—nomen autem cum dicimus, cognomen quoque intellegatur oportet; de hominis enim certo et proprio vocabulo agitur—ut si dicamus idcirco aliquem Caldum vocari quod temerario et repentino consilio sit; aut si ea re hominibus Graecis imperitis verba dederit quod Clodius aut Caecilius aut Mutius vocaretur. (*Inv.* 2.28)

> An inference will be made from one's person, if those qualities that have been attributed to persons will be carefully considered. . . . For example, a

---

[65] For the negative reactions of more recent critics, see Haury 1955: 113; Mitchell 213. Ahl cites other areas in which Quintilian's standards differ from those of the Republic (24, 29).

degree of suspicion sometimes arises even from a name—when I say "name," one should also understand "cognomen," for this is a matter of a person's fixed and particular (*proprio*) designation—for instance, if we should remark that a man's name is "Hot" (*Caldus*) because he has a rash and fiery temperament; or if inexperienced Greeks have been deceived because people are named "Gimpy" (*Clodius*) or "Blind Man" (*Caecilius*) or "the Mute" (*Mutius*).

This passage marks one of the few occasions when the young Cicero emphasizes a difference between Greek and Roman rhetorical practice. At Rome, children learned from an early point in their rhetorical education how to analyze the literal denotation of cognomina (Quint. *Inst.* 1.4.25). Greek orators, in contrast, must *alter* names to mock an opponent since, unlike the Romans, they cannot rely on a pejorative connotation already present: when Demosthenes ("the People's Strength") wishes to mock a certain Atromes ("the Fearless"), he must allege ironically that the man's name is in fact Tromes ("Trembler").[66] The Romans, as the Ciceronian passage makes clear, did not need to resort to such transparent tactics. The very fact that Roman culture admits pejorative names attests that the orator can exploit his audience's bias regarding them. For as Cicero notes, the Greeks, who are not accustomed to this type of naming practice, become confused when a Roman orator refers to the literal meaning of a name. The Greeks do not recognize that *Mutius* ("the Mute"), for example, denotes a "fixed and particular designation" that can raise suspicion in a hearer's mind regarding its bearer's physical (and therefore moral) character.[67] Hence the humorous mockery of names represents a peculiarly Roman phenomenon, allowing the orator to degrade his opponent in a way that was unavailable to the Greeks.

Twenty-five years later in his career, Cicero still advises the public speaker to exploit a name's meaning. In the analysis of wit found in the second book of *On the Orator*, the interlocutor Julius Caesar Strabo discusses the rhetorical use of an opponent's name: "the interpretation of a name has point when you make a joke of why someone is so called" (*interpretatio nominis habet acumen, cum ad ridiculum convertas, quam ob rem*

[66] Demosthenes 18.130; cf. Aristotle *Rhet.* 1400b, where one finds name puns being used primarily for praise. I shall discuss below how extant evidence indicates that Republican orators rarely altered a name to make a pun.

[67] I agree with Douglas 65–66, in his critique of Hubbell's note on the "inexperienced" Greeks, but I cannot accept his conclusion that Cicero refers here to Greeks who can be fooled "by the belief that the ancient *nomina* of Clodius, Caecilius, and Mutius alluded to the lameness, blindness, or dumbness of their bearers" (65). Douglas assumes without foundation that the Greeks would have automatically made a connection between a name and physical appearance. I think, rather, that Cicero intends by this confusing reference to "inexperienced Greeks" to acknowledge that the rhetorical tactic is distinctly Roman; see n. 66 above.

ita quis vocetur). Strabo presents the following anecdote as his sole example:

> ut ego nuper Nummium divisorem, ut Neoptolemum ad Troiam, sic illum in campo Martio nomen invenisse; atque haec omnia verbo continentur. (*De orat.* 2.257)

> As when I recently [remarked] that the distributing agent (*divisor*) Nummius had received his name in the Campus Martius in the same way Neoptolemus had received his at Troy; all these things are contained in the word.

Pyrrhus, the son of Achilles, received the name *Neoptolemus* because he came to Troy as a very young man (νέος, "young," πτόλεμος, "battle"). Nummius, Strabo jokes, also received his name on a "field of Mars." The *Campus Martius* at Rome, however, does not contain battles, but fraud: Nummius, as a *divisor*, distributed bribes in order to fix elections and so one finds a Roman coin, the *nummus*, buried in his name. Strabo presumably made this pun in a public speech at a time when Nummius was being tried for fraud.[68] The evidence for Nummius' guilt becomes clear to the people in attendance once they consider his name: "all these things are contained in the word" (*haec omnia verbo continentur*).

Cicero's advice in his treatises *On Rhetorical Invention* and *On the Orator* contributes to understanding the biases the Roman audience felt concerning the relationship between a name and its bearer. For the abuse of an individual's name not to be dismissed as sophistry, the audience must believe that the subject's name designates its bearer's internal state—even if he is not the first to bear the name.[69] As noted earlier, once an individual received such an appellation, it usually passed on to his descendants, regardless of the original reason behind the name's bestowal.[70] And yet this temporal distance did not protect a descendant from any potential abuse directed toward his cognomen. For the Romans were disposed to believe that an heir received from his ancestors not only a name but a moral character as well. An entire family could become marked by an incident from its ancestral past.

In his speech on behalf of Quintus Roscius, Cicero wishes to demonstrate that the slave Panurgus, although owned by the accuser Fannius,

---

[68] Rabbie ad loc.

[69] Douglas 64–66 observes that some Romans in the late Republic will have been the first holders of their cognomen and, as a result, in these particular cases the descriptive epithet of the name could have actual relevance. This would certainly not be true, however, in the majority of cases where a cognomen is mocked. For such abuse to have meaning, therefore, one must assume a tendency among the Romans to believe that character was inherited together with one's name.

[70] Kajanto 64. What conditions prompted (or allowed?) a son not to accept his father's cognomen are entirely unknown.

nevertheless owes his fame to an education from the great actor Roscius. Cicero, to prove his claim, offers the following comparison:

> nemo enim, sicut ex improbo patre probum filium nasci, sic a pessimo histrione bonum comoedum fieri posse existimaret. (*Q. Rosc.* 30)

> For no one would think that a good comic actor could be created by a very bad actor any more than that a moral son could be born of an immoral father.

It is significant that here Cicero is not trying to *prove* that the character of a father is visited upon the son; if so, I could not cite this passage as indicating a common belief. Rather, he uses this statement as a given to prove a slightly different point concerning teacher/pupil relationships for which other negative comparanda would certainly seem equally suitable (such as the training of orators or the discipline of soldiers).[71] In order for Cicero's claim to be effective, his audience must agree on the unlikelihood of an immoral father producing a moral son.[72] The elder Cato appeals to a related bias when he implies that those born of a good family work only for good.[73] In a nonpolitical context, Varro uses an analogy similar to Cicero's: while discussing noun declensions, Varro remarks that one can derive a nominative from an oblique case—and vice versa— in the same way one can predict a son's qualities from his father's (*Ling.* 10.59). Each of these texts presupposes a common belief that a man's character is derived from that of his ancestors.

This tendency to equate the moral integrity of a son and father informs a joke from the second century BCE. Cicero's retelling, in the humor section of *On the Orator* book 2, demonstrates that the prejudices underlying the joke still had persuasive force in the late Republic:

> censor Lepidus, cum M. Antistio Pyrgensi equum ademisset amicique cum vociferarentur et quaererent quid ille patri suo responderet, cur ademptum sibi equum diceret, cum optimus colonus, parcissimus, modestissimus, frugalissimus esset, "me istorum" inquit "nihil credere." (*De orat.* 2.287)

---

[71] Cicero sometimes takes exception to the "rule" of inherited character implied here in *Q. Rosc.*; see *Verr.* 2.3.162 and *Planc.* 31. For the father/son pairs mentioned in those passages, however, Cicero elsewhere argues the opposite, that the son has in fact inherited his father's moral character (*Verr.* 2.1.32; *Planc.* 32).

[72] Unfortunately, the composition of the audience at this time is unknown, as the speech can be dated only between the years 76 and 66 BCE.

A belief in inherited morality occurs in many cultures and can perhaps be attributed to an early conception that an ancestor lives on in the body of a child. See Bächtold-Stäubli 6:952–54, where this belief is traced in a number of societies, including that of the early Greeks. For Rome, see the story of Hortensia, daughter of Hortensius (Val. Max. 8.3.3) and Hor. *Carm.* 4.4.29: *fortes creantur fortibus et bonis* ("the strong are made from the strong and good").

[73] May 6 discusses *ORF* 8.58 and 8.173 in this context.

When the censor Lepidus had demoted Marcus Antistius of Pyrgi by taking
away his horse, [Marcus'] friends shouted out, asking what he should say to
his father [when asked] why he had lost his horse; [for they said his father]
was the best type of farmer—very thrifty, unassuming, and frugal. [Lep-
idus] replied, "[Tell him] I believe nothing of what you're saying."

The censor Lepidus clearly does not know the farmer personally. The
lack of acquaintance does not, however, prevent the censor from making
conjectures about the man's character. The actions of the son Marcus
prevent Lepidus from believing that the father is worthy of the superla-
tives with which he has been described. For the humor of the censor's
remarks rely on a bias he shares with his audience: an immoral son cannot be born of a moral father.

LIVING YOUR NAME

Romans living under the Empire were uncertain whether the cognomen
Cicero (from *cicer*, "chickpea") referred to a physical peculiarity of its
original bearer—a misshapen nose?—or to an exceptional capacity for
growing garbanzo beans.[74] According to Plutarch, Cicero's friends had
advised him to change his name if he wished to succeed in politics (*Cic.*
1.5). He did not, of course. Yet the only surviving contemporary joke on
the name belongs to Cicero himself:

> ταμιεύων δ᾽ ἐν Σικελίᾳ καὶ τοῖς θεοῖς ἀνάθημα ποιούμενος ἀργυροῦν, τὰ
> μὲν πρῶτα δύο τῶν ὀνομάτων ἐπέγραψε, τόν τε Μάρκον καὶ τὸν Τύλλιον,
> ἀντὶ δὲ τοῦ τρίτου σκώπτων ἐρέβινθον ἐκέλευσε παρὰ τὰ γράμματα τὸν
> τεχνίτην ἐντορεῦσαι. (Plut. *Cic.* 1.6 = *Mor.* 204f)

> When he was presenting a silver offering to the gods during his quaestorship
> in Sicily, he had his first two names inscribed upon it—Marcus and
> Tullius—but instead of his third name, he jokingly had the engraver sketch
> out alongside these letters a chickpea.

An odd anecdote;[75] one can only wonder whether the young Cicero is
here displaying pride over his background or awkwardly confessing his
family's rural origins, origins he had to defend throughout his political

---

[74] Plut. *Cic.* 1.4 (cf. Priscianus *Gramm.* 2.58.11 [Keil]); Plin. *Nat.* 18.10. Amy Richlin has
drawn my attention to *cicer* at Iuv. 6.373b, where the word denotes an erect penis, and to
the parallel use of the Greek *erebinthos* (see Henderson, s.v.).

[75] But not without parallel: from the imperial age, Ritti has collected over one hundred
examples of tomb monuments that contain an illustration of the name of the deceased. She
concludes that in many cases the figures are intended to preserve an aspect of the dead
person's character (375). For living persons, I have found a political graffito from Pompeii,
proclaiming that the Balbi endorse their candidate "with a stammer" (*balbe; CIL* 4.935i).

career. I am disposed to believe the latter. Cicero was well aware of the extent to which an inherited name could work to its bearer's disadvantage.

Five years after the incident recorded by Plutarch, Cicero composed a series of invective-filled speeches against Gaius Verres, a former governor of Sicily. In these orations, Cicero puns frequently on the name *Verres*—"an uncastrated boar." At one point, the orator compares Verres' administrative rapacity to the moderate rule of a former governor of Spain, Lucius Calpurnius Piso Frugi:

> nimirum ut hic [Verres] nomen suum comprobavit, sic ille [Frugi] cognomen. (*Verr.* 2.4.57)

> And clearly, just as [Verres] has lived up to his name (*nomen*), so too has [Frugi] lived up to his cognomen.[76]

Verres "the Pig" was, predictably, a brutish governor; Piso's cognomen *Frugi* ("Sober"), on the other hand, betokened an honest administration. The concept "to live up to one's name" survives in the English idiom and denotes an individual's ability to match the achievements—physical, intellectual, or both—of a parent or ancestor. In Cicero's remarks, however, the name of an individual prophesied that ability.

Not every situation provided as clear a case as those of Verres and Frugi. Occasionally name and behavior do not coincide. Since cognomina denoting positive characteristics appear to be relatively infrequent, the failure to live up to a positive name often brought special censure. An oratorical fragment of Cicero yields a pun on *Pulcher* ("Beautiful"), the cognomen of Publius Clodius. This speech included a detailed description by Cicero of Clodius dressing up as a woman in order to penetrate the rites of the Bona Dea, rites traditionally restricted to Roman matrons. The following fragment seems to have constituted the climax of that description:

> sed, credo, postquam speculum tibi adlatum est longe te a pulchris abesse sensisti. (*In Clod.* 25)

> But I'll bet that after the mirror was handed over you realized you were far from being among the beautiful (*pulchri*).[77]

---

[76] For this meaning of *comprobo*, see *OLD*, s.v. 2. L. Calpurnius Piso Frugi (consul 133), the father of this Piso and, apparently, the first bearer of the cognomen *Frugi*, receives praise for the aptness of his name at *Tusc.* 3.16. Note that *Frugi* is a second cognomen; the earlier, *Piso* ("Pea"), apparently derives from agriculture.

[77] As one would expect, Cicero did not invent this pun. In Plautus (*Mil.* 1037–38) Pyrgopolynices answers the greeting *Pulcher, salve*—"Hello, beautiful/Pulcher"—with *meum cognomentum commemoravit*—"He remembered my nickname!" (for a different interpretation, see Monteil 78). According to the Scholia Bobiensia (p. 90, 1–8 [Stangl]), the line of

This pun on *pulcher* functions on two levels. First, the adjective's literal meaning mocks Clodius as a "pretty boy" who strives to become something he is not—a woman.[78] But at the same time, the pun foregrounds the extent to which Clodius differs from his ancestors, the illustrious Pulchri: in perversely interpreting what constitutes a Pulcher, Clodius misses the point. Cicero's humor serves as a corrective.

While Clodius inherited his cognomen, other figures were the first to bear theirs. The great strongmen of the late Republic bore names that were their particular possession—Sulla *Felix* ("the Lucky"), Pompeius *Magnus* ("the Great"). Unlike honorific cognomina such as *Asiaticus* or *Africanus*, these names were not bestowed by an official state act but were adopted independently, as a boast of personal achievement.[79] These special labels exposed their owners to special risk; the public flaunting of a laudatory name could result in public ridicule.

Up until now, my examples of the mockery of names have concentrated on their manipulation by political figures, who attempt to provide their audience with insight into an opponent's character. A letter of Cicero from 59 BCE, however, provides a rare instance of the people themselves mocking a cognomen. The occasion involves neither a courtroom nor the senate but a public stage:

> populi sensus maxime theatro et spectaculis perspectus est; . . . ludis Apollinaribus Diphilus tragoedus in nostrum Pompeium petulanter invectus est: "nostra miseria tu es magnus" miliens coactus est dicere; "eandem virtutem istam veniet tempus cum graviter gemes" totius theatri clamore dixit, itemque cetera. (*Att.* 2.19.3 = SB 39)

> The sentiments of the people were felt most of all in the theater and at the games; . . . at the games in honor of Apollo, the tragic actor Diphilus inveighed impudently against our friend Pompeius; a thousand times he was compelled to say "You are great (*magnus*) to our misery"; he said to shouts

---

the Pulchri began with P. Claudius Pulcher, consul in 249 BCE, and had attained prominence by Plautus' day.

[78] Hence the nickname *Pulchellus*, which Cicero uses to refer to Clodius in his private correspondence with Atticus (*Att.* 1.16.10 = SB 16; 2.1.4 = SB 21; 2.22.1 = SB 42). The cognomen *Pulcher*, in fact, may have originally connoted effeminacy; see Marx on Lucilius 24 and my discussion of *De orat.* 2.262 in chapter 1. For more examples of this pun in the late Republic, see Catull. 79.1, 86.5, and the discussion by Skinner; also, perhaps, *CIL* 1².2.1211.

[79] Plutarch says Pompeius received his cognomen *Magnus* around 80 BCE, either by direct action from Sulla or through the acclamation of his troops (*Pomp.* 13.4–5); Livy, on the other hand, says it arose from the flattery of close friends (30.45.6). For Sulla Felix, see Plut. *Sull.* 34.2.

of the whole theater, "The time will come when you will mourn heavily for this same courage of yours," and other things as well.[80]

The populace is so sensitive to the value of a name that it clamors for an encore when Diphilus' verses contain a double meaning. The fictional world of the stage spills into the real world of politics. Pompeius' laudatory cognomen *Magnus* ("Great") becomes a vehicle for his ridicule since, like Clodius', his name is a label whose applicability he must continually prove. This same audience includes, presumably, those who laughed about the babbling Bambalio and the pretty boy Pulcher. A name bears with it a responsibility not only to one's family but to the community at large.

Magnus also prompts sarcasm in the personal remarks Cicero addresses to Atticus. In fact, it appears that Cicero "perhaps never uses [*Magnus*] as a mere name except in letter headings."[81] Whenever Cicero does use this honorific title, he frequently qualifies it with adjectives such as "our" (*noster*) or "this" (*hic*), and employs it in contexts that clearly signal that the writer intends his remarks to comment ironically upon the cognomen's meaning. Cicero on one occasion even becomes explicit in his feelings toward the military leader in a passage where he also mocks a certain Crassus:

> quanto in odio noster amicus Magnus! cuius cognomen una cum Crassi Divitis cognomine consenescit. (*Att.* 2.13.2 = SB 33)

> In how great a hatred is our friend Magnus held! His nickname is growing old along with that of "Rich" Crassus.[82]

This passage seems to point to occasions of public mockery of *Magnus* akin to the Diphilus episode. The people continued to express disap-

---

[80] Val. Max. 6.2.9 records that the actor said *miseria nostra magnus est* and pointed to Pompeius as he spoke the lines. But the general was at Capua, as Cicero makes clear later in this same letter: "they were said to fly to Pompeius at Capua" (*Capuam ad Pompeium volare dicebantur*). For similar instances of verse being applied on stage to contemporary issues of the late Republic, cf. *Sest.* 117–26, *Phil.* 1.36, *Att.* 14.3.2 (SB 357); Suet. *Iul.* 84.2; and, more explicitly, the moving address to *necessitas* by the mime Laberius (Macr. *Sat.* 2.7.2–3).

[81] Shackleton Bailey on *Att.* 1.16.11 (SB 16).

[82] This Crassus is not, apparently, the triumvir; see Shackleton Bailey ad loc. For more puns on *Magnus* see *Att.* 1.16.11–13 (SB 16), 6.1.22 (SB 115), and Caelius at *Fam.* 8.13.2 (SB 94); Plut. *Crass.* 7.1; Vell. 2.32.6; and Lucan passim. In Cicero, the irony ranges from the pathetic to the pejorative, depending upon his relations with Pompeius at each particular time. Nonironic instances of the name occur primarily in works intended for the public, e.g., *Arch.* 24, *Manil.* 67, and *Leg.* 2.6; in the letters, it is used at *Att.* 6.1.25 (SB 115) to distinguish Magnus from Pompeius Vindillus.

pointment over the failed promise inherent in the name of Pompeius "the Great."

Clodius acquired the epithet *Pulcher* from his ancestors; Pompeius became *Magnus* from his achievements. Lesser figures also entertained hopes of improving their reputation by adopting flattering labels. In his *Sixth Philippic*, Cicero deflates the pretensions of one such person—Trebellius "the Honest" (*Fides*):

> audisse enim vos arbitror, Quirites, quod etiam videre potuistis, cotidie sponsores et creditores L. Trebelli convenire. o Fides!—hoc enim opinor Trebellium sumpsisse cognomen—quae potest esse maior fides quam fraudare creditores, domo profugere, propter aes alienum ire ad arma? (*Phil.* 6.11)

> Now I believe you have heard, citizens, something that you could even see, that the sponsors and creditors of Lucius Trebellius are gathering together every day. O Trust (*Fides*)!—for I think Trebellius has adopted this cognomen—what greater trust can there be than to defraud creditors, run away from home, and take up weapons because of your debt?

Cicero pretends to reject the validity of Trebellius' *fides*; a debtor like Trebellius can hardly be trustworthy. The name allows Cicero to chide his opponent for bankruptcy, a common topic of Roman humor. The verb "to adopt" (*sumpsisse*) implies that Trebellius has dishonestly adopted this flattering sobriquet in order to present a false image.[83] The manipulative use of proper names appears to have been a common practice in the late Republic. In a letter to Trebonius of April 44, Cicero mentions the candidates for political office who adopt an uninherited name (*cognomen*) for the elections in an attempt to secure popular favor (*Fam.* 15.20.1 = SB 208). This type of name change further attests to the influence that the connotation of certain names could have over the general populace.[84] Cicero refers to a similar practice in his speech for Cluentius when he says Staienus chose the cognomen Paetus over Ligus "so that, if he had made himself a *Ligus*, he wouldn't seem to use the cogno-

[83] It is uncertain whether the cognomen *Fides* derives from the idea of loyalty; the only two parallels extant from the Republic of cognomina taken from such abstracts are *Pietas* and *Sermo* (Kajanto 97). Alternatively, the name may derive from the musical instrument (cf. *Bucina* and *Fistula*). Kajanto solves the problem by including the name under both headings (254, 343). Nevertheless, the passage cited in the text from *Phil.* 6 leaves no doubt as to how Trebellius and Cicero did, and the people would, interpret its meaning.

[84] For other apparent examples of deliberate name change during the Republic "to capitalize on . . . distinguished ancestry, real or fictive," see Hopkins 51.

By the time of the triumviral civil wars, the practice of adopting new cognomina had become especially important. Sextus Pompeius, for example, began calling himself *Magnus Pius*. According to Syme, Octavian eventually secured the ultimate name with the praenomen-nomen combination *Imperator Caesar*; see Syme 1979 1:361–99.

men of his tribe rather than his family" (*ne, si se Ligurem fecisset, nationis magis suae quam generis uti cognomine videretur; Clu.* 72).[85] In addition to explaining the significance of Cicero's remarks about Trebellius' name change, these two passages further demonstrate that descriptive names had potential appeal to prejudices latent among the Roman people. Changing a name changes one's image.

Trebellius intentionally manipulated his name as an advertisement to the populace. Cicero treats the use of names as popular labels on two other occasions. In his defense of Sestius, the orator has occasion to reprove the demagoguery of Lucius Gellius Poplicola: "He married a freedwoman not out of desire, I think, but so that he might seem a 'devotee of the people' [*plebicola*]" (*qui, ut credo, non libidinis causa, sed ut plebicola videretur, libertinam duxit uxorem; Sest.* 110). Gellius absurdly lives even his private life in accordance with his famous name. Trying to outdo the well-known fifth-century politician Publius Valerius Publicola, Gellius simply demonstrates that he does not know what "serving the people" means: it is not, Cicero asserts, to marry a woman of lowly birth.[86] A passage from Cicero's treatise *On the Republic* shows, on the contrary, the type of citizen who truly works for the populace. In passing laws to protect the rights of the common people, Publius Valerius "was *publicola* to the highest degree" (*fuit Publicola maxime; Rep.* 2.53). By misusing a name, Gellius abuses an important Roman tradition.

To a Roman, a king (*rex*) must have provided the antithesis to *publicola*. The charge of being a *rex* implied disdain for the offices and institutions of the Republic, the government established after the Romans drove out their own kings in the late sixth century BCE.[87] Cicero was himself accused of aiming at kingship as a result of his actions in the Catilinarian conspiracy (*Sull.* 21, *Catil.* 1.30). One such accusation occurred in 61 during a vicious debate in the senate with his opponent Clodius. Cicero, in relating the episode verbatim to Atticus, includes the following exchange:

> "quousque" inquit [Clodius] "hunc regem feremus?" "regem appellas" inquam "cum Rex tui mentionem nullam fecerit?"; ille autem Regis hereditatem spe devorarat. (*Att.* 1.16.10 = SB 16)

---

[85] On Staienus' adoption of his cognomen, see now Badian 9–10.

[86] Cicero probably alludes to this cognomen a few sentences earlier in the speech when he quotes a possible objection to his criticism of Gellius: "For he is a person devoted to the Roman people" (*est enim homo iste populo Romano deditus*). The orator then proceeds to demonstrate the opposite: *non fuit popularis*. Neudling 75 discusses whether this is the Gellius of Catullus' epigrams. For other examples of the cognomen Publicola being used for propaganda, see Liv. 2.8.1; cf. Plut. *Publ.* 1.1, 10.4.

[87] Opelt 129–30; Rawson analyzes the complex attitude of Romans toward kingship in the period before Caesar's death.

[Clodius] said, "How long shall we endure this king?" "You call [me] a
king," I said, "when King made no mention of you [in his will]?"
    That man had squandered (*devorarat*) King's inheritance in his expectation
of it.

Cicero employs the cognomen *Rex* ("King") in order to evade Clodius'
accusation. The witticism probably does not strike many modern readers
as funny. Cicero, however, not only made the joke but even considered it
worth sharing with Atticus. Quintus Marcius Rex was Clodius' wealthy
brother-in-law, who left a legacy to Clodius' elder brother but not to
Clodius himself.[88] Cicero's joke turns the tables on his opponent's accusation by asserting that Clodius is the one acting like a "king." Clodius is
cast as a financially profligate feaster (*devorarat*), who proves his un-
worthiness to inherit through his premature actions.[89] Suetonius relates
how Julius Caesar also learned the art of one-upmanship in this context:

> neque . . . infamiam affectati etiam regii nominis discutere valuit, quan-
> quam et plebei regem se salutanti, Caesarem se, non Regem esse respon-
> derit. (Suet. *Iul.* 79.2)

> And he was unable to shake off even the rumors that he wished to be called a
> king, even though when the plebs saluted him as king he replied his name
> was Caesar, not King.

These rumors of the plebs would have special irony if their authors were
recalling a theme from Caesar's funeral speech for his aunt Julia, in which
he traced the lineage of his family back to the early Roman king Ancus
Marcius (Suet. *Iul.* 6.1). If this is so, the plebs are doing more than attempting to bestow the kingship on Caesar. They are appealing to the
name *Rex* in Julius Caesar's family line. The name is its history and that
history includes Ancus Marcius. Julius Caesar earns the title *Rex* not simply through his actions but through family right.
    Names represent a standard that the named must continually observe.
If a person does not meet the expectations of society he can be attacked
verbally, his name providing the corroborating evidence for wrongdoing. Quintilian, as I have already mentioned, censures this type of abuse,
suggesting that only positive names such as *Pius* ("Pious") or *Sapiens*
("Wise") provide valid indication of character (*Inst.* 5.10.30). In a few
passages Cicero does pun on names in a complimentary fashion, yet the
context of these jokes only serves to underscore the discrepancy between
oratorical practice during the Republic and rhetorical theory under the
Empire. In one of his letters, the phrase "Latin Atticism" (*Latinus* 'Aτ-

---

[88] Shackleton Bailey ad loc.
[89] I discuss the connection between feasting and improper civic behavior in chapter 4.
See further Edwards chap. 5.

τιχισμός) conceals a compliment to Atticus' learning (*Att.* 4.19.1 = SB 93; cf. *Att.* 1.13.5 = SB 13). In another letter, Sabinus' "unassuming countenance and steady speech" bespeak the aptness of his name—he has inherited the qualities commonly attributed to the Sabine people (*modestus . . . vultus sermoque constans*; *Fam.* 15.20.1 = SB 208). When writing to Publius Volumnius Eutrapelus, Cicero remarks about an unsigned letter he had received that "the witty tone [εὐτραπελία] of the epistle made me realize it was yours" (εὐτραπελία *litterarum fecit ut intellegerem tuas esse*; *Fam.* 7.32.1 = SB 113). In a less straightforward manner, Cicero compliments the Bruti by denying the implications of their name. He is complaining to Atticus of the inaction of Julius Caesar's assassins after the Ides of March:

> ista culpa Brutorum? minime illorum quidem, sed aliorum brutorum, qui se cautos ac sapientis putant. (*Att.* 14.14.2 = SB 368)

> Is this the fault of the Bruti? No, it's hardly theirs, but it's the fault of other stupid brutes (*brutorum*) who consider themselves cautious and wise.

These four examples constitute all the complimentary puns on names I have found in the Ciceronian corpus. Their relationship is clear—and telling. Each instance occurs not in the orations, where names can carry special polemical force, but in the orator's private correspondence.[90] This phenomenon reintroduces an earlier theme: the public speaker of the late Republic employs political humor not for flattery, as Quintilian will later advise, but to make his opponent small.

Reading Names

The Romans could conceive of names as representing a desired standard of character. To be called *Frugi*, *Pulcher*, or *Magnus* meant accepting the responsibility for possessing honesty, beauty, or courage. Yet most cognomina, the class of names generating the majority of name puns from this period, describe unattractive features or actions. In oratory of the late Republic, the proper interpretation of these pejorative names facilitates

---

[90] The following name puns from the letters, more in keeping with Cicero's hostile wit, are not discussed in the text. Balbus: *Fam.* 9.19.2 (SB 194), *Att.* 12.2.2 (SB 238); Lepidus and Brutus: *Att.* 6.1.25 (SB 115); Lentulus (*lens*): *Att.* 1.19.2 (SB 19); Pulcher: *Att.* 1.16.10 (SB 16), 2.1.4 (SB 21), 2.22.1 (SB 42); Pollex: *Att.* 13.46.1 (SB 338); Calidius: *Fam.* 8.9.5 (SB 82).

The pun on *Calidius* is my own conjecture. I have already cited the similar pun at *Inv.* 2.28. Admittedly, the dissimilar quantities of the *i* in *Calidius* and *calidus* argue against this interpretation, but see Shackleton Bailey ad *Att.* 1.16.5 (SB 16), to which one can add the following possible exceptions: *Fam.* 9.20.1 = SB 193 (*malum*; cf. Plaut. *Amph.* 723), *De orat.* 2.284 (*liberum/libet*), *Clu.* 71 (*conditor*), and Vell. 2.108.2 (*natione/ratione*); see also Ahl 56.

the exclusion of the bearer of that name from active participation in society. In the examples cited in this section, names reveal otherness—another nationality, another heritage, and even, when it comes to animal names, another species. The examples that follow find Cicero expounding on the art of interpreting these pejorative labels. The orator shows how names speak and explains to his audience what they are saying. At the same time, Cicero shows that when his opponents attempt to use names in their favor, they do so improperly and ineptly.

Cognomina referring to ethnic or geographical origin were commonly exploited by orators as a negative label, intended to separate a name's bearer from true Roman society.[91] I begin with a subtle example to show the sensitivity that existed regarding this type of abuse. Numerius Quintius Rufus, as tribune of the plebs, had opposed the recall of Cicero from exile. In the oration for Sestius, his names come under scrutiny:

> ex iis princeps emitur ab inimicis meis is quem homines in luctu inridentes Gracchum vocabant, quoniam id etiam fatum civitatis fuit ut illa ex vepreculis extracta nitedula rem publicam conaretur adrodere. (*Sest.* 72)

> And of these [witnesses against me], the main one to be bought by my opponents was the man whom people, joking in their misery, were wont to call Gracchus, because it has been the fate of our state in this case too for that little red rat (*nitedula*), [who was] taken from the bramble bushes, to attempt to nibble away at the state.

Cicero simultaneously twists two of his opponent's names. First, he comments on the appropriateness of the nickname *Gracchus* by implying that Rufus will present as great a danger to the state as the popular tribunes Tiberius and Gaius Gracchus had in the previous century. He then further belittles Rufus through a complicated etymological game: Cicero compares him to a *nitedula*, the name for a red (*rufus*) field mouse. An ancient scholiast on this passage recognizes the significance of Rufus' mouselike qualities: "he called him *nitedula* because he was not only short in stature, but red in color" (*quod esset non tantum statura depressus, verum etiam colore rubidus, nitedulam nominavit*; Schol. Bob. p. 134, 28–29 [Stangl]). The cognomen *Rufus*, ancient sources seem to indicate, is likely to have originated as a label for a "red"-haired non-Roman.[92] By punning on this name, Cicero indicates that his opponent not only is of foreign descent but is in fact an animal that wishes to overwhelm the state. The diminutive ending of *nitedula*, however, highlights the irony of Cic-

----

[91] In addition to the jokes treated below in the text, see my discussion of *Semiplacentinus* (*Pis.* 14) at the end of chapter 4.

[92] Quint. *Inst.* 1.4.25 and Plut. *Cor.* 11.6 both state that the name *Rufus* originated as physical description. *Rufa*, moreover, was a common slave name, a fact that further indicates the ancient association between red hair and foreign descent (Kajanto 134).

ero's formulation: Quintius is simply an impotent mouse. Again, this joke may strike us as slight, but the associations involved are distinctly Roman. As in the case of the stutterer Bambalio, a name (*Rufus*) introduces a physical peculiarity (red hair), thereby allowing Cicero to portray the bearer of the name as a likely outcast.

In his *Eleventh Philippic*, Cicero similarly appeals to biases against persons of non-Roman origin.[93] The cognomen of Titus Annius Cimber indicates descent from the Germanic tribes of the Cimbri. In this instance of wordplay, moreover, to take effective advantage of Roman xenophobia the orator also exploits the belief in inherited moral character:

> lumen et decus illius exercitus paene praeterii, T. Annium Cimbrum, Lysidici filium, Lysidicum ipsum Graeco verbo, quoniam omnia iura dissolvit, nisi forte iure Germanum Cimber occidit. (*Phil*. 11.14; cf. Quint. *Inst*. 8.3.29)

> I almost forgot the pride and joy of Antonius' army, Titus Annius Cimber, the son of Lysidicus. In fact, he's a "Lysidicus" himself in the Greek sense since he has "dissolved all justice"—or maybe it's justice for a Cimber to kill a German/his own brother (*germanus*).[94]

A complex combination of name puns occurs here. First, Cicero explains that Cimber fulfills the prediction concealed in the name of his father Lysidicus (λύω, "to dissolve," δίκη, "justice"): by murdering his own brother, Cimber violates the basic principles of justice. Then, almost in mockery of the tenuous connection he has made, the orator offers Cimber a potential defense, a defense that is also based upon the belief in the relation between name and character: "or maybe it's justice for a Cimber to kill a German." Through this pretended defense, Cicero in fact incriminates his opponent further, transforming him into a Teutonic savage—the name *Cimber* literally denotes a non-Roman heritage. At the same time, by punning on *germanus* ("German" and "brother"), the orator recalls Cimber's act of murder. His opponent, Cicero demonstrates through these puns, embodies a true *Cimber*, a savage who has violently perverted familial duty.[95]

---

[93] Opelt 149–51 catalogues other instances in late Republican authors where municipal or provincial origins are referred to disparagingly.

[94] Cicero often uses the phrase *nisi forte* (as well as *nisi vero* or just *nisi*) to signal an ironic comment; see Haury 1955: 81–82. In addition to the passages Haury cites, cf. *Har. resp.* 5 (quoted below in the text); *Att*. 13.40.1 (SB 343).

[95] Cicero later gives Cimber the mock epithet *Philadelphus* ("brother lover"; *Phil*. 13.26). For a similar pun on *germanus* see the song of the triumphant soldiers of Lepidus and Plancus, both of whom included brothers in the proscription lists of 43 BCE: "the two consuls are celebrating a triumph over Germans/brothers, not Gauls" (*de Germanis, non de Gallis, duo triumphant consules*; Vell. 2.67.4); cf. also *Hist. Aug. Caracalla* 10.6 (Caracalla "Geticus").

Cultural prejudice informs two other name puns found in Cicero's oratory. Both these instances find the orator exploiting the cultural connotations, as opposed to the literal denotation, of an opponent's name. In one of the speeches he delivered upon returning from exile, Cicero attributes his past reluctance to prosecute Publius Clodius to the man's status as a public enemy, not a private one. He continues:

> itaque eum [Clodium] numquam a me esse accusandum putavi, non plus quam stipitem illum qui quorum hominum esset nesciremus, nisi se Ligurem ipse esse diceret. (*Har. resp.* 5)

> And so I never thought I should accuse [Clodius] any more than that stump [Aelius], whose heritage we would be ignorant of—if he didn't himself claim he was a Ligurian.

Ligus, the cognomen of Aelius, advertised his family's ancestral origins. Yet a Roman proverb proclaimed the Ligurians to be proverbial deceivers: "all Ligurians are liars" dates back as early as the elder Cato (*Ligures . . . omnes fallaces sunt*; *Orig.* 32 [*HRR*]). Hence, Cicero argues, Aelius' cognomen indicates a deceptive nature. The orator aims his appeal once again to the Roman distrust of anything alien or non-Roman.

A similar bias equips the following joke with its barb:

> [dixit] argentarius Sex. Clodius, cui nomen est Phormio, nec minus niger nec minus confidens, quam ille Terentianus est Phormio. (*Caecin.* 27; Quint. *Inst.* 6.3.56)

> The banker Sextus Clodius [has spoken]. His name is Phormio, and he is no less black nor less bold than Terence's Phormio.

The humor of this passage resides in the connotations Clodius' nickname *Phormio* has for the audience; here, specifically, Cicero relies on their familiarity with the parasite of Terence's comedy of the same name. Ugly and distorted, the mask of the parasite indicates both moral and physical deviance.[96] These stock comic characters, of lowly origin and concerned only with appeasing their appetites, play no active role in the united society that forms at a comedy's conclusion. The name Phormio, Cicero implies, labels Sextus Clodius as a social misfit, an outcast of the type known to any member of the Roman audience.

Erich Gruen suggests to me that the name *Lysidicus* may represent a distortion of *Luscus*, a cognomen found among the Anii. For more puns on Greek names in Cicero, see *S. Rosc.* 124, where Chrysogonus is taunted for the theft of Roscius' land with the simple pun "I come now to that golden name of Chrysogonus" (*venio nunc ad illud nomen aureum Chrysogoni*). This is an old type of joke: see Plaut. *Bacch.* 240; Ter. *Ad.* 168–70; and *Att.* 6.9.2 (SB 123), where Terentia's freedman Philotimus is accused of *philotimia* ("ambition"). Cicero puns on the foreign name *Sardanapallus* at *Rep.* 3 frag. 4 (see Adams 64).

[96] Plates and discussion are in Bieber 100.

Another class of puns centers on those puzzling cognomina obtained from the names of animals. Although one cannot always discern the original connotation of appellations of this type, it seems plausible that, as with adjectival cognomina, the original naming must often have had the intention of highlighting "unwelcome traits of character"—it is difficult to account for cognomina such as *Musca* ("Fly") or *Asinus* ("Ass") otherwise.[97] Indeed, in colloquial Latin and Roman comedy, animal names are often employed as terms of abuse.[98] Hence, as with the cognomina describing non-Roman heritage, an animal name can present its bearer as an unfit member of the community. The type of mockery was important enough for Cicero to include examples of in the humor section of *On the Orator*. An analysis of these instances demonstrates that, as was the case with physical peculiarities, names offer fine material for degrading an opponent. The restrictions to be observed in their employment are purely rhetorical, the interlocutors of the dialogue indicate, and have nothing to do with any potential inefficacy of a name joke per se. While discussing the use of humor as a means of gaining rhetorical advantage (*ut proficiamus aliquid*), the speaker Strabo presents the following as a negative example:

> quid enim est Vargula adsecutus, cum eum candidatus A. Sempronius cum Marco suo fratre complexus esset, "puer, abige muscas"? (*De orat.* 2.247)

> For what did Vargula achieve when [he remarked], after the candidate Aulus Sempronius [Musca] and his brother Marcus had embraced him, "Boy, drive away the flies (*muscae*)"?

These two Sempronii bore the cognomen *Musca* ("Fly"). The wit does not strike one as markedly different from other Republican name puns, and yet Cicero portrays Strabo as disapproving of Vargula's remark. Strabo's expressed objection—that Vargula "went for the laugh" (*risum quaesivit*)—only provides half an explanation, for, as Strabo himself admits, this offers only a subjective judgment (*mea sententia*). If his discourse intends to instruct, he must provide more objective criteria.

Another example from this section of *On the Orator* clarifies Strabo's intentions. Using a justly famous joke about the name Catulus that Quintilian later chose to include in his own discussion of rhetorical

---

[97] Kajanto 85; Chase 112 compares the German "zoological *Schimpfwörter.*" Rose 174–75 rejects the possibility that the names could have originally been totemic.

Animal names related to farming seem to provide an exception. Varro's *On Agriculture* abounds in such appellations, most of which Varro, sooner or later, puns upon: Scrofa (2.4.1–2), Vaccius (2.5.2), Equiculus (2.7.1), Orata and Murena (3.3.10), Parra (3.5.18), and, finally, Merula, Pavo, Pica, and Passer make up the "aviary" of an *augur* (3.2.2). In fact, the one clearly pejorative name in the dialogue—*Varro* ("Knock-kneed," or, perhaps, "Blockhead")—is, interestingly, never mocked.

[98] Colloquial Latin: Hofmann 88, 194; Roman comedy: Lilja 30–35.

humor, Strabo explains how wit can be employed profitably in the court-room (*De orat.* 2.219). The skill, however, cannot easily be taught:

> quid enim hic meus frater [Catulus] ab arte adiuvari potuit cum a Philippo interrogatus quid latraret, furem se videre respondit? (*De orat.* 2.220; cf. Quint. *Inst.* 6.3.81)

> For how could my brother [Catulus] here have been helped by training on the occasion when he was asked by Philippus why he was barking and he responded, "Because I see a thief"?

Philippus alludes derisively to the cognomen of Catulus ("Puppy"), and compares his opponent's rhetorical pleading to the barking of a dog.[99] Catulus turns the joke around by transforming himself from a yapping puppy into an astute watchdog. Part of the effectiveness of Catulus' re-mark rests in the fact that he has responded to a direct insult: Quintilian categorizes the joke as an effective type of counterattack (*genus repercu-tiendi*) and Strabo later refers to it as a fine example of a witty rejoinder (*De orat.* 2.255). But it is important to recognize that Strabo initially labels the remark as an example of the profitable use of wit in oratory. In fact, it is the first anecdote he relates in a lengthy digression devoted to how an orator can most effectively employ wit, where it is not charac-terized as an example of humor given in response. The attack on Phil-ippus, therefore, is showcased not simply for its verbal cleverness but for its applicability to the situation in the courtroom.

These observations on the joke of Catulus help explain Strabo's objec-tion to Vargula's failed joke "Boy, drive away the flies" (*"puer, abige muscas"*). The remark's "uselessness" (*sine causa*; 2.247) does not involve its quality as humor but rather its gratuitous nature. It aims only for laughter (if not merely a clever insult) and as such has no rhetorical value. As Strabo asserts later, "it must also be noted that not everything laugh-able is clever" (*hoc etiam animadvertendum est, non esse omnia ridicula faceta*; 2.251). In fact, if a joke makes no rhetorical point, it may even provoke the censure of an audience. Strabo teaches not only that one can effec-tively employ wit in oratory but that its misuse can be counterproduc-tive. There seems, then, to have existed guidelines for the public employ-ment of name jokes, and these guidelines attest to the efficacy of names in revealing character faults.

Cicero had bestial foes as well. In a scathing attack on the companions of Marcus Antonius, Cicero gets in a dig at Decius Mus ("the Mouse"):

---

[99] Strabo and Quintus Lutatius Catulus shared the same mother, hence *frater*. Kajanto 24, 326, and Chase 112 both derive *Catulus* from the Latin word for "puppy," and not from *catus*, "wise." Varro *Ling.* 5.99 seems to derive the name from both words.
Philippus' initial remark itself contains a good pun: *latrare* was a common term of abuse applied to shrill-sounding orators (Rabbie ad loc.; cf. English "yap").

est etiam ibi Decius, ab illis, ut opinor, Muribus Deciis; itaque Caesaris munera erosit. (*Phil.* 13.27)

He also has in his presence a Decius, descended, I believe, from the Mures ("mice") Decii; that's why he's devoured Caesar's gifts.

The remark recalls the pun on *Rufus* already discussed (*Sest.* 72): a cognomen reveals the nonhuman, destructive tendencies of its bearer and at the same time belittles the opponent by figuring him as a rodent. This particular example stresses the importance placed on the ridicule of a name since Cicero may in fact be inventing—as he hints at with his parenthetical "I believe" (*ut opinor*)—the familial connection of this Decius to the Mus branch of the family.[100] This animal metamorphosis also enables Cicero to describe vividly Decius' profligacy. Like Clodius, who "devoured" an inheritance he never received, the rodentlike Decius has helped Antonius eat away (*erosit*) Caesar's legacy.

PUNNING WITH THE PEOPLE

One animal in particular fascinated Cicero—a certain uncastrated male pig that provided the orator with his first major victory in the political courts. In a series of speeches written in 70 BCE, Cicero showcases the name Gaius *Verres* ("the Boar") as a way of expressing his own affinity with notions of names and naming that were common among the general Roman populace. I opened this chapter by considering the magical effects names were considered to have on external reality. Orators exploit this belief by making jokes that assume a connection between the meaning of a name and the internal character of the person named. Clamor for encores in the theater and choruses of approving laughter in the courtroom demonstrate popular appreciation of this humor. In the *Verrines*, Cicero highlights how the people themselves employ these beliefs in criticizing their superiors. In this way, he is able to portray himself as an extension of the people's voice.

Verres' piggish persona first appears in the preliminary hearings to the main trial. While narrating the early portion of Verres' praetorship, Cicero relates that for a short time it seemed as if the governor might develop into an honest administrator. Cicero quickly checks himself; Verres had not in fact been his true self at this time, he maintains, but was in reality Quintus Mucius, his predecessor in Sicily and an honest man (*Div. in Caec.* 57). Soon, however, Verres' true character emerges; he once again "comes to himself," a self that had always been knowable through his name:

---

[100] Cf. Shackleton Bailey ad loc.

sed repente e vestigio ex homine tamquam aliquo Circaeo poculo factus est
Verres; redit ad se atque ad mores suos. (*Div. in Caec.* 57)

But suddenly, as if through some potion of Circe, he was transformed from
a human being into a boar (*verres*); he returned to himself and to his proper
character.

Verres reacquires his name as if through magic. Unlike Odysseus' men,
who became their true selves when Circe transformed them back into
human beings, Verres exhibited human qualities only when masquerad-
ing as an honest man. The metamorphosis, which Cicero represents as a
supernatural feat, is activated by the power of a name—"Verres" is not
simply a label but an expression of the man's own self.[101]
Considering both the emphasis placed on Verres' name in the preliminary hearing and the frequency of name jokes elsewhere in oratory, it
comes as a surprise when, during the actual prosecution of his opponent,
Cicero apologizes for quoting some puns on Verres' name. The orator
records the complaints people had about Verres' urban praetorship in
Rome:

> hinc illi homines erant qui etiam ridiculi inveniebantur ex dolore; quorum
> alii, id quod saepe audistis, negabant mirandum esse ius tam nequam esse
> verrinum; alii etiam frigidiores erant, sed quia stomachabantur ridiculi vide-
> bantur esse, cum Sacerdotem exsecrabantur qui verrem tam nequam reli-
> quisset. quae ego non commemorarem—neque enim perfacete dicta neque
> porro hac severitate digna sunt—nisi vos illud vellem recordari, istius ne-
> quitiam et iniquitatem tum in ore vulgi atque in communibus proverbiis
> esse versatam. (*Verr.* 2.1.121)

And so there were those people who were found to be even ridiculous in
their grief. Some of them, as you've often heard, used to say that it was no
wonder that the pork gravy/justice of Verres (*ius verrinum*) was so bad.
Others were even more tedious, but because they were angry they seemed
laughable as they cursed Sacerdos/the priest for having neglected [to sacri-
fice] such a foul boar/Verres. I wouldn't be recounting these stories, since
they're not particularly witty and, in addition, are unworthy of the serious
nature of this place, if it weren't that I'd like you to remember that at this
time this man's evil and foul nature was always on the lips of the masses and
in the common proverbs.

---

[101] A one-liner from Plutarch punning on the name *Verres* also dates from the time of
this speech. The Κεκίλιος of the anecdote is most likely the Caecilius of Cicero's *Speech
against Caecilius*: "And when a freedman by the name of Caecilius, an adherent of Judaism,
wished to slight the Sicilians to accuse Verres, Cicero remarked, 'What [business can a]
Jew have with a pig?'" (ὡς οὖν ἀπελευθερικὸς ἄνθρωπος, ἔνοχος τῷ ἰουδαΐζειν, ὄνομα
Κεκίλιος, ἐβούλετο παρωσάμενος τοὺς Σικελιώτας κατηγορεῖν τοῦ Βέρρου "τί Ἰουδαίῳ
πρὸς χοῖρον;" ἔφη ὁ Κίκερων; *Cic.* 7.6).

Cicero, in his stance as a representative of the seriousness (*severitas*) of the courtroom, pretends to disapprove of these witticisms, yet the ascription of one of these puns (the *ius verrinum*) to Cicero himself by a later student of rhetoric attests to their Ciceronian flavor.[102] In fact, Cicero's false hesitation, rather than detracting attention from these instances of popular humor, allows him to highlight them. As in other examples of this rhetorical device of *praeteritio*, by which an orator pretends to "pass by" an item of information through a feigned sense of modesty or propriety, the emphatic lack of emphasis only underscores the point the orator is allegedly trying to evade.[103] In this particular case, the actions of Verres have had a telling effect on the authors of these jokes: the Roman people do not appear as witty (*faceti*), but as ridiculous (*ridiculi*);[104] the jokes emerge not from gaiety, but from grief (*ex dolore*) and anger (*stomachabantur*). These same emotions are represented as inspiring other name puns from the political arena: people mocked Rufus in their grief (*in luctu; Sest.* 72); Cicero's humorous abuse of Bambalio springs from contempt (*nihil illo contemptius; Phil.* 3.16). In the *Verrines*, Cicero includes these witticisms because, in the reality of Roman rhetoric, they serve a powerful function. Even in the talk of the common people, the evil of Verres finds apt expression in jokes on his name. The corrupt politician stands exposed by popular sentiment, a sentiment conveyed through the voice of Cicero, the upright and proper orator.

The citizens of Rome took notice of Verres' name on another occasion. Before leaving for his year in Sicily, Verres had busily studied and plotted in advance how most effectively to plunder his new province. The preparations were not lost on the Romans, who had suffered through the same man's praetorship. Cicero praises the astuteness of the urban populace:

> o praeclare coniectum a vulgo in illam provinciam omen communis famae atque sermonis, cum ex nomine istius quid iste in provincia facturus esset perridicule homines augurabantur! . . . videte satisne paratus ex illo omine urbano ad everrendam provinciam venerit. (*Verr.* 2.2.18–19; cf. Quint. *Inst.* 6.3.55)

> What a wondrous omen about that province the masses have spread about in their rumors and everyday gossip; for people were laughably prophesying from this man's name what he would do in his province! . . . Ask yourself whether that omen in the city had prepared him well enough to come sweep out (*everrendam*) the province.

The popular origins of the omen demonstrate the extent of Verres' guilt—the Roman people, Cicero alleges, anticipated that guilt even be-

---

[102] Tac. *Dial.* 23.1; cf. Quint. *Inst.* 6.3.4, 55.
[103] *Rhet. Her.* 4.37; Quint. *Inst.* 9.2.75
[104] For the negative connotations of *ridiculus* when used of a person, see Rabbie 218.

fore Verres had left Italy. His name provided a kind of omen for his future actions, an omen that Cicero claims was known throughout the city. Verres' voracious appetite must manifest itself in the action of sweeping (*everrere*), a verb phonetically similar to Verres' name.[105] While in Rome, the populace provides evidence for Cicero of Verres' unmitigated cruelty. His *nomen* ("name") provides an *omen*; as in religious and medical texts, names are represented as providing access to the supernatural.

When the narrative of the speeches moves to Sicily, Verres' designated province, Cicero continues to voice popular sentiment by quoting the jokes of the people. The Sicilians were renowned for their great wit.[106] As prosecutor of Verres, Cicero's task was to speak on behalf of these provincials, and he uses this reputation to demonstrate their resilient character. As with the jokes from Verres' urban praetorship that Cicero quoted earlier in the speeches, the orator sympathizes both with how the Sicilians have suffered and with how they have used humor to alleviate that suffering. Verres—"that plunderer of religious scruples" (*iste praedo religionum*)—has just failed to steal a statue of Hercules from the people of Agrigentum. Cicero concludes his narration of the episode as follows:

> numquam tam male est Siculis quin aliquid facete et commode dicant, velut in hac re aiebant in labores Herculis non minus hunc immanissimum verrem quam illum aprum Erymanthium referri oportere. (*Verr.* 2.4.95; cf. Quint. *Inst.* 6.3.55)

> The Sicilians have never had it so bad that they don't make some apt joke. Just as in this case, when they were saying that this gigantic boar (*verres*) deserves to be counted among the labors of Hercules no less than the famous Erymanthian boar does.

Beyond their value in entertaining the jury, the jokes on Verres' name serve two additional ends. First, on a rhetorical level, they ally the victims of Verres with their legal spokesman, Cicero, who will continue in these speeches to mock Verres' name in order to draw inferences about his behavior.[107] Second, the humor derives persuasive strength from the

---

[105] Additional plays on Verres as a greedy "sweeper" occur at *Verr.* 2.2.52 (*quare appellentur sane ista Verria, quae non ex nomine sed ex manibus naturaque tua constituta esse videantur*—"Sure, let the [festival] be called the Verria; it does not seem to have arisen from your name, but from your hands and nature"); *Verr.* 2.4.53 (*quod umquam, iudices, huiusce modi everriculum ulla in provincia fuit?*—"Was there ever, gentlemen of the jury, a dragnet [*everriculum*] of this kind in any province?"). Other passages where emendation could yield a pun include *Div. in Caec.* 57 (*vertit* > *verrit*); *Verr.* 2.2.19 (*evertendam* > *everrendam*); 2.3.137 (*avertentem* > *averrentem*); 2.4.53 (*avertere* > *averrere*); does the *eversum* at 2.2.52 derive from *everto* or *everro*?

[106] *De orat.* 2.217; Quint. *Inst.* 6.3.41 (Caelius speaking).

[107] *Verr.* 2.2.191 (*videtis VERRUCIUM? videtis primas litteras integras? videtis extremam partem nominis, codam illam Verrinam tamquam in luto demersam esse in litura?*—"See the name

bias regarding a name's meaning in Roman culture. Verres' name can act only to reaffirm his boarish nature.

Throughout the remainder of his career as a public speaker, Cicero continues to believe what he asserted in his early treatise *On Rhetorical Invention*: name puns are "a matter of a person's fixed and particular designation" (*de hominis . . . certo et proprio vocabulo*; *Inv.* 2.28). The name of an opponent could be employed as corroborative proof of his guilt. Other examples demonstrate the wide range of these witticisms, a range that can be paralleled in other contemporary literary genres where, it has recently been argued, etymologizing and differing forms of soundplay and wordplay are central to the meaning of a text.[108] Oratory, however, exhibits traits peculiar to its genre. The relationship between oratory and wordplay resembles that between the orator and theater. Just as the public speaker should temper his imitation of the actor, avoiding excessive mimicry and gesticulation, so too he had observable limitations in his use of name puns.[109] Rhetorical precepts are not intended, asserts the orator Antonius in *On the Orator*, to "lead us to discover what to say through artistry, but to make us confident that those things we pursue through rational talent, study, and practice are correct" (*non ut ad reperiendum quid dicamus, arte ducamur sed ut ea, quae natura, quae studio, quae exercitatione consequimur . . . recta esse confidamus*; *De orat.* 2.232). Certain jokes on names, I shall argue, were not correct.

DISTORTING NAMES

I noted earlier how the Greek orator Demosthenes, wishing to deride a man named Atromes ("Fearless"), ironically pretended his name was actually Tromes ("Trembler"). The Roman rhetorician Quintilian censures this practice as "feeble" (*frigida*) and provides the following examples:

VERRUCIUS? See how the first letters have not been tampered with? See the last part of the name, that pig's tail [*codam illam Verrinam*], stuck in the erasure just as if it were immersed in mud?"); *Verr.* 2.4.53 (*nam nos quidem quid facimus in Verre, quem in luto volutatum totius corporis vestigiis invenimus?*—"For what are *we* doing in the case of Verres, whom we discovered from the traces of his entire body after he rolled around in the mud?").

[108] Ahl, esp. 1–63. I append a list of other name puns I have come across in my reading: (1) *Verr.* 2.1.104: *Chelido*; (2) *Verr.* 2.3.23: *Apronius/aper*; (3) *Clu.* 71–72: *Gutta, Bulbus*; (4) *Catil.* 3.6: *Lentulus/tardissime*; (5) *Flacc.* 41: *frugi/Phrygi*; (6) *Vat.* 6: *Vatinius/vaticinando*; (7) *Sest.* 135: *Leo* (cf. Schol. Bob. p. 140, 11–17 [Stangl]); (8) Shackleton Bailey's conjectures at *Ad Q. fr.* 2.11.3. McCartney has located many more examples, the existence of which I doubt: *Leg. agr.* 2.59 (Iuba); *Mur.* 19 (Servius); *Dom.* 116 (Scato); *Balb.* 45 (Aquilius); *Sest.* 132 (Caesar); *Planc.* 34 (Plancius) and 58 (Iuventius); *Phil.* 2.106 (Laco), 12.14 (Tiro), 12.20 (Aquila).

[109] Of the many passages comparing orators to actors, see *De orat.* 2.242, *Off.* 1.130; Quint. *Inst.* 6.3.29; and the discussions in Graf 1992: 48–51 and Edwards 117–19.

ut Acisculum, quia esset pactus, "Pacisculum," et Placidum nomine, quod
is acerbus natura esset, "Acidum," et Tullium cum fur esset, "Tollium"
dictos invenio. (Quint. *Inst.* 6.3.53)

I find that Acisculus, for example, was called "Pacisculus" because he made
a pact and Placidus "Acidus" because he had a sharp nature, and Tullius,
since he was a thief, was called "Tollius" [i.e., "Lifter"].

None of the persons cited here by Quintilian can be accurately identified
and, consequently, it is uncertain whether these puns belong to Republic
or Empire.[110] Seneca the elder also seems to disapprove of this practice,
labeling one instance as "far from eloquent."[111] In the section of Cicero's
treatise *On the Orator* that covers the alteration of a word's meaning
through the change of one letter (*parva immutatio*, or paronomasia),
Strabo seems to offer from the elder Cato another example of a name
being distorted for the sake of humor: *Nobiliorem mobiliorem*—"the
mobile-er Nobilior" (*De orat.* 2.256 = ORF 8.151). An apparent echo in
the grammarian Rutilius Lupus seems to indicate, however, that Cato is
likely to have used the two words together in rhyming mockery and not
to have simply used *Mobilior* as a feigned proper name.[112] Quintilian,
then, may not have been disturbed by Cato's wit on this occasion.

In Cicero's speeches, only one example of a distorted name occurs.
Cicero does not claim credit for the joke; it is, predictably, another product of Sicilian wit. While gathering evidence for the prosecution of
Verres, Cicero attempted to examine the personal copies of senatorial
decrees that Verres had made during his tenure. A friend of the governor
intervenes:

retinere incipit tabulas Theomnastus quidam, homo ridicule insanus, quem
Syracusani Theoractum vocant. (*Verr.* 2.4.148)

A certain Theomnastus began to hold on to the records. The man is ridicu-
lously insane; the Syracusans call him Theoractus.

Instead of being "remembered by the gods," (θέος + μιμνήσκω), the
Syracusans have more aptly renamed their madman "beaten by the gods"
(θέος + ῥάσσω). This type of nicknaming, relying on similarity of
sound rather than etymology, occurs elsewhere as a form of popular
mockery: the soldiers of the future emperor Tiberius commented on
their commander's great love of drinking by changing his name from
Tiberius Claudius Nero to Biberius Caldius Mero (approximately

---

[110] Monaco 1970: 126.
[111] Sen. *Contr.* 10.praef.11. Seneca only mentions that someone altered the name *Pas-
sienus* into a Greek obscenity. Most likely the change implied passive homosexuality (perhaps Paschianus or Pathianus?).
[112] Rutilius Lupus 1.3; cf. Carm. *De fig.* 110.

"Drinker of warm undiluted wine"; Suet. *Tib.* 42.1); Labienus, a particularly vicious orator under Augustus, was redubbed Rabienus, "The Frenzied" (Sen. *Contr.* 10.praef.5). Such puns also occur frequently in Greek and Roman comedy.[113]

Nowhere, however, does Cicero employ this device in his extant speeches. The practice would appear to be a literary "trick" the orator deemed unworthy of the dignity of the courtroom or senate. The absence of such wordplay provides another indication of his regard for the supernatural association of names: he eschews name puns that are not etymologically significant.[114] In his letters, Cicero also does not distort names. Yet he does invent nicknames that do not properly belong to their bearer. All examples of this device occur in the collection addressed to Atticus and all fall into the pejorative category. There is no need to discuss them at length since they are not directly related to the present subject of jokes on names in the public arena. Crassus is called *Calvenna* (*Att.* 14.5.1 = SB 359) and, perhaps, *Calvus ex Nanneianis* (*Att.* 1.16.5 = SB16), presumably as a joke on his being bald (*calvus*); the epithet may also represent a nickname that the correspondents had adopted when seeking to avoid direct mention of Crassus in their letters. Pompeius receives the titles of *Sampsiceramus* (*Att.* 2.14.1 = SB 34) and *Hierosolymarius* (*Att.* 2.9.1 = SB 29, probably a pun on Marius; see Shackleton Bailey ad loc.). The most antagonistic example refers, predictably, to Clodius, deemed *illa populi Appuleia*, Appuleius being the nomen of Saturninus, a famous tribune of the people (*Att.* 4.11.2 = SB 86). The feminine termination implies that Clodius plays the submissive role in a homoerotic relationship.[115]

THE NAME IS THE NAMED

The Roman cognomen possessed peculiar status in the late Republic. In society, the name marks off the more prominent political families from the rest of the community; yet the descriptive meanings of these cog-

[113] See the bibliography in Hijmans 119 nn. 9, 10. The fact that Sicily was the home of Epicharmus, a fifth-century writer often associated with the rise of Old Comedy, may contribute to the reputation of the Sicilians.

[114] By the phrase "etymologically significant" I refer to associations that one finds corroborated in nonoratorical evidence from the Roman world. Although I largely agree with Ahl 1–63 about the elasticity of ancient etymological practice (which can include multiple derivations, as with the two "etymologies" of *Verres*, from both *verres* and *everrere*) and its potential relevance to a proper appreciation of Roman poetry, I believe that in public oratory the degree of wordplay that Ahl claims for literature does not occupy nearly so prominent a role, at least in the area of name puns.

[115] Cf. *duce filiola Curionis* as a slur on *Curio filius* (*Att.* 1.14.5 = SB 14) and the apparent references to the future Augustus as *Octavia* on the Perusine sling bullets (Hallett 1977: 152–53, 157–60). Further references in Richlin 1992a: 97, 283.

nomina are usually less than complimentary. In oratory, handbooks advise the public speaker to mock these names as a way of persuading an
audience; and, indeed, in Cicero one finds this device employed frequently. I have proposed that an explanation of these phenomena can be
found in the importance that the Romans placed in names and naming,
an importance observable in many aspects of society. Name puns are not
simply another aspect of sophistry that has become sanctioned by the
special arena of Roman rhetoric: it was thought that names, in being
passed down from ancestors, also transmitted moral character to descendants. Anecdotes demonstrate that the Roman people were sensitive to
the connotations of a name. In fact, politicians were known to change
their names as a means of persuading the populace of their sincere character. A final—and perhaps the most important—indication that names
constituted serious evidence for character is offered in the previous chapter, on the public mockery of physical peculiarities. Most cognomina
describe bodily peculiarities in a pejorative manner. The undeniable rhetorical power in mocking these deformities causes further doubt that a
Roman of the late Republic would have chosen, of his own volition, to
adopt a name that described such features. At Rome a name, no less than
a physique, constituted part of the definition of the public self.

A final point to be considered concerns the eventual fate of the Roman
cognomen. The cognomina of the late Republic began as a peculiarity of
the aristocracy. Then, around 100 BCE, freedmen began to bear such
names; beginning with the Augustan era, all distinction rapidly breaks
down, as cognomina are applied to the plebs and women.[116] At the same
time, names describing physical peculiarities show a marked decrease
among senatorial families, as do pejorative names in general.[117] It is a
truism of both ancient and modern scholarship that the end of the Republic brought with it an end to classical rhetoric as Cicero knew and practiced it. The agonistic atmosphere of the Republic dissipates, it is argued,
as the government comes under the control of a single man. Similarly, as
the need to maintain balance within an oligarchy diminishes, the cognomen loses significance as an effective rhetorical device and so becomes
meaningless as a check upon political success. Its original function lost,
the name spread quickly across the spectrum of Roman society.

[116] However, the cognomina of slaves and freedmen less commonly carried pejorative
connotations in the early first century BCE (Kajanto 64). On their later application to plebs
and women, see Kajanto 19.

[117] Kajanto 133; the percentage of total pejorative cognomina declines from approximately 24 percent in the late Republic (a conservative estimate; see n. 3 above) to 11.5
percent in the Empire (132).

Chapter 3

MORAL APPEARANCE IN ACTION: MOUTHS

> quemadmodum quis ambulet, sedeat, *qui ductus oris,*
> *qui vultus in quoque sit*—nihilne est in his rebus, quod
> dignum libero aut indignum esse ducamus? nonne
> odio multos dignos putamus, qui quodam motu aut
> statu videntur naturae legem et modum contempsisse?

> (And as for how someone walks and sits, or *the type of*
> *facial features and expression each person has*—is there
> nothing in these matters that we consider either
> worthy or unworthy of a freeborn person? Isn't it true
> that we consider many people worthy of our
> contempt who, through a certain kind of movement
> or posture, seem to have scorned the law and limit of
> nature?)
> —Cicero, *De finibus* 5.47

THIS QUOTATION from Cicero's moral treatise *On the Limits of Good and Evil* could not be more clear. During the late Roman Republic, physical appearance provided evidence for moral character. In chapter 1, I analyzed how Cicero exploits this bias in his public ridicule of an opponent's physical peculiarities. Never far removed from Cicero's humor lurked the notion that bodily deformities reflect a deviance from nature and hence signal to the onlooker an inherently evil character. In the next two chapters I examine a similar phenomenon. An orator can use less permanent aspects of an opponent's physique—his physical expressions, affectations, and posture—as evidence that the opponent will exhibit types of behavior that stand opposed to accepted Roman concepts of propriety. Each person's appearance has the potential for interpretation. To the informed orator, specific sets of externalized characteristics can offer effective material for public mockery and ridicule. In contrast to physical peculiarities, these signs do more than simply indicate deviance; they also provide the orator with evidence for predicting illicit behavior. That is, these physical characteristics not only result from illicit activity, but they also indicate a likelihood for such activity in the future.

In the epigraph cited above, facial expression—*ductus oris*—ranks among the external indicators of freeborn status: persons having an improper look, the speaker asserts, "seem to have scorned the law and limit of nature." In this chapter I analyze some Roman mouths to show how linguistic categories shed light on moral and political categories. The essentializing claim that certain facial expressions are more "natural" than others finds confirmation in the invective Cicero uses in his public speeches. The orator repeatedly emphasizes an opponent's *os impurum*—the impure mouth tainted by "unspeakable" activities ranging from drinking and eating to fellatio and cunnilingus—until the opponent becomes caught in a double bind, an inescapable circle of excess.[1] The activities of the mouth are represented as effecting certain types of evil while at the same time transforming the mouth into a sign of corruption visible to the properly discerning viewer. In particular, I discuss how Cicero, in the orations *Against Verres* (*In Verrem* 2.3) and *On Behalf of His Home* (*De domo sua*), exploits the oral activity of an opponent both to create and to reinforce class distinctions in Rome. As we shall see, the shape and appearance of the mouth constituted an important part of the elite Roman's elocutionary style.

The physical appearance of Publius Vatinius occupied our attention in chapter 1. The evidence for his evil, Cicero demonstrated, was visible to all, on a face and neck covered with swellings and pustules. Unfortunately for Vatinius, another part of his body also spoke out in condemnation. Cicero takes leave of his opponent as follows:

> quod si ipse, qui te suae dignitatis augendae causa, periculo tuo, nullo suo delicto, ferri praecipitem est facile passus, tamen te omni honore indignissimum iudicat, si te vicini, si adfines, si tribules ita oderunt ut repulsam tuam triumphum suum duxerint, si nemo aspicit quin ingemescat, nemo mentionem facit quin exsecretur, si vitant, fugiunt, audire de te nolunt, cum viderunt, tamquam auspicium malum detestantur, si cognati respuunt, tribules exsecrantur, vicini metuunt, adfines erubescunt, *strumae denique ab ore improbo demigrarunt et aliis iam se locis conlocarunt*, si es odium publicum populi, senatus, universorum hominum rusticanorum,—quid est quam ob rem praeturam potius exoptes quam mortem? (*Vat.* 39)

> But if the very man [Caesar] who readily allowed you to be carried headlong in order to increase his own importance—at your own risk and with no problems for himself—if even he considers you most unworthy of any office; if your neighbors, in-laws, and fellow tribesmen hate you so much that they considered your defeat their triumph; if no one looks at you without groaning, no one mentions you without cursing, if they avoid you, flee from you, don't want to hear about you, [and], when they have seen you, they curse you like some bad omen; if relatives reject you, fellow tribesmen

---

[1] Richlin 1992a: 26–30 discusses how in Roman invective various parts of the body, including the mouth, are perceived of as "staining" the character of their owner. References to the impure mouth (*os impurum*) recur throughout her study; see especially 99 (Cicero) and 149–51 (Catullus).

curse you, neighbors fear you, in-laws feel ashamed; [if], finally, your swellings have moved away from the wicked area around your mouth (os) and have
already located themselves in other parts, if you are the common object of hatred
from the people, senate, from all the men of the countryside—what reason
could you have for preferring the praetorship to death?

As Vatinius' physical blemishes (strumae) flee the area surrounding his
mouth (os), thematic details and grammatical syntax share a crescendo.
On a syntactic level, the clause forms the final component (denique) of a
protasis that lists the several arenas of life in which Vatinius is despised,
and thereby introduces the final expression of his popular hatred—he is
reviled by all residents of both city and country (odium publicum populi,
senatus, universorum hominum rusticanorum). Thematically, the passage
unites two prominent motifs of the speech: the tribune's ugly exterior
and his universal unpopularity. The equation of interior and exterior
feeds into popular biases concerning the origin of an individual's evil and
the effect this evil has on physical appearance. In addition, however, this
passage introduces a new, but associated, network of ideas suggesting
that the mouth area serves as the locus of improper behavior. Unlike the
other physical peculiarities I examined, Vatinius' "wicked mouth" is not,
strictly speaking, a static deformity that represents its bearer's inner evil.
To be sure, it includes this function: the evil emerges from within
Vatinius' body to escape through the mouth, thereby causing his sores to
flee from his face. Through this description, the orator directs attention
toward the mouth as a participant in an evil that, in turn, can be read by
the viewer. But in spite of this attention, the nature of these emanations
of evil remains unspecified. For, as other portrayals of the os in Cicero
demonstrate, the mouth does not simply represent inner depravity, as
did, for example, Vatinius' facial swellings (strumae); rather the os, because of its continual interaction with the world external to the body, acts
as a kind of two-way mechanism for evil. While as a physical feature the
os stands as a symbol of an inner moral turpitude, the mouth at the same
time has created this immoral character through its external actions,
which include eating, drinking, and various types of sexual activity. By
contrast, the commonest Latin word for "facial expression"—vultus—
since it does not describe a specific part of the body, never plays an active
role in creating its bearer's immorality. The mouth, then, leads a dual
existence both as symbol (externally representing to the viewer internal
evil) and as vehicle (creating that evil through its actions).

Os As Metaphor

A lexical study of the word os supports a model in which the Roman
mouth acts as both symbol and source of moral turpitude. An examina-

tion of the word's occurrences up to the time of Cicero suggests that the Romans regarded the *os* as the most prominent part of the human head. Its original, literal meaning encompassed the physical manifestations of the mouth—mouth both as facial feature and as organ involved in speaking, chewing, swallowing, and other oral activities. Outside the realm of human action *os* can, like the English word "mouth," describe a link between exterior and interior: an animal, for example, has an *os* (*TLL* 9.2:1088–89), as do inanimate objects such as vases, bodies of water, and tombs (*TLL* 9.2:1090–91). In relation to human anatomy, however, the word acquires a particular meaning. Unlike any other part of the body, *os* can refer by synecdoche to the entire face or head: when one cries, for example, the *os* fills with tears; or turning the head can be described as turning the *os* (*TLL* 9.2:1082–87). This extended meaning of *os* demonstrates the mouth's significance for ascertaining the characteristics of a face. The mouth can dominate and define its bearer.

The works of Cicero, the orations in particular, reveal an interesting consequence of the predominance of *os* as a facial feature. Since the word can signify the entire face, the orator often refers to the *os* to indicate character. Yet in only two passages from his orations does Cicero tell the audience to consider a person's *os* to discover a morally positive character (*Sull.* 74; *Marc.* 10). However, more than a dozen examples figure the *os* as reflecting a potential for deviance.[2] This tendency for a person's mouth to signify predominately negative internal qualities extends to *every* occasion Cicero uses the word in his orations to refer to an opponent. And among those cases where Cicero fixes on an adversary's mouth, two distinct levels of reference are discernible. Without adjectival or adverbial modifiers, *os* often occurs in a context where the feature clearly indicates audacity or contumacy (*Verr.* 2.4.66: *os hominis insignemque impudentiam cognoscite*—"consider the *os* and the outstanding shamelessness of the man"; *Rab. Post.* 34: *quod habent os, quam audaciam!*—"what an *os* they have, what boldness!").[3] But when accompanied by a modifier *os* receives an added dimension and tends to refer more specifically to vices or reprehensible actions—perhaps they are actions that were originally considered the result of bold behavior (cf. *Phil.* 2.68, 5.16). The activation of

---

[2] In addition to the passages I cite in this chapter, see *Sest.* 17, *Phil.* 13.4 (cf. *Verr.* 2.5.161). I have not found parallels for the use of *os* as an indicator of character in the plays of Plautus or Terence.

[3] The following completes the list of Ciceronian passages: *Quinct.* 77; *S. Rosc.* 87, 95; *Verr.* 2.2.48, 2.3.5, 2.3.41; *Font.* 29; *Vat.* 5; *Pis.* 63 (cf. *ORF* 66.37 [L. Crassus]; Catull. 42.16–17). Boldness is implied in the interrogative collocation *quo ore* at *Verr.* 2.1.127, 2.4.26; *Clu.* 65; *Phil.* 2.103, 7.21. Both associations of *os* occur throughout all periods of classical Latin prose and poetry; cf. *TLL* 9.2:1085.29–37, 1086.21–46.

Cicero occasionally uses the word *os* when referring to a face in neutral terms (*Verr.* 2.1.1; *Catil.* 1.1, 4.1).

immorality occurs, moreover, regardless of the specific modifier used. The added word seems to emphasize the orator's reference to his opponent's mouth: qualifying the *os* brings it to the audience's attention and activates it as an agent of immoral action. The modifier indicates that the *os* no longer simply signifies but now actively participates in the world external to itself.[4]

These passages in which a modifier accompanies *os* often include a wordplay or witticism by which the orator further brings an opponent's appearance to his audience's attention. The evil behavior implied by *os* plus a modifier is always, however, generic and ambiguous, as in the passage of invective against Vatinius cited above, where the "wicked" (*improbum*) nature of the *os* receives no further clarification. Cicero never specifies in these instances what precisely the mouth has done to cause it to be reprehensible. He is not simply making the *os* a metaphor for evil, for in every case where Cicero attaches a modifier to *os*, he continues to emphasize its physicality. In fact, when Cicero begins to direct his attention to an opponent's *os*, it is precisely because he wishes to exploit the relationship between the physical and the moral.

The metaphorical applications of the word *os* have largely pejorative implications in Cicero's orations. As the following discussion will demonstrate, these negative connotations attach to the mouth in its purely physical capacity (eating, drinking, oral sex). This may come as a surprise when one considers that another physical function of the mouth—speaking—occupies a position of prominence for Cicero as orator. In fact in his rhetorical writings, unlike in the orations, Cicero uses *os* in its extended meanings predominately to describe the act of public speaking. Negative implications of the word rarely appear; one of the few instances occurs in *On the Orator*, when Antonius outlines the basic requirements of the aspiring orator.

> sed quia tamen hoc totum, quicquid est, sive artificium sive studium dicendi, nisi accessit os, nullum potest esse . . . (*De orat.* 2.29)

[4] *Os* occurs with an adjectival modifier (other than demonstratives or possessives) in a nonpejorative context at only two places in Cicero's speeches. One instance, where Cicero refers to "the most beautiful mouth of the Gorgon," actually supports my argument since the adjective is employed with clear irony (*Gorgonis os pulcherrimum*; *Verr.* 2.4.124). The other occurs at *Rab. perd.* 36, where Rabirius is described as having received his scars *ore adverso* (i.e., "facing" his opponent). One may contrast the twelve times when the word is modified by a descriptive adjective or adverb having a pejorative sense (*Quinct.* 77; *Verr.* 2.5.161; *Dom.* 26, 104; *Har. resp.* 11; *Pis.* 13, 63; *Vat.* 39; *Phil.* 2.68, 5.20, 11.5, 11.7). This total does not include those instances where a demonstrative or possessive adjective modifies *os* in a pejorative context (e.g., *Verr.* 2.3.62, *suum*; *Sest.* 111, *illo*; *Phil.* 5.16, *illud*) and those where negative associations are clearly signaled by a nearby word (e.g., *Sest.* 118, *in ore impuri hominis*—"in the mouth of a foul man"; *Cael.* 78, *ore . . . inquinatum*—"stained by the mouth").

But seeing that this whole business—whatever it is, whether a system of
speaking or a pursuit—can be nothing unless some "cheek" (*os*) is added
. . .

The effective *orator* uses both aspects of his *os*: the physical organ and the
daring that is its metaphorical companion. In the philosophical works
and Lucretius as well, *os* occurs only in physical descriptions, while in the
letters the metaphorical use appears but occasionally, in cases of excitement.[5] It would seem, then, that it is the public and competitive nature of
oratory that causes a speaker to manipulate his hearers' conception of *os*
in a pejorative way. The high visibility of the *os* prompted its employment in political invective as a channel between an individual's internal
makeup and external activity.

Sexual Language in Roman Oratory

Before I examine the mouths of Cicero's opponents, it will be helpful to
review the nature and function of sexual language in Roman oratory. For
in one of the speeches I analyze below—*On Behalf of His Home*—the role
of the *os* in illicit sexual activity receives particular attention. To properly
assess Cicero's technique in this case, it is necessary to recognize the parameters and restrictions that orators of his day seem generally to have
observed when mentioning, and then ridiculing, sexual practices.

There often arises a discrepancy between theory and practice in Cicero's rhetoric, and his attitude toward sexual obscenity is apparently no
exception. In *On the Orator*, Cicero's primary spokesperson on wit, Caesar Strabo, remarks that "obscenity is not only inappropriate for the public speaker, but scarcely [is appropriate] even for a banquet of free citizens" (*obscenitas, non solum non foro digna, sed vix convivio liberorum*; *De
orat.* 2.252). The sentiment is echoed by Roman teachers of rhetoric elsewhere.[6] Yet a modern reader soon realizes that, in spite of these assertions to the contrary, Cicero violates his own rule, at least in regard to the
"obscenity" (*obscenitas*) that refers to sexual behavior. The "speeches of
Cicero are full of references to sexual practices, unnatural and otherwise,
and of sexual invective."[7] One may perhaps minimize this discrepancy
by distinguishing between explicit verbal obscenities and euphemistic

---

[5] *Os* in Lucretius and in Cicero's philosophical writings always means "mouth" or
"face/head"; *os* is used pejoratively in Cicero's correspondence for "daring" at *Fam.* 5.10a.2
(Vatinius to Cicero), 9.8.1; *Att.* 12.5.1. Lax morals are implied in the word's application at
Att. 15.29.2 and perhaps 1.18.5 (see Shackleton Bailey ad loc.).

[6] E.g., *De orat.* 2.242; *Off.* 1.144; Sen. *Contr.* 1.2.23; Quint. *Inst.* 6.3.29.

[7] Adams 222; cf. Richlin 1992a: 96–104.

references to sexual activity. Extant Roman oratory clearly demonstrates that the latter were permissible in certain contexts.[8]

Cicero's practice concerning the *os* of his opponents illustrates well the orator's caution about the boundary between euphemistic and direct obscenities. In addition to having this verbal constraint, the orator felt himself limited in whom he could choose as the object of his attacks. It has been noted that the accusation of an "impure mouth" (*os impurum*), "particularly vile to a Roman, Cicero reserves for the lowly, less powerful victims."[9] I shall speculate at the end of this chapter about how this restraint on Cicero's part both stems from and contributes to an "ideology of the mouth," a set of beliefs and practices that distinguishes among people of different social groups—such as those born free and those not—and in so doing enforces social and political categories. For now, I simply emphasize the two principal rhetorical considerations that characterize Roman invective involving sexual practices and the *os*: First, the orator must limit himself to double entendres, vague references that allow him to cast aspersions on an opponent while maintaining his own dignity as a public speaker. Second, the orator cannot directly accuse his more prominent opponents of improper social and sexual activity. These restrictions do not, however, prevent Cicero from manipulating context in order to disambiguate his innuendo. A clear example of Cicero's care at ensuring deniability for himself occurs in his invective against Marcus Antonius. After relating how Antonius had been sexually subservient to the younger Curio, Cicero pretends to stop before becoming too explicit:

> sed iam stupra et flagitia omittamus; sunt quaedam quae honeste non possum dicere, tu autem eo liberior quod ea in te admisisti quae a verecundo inimico audire non posses. (*Phil.* 2.47)

> But let's forget about his acts of sexual misconduct. There are certain things that I cannot honorably mention. And for this reason you are allowed more license, since you can't hear from a discreet enemy the kinds of things you've allowed to be done to yourself.

---

[8] Adams 222: "the orator (and declaimer) had to be euphemistic. Lexical obscenities and mildly risqué words are absent from the speeches of Cicero, and there is no evidence that they were admitted by other orators in formal speeches." For Cicero's awareness of the different levels of obscene language, see *Fam.* 9.22 and the analysis in Richlin 1992a: 18–26.

[9] Richlin 1992a: 99. Marcus Antonius provides a notable exception to this tendency (cf. *Phil.* 2.68). My examination of the *os impurum* is in many ways an expansion of the views that Richlin is here admirably able to confine to one paragraph. My discussion differs in that it shows the ways in which Cicero thematizes this conceit, eliciting the cooperation of his audience to reinforce political categories.

The phrase "allowed to be done to yourself" (*in te admisisti*), with its apparently neutral overtones, seems to continue Cicero's pose of discreet reticence. But other occurrences of the verb *admitto* indicate that Cicero is further incriminating Antonius at the very moment he claims to be exercising discretion. This verb "was the technical term for the bringing of one animal to the other (usually the male to the female)"; more significantly, *admitto* can refer euphemistically to a pimp allowing his prostitute access to a man.[10] The portrayal of Antonius pimping for himself as a young male whore coincides with imagery Cicero employed earlier in the speech (2.44–45). This technique of Cicero, by which he enables innuendo to say more than his own position as dignified orator can allow, recurs throughout his orations *Against Verres* (2.3) and *On Behalf of His Home*. In these speeches, the object of Cicero's most violent attacks are the relatively unimportant figures of Apronius and Sextus Cloelius. Yet by the end of each speech, the orator has caused the mouths of the leaders Verres and Clodius to become as tainted as those of their assistants.

CICERO BAD-MOUTHS HIS OPPONENTS

Against Verres 2.3

I showed in chapter 1 how the physiques of Fannius Chaerea and Publius Vatinius enabled Cicero to reveal to his audience their inherent evil nature. The physical appearance of Gaius Verres apparently did not accommodate such abuse; or at least Cicero did not feel compelled in this case to resort to tactics that were quite so direct. Yet in the third part of the second set of speeches against Verres (*In Verrem* 2.3 [*De re frumentaria*]), the body and, in particular, the mouth and its associations do play a significant role in the representation of Verres' character. I do not intend to suggest that Cicero's mockery of the *os* of his opponent represents the primary mode of invective employed in this speech; many kinds of abuse occur throughout the oration. Rather, I wish to show not that Cicero is creating this motif of the *os* but that he is exploiting biases already present in his audience against certain types of oral activity. For since these activities are figured as shaping not only moral character but also physical appearance, Cicero offers in the orations empirical proof for his philosophical claim that facial expressions (*ductus oris*) reflect freeborn status.

Verres went into voluntary exile after Cicero's first speech against him and thereby prevented the orator from actually delivering any part of the second set of speeches (the so-called *actio secunda*). Cicero nevertheless proceeded to complete and publish its five parts, which were written as if their delivery had occurred. When viewing the speech from this perspec-

---

[10] Adams 206–7. For prostitutes, see Plaut. *Asin.* 236; cf. Prop. 3.21.7, Sen. *Nat.* 1.16.5.

tive, as a written text that contributed to Cicero's successful bid for primacy among his fellow advocates, one would expect the orator to be especially conscious of the image he projects to his readers. The legalities, after all, have been resolved; in publishing more speeches against Verres Cicero primarily wishes to advance his forensic and political standing. In this respect, *Against Verres* 2.3 sheds an interesting light on the mature Cicero's later use of the mouth in his invective against Clodius. For in this speech, the physique that receives the orator's attention belongs not to Verres himself but to his henchman Apronius, a minor magistrate in charge of collecting tithes from the Sicilian farmers. By manipulating themes related to orality and by extending to moral action the boundaries of agency recognized in Roman law, Cicero fashions his opponent's political representative into his moral representative.[11] As a result, Verres emerges as equally culpable of any accusations—either legal or moral—raised against his assistant.

Cicero begins the speech by considering his own situation, that of a man who takes on the role of prosecutor for the sake of his country. Such an individual, he observes, must forever after run the risk of being accused of the very vices he has publicly reprehended (*Verr.* 2.3.1–5). In the prosecution of Verres, however, such a restriction produces positive results: it provides Cicero with a negative example by which he may conduct his life.

> ergo in isto reo legem hanc mihi, iudices, statuo, vivendum ita esse ut isti non modo factis dictisque omnibus, sed etiam oris oculorumque illa contumacia ac superbia quam videtis, dissimillimus esse ac semper fuisse videar. (*Verr.* 2.3.5)

> And so in the case of this defendant here, judges, I am setting up this condition for myself: I must live in such a way that I will seem to be (and will seem always to have been) very unlike this man not only in all his actions and words, but even in that defiant and haughty behavior that you see in his mouth (*os*) and eyes.

By exploiting the metaphorical resonance of the mouth that I have discussed earlier, by which the mouth constitutes the outward reflection of its bearer's audacity, Cicero encourages the jurors to assay Verres' daring through their own powers of observation. The coexistence of the metaphorical aspects of the mouth and eyes (*contumacia ac superbia*) and their physical manifestation (*quam videtis*) provides the means for discovering Verres' character.

Cicero represents his second main character as also physically present

---

[11] In Roman law, a principal was liable in full for any business conducted by his agent (Nicholas 201–4).

in the courtroom. The orator describes Quintus Apronius as the chief agent (*princeps*) of Verres' "aides and ministers of desires" (*ministros ac satellites cupiditatum suarum*; 2.3.21). Cicero points to Apronius' presence through the appositional *quem videtis* (2.3.22)—"whom you see [before you]"—and thereby achieves a double purpose. First, he strikes an air of verisimilitude for his readers—and perhaps also irony, since the emphasis on seeing represents an attempt to create a court setting that never in fact existed. At the same time, the phrase reminds the hypothetical jury members of the only other person in court that had been referred to so specifically—Verres—and thus recalls their earlier recognition of Verres' defiance as exhibited by his physical appearance (*contumacia . . . quam videtis*; 2.3.5).

The orator here directs attention to Apronius in the same way he had done with Verres, by straightway bidding the judges to examine his subject's facial features:

> aspicite, iudices, vultum hominis et aspectum, et ex ea contumacia quam hic in perditis rebus retinet illos eius spiritus Siciliensis quos fuisse putetis [cogitate ac] recordamini. (*Verr.* 2.3.22)

> Look at the expression and look of this man, judges, and from the defiance which he retains now, in a desperate cause, recall those gusts of rage (*spiritus*) that you would imagine to have occurred in Sicily.

With this exhortation regarding Apronius, Cicero recalls further his earlier description of Verres: even when confronted with a criminal prosecution, both men exhibit defiance (*contumacia*) in their faces. Through the paronomasia *aspicite . . . aspectum* ("look at the . . . look"), Cicero again underscores the inside/outside exchange of the morally bankrupt: their "look" (*aspectus*) reflects their inner spirit, which can be "looked at" (*aspicite*), and thereby critiqued, by others. One can compare the less emphatic contrast at 2.3.5 (quoted above), where "the defiance and haughtiness in Verres' eyes" (*oculorum . . . illa contumacia ac superbia*) meets the inspecting glance of the judges (*quam videtis*). Yet this examination of aspect does not lead merely to an appreciation of the subject's character. By placing *recordamini* ("recall") in this context—where none of the judges could be expected to have actually seen Apronius' actions firsthand (as indeed *quos fuisse putetis* testifies)—Cicero suggests that by examining physical appearance, the judges can virtually see past actions at which they were not physically present.[12] This exhortation is especially

---

[12] I have found no other example in the orations where *recordor* means "remember something you have *not* witnessed." Forcellini does record two instances where *recordor* refers to the future—Ov. *Epist.* 10.79 and Justin 5.7.9—but in both passages *recordor* means to predict a future event by recollecting similar past events. Later scribes seem to have been confused by Cicero's use of *recordor*, as evidenced by the supplement *cogitate ac* that has crept into the tradition.

odd from a legal standpoint since, in normal court proceedings, a witness was expected to report even firsthand testimony as only personal opinion.[13] In this case the converse happens: Apronius' silent presence has the power to restage his past as visible fact.

Cicero continues to equate Verres and Apronius through an interesting variation on his opening remarks. Whereas the prosecutor will consider it a pleasure to live a life as unlike Verres' as possible (*dissimillimus*; 2.3.5), the governor conversely had chosen Apronius as his right-hand man on account of their similarly base characters: "Verres judged [Apronius] to be most like himself (*simillimum*) in evil, profligacy, and contumacy" (*Verr.* 2.3.22).[14] The mock-legal language of "judged" (*iudicavit*) plays off the vocative "judges" (*iudices*) in the previous sentence: Verres has employed for his own low ends the very skills Cicero wishes his fictional audience of jurors to use in convicting the former governor. In this way Verres himself has shown the judges how to construe his and Apronius' moral relationship: the two men are as close as Verres himself could ensure through his own judgment.

Cicero continues by reformulating yet again his observations on the similarity between Verres and Apronius. He now encourages the judges to take an active role and use their own familiarity with reading character. Cicero bids them to create in their minds, if they can, a man who could match the notorious character and wicked lusts of Verres (2.3.23). The orator then describes for the jurors the inevitable result of this mental exercise:

> is erit Apronius ille, qui, ut ipse non solum vita sed corpore atque ore significat, immensa aliqua vorago est aut gurges vitiorum turpitudinumque omnium. (*Verr.* 2.3.23)

> That man will be Apronius, the one who is, as he himself shows not only by his way of life but by his body and mouth (*os*), a measureless abyss or whirlpool (*vorago . . . aut gurges*) of all vices and indecencies.

The meaning remains the same as before—Verres and Apronius are equals in sin. The mouth resurfaces, coupled with the body (*corpore atque ore*), to represent not just defiant and haughty behavior but a morally base character and action. The metaphor of the whirlpool was still very much alive in Cicero's day: the words *vorago* and *gurges* could describe the insatiable oral activity of gluttonous spendthrifts or of "bloodthirsty"

[13] Cic. *Ac.* 2.146, *Font.* 29; Greenidge 274.

[14] *Hic est Apronius quem . . . Verres . . . nequitia, luxuria, audacia sui simillimum iudicavit*; cf. 2.3.60: *a Q. Apronio . . . ad Verris flagitia libidinesque accommodato* ("by Quintus Apronius . . . who was well-fitted for Verres' disgraces and lusts").

McCartney 353 n. 1 suggests that another aspect of the similarity between these two men resides in their "piggishness" (*verres* means "uncastrated boar," while *Apronius* suggests *aper*, a "wild pig").

criminals.[15] Applied to Apronius, the image inverts Cicero's characterization of Vatinius' revolting face: the mouth, a "whirlpool of all vices and indecencies," both swallows external vices and becomes a kind of repository of depravity as it whirls in endless, insatiable motion. Cicero frames the metaphor to show that he is not alone in recognizing this facet of Apronius' character, for he has also guided his audience to make this new connection through their mental exercise. By his mere physical appearance (*corpore atque ore*), Apronius provides the signifiers (*significat*) that allow a viewer to interpret his character.

One certainly cannot accuse Cicero of understressing his point here. Having first read Apronius' character before his audience and then having led them through their own reading, he now steps back and explains in a lengthy period that in fact *everyone*—with one significant exception—has been able to recognize, and unable to tolerate, Apronius' evil:

> tantamque habet morum similitudo coniunctionem atque concordiam ut Apronius, qui aliis inhumanus ac barbarus, isti uni commodus ac disertus videretur; ut quem omnes odissent neque videre vellent, sine eo iste esse non posset; ut cum alii ne conviviis quidem isdem quibus Apronius, hic isdem etiam poculis uteretur; postremo ut odor Aproni taeterrimus oris et corporis,—quem, ut aiunt, ne bestiae quidem ferre possent,—uni isti suavis et iucundus videretur. (*Verr.* 2.3.23)

> And the similarity of their character has so great a union and harmony that Apronius, who seems to others inhuman and uncultivated (*barbarus*), seems to this [Verres] alone agreeable and eloquent (*disertus*); that this man whom all hate and do not wish to see, Verres cannot be without; that when other men do not enjoy even the same banquets as Apronius, this fellow uses the very same drinking cups; finally, that the extremely foul smell of Apronius' mouth (*os*) and body—which, they say, not even beasts can stand—seems to this man alone fine and pleasurable.

This description of Apronius focuses on aspects of his mouth that render him unfit for human society: his inability to speak properly (*barbarus*; cf. the apparent contrast in *disertus*), his unattractive behavior at banquets (as figured in the oral connection he and Verres have in sharing drinking cups), and finally the odor that reeks from his mouth and body.[16]

---

[15] *Sest.* 111: *gurges ac vorago patrimonii* (of Gellius); *Phil.* 11.10: *quem gurgitem, quam voraginem! quid eum non sorbere animo, quid non haurire cogitatione, cuius sanguinem non bibere censetis?* ("What a whirlpool! What an abyss! What do you imagine that he isn't planning to suck up and gulp down? Whose blood do you think he isn't drinking?"); *Phil.* 2.67; Macr. *Sat.* 3.13.6.

[16] Krenkel 1981: 42–43 thinks that Cicero refers here specifically to Apronius' reputation as a *cunnilinctor*. He cites many passages to support this theory, including a number that refer to how *cunnilinctores* were thought to taint cups. For the use of *os* to refer elliptically to oral sex, see *TLL* 9.2:1075.31–50.

Through these oppositions, Cicero completes the alienation of his two principal opponents. The prosecutor has shown the jury that it is united in its judgment with all members of the community—all, that is, but Verres.

As the oration continues after the mention of Apronius' bodily and oral smells, it becomes clear why Cicero has equated Verres and his henchman in the speech's opening sections. After introducing Apronius, the orator proceeds with his narration of the many crimes this tax collector has committed against the Sicilian farmers. Since Verres and Apronius have been linked so closely in the speech's introduction, the two men can now freely interchange as actors in the abuse of duties that, strictly, were Apronius' alone. As a result, Verres not only becomes responsible for entrusting to Apronius the power of harassing the farmers unjustly, but he also, in his position as his aide's ideological ally in vice, now shares direct responsibility for all Apronius' own actions.[17] It was a reading of their external features, especially the mouth, that forged Apronius' role as not only a political but also a moral representative of Verres.

Part of the taint attached to Apronius' mouth stems from drink: "he would have filled everything with his breath [and] the smell of wine" (*spiritu suo vini . . . odore complesset*; *Verr.* 2.3.31). It is, significantly, in this compromising position that Cicero has Apronius, Verres' political representative, deny his own identity and claim himself to be a "second Verres" (*Verrem alterum*; *Verr.* 2.3.31). Without explicitly bringing Verres into the picture, and without having to marshal any evidence, Cicero makes Verres share with the man most like himself (*sui simillimum*) the taint attached to illicit feasting. In a later context in which the similarities between Apronius and Verres are again emphasized, another reference to Apronius' mouth occurs. He was "the sort of man who could not only not keep his spirit pure, but not even his respiration" (*qui non modo animum integrum sed ne animam quidem puram conservare potuisset*; 2.3.134). The pun on *animus/anima* ("spirit/respiration") stems from Apronius' (and by extension Verres') tendencies to drunkenness and the bad breath associated with this action. As with Vatinius (*Vat.* 39), the inside emerges through the mouth to indicate on the exterior a person's previous base activities.[18]

[17] Several times in the speech Cicero attributes to Verres actions for which only Apronius is strictly accountable; cf. especially sections 110, 121, 129, 133, 135–37, 153, as well as the passages discussed in the text below.

[18] If one can assume *hiscas* does not refer to an affectation of speech (see Neudling 186), then oral odors play a role in Catullus' mockery of Victius at poem 98. However, in abusing Victius' bad breath Catullus does not seem to be attacking his moral character in the manner of popular mockery of body odors. Catullus rather plays on reifying a metaphorical proverb (*putide* moves from the realm of the figural to the literal).

Cicero's treatment of the mouth in *Against Verres* 2.3 anticipates the similar but more developed tactics he adopts in the speech *On Behalf of His Home*. In the present speech, he uses the *os* in describing Verres only to indicate contumacy, a usage that is not foreign to Cicero even in his noninvective texts. When *os* bears stronger connotations, either of excessive bibulousness or vague but intense wantonness, Verres' henchman Apronius carries the direct guilt. But Cicero early in the speech had triply stressed (and allowed the judges to concur actively in this assessment) that the character of these two men is identical. In this way the orator, although he avoids directly attacking Verres, nevertheless incriminates him indirectly in two ways: First, Cicero shows his opponent to be an improper judge of character—uniquely improper in fact, as he is the only human being to converse with Apronius. Second, and more importantly, Verres' similarity and close contact with Apronius confirm that he too is guilty of any contagion that may attach to the mouth. By manipulating the mouth, Cicero also preserves deniability: he implicates Verres in a vast array of crimes while avoiding any charges of introducing false evidence. This same structural relationship recurs in the next speech I analyze: the *os* serves to link a prominent opponent (Publius Clodius) with a person of lower social standing (Sextus Cloelius), a person who can be directly attacked with allegations of oral immorality. Once Clodius is implicated in nonelite behavior, thereby becoming the social equivalent of Cloelius, the orator easily severs the pair from the rest of the community.

On Behalf of His Home

In 62 BCE, Publius Clodius intruded upon the rites of the Bona Dea, a ceremony restricted to Roman matrons. Five years later, in the final portion of the speech *On Behalf of His Home* (*De domo sua*), Cicero mocks the inappropriateness of a situation in which Clodius deems himself capable of sanctifying the site of Cicero's former residence. The orator turns to address his audience, which consists entirely of members of the college of priests:

> hic non illudit auctoritati horum omnium, qui adsunt, summorum virorum? non vestra, pontifices, gravitate abutitur? ex isto ore religionis verbum excidere aut elabi potest? quam tu eodem ore accusando senatum, quod severe de religione decerneret, impurissime taeterrimeque violasti. (*Dom.* 104)

> Doesn't this man mock the authority of all these men who are present, men [who are] of the highest stature? Doesn't he misuse your dignity, priests? Can any word of religious scruple fall or slip from this mouth of yours

[Clodius] (*ex isto ore*)? With the same mouth (*eodem ore*) you have violated these scruples most uncleanly and most foully by accusing the senate because it made a severe decree concerning religion.

This is the first and only mention of Clodius' mouth (*os*) in the speech. The taint of his mouth renders Clodius inappropriate to utter a word of religion and, in its attempts to convey religious piety, his mouth even violates religion. Clodius' speaking ability is not, however, the only element used to characterize the impurity of his mouth. The oral activity of others besides Clodius has received detailed attention in earlier passages of this speech, passages that the audience of priests surely recalled upon hearing the remarks of Cicero just quoted. For in the speech *On Behalf of His Home* Cicero employs rhetorical techniques similar to those I have already noted in the speech against Verres and Apronius. As part of his diatribe against Clodius, the orator highlights many of the unsavory aspects of his opponent by emphasizing the relationship he has with his assistant, Sextus Cloelius.

When Cicero returned from exile in 57 BCE, he found his land on the Palatine confiscated and his home demolished. The damage had been done by his neighbor, Publius Clodius, the tribune of the plebs who had contrived the orator's banishment in the previous year. Cicero could not easily reclaim the property: Clodius, anticipating his opponent's eventual recall, had erected on the site a shrine to *Libertas*, the goddess of freedom, thereby consecrating the property and preventing its former inhabitant from resuming residence. The subsequent conflict between the two men produced Cicero's speech *On Behalf of His Home*, in which the orator argues before members of the Roman priestly college that Clodius had conducted a technically improper consecration and that, as a result, Cicero should regain his property. These technical points make up less than one-third of the entire speech (chiefly sections 104–41); the remainder contains Cicero's self-justification—and self-laudation—of his actions before, during, and after exile, a subject that necessarily accompanies an attack on Clodius not only as a tribune but as a human being.[19]

The speech opens with Cicero defending his most recent actions: he has proposed that the senate accord Pompeius an extraordinary commission in charge of the grain supply not, as Clodius has alleged, simply to conciliate the people, but to meet a real and severe food shortage (*Dom.* 4). His position taken and the merits of Pompeius reviewed (cf. especially 18–19), Cicero underscores the contrast he has created between himself and Clodius by presenting the former tribune—"the pirate chief himself with his totally despicable band of thieves" (*ipse archipirata cum grege prae-*

---

[19] For the historical details of this speech and a discussion of its order of argumentation, see the commentary of Nisbet 1939: vii–xxix.

donum impurissimo; 24)—with a partner to represent, in a sense, Clodius' "Pompeius." Enter Sextus Cloelius, the man whom Clodius' grain laws of 58 BCE had put in charge of grain distribution:[20]

> hic vir [Pompeius] extra ordinem rei frumentariae praeficiendus non fuit? scilicet tu helluoni spurcatissimo, praegustatori libidinum tuarum, homini egentissimo et facinerosissimo, Sex. Cloelio, socio tui sanguinis, qui sua lingua etiam sororem tuam a te abalienavit, omne frumentum privatum et publicum, omnis provincias frumentarias, omnis mancipes, omnis horreorum clavis lege tua tradidisti. (*Dom.* 25)

> Was a man such as this [i.e., Pompeius] not to be entrusted with an exceptional command of the grain situation? While you yourself, of course, have through your own law given over to a totally despicable glutton (*helluoni*), the taste-tester (*praegustatori*) of your lusts, a person completely impoverished and wicked—Sextus Cloelius, the sharer of your blood, who has used his own tongue to alienate even your sister from you—[to this man you have given] all the grain both public and private, all the grain-producing provinces, all the contractors, and all the keys to the granaries.

Oral images dominate the description of Cloelius. *Helluo* introduces the stock charge of gluttony—an obviously oral activity and, as I shall discuss in the next chapter, one that in Roman invective carries implicitly the associations of the banquet and its necessary accompaniments: dancing, the excessive use of drink and perfumes, and disgraceful (although vaguely expressed) sexual activity. A banquet needs guests. Cicero had incriminated Verres by making him not only a fellow banqueter with Apronius but also a sharer of his cups (*Verr.* 2.3.23). Through the word "taste-tester" (*praegustator*) Cicero creates a similar linkage between Clodius and Cloelius. Again the activity is oral and moves from the ostensible realm of eating (*gustare* means literally "to taste") to one of more general physical pleasures—Cloelius tests out in advance Clodius' lusts. Cicero thus makes explicit the sexual connotations only implied by *helluo*. The epithet "a person completely impoverished and wicked" (*homini egentissimo et facinerosissimo*) and the naming of Cloelius intervene before the orator provides further details. The description seems to tease the audience of priests, who await explication of how precisely Cloelius pre-tastes his friend's lusts.

---

[20] Evidence for this commission rests solely on the passage cited. For the name Sextus Cloelius see Shackleton Bailey 1960: 41–42 (misprint: on p. 41, read *Har. resp.* 11 for *Har. resp.* 6), and his later addendum in 1981: 383. Before Shackleton Bailey's correction, the man's name was believed to have been Sextus Clodius. All my subsequent quotations take into account this emendation, which has been generally accepted; see, however, Flambard 235–45 and Loposzko 498–503 (esp. nn. 30–31).

An apposition links the two men further: Cloelius is called "the sharer of Clodius' blood" (*socio tui sanguinis*). The expression is strange; scholars have long assumed Cicero refers to some kind of otherwise unknown blood relationship. The revelation that Sextus in fact has the nomen Cloelius and not Clodius (see n. 20) has made scholars less secure of this interpretation. However, another is available. The ancients believed semen to have arisen from the altered physical state of blood. When Propertius complains of being of "small blood" (*parvum sanguen*), then, he remarks on his excessive sexual activity and resultant weakness.[21] A similar pun relating Clodius' physical condition to his sexual wantonness occurs in the speech *On Behalf of Sestius*:

> qui tribunus plebis felix in evertenda re publica fuit, nullis suis nervis—qui enim in eius modi vita nervi esse potuerunt hominis fraternis flagitiis, sororiis stupris, omni inaudita libidine insani [*or* exsanguis]? (*Sest.* 16)

> A tribune of the plebs who was fortunate in his destruction of the state, with no muscles (*nervi*) of his own—for what muscles could a person have in a life of this kind, when he is insane (*insani*, or *exsanguis*, "bloodless") from repeatedly abusing his brother[s], having sex with his sister[s], and every [other] unheard of lust?

The play on *nervi*—literally meaning "muscles," but also a slang for "penis"[22]—works like the blood and mouth in revealing to an observer excessive sexual indulgence. Clodius' observable state of weakness indicates a depraved moral character. In addition to the pun on *nervi*, some wish to find further reference to sexual excess by reading *exsanguis* here, rather than the codices' *insani*, in light of Cicero's later reference to Gabinius and Piso as "enervated and bloodless" (*hominibus enervatis atque exsanguibus*; *Sest.* 24).[23] My interpretation of *On Behalf of His Home* 25 would support such an emendation. In any event, the passage cited provides a parallel for the notion that excessive sexual activity was portrayed in invective as enervating.

[21] Shackleton Bailey first offered this interpretation in a Latin footnote (1960: 41 n. 2), where he refers to his own *Propertiana* (1956: 188), which contains an explanation of *parvum sanguen* (Prop. 3.16.19) and the passages from ancient authors he uses for support. For an exhaustive account of the haemotogenic theory of semen among the ancient Greeks and Romans, see Lesky 1344–417, who traces the development of this theory from its origin in the fourth century BCE on through Galen. Héritier-Augé offers comparative material.

Catullus 80 (on Gellius' pale complexion) also exploits this association between "blood" and sexual activity. Krenkel 1981: 47–48 argues that Cicero implies by *socio tui sanguinis* that Clodius and Cloelius perform cunnilingus on Clodia while she is menstruating.

[22] Adams 38, who cites Grassmann 66 with n. 154.

[23] First proposed by Koch 384, and accepted by Clark in the OCT. T. Maslowski retains *insani* in the most recent Teubner edition of *Pro Sestio* (1986).

If one grants that the phrase "sharer of your blood" (*socio tui sanguinis*) has sexual connotations, how then is the phrase to be interpreted? Clearly the epithets implying Cloelius' excessive sexual activity (*helluoni, praegustatori tuarum libidinum*) show that Cloelius suffers from a lack—not an overabundance—of *sanguen*. By making Clodius an "ally" (*socius*) of this physical state, Cicero points to the excessive sexual tendencies of both his opponents.[24] Nothing unusual so far; many passages, including *On Behalf of Sestius* 16 just cited, demonstrate that Cicero felt no compunction in impugning Clodius with this charge. It is in the relative clause that he levies the more serious accusation.

"Who has used his own tongue to alienate even your sister from you"—*qui sua lingua etiam sororem tuam a te abalienavit*. Has Cloelius been telling Clodia bad things about her brother? Cicero does in part intend his audience to construe the phrase "with his own tongue" (*sua lingua*) as a reference to speaking; in fact it is precisely the ambiguity of the words that allows him to make this statement in the first place. For the previous discussion has shown that Cicero depicts Cloelius as a wanton partaker of sex and as a partner of Clodius in this pursuit. The relative clause indicates a breach in this relationship; Cloelius excels over Clodius in the art of cunnilingus and so has caused Clodia to require her brother's services no longer. The two men's sharing of blood takes on another dimension: the "blood" represents Clodia, Clodius' blood sister. Once again it is the action of the mouth that unites (*praegustatori*) and, conversely, divides (*sua lingua abalienavit*) the two men. But Cicero's language does not refer here only to Sextus' sexual activities; the context of the charge also implicates Clodius. In light of the relationship established between the two men prior to the relative clause, the adjective limiting the tongue—*sua* (his own)—is not otiose; it implies another tongue, a *tua lingua*— Clodius'—that has been active at some time in the past. The particle *etiam* also takes on a new dimension: "even" his sister, with whom Clodius has so close an "attachment," has been severed from him. Recollection of Cloelius' position as Clodius' taste-tester confirms our suspicion of Clodius' participation in this affair: One of Cloelius' functions is to use his tongue to sample sex for Clodius.

As noted in my earlier section on sexual language in Roman oratory, the "impure mouth" (*os impurum*)—here as employed in cunnilingus— constitutes a charge that the orator refrained from levying publicly against prominent individuals. Through a manipulation of word association (*helluo*) and double entendres (*praegustator, sanguen, lingua*), Cicero succeeds in overcoming this restriction. As in his similar treatment of

---

[24] For *socius* meaning "a sharer in a specific type of state," cf. *Catil.* 1.8, where the Catilinarian conspirators are described as *amentiae socii* ("allies in madness").

Verres and Apronius, Cicero's technique consists of equating in morality a less powerful (and hence more assailable) assistant with his prominent leader. And the bodily part that was conspicuous in making these equations stands visible to all: the mouth, whose physical activities—eating (*helluo*), tasting (*praegustator*), licking (*lingua*)—taint its bearer. In accordance with the model of the mouth I sketched at the beginning of this chapter, the *os* becomes tainted in turn as a result of direct participation in the external world. It is not surprising then that Cicero refers to the mouth, the physical manifestation by which one can read its bearer's guilt, when next he mentions Sextus Cloelius.

In the section that follows Clodia's sexually induced alienation from her brother, Cicero describes Clodius as complaining that Cloelius has been deprived of control over grain supplies: the grain administration has been snatched "from the very impure mouth of Sextus Cloelius" (*ex ore impurissimo Sexti Cloelii*; *Dom.* 26). Cicero identifies Cloelius for his audience of priests by referring to that part of him most conspicuous in his immoral dealings: his impure mouth. The equation apparently made a great impression. In the year following his delivery of *On Behalf of His Home*, Cicero can speak of the pen Clodius used to write the bills of his tribunate as "dipped in/stained by the impure mouth of Cloelius" (*stilo illo impuro Sex. Cloelii ore tincto*; *Har. resp.* 11); again Sextus becomes identified with his mouth as a result of the actions described at *On Behalf of His Home* 25. As we have seen, for a Roman *os* could often refer by synecdoche to the entire face or head. In a similar manner, the mouth of Cloelius has by itself become a sufficient representative of Cloelius and his character.

Having used Cloelius to sever Clodia from Clodius, Cicero immediately employs a series of risqué puns to reunite the siblings. The epithets he directs at Clodius—*patricida, fratricida, sororicida* (*Dom.* 26) "father killer [*or* traitor], brother killer, sister killer"—represent neither empty slander nor literal descriptions from which to reconstruct historical events, as some have attempted. Rather, beginning with the common rhetorical slander *patricida*, "traitor," Cicero exploits the popular etymology of this word—"father killer"—and the slang meaning of *caedo*—"to cut down (with one's penis)"—to suggest with the following two words (*fratricida, sororicida*) that Clodius engages in incest with both his brother and sister (cf. *Sest.* 16, cited above: *fraternis flagitiis, sororiis stupris*).[25] The

---

[25] On the popular etymology of *parricida* see Priscianus *Gramm.* 2.26.7 (Keil) and *OLD*, s.v. *parricida* 1a. For the obscene use of *caedo* see Catull. 56.6–7 (*hunc . . . rigida mea cecidi*—"I cut him down with my rigid member") and Adams 145–46. Nisbet 1939 appears to be the first to give the interpretation offered in the text for *fratricida* and *sororicida*, and he cites as historical support the Bobiensia scholiast on *Sest.* 16 (p. 127, 26–27 [Stangl]). The interpretation of *patricida* given in the text represents my own contribution.

insinuations may not stop here; *patricida* seems to conceal a similar reference. Indeed, the presence of a sexual pun in *fratricida* and *sororicida* almost
demands such an allusion. When Cicero has occasion later in the speech
to impugn Clodius' adoption into the plebs by Fonteius, a man younger
than Clodius, he refers to their peculiar father/son relationship as
follows:

> dico apud pontifices: nego istam adoptionem pontificio iure esse factam:
> primum, quod eae vestrae sint aetates, ut is, qui te adoptavit, vel filii tibi
> loco per aetatem esse potuerit vel eo, quo fuit. (*Dom.* 36)

> I am speaking before the priests: I say, [Clodius,] that that adoption of yours
> was not conducted in accordance with pontifical law: first, because the ages
> of the two of you are such that the man who adopted you could, by dint of
> his age, either occupy for you the position of a son or that [position] in
> which he used to be (*eo, quo fuit*).

Cicero implies with the phrase *eo, quo fuit* ("in that position in which he
used to be") that Clodius' adoptive father has already served Clodius as
an object of the man's lusts. As the younger man, Fonteius could fill the
role either of Clodius' son or, as Cicero asserts has in fact been the case,
of his boy lover. The epithets *patricida, fratricida, sororicida*, then, indicate
Clodius' sexual aggression toward all members of his family. The most
important function of these vocatives for our purposes, however, is their
ability to reunite sexually brother and sister. Cicero recognized in the
subject of incest an important element of the theme of the *os* that he
would continue further to exploit in this speech. Oral sex and incest serve
to unite the three primary antagonists—Clodius, Clodia, and Cloelius.

Cicero resumes the narrative by giving his reasons for entrusting the
grain commission to Pompeius (26–31). In this way the orator underscores the contrast he has set up between the pairs of himself/Pompeius
and Clodius/Cloelius. By degrading his pair of opponents, Cicero further justifies the program that he and Pompeius have adopted.

The "foul-mouthed" Cloelius makes his next appearance in Cicero's
argument for the illegality of his own exile. Cloelius, the draftsman of
Clodius' original bill, is taken to task for the imprecision of his language:

> non tulit ut [m. tullio aqua et igni] interdicatur. quid ergo? ut inter-
> dictum sit. o caenum, o portentum, o scelus! hanc tibi legem Cloelius
> scripsit spurciorem lingua sua, ut interdictum sit cui non sit interdictum?
> Sexte noster, bona venia, quoniam iam dialecticus es et haec quoque liguris
> . . . (*Dom.* 47)

> He did not propose "that [Cicero] be denied [fire and water]." Then what
> [did he write]? "That he *has been* denied." A filthy and unnatural crime! Did

Cloelius write for you this law, dirtier than his own tongue, so that a man shall have been denied who has not been denied? Sextus my friend, I beg your pardon, since you are now a master of logic and you are lapping up (*liguris*) these matters too . . .

The orator resorts to humorous abuse at the crucial point in which his own argument becomes most sophistic: the grammatical "error" for which he reproaches Cloelius—using a perfect subjunctive (*interdictum sit*) for a present (*interdicatur*)—is not only permissible Latin, but it is used by Cicero himself later in this same speech.[26] The metaphorical connotations of eagerness expressed in *ligurio* ("lapping up") appear to have been colloquial. Suetonius preserves a passage from an Atellan farce that employs the same pun in mocking the "oral obscenity" (*obscaenitas oris*) of the emperor Tiberius.[27] Cicero unquestionably refers here to Sextus' appetite for cunnilingus: earlier references to Cloelius' impure mouth had set a precedent (*Dom.* 25–26), the phrase "dirtier than his own tongue" (*spurciorem lingua sua*) arouses expectations here (which, as with *sua lingua* at *Dom.* 25, can be alternatively interpreted as referring to Cloelius' speech, as here opposed to his writing), and *quoque* ("too") points to a meaning of *ligurire* beyond the ostensive metaphor for eagerness.[28] In spite of the clear references here, it is nevertheless worthy of note that, just as at *On Behalf of His Home* 25–26, Cicero's words are capable of a surface explanation that would not require his audience to pick up obscene connotations, or at least would allow him to deny that any such connotations were intended. Cicero once again seems to honor oratorical propriety at the very moment he violates it.

Having once again exposed Cloelius' indecent behavior, Cicero reunites Cloelius and Clodius as he has reunited brother and sister. It is important that all his opponents be excluded from society; but it is equally important that they be excluded together. His description of the relationship between master and underling that follows—that Cloelius is

[26] See the appendix to Nisbet's commentary (1939: 204–5), where he demonstrates that the use of a perfect subjunctive to denote a future wish, whereby *ut M. Tullio interdictum sit* means "that M. Tullius shall be deemed to have been outlawed," is perfectly acceptable Latin. Cicero uses an analogous construction at *Dom.* 106.

[27] Metaphorical occurrences of *ligurio* in the Ciceronian corpus: *Verr.* 2.3.177, *Fam.* 11.21.5 = SB 411 (both arise, moreover, in figurative contexts, indicating that the word was not yet a dead metaphor); Suet. *Tib.* 45: *hircum vetulum capreis naturam ligurire* ("the old goat longs for nature at Capri/licks the cunts of the roe deer").

[28] Nisbet 1939 ad loc. also notes Immisch's suggestion of a pun *dialecticus*/διαλείχειν ("to lick thoroughly"), but remarks that it is "doubtful." I have been unable to find a similar pun on *dialecticus* or its cognates to support Immisch's claim (the difference in vowel quantities perhaps argues against it), and Adams's point that *quoque* "shows that the referent was a 'licker up' of something else apart from what is implied in *dialecticus*" further indicates that one should read *dialecticus* as simple irony, without obscene connotations (140).

"an assistant most impure, not only of all two-footed but also of all four-footed creatures" (*ministro omnium non bipedum solum, sed etiam quadrupedum impurissimo*; *Dom.* 48)—recalls Cicero's verbal exclusion of Apronius from, successively, the realm of humans and then of animals (*Verr.* 2.3.23). The ambiguous syntax of the genitive construction "of all . . . two-footed . . . [and] four-footed" (*omnium . . . bipedum . . . quadrupedum*) also calls into question Clodius' human status. Initially these words would have been construed by Cicero's audience as possessive genitives—"an assistant *for*"—a common construction in Cicero. Only with the adjective *impurissimo* ("most impure")—an interesting word in itself, having been used thus far only in describing Clodius' gang (24) and Cloelius' mouth (26; cf. *Sest.* 16, *Har. resp.* 11)—does the "intended" syntax become clear (viz., "who is the most impure of . . .").[29] By using an adjective having associations with the impure mouth, Cicero portrays Clodius and Cloelius as unfit for human society.

After reuniting master and minion, Cicero continues to follow the familiar stratagem of excluding both individuals from human (Roman) society. His tactics resemble those employed in the orations against Verres, where parataxis and periodicity combine in listing the facets of humanity from which Verres and Apronius are excluded (*Verr.* 2.3.23). Clodius' poor judgment in choosing Cloelius extends to all the assistants with whom he surrounds himself:

> neque tu eras tam excors tamque demens ut nescires Cloelium esse qui contra leges faceret, alios qui leges scribere solerent; sed neque eorum neque ceterorum, in quibus esset aliquid modestiae, cuiusquam tibi potestas fuit; neque tu legum scriptoribus isdem potuisti uti quibus ceteri, neque operum architectis, neque pontificem adhibere quem velles, postremo ne in praedae quidem societate mancipem aut praedem extra tuorum gladiatorum numerum aut denique suffragi latorem in ista tua proscriptione quemquam nisi furem ac sicarium reperire potuisti. (*Dom.* 48)

> And you were neither so senseless nor so insane as to be unaware that Cloelius is a man who acts contrary to the laws, [while it is] others who usually write the laws; but you have no power either over these men or over the rest of men who have some degree of shame; and you were also unable to use the same scribes as everyone else, and the same architects, and to employ the priest that you wanted; finally, not even in the sharing of your loot could you find an agent or representative, except for your group of

---

[29] Merguet gives six examples in the speeches of *minister* with a possessive genitive; for the "actual" construction of *impurissimo*, Nisbet 1939 ad loc. cites Kühner-Stegmann 2.1:425, none of whose examples allows the room for ambiguity Cicero does here. Richlin believes it "probable . . . that *impurus* always carried at least the suggestion of the meaning 'contaminated by oral-genital contact'" (1992a: 29).

gladiators, or, last of all, anyone to put the law to a vote in this proscription of yours except for a thief and assassin.

Clodius stands apart from the rest of the civilized Roman community, which follows recognized rules of state (*lex*) and society (*modestia*). His only companions are Cloelius, who stands outside of these laws (*qui contra leges faceret*), and other nameless persons, presumably the members of the *impurissimus* band of gladiators over whom he lords as pirate chief (*tuorum gladiatorum numerum*; cf. *Dom.* 24).

Cicero has occasion soon after this passage to mention specifically one of Clodius' gladiators, in order to show how society has prejudged this man for his friendship with Clodius. It appears that this person had declined to pursue a court action for fear of losing on account of his relationship with Clodius. Cicero does not use a name, but cryptically refers to him as "that new kind of Ligurian" (*ille novicius Ligus*; *Dom.* 49). The meaning of *novicius* remains unclear in this context. Apparently *Ligus*, both a Roman cognomen and the name of an Italian tribe, contains a slight on recent citizenship. The ethnic bias—"all Ligurians are liars"—is also surely present.[30] But the emphasis Cicero places on the orality of Clodius' attendants points to yet another connotation—*novicius Ligus* hides a pun on the verb *ligurio* ("to lick"). This unidentified brother of Marcus Papirius is a "new licker" who has been imported like a new "citizen" (*novicius*) into Clodius' private society. This interpretation of *novicius* receives some support from a later mention by Cicero of this Ligus. In *On Behalf of Sestius* the orator describes him again as a new element of Clodius' society: "that someone of yours [i.e., of Clodius], a supplement to my enemies" (*iste nescio qui, additamentum inimicorum meorum*; *Sest.* 68). In *On Behalf of His Home*, Cicero showed the implications of his joining this new group. A tainted mouth characterizes even mere association with Clodius.

The rift between Clodius and Clodia over Cloelius' superior sexual technique has been mended verbally by their union against society. The taint attached to the mouth, however, has not been forgotten. In his final mention of Cloelius in the speech *On Behalf of His Home*, Cicero resumes this early motif. The context is again the supposedly prejudiced wording of Cloelius' draft of the bill confirming Cicero's exile, *UT M. TULLIO*

---

[30] For the trope of the "Ligurian liar," see chapter 2. Nisbet 1939 ad loc. discusses the uncertainty of interpretation regarding Ligus here: "Cicero generally hints that he had intruded himself into the Aelian *gens*, and that though not a Ligurian, he shared the treacherous character of the Ligurians." I do not reject this interpretation (*Sest.* 69, quoted in chapter 2, would seem to confirm it). If both Nisbet's conjecture and the one I offer in the text were true, this would merely be a further instance of Cicero supplying a surface insult that can also be construed more damningly by the audience (while capable of being denied by himself).

INTERDICTUM SIT. The orator asks Clodius why he had not mentioned in the bill Cicero's own removal from the senate, a common clause inserted in the case of exiles. He then supplies Clodius with the means of finding the answer:

> quaere hoc ex Cloelio, scriptore legum tuarum: iube adesse: latitat omnino, sed si requiri iusseris, invenient hominem apud sororem tuam occultantem se capite demisso. (*Dom.* 83)

> Find out why from Cloelius, who writes up your laws. Order him to appear here: he's no doubt in hiding, but if you have him sought out, they'll find the man with your sister, concealing himself, face down (*capite demisso*).

By using quasi-legal language, Cicero mocks Clodius' presumption in composing his bill. The phrase *iube adesse* ("order him to appear") is the normal expression by which a magistrate orders someone to appear in court, and the legal tone continues as the orator intimates Cloelius' guilt through his choice of the word *latito* ("in hiding"), a technical term describing someone who avoids a summons to trial.[31] This air of formality deflates slowly as sentence end approaches. First Cloelius is called a *homo*, a term often used to convey sarcasm or irony.[32] Then his whereabouts are revealed—he is at Clodia's house. If the audience has not yet guessed the implications of this hiding place, they become clear with the final descriptive ablative absolute *capite demisso* ("face down"). The phrase exhibits an ambiguity such as I have often had occasion to note in my discussion. Literally meaning "with head lowered" and connoting dejection or humility, the words are quite capable of yielding an innocent interpretation.[33] But at the same time a passage from Catullus, in which Gellius is imagined in self-fellation, indicates that the phrase also had currency in the erotic sense that Cicero has led his hearers to anticipate here (Catull. 88.7–8: *nam nihil est quicquam sceleris, quo prodeat ultra, / non si demisso se ipse voret capite*—"for there's no more vices he could commit, not if he ate himself with his head lowered"). Similarly, Seneca disdainfully describes the act of one man fellating another as "sinking the head" (*caput merserat*; Sen. *Nat.* 1.16.4). These passages from Catullus and Seneca provide double evidence. They not only reveal why Clodius is lying "face down" at Clodia's house, but they also show that an allusion

---

[31] *Iube adesse*: see *Dom.* 54 and 62, where the phrase refers to Clodius' actions as tribune; *Verr.* 2.2.41. *Latito*: Cicero always uses the word in a legal sense (Kinsey 141). For the combination *latitare/occultare* cf. Cic. *Frg. or. inc.* 24: *("latitare") turpis occultatio sui.*

[32] For *homo* in a derogatory sense, see Shackleton Bailey on *Fam.* 12.22.1 (SB 346); Landgraf on *S. Rosc.* 8.

[33] Cf. *Clu.* 58; Caes. *Gall.* 1.32.2; Sen. *Contr.* 1.3.1, 9.2.7; Sen. *Epist.* 65.20. A similar double entendre implying cunnilingus occurs at *Phil.* 13.24.

to oral–genital contact could be used to publicly degrade an opponent.[34] Once again, by implying sexual activity of the mouth, Cicero ridicules Cloelius (and, by association, Clodius) and thereby renders both of them incapable of countering Cicero's assertion that he was exiled illegally.

This discussion of *On Behalf of His Home* opened with Cicero's only direct references to Clodius' *os* (*Dom.* 104). The criticism of Clodius' legitimacy as a representative of the public religion occupies the final portion of the speech. Although Clodius' mouth does not receive direct mention prior to this passage, oral activity has nevertheless played a prominent role in coloring Cicero's invective of his opponent.

The first question directed at Clodius in this passage concerns the propriety of him even speaking on religious matters: "Can any word of religious scruple fall or slip from that mouth (*os*) of yours?" (*ex isto ore religionis verbum excidere aut elabi potest?*). The deictic adjective accompanying *os*, *iste* ("that mouth of yours"), brings Clodius' mouth to the attention of the jurors and signals the cathexis in the relationship among Cloelius, Clodius, and Clodia that Cicero has woven throughout the earlier portions of the speech. The former tribune shares the taint of the mouth by association, a taint that affects even his ability to communicate. Cicero also mentions the mouth in the sentence immediately following: "With the same mouth you have violated these scruples most uncleanly and most foully by accusing the senate because it made a severe decree concerning religion" (*quam tu eodem ore accusando senatum, quod severe de religione decerneret, impurissime taeterrimeque violasti*). The modifier attached to *os* here, *idem* ("same"), emphasizes Clodius' impropriety in using the same mouth for engaging in sexual activity, for carrying out a religious ceremony, and for protesting the punishment of his involvement in the Bona Dea incident. These three realms of Clodius' activities had already been interlinked earlier in the speech through Cicero's jokes concerning Cloelius as the impure "taste-tester" and through the union of both these men to Clodia through the motifs of incest and oral sex. *Impurissime* ("most uncleanly"), lastly, further recalls the dirtiness of Cloelius' "impure mouth" (*os impurum*; *Dom.* 26). The word *impurus* had been used earlier to describe Clodius' gang (*Dom.* 24) and to describe Cloelius again, "the most impure assistant" (*minister impurissimus*; *Dom.*

---

[34] For the negative terms with which the female genitalia are described in Latin literature, see Richlin 1992a: 67–69, 115–16, 122–23. A possible allusion to Clodius as a cunnilinctor occurs in Catullus poem 79; see Skinner, esp. 197–200. I discuss in the next chapter additional reasons for the undesirability of a man performing fellatio or cunnilingus: it was conceived as putting the man in the submissive role, as the one providing pleasure to another without receiving pleasure himself.

48). Other passages outside of *On Behalf of His Home* also attest to the associations that would have been suggested by the proximity of *os* and *impurus* (*Pis.* 8; *Sest.* 118; *Phil.* 2.68, 5.16, 5.20, 11.7).

By using vocabulary that recalls other contexts of oral activity, Cicero colors the only passage in *On Behalf of His Home* in which he directly touches upon Clodius' mouth. At the beginning of this chapter I hypothesized that, for a Roman, the mouth acts as a channel between the outer world and one's inner being; I further suggested that the mouth can be tainted by the worldly activity that it touches upon as well as by the internal evil that rises up from within. In his treatment of Clodius in *On Behalf of His Home*, Cicero translates this conception of the *os* into a linguistic realm. The reprehensible oral activity attached to his assistant Cloelius becomes associated by the end of the speech with Clodius' own mouth. Once Clodius' *os* has been identified as evil, his mouth proceeds to attract the modifiers that point up the nature of that evil (*ex isto ore; eodem ore*). His mouth speaks without words, revealing its inability to communicate with the outside world.

The Mouth and Political Ideology

Cicero's performance in *On Behalf of His Home* suggests that descriptions of, and responses to, particular mouths assisted in forming a Roman ideology of body parts. As noted already, the *os impurum*—the mouth tainted by sex and drink—is a charge that hinges on class. Only by connecting Clodius with a member *outside* the elite—Cloelius—can Cicero eventually implicate Clodius himself in the lowly activity of cunnilingus.[35] Having analyzed how Cicero exploits the connotations of mouths, I can now return to the statement from *On the Limits of Good and Evil* that is the epigraph to this chapter. Could the educated Roman of Cicero's day tell simply by looking at a person's face whether that person has in fact "scorned the law and limit of nature"?

Roman society was structured in a number of ways to control access to the elite. Jean-Michel David has studied the elocutionary style that came

---

[35] A wall painting depicting male-female cunnilingus was found recently in the suburban baths at Pompeii. Previously the depiction of this subject had been known only from gems and lamps (Jacobelli 45–46 cites the relevant literary and artistic evidence). The "rough-and-ready" style of the Pompeian paintings may provide further evidence for the lower-class connotations of this sexual practice (Clarke 286–87).

Hallett 1978 argues that a wall painting especially prized by Tiberius of Atalanta and a male lover depicts the sexual position "sixty-nine" (Suet. *Tib.* 44.2; cf. Ov. *Ars* 3.775, *Am.* 3.2.29–30).

to be designated as *eloquentia popularis*—the "popular way of speaking" that arose in contrast to the more urbane elite style.[36] David has shown that this "popular eloquence" was normally associated with political newcomers, people who may have been important in their native communities but who, upon arriving in the big city, stood out because of their non-Roman style of pronunciation, use of vocabulary, and even sense of humor. The patron/client system established at Rome also often marked these men. Lacking the connections necessary to speak in defense of prominent Romans, they were often forced early in their careers to prosecute important aristocrats, thereby being further labeled as a group of malcontent challengers to the status quo. Moreover, Ciceronian invective indicates that some "popular speakers" were often marked by an external appearance determined in contradistinction to the elite—they wore baggy clothes, sported foppish hairstyles and skinny beards, and even seem to have had their own style of walking.[37] What we would call "acquired" characteristics became constructed by invective as a function of a person's inner nature and, by extension, political affiliation.

It would not then be so unusual for these individuals to have distinct mouths. Parallels exist in other cultures for what might be termed "class-specific" mouths. Pierre Bourdieu, a French sociologist concerned with how different social and political situations affect our bodily dispositions, has noted that in contemporary France the mouth both reflects and helps define inherent differences between the bourgeoisie and the lower class. The bourgeois mouth (*la bouche*) "is more closed, pinched, i.e. tense and censored" whereas the working class mouth (*la gueule*) is "unashamedly wide open, . . . i.e. relaxed and free."[38] This contrast manifests itself throughout the entire range of each class's lifestyle. In diet, lower-class men reject the upper-class love of fish—a food that must be chewed with a small mouth, with the front teeth—preferring instead the vigorously chomped steak. These differences find expression in daily metaphor: popular phrases describing fastidiousness and uptightness utilize the bourgeois *bouche*, whereas the lower-class *gueule* is used in metaphorical phrases describing outspokenness, verbal strength, and even physical violence.[39] The French mouth, like the Roman, draws attention to itself

[36] David 1980 and especially 1983.

[37] I discuss the clothing and appearance of the nonelite in my next chapter. For indications that different politicians had different and identifiable walks, see *In Clod.* 22; *Sest.* 17, 105; *Brut.* 225; *Phil.* 13.4.

[38] Bourdieu 1991: 86.

[39] Diet: Bourdieu 1984: 190–91; metaphor: Bourdieu 1991: 86–87. Similar observations have been made by Labov concerning the mouths of male speakers in New York City (cited in Bourdieu 1991: 86).

both verbally and visually, until it dominates the head and allows conclusions to be drawn about social position and internal character.

At Rome, then, a natural structure—the mouth—becomes constitutive of social structures. As with their treatment of physical peculiarities, Romans appealed to the natural world for evidence that the activity of the mouth is indicative of internal states of being. As a result, the physical mouth, an apparently objective entity that always existed, comes to act as a structuring structure—a constructed, objective part of reality that simultaneously creates and reinforces distinctions both between and within classes.[40]

The situation of the mouth can be compared to a more commonly recognized phenomenon. Proper speech is an aspect of proper Roman (urban) education, and improper speech was readily detectable and readily mocked—readers of Catullus will recall Arrius and the "Hionian Sea."[41] Although hearing when the proper norms of speech were violated was an easy manner, defining precisely what constituted such speech was not. "But what is this 'urbane' flavor (*urbanitatis color*) you're talking about?" Brutus asks in one of Cicero's rhetorical dialogues. "I don't know," Cicero replies, "I only know it's *something*."[42] The essence escapes description but not detection. In rhetorical training, the upper classes use their economic capital (the money to educate themselves) to create symbolic capital (the proper etiquette of the Roman elite). *Romanitas* can be bought: an obvious point, of which Horace's father was well aware.[43] This symbolic capital serves, in turn, to mask the importance of economic capital. The ways one acts, speaks, and moves—not financial resources—become perceived as the natural determinants of a person's social and political position. The orators from the provinces, with their unnatural gestures and speech patterns, embody what is improper for the elite Roman. As a result, the social hierarchy becomes legitimated, and only those with access to a proper training remain in power.

This scenario, I suggest, also applies to the mouth. Passages such as the one I quoted from *On the Limits of Good and Evil* prove that social stratification *was* practiced by appealing to nature (*natura*). People are this way because this is the way they are. Anyone who is not this way is not like us

[40] I borrow the notion of a "structuring structure" from Bourdieu 1990: 53.

[41] Catull. 84; cf. Lucilius Hirrus, whom Cicero mockingly calls "Hillus" in allusion to Hirrus' speech defect (*Fam.* 2.10.1 = SB 8).

[42] *Brut.* 171: *Et Brutus: "Qui est," inquit, "iste tandem urbanitatis color?" "Nescio," inquam; "tantum esse quendam scio."* Ramage offers a thorough discussion of what constituted this elusive *urbanitas*.

[43] Hor. *Sat.* 1.6.76–78; fortunately, Horace's father had sufficient economic capital.

and therefore should not presume to take over our roles. The issue at stake for the elite Roman is not one of class but of who is a proper representative of the natural order. And every time Cicero opens his mouth to talk about another person's mouth, he uses a public context to further legislate and reinforce political and social categories.

Chapter 4

MORAL APPEARANCE IN ACTION: EFFEMINACY

OVEREATING, naked dancing, telling jokes—three activities guaranteed to
curtail any young Roman's political aspirations. The connection between
moral profligacy and extravagant feasting constitutes a stock charge in
invective texts from the late Republic, a charge that frequently surfaced
in chapter 3 when Cicero took to scrutinizing the mouths of Apronius
and Cloelius (*Verr.* 2.3.23, 31, 62, 134; *Dom.* 25). This chapter explores
the foreboding environment of the banquet room and examines those
features recurring most frequently in Roman representations of perverted
feasters. The discussion will of necessity be very schematic and the conclusions will apply only to a particular area within this type of invective:
many elements inform the illicit character of convivial excess and any
single explanation for all these elements would necessarily oversimplify. I
shall not, therefore, consider the standard explanation for the danger represented by excessive banqueting, namely that banquets reflect a Greek
or Eastern way of life that will slowly infiltrate and destroy Roman *grav-
itas*. Without doubt this account contributes much to understanding why
banqueting themes are so prevalent in moral critiques written by Roman
authors from the late Republic.[1] In fact, Greek loan words dominate the
very vocabulary of the banquet, thus creating the impression of "a way of
life imported as a package."[2] Yet these alleged origins fail to explain fully
the Romans' perverse fascination with banqueting practices. The power
in the rhetoric of banqueting lies not simply in a clever manipulation of
xenophobia but in Roman concerns about the nature of the masculine
self.

The effeminate male actively participates in the banquet's debauchery.
In the invective directed at the feast, the Roman orator consistently fas-
tens upon specific, externally visible traits to indicate to his audience the
effeminate character of an opponent. Thus a double phenomenon occurs
similar to that which I observed in analyzing the mockery of the mouth
(*os*): physical traits or affectations of a person not only reveal past involvement in an immoderate feast, but they also presage future affiliation with a convivial setting. An analysis of these external indicators
of feasting reveals their distinctly Roman significance: the stigma of

---

[1] See, for example, the texts discussed by Edwards 186–88.
[2] MacMullen 486–87.

convivial excess stems from anxiety over what constitutes—and what deconstitutes—Roman masculinity.

The effeminate banqueter does not inhabit only rhetorical invective; the combination of food, dance, and effeminate or sexually submissive behavior occurs in comedy and epigram as well.[3] The generic character of these effeminate feasters tempts modern readers to attribute to them a purely literary existence, one that the Romans have simply borrowed from Greek antecedents. This scholarly tendency, originating from a compulsion to rid Roman society of the slightest traces of male homo-eroticism, is best exemplified by certain modern attitudes toward the homoerotic poems of Catullus and Horace: their expressions of love for young boys derive not from real affection, some scholars claim, but from literary influence.[4] Such assertions promise to be replaced by more balanced assessments; rather than reflecting a debt to literary ancestors, the poets seem instead to be responding to the very real Hellenization of their society.[5] One might even argue what intuitively seems probable, that the apparent Greek legacy of the banquet simply came to occupy a space already present in Roman society and that the process of assimilation obscured traces of original Roman attitudes and practices.[6] And the possibility that life, at least in part, imitates art should not be ignored out of hand. Recent research into the role of spectacle in Roman society reveals how the Romans tended to blur rather than highlight this distinction between life and art.[7] Such practices strengthen the possibility that the very stigma of the banquet as perpetuated in invective helped shape the identity of an already existing subculture.[8] Hence a process of cultural

[3] E.g., Plaut. *Men.* 197–98, *Mil.* 666–68, *Poen.* 1298, 1317–18, *Stich.* 769–72; Catull. 29.1–5, 47.3–6 (cf. the chart in Richlin 1988: 362).

[4] Horace: Williams 1962: 39–42; Catullus: Arkins 106–7.

[5] Griffin offers an excellent survey of how "Roman life, and particularly the life of luxury and pleasure, was so strongly Hellenistic in colouring and material that no simple division into 'Greek' and 'Roman' elements is possible" (88). Recent handbooks and commentaries follow Griffin's assessment in at least allowing the possibility of genuine homoerotic passion among the poets, e.g., *The Cambridge History of Latin Literature* 409 (Luck). Although Griffin focuses on the Augustan period, his discussion includes texts from the late Republic, and his conclusions would seem valid for this earlier period as well.

[6] See Edwards 94–97, who maintains that "the 'anti-Greek' rhetoric that has come to be associated with effeminacy was grafted on an established Roman practice" (94).

[7] Dupont 119–23 comments on the fine line between theatrical and oratorical performances. Barton 54–65 discusses the intersection or blurring of theatrical violence and reality in the early Empire. See also Versnel 371–97 on the Roman triumph. For modern parallels, see Rogin, especially chap. 1, "*Ronald Reagan*: The Movie" (1–43), and the remarks of Greenblatt 263–72.

[8] Weeks discusses the effects that social representations of homosexuals have had on actual practitioners of homoerotic behavior. See especially his discussion of the distinction between "primary" and "secondary" deviation (107–10). Richlin 1993 offers a detailed analysis of whether a homosexual subculture could have existed in ancient Rome.

transmission is operative here that is more complex than a simple matter of literary influence. As I shall demonstrate below in more detail, the effeminate banqueter represents not simply a literary inheritance but the hybrid product of social realities and imaginative forebodings.

A further consideration encourages the use of invective texts as a gauge of actual Roman behavior. As we have seen, orators use the process of invective to construct an ideology that necessarily entails a certain level of complicity on the hearers' part. In the particular process of defining and enforcing the importance of masculinity in Roman culture, public speakers found an easy target for their insecurities in the person of the effeminate male.[9] Since the effectiveness of an orator's persuasive ability depended in large part upon his credibility, one would expect the orator to form in his invective as coherent and realistic a picture as possible. Thus we would be extremely credulous to believe that a Roman audience would allow constant references to practices entirely alien to its experience, especially when these practices are mentioned only in order to be censured. Hence the rhetorical power of invective against banquets and effeminacy, a power attested to by its frequency—if by nothing else— virtually ensures that some reality supports these hostile accusations. Recent scholarship has begun to clarify the relationship at Rome between political ideology and actual sexual practices, confronting the evidence at face value rather than simply explaining it away.[10] If one applies this approach to the effeminate banqueter, he is found to occupy a liminal world between literature and reality: the literary aspect allows the orator to employ caricature, thereby ensuring that his audience will recognize the figure he describes, while the element of reality allows, I believe, the real threat of this figure to be felt. In the following discussion, I recreate a context within which this particular mode of invective alternately appealed to and appalled its hearers. I begin by bracketing questions of historicity, focusing instead on how the banquet and its attendant vices are constituted in our extant texts as a reality directly opposed to proper Roman behavior. These observations will then allow me to concentrate on why this counterreality was construed as an already present threat to society. Finally, the qualities associated with the effeminate male lead to a consideration of the nature of male homoerotic behavior at Rome. Extant

[9] I disagree with the claims of Boswell 1990: 70–72 that "'sexual identity' had little to do with expected social roles in the community" (71). This assertion is said to apply broadly to "Mediterranean city-states of the ancient world (ca. 400 BC–400 AD)" (70).

[10] See most recently Richlin 1993; Cantarella 120–41. MacMullen's discussion covers the "exceptions, contradictions, and tensions" (485) in trying to posit a "Roman attitude" toward male homosexuality, uncovering along the way "various pressures to conform and counter-pressures which obliged people to conceal a part of themselves" (496).

evidence strongly supports the notion that our constructed effeminate male constitutes a real category of person to whom distinguishing and distinctive codes of behavior can be ascribed.

FEASTING WORDS

On both a moral and a semantic level, Romans linked gluttony with ineffective self-management. The popular vocabulary of bankruptcy and financial profligacy derives from words that describe excessive indulgence in food and drink: a person who squanders wealth "devours" it (*comedo* or *devoro*); to declare oneself bankrupt is to "overcook" or "boil away" (*decoquo*), and so a bankrupt person is an "overcooker" (*decoctor*).[11] It is not difficult to discover the relationship between the financial and convivial domains: wasting away time and money in the sensual pleasures of food prevents a person from maintaining control of an estate. This equivalence provides a paradigm for humorous invective. The elder Cato, for example, exploited the similar semantics of gluttony and financial mismanagement. Macrobius preserves one instance:

> sacrificium apud veteres fuit quod vocabatur propter viam. in eo mos erat ut, siquid ex epulis superfuisset, igne consumeretur. hinc Catonis iocus est. namque Albidium quendam, qui bona sua comedisset et novissime domum quae ei reliqua erat incendio perdidisset, propter viam fecisse dicebat: "quod comesse non potuerit, id combussisse." (Macr. *Sat.* 2.2.4)

> Among the ancients there was a sacrifice called "beside the road." In this type of sacrifice it was the custom to consume by fire anything left over from feasting. From this practice comes Cato's joke. When a certain Albidius had squandered his own goods and had recently lost in a fire his only remaining house, Cato said Albidius had conducted a "sacrifice beside the road": what he couldn't squander/devour (*comedo*), he burned up.

Cato literalizes the bankruptcy metaphor: since Albidius could not "eat away" his whole estate, he conducts the sacrifice appropriate for one setting out on a journey (*propter viam fecisse*; cf. Fest. p. 229 [Mueller])— what cannot be eaten is set on fire. A similar connection between the

---

[11] *comedo*: Plaut. *Pseud.* 1107; Catull. 29.14; Cic. *Phil.* 11.37; Hor. *Epist.* 1.15.40; Martial 5.70.5; *TLL* 3:1767.25–72. *devoro*: Catull. 29.22; Cic. *Phil.* 2.67, *Verr.* 2.3.177, [Cic.] *Inv. in Sall.* 20; Quint. *Inst.* 8.6.25; Macr. *Sat.* 3.13.6: *Gurgitem a devorato patrimonio cognominatum* (Gurges received his name from his devoured patrimony); *TLL* 5.1:876.21–50. *decoctor*: *TLL* 5.1:197.65–198.7; Crook 375–76 agrees that in situations of debt *decoquere* must mean "to squander," in spite of the scholiast to *Catil.* 2.5 (Schol. Gron. p. 281, 7–10 [Stangl]), who claims that a *decoctor* is one who "cooks away" a debt, as opposed to a patrimony.

glutton and the spendthrift underlies a joke of Cato preserved by Plutarch:

τὸν δὲ πεπρακότα τοὺς πατρῴους ἀγροὺς παραλίους ὄντας ἐπιδεικ-
νύμενος προσεποιεῖτο θαυμάζειν ὡς ἰσχυρότερον τῆς θαλάττης, "ἃ γὰρ
ἐκείνη μόλις ἔκλυζεν, οὗτος," ἔφη, "ῥᾳδίως καταπέπωκεν." (Plut. Cato
Ma. 8.7)

Pointing to a man who had sold the seaside estates of his ancestors, [Cato] pretended to marvel that the man was stronger than the sea. "For what the sea washed away with difficulty," he said, "this man has easily drunk down."

Καταπίνω ("drink down") presumably translates the Latin verb *ebibo*, another word from the domain of the feast that the Romans metaphorically applied to financial profligacy.[12] These two dicta of Cato do not represent merely cheap jokes. In fact, the attribution to Cato attests to their profoundly Roman character.[13] Another pair of anecdotes preserved by Plutarch conveys the former censor's feelings about preserving patrimony: he once remarked that one of his three regrets in life was to have been intestate for an entire day (Plut. *Cato Ma.* 9.6); on another occasion he notes that to lessen patrimony befits not a man but a widowed woman, whereas to increase patrimony reveals a "godlike paragon" (θαυμαστὸν ἄνδρα καὶ θεῖον; *Cato Ma.* 21.8). The importance Cato placed on the proper management of finances helps to explain his humorous abuse of gluttonous spendthrifts.[14]

Cato's conceptual matrix of gluttony, financial profligacy, and the proper role of a man (as opposed to a woman) reemerges in the time of Cicero with explicitly political connotations. The activities of the immoderate feast come to occupy a position opposed to that of a proper Roman statesman. In his speech *On Behalf of Sestius*, the orator highlights

[12] *ebibo*: Plaut. *Trin.* 250; Hor. *Sat.* 2.3.122; Ulp. *Dig.* 5.3.25.16. Edwards 175 cites the similar use of *effundo* and *profundo* ("pour out").

[13] The elder Seneca speaks of Cato as an oracle of morality (Sen. *Contr.* 1.praef.9); see further Edwards 1–2, 139, 177.

[14] Another example of an orator exploiting the connection between gluttony and poverty before Cicero's day is preserved at *De orat.* 2.265: *ille Gallus olim testis in Pisonem, cum innumerabilem Magio praefecto pecuniam dixisset datam idque Scaurus tenuitate Magi redargueret, "erras," inquit "Scaure; ego enim Magium non conservasse dico, sed tamquam nudus nuces legeret, in ventre abstulisse"* ("A man named Gallus once testified against Piso. After he had said that an inestimable sum of money had been given to the prefect Magius, and Scaurus was attempting to refute this by pointing to Magius' financial straits, Gallus replied, 'You don't understand, Scaurus; I'm not saying Magius has saved it but rather, just like a man in a tunic [*nudus*] gathers nuts, he has stored it away in his stomach'").

the questionable morality of the former consul Gabinius by referring to his penchant for feasting and sex:

> me ipsum ut contempsit helluo patriae! nam quid ego patrimoni dicam, quod ille tum cum quaestum faceret amisit? (*Sest.* 26)

> How this consumer of the fatherland (*patriae*) spurned even me! For why should I say [consumer] "of his patrimony" (*patrimoni*), something he lost when he was out selling his favors (*quaestum faceret*)?

The abuse reveals an interesting thought progression. After alluding to Gabinius' inability to govern the state (*helluo patriae*), Cicero segues into remarks on the inability to control financial affairs. The relationship becomes more concrete through the etymological link Cicero exploits with his play on *patriae* and *patrimoni*. Abandoning the *father*land and squandering a *father*'s estate expose similar faults of character. Catullus' lampoon of Mamurra in poem 29 depends on similar associations. Mamurra's treatment of his inheritance anticipated his exploits as governor: "first his father's property was ripped to shreds" (*paterna prima lancinata sunt bona*; 29.17). After enumerating Mamurra's plundering of the provinces, Catullus encapsulates all these exploits in one phrase: "what can this man do other than devour a well-oiled patrimony?" (*aut quid hic potest / nisi uncta devorare patrimonia?*; 29.21–22). Like Gabinius, Mamurra recapitulates in a corrupt public career his incapacity in private affairs.

These short outbursts of Cicero and Catullus against their political opponents reveal a close correspondence between representations of the public and the private, a concern reflected in legal texts that treat financial prodigality.[15] As has been noted, Cicero translates the charge of gluttony into a danger to the state (*helluo patriae*); Catullus uses the corresponding verb form to characterize Mamurra's actions (*elluatus est*; 29.16). A similar association between Gabinius' immoderate private life and his neglect of state matters occurs elsewhere: Cicero describes him in *Against Piso* as "that whirlpool and glutton, born for his belly, not for praise and glory" (*ille gurges atque helluo, natus abdomini suo, non laudi et gloriae*; *Pis.* 41)—praise and glory constituting, of course, traditional goals of the Roman aristocrat.[16] The passage from *On Behalf of Sestius* also shows the orator ridiculing Gabinius for wage earning, an activity deemed beneath the dignity of a statesman.[17] The phrase he uses, however, contains a double

---

[15] Edwards 180–83.

[16] Earl 11–43 discusses the importance of the values *laus* and *gloria* in the late Republic.

[17] *Off.* 1.150–51 provides the *locus classicus* for this view. The reasons behind the distinctions Cicero makes in this passage are examined by Finley 35–61. The Romans did not,

entendre and thereby adds another dimension to the complex of charges levied: *quaestum facere* ("to profit") can stand as an abbreviated form of *quaestum [corpore] facere* ("to profit from one's body"). Hence Cicero implies not only that Gabinius had to support himself financially but that he did so through prostitution.[18] The connection in invective between financial and sexual profligacy also occurs in Catullus' attack (29.7, 13–14, 16). One may trace this motif in Roman political discourse back to at least the middle of the second century.[19] Yet another element of Cicero's attack here will recur in the invective connected with feasting: Gabinius' reputation as a catamite points to the sex of his clientele, thereby further degrading the former consul as being something less than a man.[20] All these charges characteristic of political invective—gluttony, financial mismanagement, political ineptitude, and sexual (especially homosexual) profligacy—intersect in the dark and mysterious arena of the banquet.

THE ACTIVITIES OF THE FEAST

Cicero and other Roman orators repeatedly find in the feasting motif fertile material for invective. Yet it often becomes difficult to distinguish among the precise activities to which the speaker could refer in these situations. The description of these activities is often as obscure as the shadowy settings in which the activities allegedly occur.[21] The confusion stems in part from the orator's stance as an upright man (*vir bonus*): were he able to describe in detail what happens at these private feasts, he could potentially implicate himself in the activity. The obscurity resulting from

---

however, disdain the accumulation of wealth so much as the means of accumulation: see *Off.* 1.92, 2.87; D'Arms 20–24.

[18] Cicero formulates this charge against Gabinius more explicitly at *P. red. in sen.* 11— *cum suam rem non minus strenue quam postea publicam confecisset, egestatem et luxuriem domestico lenocinio sustentavit* ("After he had squandered his own wealth with no less vigor than he had later squandered the public's, he supported his poverty and luxury with a brothel at home").

For the phrase *quaestum facere* signifying prostitution, see Ulp. *Dig.* 23.2.43 (*CIL* I².593.122–23 [*tabula Heracleensis*] refers specifically to male prostitution). Cf. Plaut. *Poen.* 1140; Ter. *Hau.* 640; and perhaps Cic. *Quinct.* 3.12.

[19] *ORF* 21.19 = Gell. 6.11.9: *si tu plus tertia parte pecuniae paternae perdidisti atque absumpsisti in flagitiis, si hoc ita est: qui spondet mille nummum?* ("If you have lost more than one-third of your father's money and have squandered it in disgraceful actions, if this is true: who promises a thousand silver pieces in surety?"). In this, the third of four similarly constructed rhetorical questions Scipio Aemilianus addresses to Asellus, losing patrimony and being wanton not only are given equal emphasis but are also each predicated upon each other. See also Sall. *Cat.* 14.2.

[20] Cicero alludes to Gabinius' reputation at, e.g., *P. red. in sen.* 11–12; *Sest.* 18; *Pis.* 20.

[21] For the dark surroundings of the immodest banquet, see e.g. *S. Rosc.* 134; *Catil.* 2.22; *Sest.* 20; *Pis.* 18, 53, 67; *Prov.* 8. It is a common motif that one who frequents the banquet is unaccustomed to daylight (see Cic. *Fin.* 2.23 and Otto n. 1662).

this necessary ignorance increases the efficacy of the motif: the allusive-
ness of many of these descriptions titillates the listeners' imaginations and
encourages them to envision the precise details of the occasion that the
orator presents in bare outline. In this way the speaker allows his audience to play the voyeur, to satisfy its fascination with the forbidden: "the
speaker should manipulate the description of reality so that the audience
imagines more than it sees" (*orator surripiat oportet imitationem ut is qui
audiet cogitet plura quam videat*; *De orat.* 2.242).[22] Nevertheless, in spite of
this mannered ambiguity certain themes emerge with consistency.

Five basic areas of activity commonly surface in association with the
immoderate feast: excessive eating, drunkenness, the telling of jokes,
dancing and singing (including poetry recitation), and various forms of
sexual intercourse.[23] Constructed as vices, these activities frequently occur in combination: Cicero describes his enemy Gabinius in a largely
asyndetic series as "done in by wine, eating houses, pimping, and adultery" (*vino ganeis lenociniis adulteriisque confectum*; *Sest.* 20). Often the practices are alluded to even more elliptically: Piso's teachers of philosophy—
who also arrange his banquets (*conditores instructoresque convivi*)—instruct
their student that "every part of the body should always be involved in
some sort of pleasure or sensual stimulation" (*in omni parte corporis semper
oportere aliquod gaudium delectationemque versari*; *P. red. in sen.* 14–15).
Vague lists of intertwining vices abound in invective of this type.[24] Yet
despite the frequency of these sorts of allegation, any attempt to differen-
tiate between the activities of the feast proves not only impossible but
misguided, since their confusion and conflation are precisely the point:
the rhetorical handbooks instruct that if an opponent can be shown to be
guilty of one vice, it is then possible to implicate him in any.[25] Therefore,
rather than attempting to distinguish artificially between these activities,
I shall be considering their common features. In particular, I shall concentrate on the most prominent guest figured in the Ciceronian representation of the feast: the dancing, effeminate male.

THE DANCER IS THE DANCE

The dance characterizes the feast so well that it is mentioned in Roman
invective only in a banqueting context. Yet the abuse directed at dancing

---

[22] See Barton, chap. 3, "Fascination" (85–106).

[23] These points are also covered in Richlin 1992a: 86–93. Edwards 173–206 analyzes
banqueting motifs in Roman moralizing texts.

[24] Examples not discussed elsewhere in the text or notes and involving the different
elements of the banquet in various combinations include *Verr.* 2.5.92–94, 137; *Pis.* 42; *Phil.*
2.104–5; *Sal. Cat.* 13.3; *Liv.* 39.15.9; *Suet. Gramm.* 15.

[25] *Inv.* 2.33; cf. 2.50 and *Rhet. Her.* 2.5.

feasters could not simply be wielded at random. The orator needed to provide a substantial and verifiable foundation to his accusations. To be effective in accusing an opponent of connections with the immoderate feast, the speaker had to present evidence visible to his audience. Believing requires seeing.

In the midst of a typical account of the breakdown of morality in the Republic, Cicero in *On the Laws* attributes moral decline in part to the seductive tendencies of music and dancing:

> illud quidem video, quae solebant quondam compleri severitate iucunda Livianis et Naevianis modis, nunc ut eadem exultent et cervices oculosque pariter cum modorum flexionibus torqueant. graviter olim ista vindicabat vetus illa Graecia, longe providens quam sensim pernicies inlapsa in civium animos malis studiis malisque doctrinis repente totas civitates everteret. (*Leg.* 2.39)

> I do see one thing in particular: that those same people[26] who at one time were accustomed to be filled up with a pleasurable feeling of austerity at the measures of Livius and Naevius are nowadays jumping around and twisting their necks and eyes in time with the changing measures. In the past, ancient Greece punished severely that kind of behavior, for it foresaw well in advance how this source of destruction, gradually creeping into the minds of citizens, would suddenly overturn entire states through its evil pursuits and teachings.

As Roman civilization declines from the period when its oldest poets, Livius and Naevius, were writing, Cicero recognizes in dancing a vice that conspires with other base activities for the potential destruction of the state. This moralizing opinion of dance also informs invective from the century preceding Cicero. In a fragmentary piece of invective written by the second-century BCE satirist Lucilius, dancing and effeminacy appear to be associated: "like a fool you went dancing with the *cinaedi*" (Lucilius 33 [Warmington]). A later grammarian, commenting on this passage from Lucilius, remarks that "among the ancients, dancers or pantomimes were called *cinaedi*" (*"cinaedi" dicti sunt apud veteres saltatores vel pantomimi*; Nonius p. 5 [Mercerus]). Indeed, this grammarian's statement is confirmed by a contemporary of Lucilius, Scipio Aemilianus.

---

[26] The manuscripts are faulty at this point, but the general meaning is clear. I cite Keyes' text. My interpretation follows Davisius et al. in construing *quae* as modifying an understood *theatra*, which then becomes personalized into *spectatores* or a similar noun with the verb *exultent*.

For additional moral judgments on dancing from the late Republic, see *Off.* 1.150, 3.75 (where dancing in the forum is described as the ultimate act of shamelessness; cf. 3.93); Nepos *Epam.* 1.2; my discussion of effeminacy concludes with a reconsideration of the invective against dancing.

Scipio complained how the freeborn young Romans of his day "are learning to sing, something our ancestors wanted to be considered disgraceful to the freeborn; they go, I say, to dancing school, freeborn girls and boys among the *cinaedi*" (*discunt cantare, quae maiores nostri ingenuis probro ducier voluerunt: eunt, inquam, in ludum saltatorium inter cinaedos virgines puerique ingenui*; Macr. *Sat.* 3.14.7 = *ORF* 21.30). Part of the stigma of the dance derives from its associations with the passive role in male-male sexual encounters; in ancient Greece and Rome, male-male homoerotic behavior was figured as nonreciprocal, consisting of a virile penetrator and a passive, penetrated partner.[27] *Cinaedus*, in fact, eventually became a standard word to describe the man who is the penetrated partner in a homoerotic relationship.[28] The dance, it seems, indicated a commitment to a specific, predetermined lifestyle.

Scipio seems to have been unaware of a previous graduate of this school of abomination. Earlier in the same century, the elder Cato instituted proceedings against a certain tribune of the plebs, Marcus Caelius. Cato mocks his opponent for dancing in public and associates the activity with singing, the recitation of Greek poetry, and joke telling (Macr. *Sat.* 3.14.9 = *ORF* 8.114–15). Even in the elder Cato's day, the charge of dancing carried with it a body of negative associations.[29]

A descendant of Cato, while prosecuting the consul designate Lucius Murena in 63 BCE, followed a tack similar to that of his ancestor. In a speech accusing Murena of electoral corruption, the younger Cato alleged that the defendant was a dancer (*saltator*). In defending Murena from this accusation, Cicero maintains that dancing constitutes a vice incapable of existing in isolation, "for almost no one dances while sober—unless perhaps he is insane—neither while alone nor in a moderate and honorable banquet. The dance is the final accompaniment to an early banquet,[30] a pleasant locale, and many luxurious activities" (*nemo enim fere saltat sobrius, nisi forte insanit, neque in solitudine neque in convivio moderato atque honesto. tempestivi convivi, amoeni loci, multarum deliciarum comes est extrema saltatio*; *Mur.* 13). Cato has not accused Murena of any of

[27] I discuss this notion, citing relevant bibliography, in the section below entitled "The Category of the Effeminate Male"; see esp. n. 55.

[28] Using archaeological and literary evidence, Colin explores the semantic development of *cinaedus* to connote a sexually passive homosexual (1952–53: 329–35). On the word's meaning in classical Athens, see Winkler 45–70; for the second century CE, see Gleason 1991: 396–99.

[29] One may add to this list an apparent piece of invective against the elder Curio, who was named after the dancer Burbuleius because he was "quick and restless in body and tongue" (Sall. *Hist.* frag. 2.25. Cf. Val. Max. 9.14.5; Plin. *Nat.* 7.55).

[30] And, as a result, scandalous; for the opprobrious associations of a *convivium tempestivum*, see, e.g., *Verr.* 2.3.62; Catull. 47.5–6. Catiline's men provide a special case; they begin their feasts before dawn (*Catil.* 2.22).

dancing's attendant vices. Therefore, Cicero maintains, the accuser can only be incorrect in calling Murena a dancer.

Cicero's rhetorical strategy here reveals his audience's assumptions. Both orators presume their audience will agree that implicating Murena in the dance will implicate him in the attendant vices Cicero later lists— disgraceful banqueting, sex, revelry, lust, and excessive expenditure (*turpe convivium, . . . amor, . . . comissatio, . . . libido, . . . sumptus*). And if Cato can succeed in establishing his opponent's associations with the feast, he will all the more easily prove Murena guilty of electoral corruption, as this charge will be construed as consistent with Murena's immoral character. Such a belief in the association between personal immorality and political corruption informs the historian Sallust's famous description of the conspirator Sempronia: her skills in the dance, poetry, and witty conversation clearly foreshadow her eventual disservices to the state (Sall. *Cat.* 25). But the younger Cato's single accusation of dancing does not suffice here. The dance presupposes a broader context of corruption, a context that Cato has failed to delineate.

To be sure, in his own invective Cicero also relies upon the multiple negative associations the dance conjures in his audience's mind.[31] Yet the orator is not simply hypocritically or opportunistically using a weapon he himself has condemned. Rather, his use of the charge is quite different from Cato's attack, as Cicero represents it in his speech *On Behalf of Murena*.

In his second oration against Catiline, Cicero muses on the military efficacy of the more luxuriant members of Catiline's group of revolutionaries:

> quo autem pacto illi Appeninum atque illas pruinas ac nives perferent? nisi idcirco se facilius hiemem toleraturos putant, quod nudi in conviviis saltare didicerunt. (*Catil.* 2.23)

> But how will they stand that frost and snow in the Appenines? Maybe they think they'll tolerate winter more easily since they've learned to dance naked at banquets.

Earlier in the speech, Cicero invested a great amount of energy in proving that Catiline's men, when not stirring up political unrest, devote their lives to feasting (see especially *Catil.* 2.22, cited later in this chapter). Dancing, then, serves to cap an already well-delineated characterization. The naked dancing of the Catilinarians, an activity threatening to overthrow Roman morality, has been falsely construed by the rebels, Cicero humorously conjectures, as a type of training designed to over-

---

[31] In addition to *Catil.* 2.23 cited in the text, see *Verr.* 2.3.23 (Verres' son); *Planc.* 87, *Pis.* 22 (both of Gabinius).

throw the Roman military. In light of Cicero's own use of the charge of dancing in the Catilinarian orations, the inadequacy of the attack on Murena becomes clear. Cato has not verified his accusations of dancing, as Cicero does, by pointing to any other signs of Murena's connection with immoderate feasting. Hence Cicero needs simply to question the truth of Cato's charge of dancing to show that it represents slanderous abuse (*Mur.* 13).

Cicero's rebuttal of Cato in *On Behalf of Murena* recalls the factors that inform the mockery of physical peculiarities and, to a lesser extent, the *os*. External indicators make these two modes of invective persuasive. At the very moment of a speech's delivery, the orator can point to those features of the accused that his audience would have associated with immorality. For example, were an audience member to doubt the accuracy of Cicero's censure of Vatinius, a perusal of the defendant's pustules would serve to legitimate the orator's invective. To be effective, therefore, the topos of the immoderate feast requires a type of external signal that can indicate, even when the accused is separate from the activity, the implicit probability of his involvement. Such a signal would provide a powerful rhetorical tool, for the passages discussed above have demonstrated that proof of involvement in merely one vice can implicate an individual in all the sordid components of the feast. Indeed, these signals were available. They derive from the ways in which the luxurious atmosphere of the banquet was thought to alter the physical appearance and affectations of its male participants.

POLITICAL HEAVIES

I begin with a negative conclusion. An overweight appearance, surprisingly, does not seem to have provided a sufficient cause for accusing an opponent of immoderate feasting. Though this may run counter to our expectations of invective, the absence can be explained by the public perception of wealth in the Roman Republic.

According to the second-century CE antiquarian Aulus Gellius, a speech of the elder Cato from 184 BCE marks the first instance of a *censor* attaching a badge of dishonor (*ignominia*) to a Roman citizen's corpulence. This particular instance involved the censure of a Roman knight (*eques*), a member of the class that originally formed the cavalry of the Roman army but that, by the time of the late Republic, comprised primarily wealthy businessmen. According to normal procedure, Gellius states, censors relieved an overweight *eques* of his duties without effecting a lowering of census class (Gell. 6.22 = *ORF* 8.78). With Cato, then, the corpulence of an *eques* expands from being simply a pragmatic issue—an overweight man cannot properly control a horse (cf. *ORF* 8.80: "he can't

sit on his quaking horse"—*sedere non potest in equo trepidante*)—to being a
moral and political issue: the personal neglect evidenced by a man's overweight appearance reflects potential neglect of his civic duties. Explicit
testimony of Cato's feelings on the subject survives in an anecdote that
Plutarch preserves, which seems to derive from the same censorial speech
mentioned by Gellius:[32]

τὸν δὲ ὑπέρπαχυν κακίζων [ὁ Κάτων] "ποῦ δ᾽ ἄν" ἔφη "σῶμα τοιοῦτον τῇ
πόλει γένοιτο χρήσιμον, οὗ τὸ μεταξὺ λαιμοῦ καὶ βουβώνων πᾶν ὑπὸ τῆς
γαστρὸς κατέχεται;" (Plut. *Cat. Ma.* 9.5)

In reproaching a fat man [Cato] remarked, "How would a body such as this
be beneficial to the state, when the part between throat and groin is entirely
taken up by the stomach?"

This formulation recalls Cato's witticisms on financial mismanagement, where he construes personal and private profligacy as manifesting
analogous faults of character. Thus, for Cato, being overweight represented a politically reprehensible condition. Yet as I have noted, Gellius
views Cato's sternness in this situation as unusual for a censor.[33]

Cato's witticism recalls Cicero's censure of Gabinius in the speech *On
Behalf of Sestius* (section 20, quoted above), where the orator presumes a
link between the former consul's ability to control his patrimony and the
state. Yet in spite of this similarity, Cicero does not follow Cato in deem-
ing corpulence an object worthy of public reproach. In fact, in the entire
Ciceronian corpus I have found only one witticism based on an opponent's overweight appearance. In the speech *On Behalf of Caecina*, Cicero
impugns the testimony of Publius Caesennius, a witness for the opposition, by describing him as "possessing not so much weighty authority as
a weighty body" (*non tam auctoritate gravi quam corpore*; *Caecin.* 27). This
unique example occurs in a speech dating from a relatively early stage of
Cicero's public career—69 BCE, when he had not yet held the office of
praetor. The situation, moreover, seems to have had little political consequence: the issue concerned a civil suit over a land dispute that was heard
by a small group of minor judges (*recuperatores*). And in fact, on a rhetori-

---

[32] This is the generally received opinion; the contents of the witticism in Plutarch accord
well with Gellius' evaluation of Cato's censorial oration (Gell. 6.22.4). Cugusi 502, however, follows Jordan in questioning this attribution on the grounds that Plutarch's anecdote
probably derives from Cato's *liber dictorum*. While it does seem possible that Cato's joke
book supplied Plutarch with this anecdote (although it is disputed whether Cato included
his own witticisms in this collection; see Astin 186–88), I nevertheless do not see why that
precludes the possibility of the dictum coming from an oration; Furius Bibaculus' collection
of Cicero's *facete dicta* includes excerpts from the orator's speeches (Macr. *Sat.* 2.1.13).

[33] As does Marache 80 n. 1. At Gell. 4.20.11, another overweight member of the eques-
trian class is relegated to a lower census ranking. The reasons cited are neglect of his horse
and disrespect for the censors; his weight is not mentioned.

cal level the pun receives little emphasis from the orator. It precedes a slightly more extended witticism on the cognomen of a certain Sextus Clodius Phormio, a second witness, which in turn introduces a more elaborate anecdote regarding the judicial bribery of yet another witness, Fidiculanius Falcula. The sole extant example of Cicero publicly mocking an opponent for his weight, therefore, provides little evidence that such an appearance constituted, in an oratorical context, a seriously reprehensible offense.[34]

The hypothesis that corpulence does not invite political reproach during the late Republic receives further support from a lexical study of the three words most commonly used to denote it—*crassus, obesus, pinguis*—and their cognates. Indeed, the last adjective tends to describe corpulence chiefly "as a sign of prosperity or well-being."[35] Cicero uses the word in juxtaposition with *valentes* ("hardy"; *Fat.* 7), while Horace describes himself as "sleek and *pinguis*, with a nice complexion" (*pinguem et nitidum bene curata cute; Epist.* 1.4.15). *Obesus*, which describes a greater degree of corpulence than *pinguis* (cf. Isid. *Diff.* 1.114), occurs five times in the imperial medical writer Celsus to describe a state that can hinder health. The word does not, however, connote reproach; it usually occurs in conjunction with the equally risky state of extreme thinness (described by *gracilis*; cf. 1.3.13, 2.1.5 [*bis*], 2.1.23, 2.10.5). The adjective *crassus*, a word with connotations of sluggishness and stupidity in nonbodily contexts, also does not have clearly pejorative overtones in any of the extant Republican texts in which it describes a person's appearance.[36] In fact, when Cicero wishes to mock someone named Crassus, he does not exploit any potential connotations of the name but invents humorous pseudonyms.[37] If *Crassus* did have an obviously negative meaning in a political context, one would have expected Cicero's jokes to reflect this. A similar argument can be made for the one Republican figure who seems to have been identifiable by his fleshy appearance. The abusive remarks against Pompeius Magnus never refer to the corpulence evidenced in depictions of him; in fact, the double chin so characteristic of

---

[34] Outside the context of internal Roman politics, Plutarch preserves a joke made by Scipio Aemilianus on the lack of care Ptolemy Physcon ("Potbelly") took regarding his body (*Mor.* 201a). Imperial writers permit this form of abuse: Juvenal 1.139–43, 8.147; Persius 6.74; and perhaps Lucan's "encomium" of Nero (1.53–59).

[35] OLD, s.v. *pinguis* 1b; similarly, Forcellini restricts the word to persons "in good condition."

[36] My search included the texts of Plautus, Terence, Cato, Lucilius, Caesar, Lucretius, Cicero, and Catullus. The passages at Plaut. *Pseud.* 659, 1218, and Ter. *Hec.* 440 seem purely descriptive, with no negative connotations clearly intended. The meaning "slow-witted" or "rustic," as found in the idiom *crassa Minerva*, best derives from the root meaning of the word ("thick" and therefore "slow moving") rather than from its use to describe the human physique.

[37] *Att.* 1.16.5, 2.13.2, 14.5.1, all of which I discuss in chapter 2.

the general's public portraits would seem to provide a further indication
that corpulence was an unobjectionable feature of the Roman aristocrat.[38]

It is always dangerous to argue from the silence of our limited (but, in
the case of the late Republic, hardly meager) sources. Yet this silence does
deserve special mention on account of the generic character of banqueting invective and the many different factors to which an orator appealed
to indicate his opponent's involvement in banquets. This area of absent
wit becomes especially interesting in light of the differences I observed in
chapter 1 between Hellenistic rhetorical and ethical treatises and Roman
oratorical practice. I attributed the Roman proclivity for abusing physical
peculiarities to the prevailing bias that a human being bears personal responsibility for all bodily faults, regardless of whether they are congeni-
tal or acquired from acts committed during a person's lifetime. As a result, a deformity such as Vatinius' facial swellings would have been
regarded by the Greek treatises as a characteristic for which the bearer
could not be held responsible; we saw in Cicero's speech against Vatinius
the opposite assumptions within which Roman invective operated. In the
case of an overweight appearance, Greek theory and Roman practice
would again appear to stand at odds. As discussed above, Romans seem
to avoid the mockery of corpulence, while Hellenistic treatises would
deem such abuse appropriate, since corpulence results from personal neglect and hence constitutes an ethically reprehensible state of being.[39] In
this particular case, however, the difference between Greek and Roman
conceptions does not seem attributable to differing notions of personal
responsibility so much as to a different set of values that the Romans
attached to social position.

It has frequently been observed that, to a Roman aristocrat, abundant
wealth constituted an admirable possession—provided that it has been
properly acquired.[40] This social value, I propose, accounts for the dearth
of public mockery of a person's weight. A grammarian preserves for us
an epigram that testifies to the identification of corpulence and wealth in
the late Republic:[41]

---

[38] For the double chin in depictions of Pompeius, see most recently Bentz 231. As I shall
discuss in chapter 5, Pompeius was certainly the object of mockery for other aspects of his
appearance: his dress, his ruddy complexion, and certain of his gestures.

[39] [Arist.] *Rh. Al.* 1426a3–11 admits invective against someone who is feeble from lack
of exercise; cf. 1440b16–23; *Rhet. Her.* 3.10; Cic. *Inv.* 2.177. For the ethical basis underlying
this type of invective, see Aristotle *EN* 1114a23–31. In the case of women, Hippocrates
asserts that obesity hinders conception (*Airs* 21).

[40] See for example *ORF* 6.2 (= Plin. *Nat.* 7.139–40); *ORF* 31.3 (= Gell. 1.13.10); Finley
35–41.

[41] The Carbo mentioned is apparently Gaius Papirius Carbo Arvina, praetor 83 BCE,
who Cicero tells us was an enemy of the orator Lucius Crassus (*De orat.* 3.10; cf. Val. Max.
3.7.6). The epigram can then be dated to soon after 91 BCE, the year of Crassus' death.

dictum est de Carbone, qui, mortuo Crasso, homine felice, inimico suo, ante obscurus florere coepit: "postquam Crassus carbo factus est, . . . Carbo crassus factus est." (*ORF* 87.3)

[The following] was said of Carbo, who was once unimportant, [but] began to flourish upon the death of his enemy Crassus, a rich man: "After Crassus became *carbo* (coal), . . . Carbo became *crassus* (fat)."

The pun on *Crassus* indicates that a Roman would readily identify a fat man as wealthy and prosperous. Conversely, *tenuis* ("thin") commonly describes a man in desperate financial straits.[42] It seems reasonable, then, that this association between wealth and an overweight appearance explains why political invective from the period contains little mockery of corpulence. I do not wish to claim that this source of invective was never used—the passage cited above from Cicero's speech *On Behalf of Caecina* indicates that it was—but simply to suggest that such claims did not have the greatest political efficacy. Corpulence would have represented wealth and its corollary, political and social esteem. To have pointed to a rival's girth would not have effectively brought about his exclusion from society; on the contrary, it could have served as an indicator of his social importance.

In public invective, the Romans did not use an opponent's overweight appearance to affix the stigma of the immoderate feast. One can reasonably attribute this omission to the associations between corpulence and wealth. Hence an absent category of invective confirms the judgment one finds expressed in more direct sources concerning the value placed on wealth in Roman society. We should now look through the eyes of this plump aristocrat as he gazes on—or conjures—his political opponent: the drunken, naked, effeminate dancer, drenched in perfumes as he jokes and sings songs.

THE CONCEPTION OF THE ROMAN MALE

Orators of the late Republic conflate the phenomena of the immodest banquet and the effeminate male. Each situation normally suggests the other, and both embody a potential threat to the state. Attendance at a feast, I have noted, anticipates political inefficacy. The Romans speak of effeminacy in similar terms. In late 44, Quintus Cicero writes despairingly to Tiro of the consuls designate, Hirtius and Pansa: "I know them thoroughly—full of lusting and lounging of the most effeminate nature. If they don't yield the helm, there's the greatest danger of everything being shipwrecked" (*quos ego penitus novi, libidinum et languoris effeminatissimi animi plenos. qui nisi a gubernaculis recesserint, maximum ab uni-*

---

[42] E.g., *Verr.* 1.1.46; *Catil.* 2.20; *Sest.* 103; *OLD*, s.v. *tenuis* 10b.

verso naufragio periculum est; *Fam.* 16.27.1 = SB 352). This picture of the effeminate feaster of the late Republic, a strangely androgynous glutton of food and sex, contributes to the modern reader's despair over whether one can glean any truth from Roman invective.[43] Yet this unstable figure can be used to advantage: the danger it represents contributes to an understanding of Roman masculine self-definition.

An effeminate man threatened the Roman male. As suggested earlier, the fear of Hellenic or Eastern influence may explain in part *what* the Romans of this time were wary of—namely, the infusion of different ways of thinking about government and society. Modes of thinking that the Romans perceived as being at odds with their own became associated with an Eastern way of manners and dress. Yet this formulation does not answer *why* Roman society fixated on the fear of effeminacy. One possible explanation lies in the Roman male's conception of self and of the natural features he felt separated him from a woman.

Medical writers of the second century CE reiterate theories of sex differentiation that date back seven hundred years to the works of Empedocles. According to these writers, conception involved the intermingling of warm male semen and cool female semen.[44] The net temperature resulting from this interaction determined the sex of the child: "males were those fetuses who had realized their full potential" by amassing the greatest amount of heat while still in the womb; insufficient accumulation of heat, on the other hand, produced a female.[45] The theory found support in empirical observation: as a result of her cooler body temperature, a woman has a softer, moister physical makeup than a man. This theory of the differing amount of heat in the sexes seems to have had currency in the late Republic; Varro, for example, affirms in his treatise on agriculture that dry plants are relatively infertile, as opposed to those that are "looser and [therefore] more fertile, as the female is [looser and more fertile] than the male."[46] The formulation of this assertion, in which the statement that the female is looser (*laxiora*) than the male is supplied as a

---

[43] See, for example, Syme 1939: 149–50; Nisbet 1961: 192; Richlin 1992a: 102.

[44] Although never accepted by Aristotle, the belief in female semen prevailed among the ancients from the pre-Socratics onward (Blayney 230).

[45] The quotation comes from P. Brown 9–10, who cites Aretaeus 2.5 in support; cf. also Galen *De usu partium* 14.6–7, *De semine* 2.5. Galen appears to follow Empedocles (Aristotle *GA* 764a1–6; cf. 723a24–25, Aetius 5.7.1). Brown's discussion of sexuality in Late Antiquity first prompted many of the connections I make in my own argument between male anxiety and the invective of effeminacy.

A caloric distinction between the sexes seems to be corroborated by modern science: female-to-male transsexuals remark on how testosterone raises the body temperature (Bloom 48).

[46] Varro *Rust.* 1.41.4: *omnia enim minuta et arida ad crescendum tarda, ea quae laxiora, et fecundiora, ut femina quam mas et pro portione in virgultis item*; I understand *femina* and *mas* to refer to male and female animals (or human beings) as opposed to plants. A similar dichotomy occurs in Polemo's treatise on physiognomy; 1.194.11–16 (Foerster).

given, implies a consensus among Varro's readers concerning what properties constitute the male as opposed to the female. Further evidence for the widespread application of this idea can be found in the rhetorician Quintilian, who conjectures that the voices of young boys are weaker than those of men because boys still retain "dampness" (*propter umorem*; *Inst.* 11.3.28).

Aside from the apparent parallelism of thought in Varro and Quintilian, there are additional reasons for supposing that the caloric theory of sex differentiation preserved by Galen was part of the collective knowledge of a Roman of this period. First, Galen was a compiler whose work "summarized all that was worthy in the medical tradition of the classical world."[47] That he does not indicate that this theory of sex differentiation had been recently contested indicates its acceptance in the late Republic. Second, Lucretius' account of conception in book 4 of *On the Nature of Things* harmonizes with the theory propounded by Galen.[48] Finally, the philosophical conceptualization of pleasure (and hence vice) as fluid, whereas virtue is dry and hard, also accords with this split in the characterization of the sexes.[49] The warm, dry male and the cool, moist female of Republican invective offered a familiar dichotomy.

An interesting consequence arises from the perceived role of heat in a human being's conception: according to Galen, if the heat of a male were to subside at any point during the course of his lifetime, he may risk blurring his sexual identity. "No normal man might actually become a woman; but each man trembled forever on the brink of becoming 'womanish.'"[50] These words, describing Roman male anxieties during Late Antiquity, apply equally well to the late Republic. For behind the humorous invective of effeminacy there continually lurks the possibility of a man undergoing a behavioral transformation. This potential threat to the socially constructed natural order, whereby the biological male is expected to exhibit specific masculine traits, becomes translated via public humor into a threat to political order.

If Galenic theories of sex differentiation had legitimacy for these Romans—and Varro indicates how farming techniques were one way such theories may have found a wider, and even practical, application—

[47] Scarborough 49.

[48] Lucretius does not, however, deal specifically with the problem of sex differentiation: R. Brown 322–23.

[49] Edwards 173–74 discusses this conception of vice and virtue, citing in particular Sen. *Dial.* 7.7.3.

[50] P. Brown 11, citing Galen *De semine* 1.16; Gleason has a similar discussion of sex types in the second century CE (see especially 390–92). Quintilian advises the orator to maintain bodily strength (*firmitas corporis*), lest "the voice be thinned out to the frailness of a eunuch, woman, or sick person" (*ne ad spadonum et mulierum et aegrorum exilitatem vox nostra tenuetur*; *Inst.* 11.3.19). Laqueur 126–27 describes Renaissance accounts of how a sudden increase in heat could change women into men.

then invective against effeminacy emerges as something more than mere
slander. The orator who accuses an opponent of feminine characteristics
—or indeed alleges that his adversary has actually undergone some form
of sexual transformation—now can be construed as not merely degrading a person's social standing: that is, in comparing a man to a woman
the attacker does not simply suggest that his opponent has the social
value of a woman. Rather, a preponderance of effeminate qualities in an
adversary would allow an opposing speaker to assert that an opponent
not only violates the boundaries of social propriety but represents a failure within nature itself. A recent study of effeminacy in Roman culture
claims that "we cannot assume that such behavior [i.e., effeminacy] was
seen as immoral only because it was associated with certain sexual practices."[51] Perhaps in a nonpolitical context effeminacy and a specific sexual stance could be separated. There is no question, however, that in late
Republican oratory effeminate qualities imply passive homoerotic activity and that this construct became represented as a marked failure in a
man with political pretensions.

The invective against physical peculiarities discussed in chapter 1 also
depends on a notion that human beings have deviated from their natural
state, or, to follow Cicero's formulation in *On the Laws*, from the workings of *iustitia*. This belief that a lapse from the natural order informs the
social danger of effeminacy finds direct expression in a text from 142 BCE,
wherein Scipio Aemilianus inveighs against Publius Sulpicius Galus:

> nam qui cotidie unguentatus adversus speculum ornetur, cuius supercilia
> radantur, qui barba vulsa feminibusque subvulsis ambulet, qui in conviviis
> adulescentulus cum amatore cum chiridota tunica inferior accubuerit, qui
> non modo vinosus, sed virosus quoque sit, eumne quisquam dubitet, quin
> idem fecerit, quod cinaedi facere solent? (Gell. 6.12.5 = *ORF* 21.17)

> For if someone, drenched daily in perfumes, adorns himself before a mirror,
> shaves his eyebrows, walks about with his beard plucked and thigh hairs
> pulled out; who, as a young boy with his lover, wearing a long-sleeved
> tunic, was accustomed to lie in the low spot at banquets, who is not only
> fond of wine, but fond of men also, then would anyone doubt that he has
> done the same thing that pathics usually do?

Galus openly flaunts effeminate traits; he wears perfumes, depilates face
and body, once banqueted with older lovers, and as an adult betrays a
fondness for other men. Aemilianus depicts Galus' natural sex struggling
against the socially constructed norms of Roman masculinity. In Aemilianus' formulation, a proper Roman observer can construe this behavior as nothing else than a perversion of nature. Galus, one must conclude,
is pathic.

---

[51] Edwards 77.

A Man for Every Woman, A Woman for Every Man

No man in the late Republic ever actually became a woman—at least so far as we know.[52] A man could, however, approach this transformation when certain characteristics commonly identified as effeminate began to affect his behavior. In humorous invective, an orator most frequently associates the manifestation of effeminate traits in an opponent with a presumed role as the penetrated male in a homoerotic relationship; the dominant partner, on the other hand, does not ever seem to have been the direct object of abuse for playing the active role.[53] Rhetorical invective against the sexually submissive male finds a parallel in the threats of anal rape (*pedicare*) and oral rape (*irrumare*) that recur in graffiti and invective poetry.[54] These two sexual threats serve similar purposes of degradation. At their most basic level, they make the opponent into an object of sexual violence, or at least into the plaything of another's sexual whims, and so expose the opponent as one who does not have control over his own body.[55] This rigid distinction between active and passive roles accounts for part of the repugnance to cunnilingus I describe in the previous chap-

[52] Plin. *Nat.* 7.36 does, however, consider cases in which women turned into men. For a modern discussion, see Bloom's account of female-to-male transsexuals, which contains many fascinating insights into the nature of a person's inherent gender.

[53] The only possible exception I know of depends upon an obscure pun on Antonius' sexual proclivities: *accessit ut, Caesare ignaro, cum esset ille Alexandreae, beneficio amicorum eius [Antonius] magister equitum constitueretur. tum existimavit se suo iure cum Hippia vivere et equos vectigalis Sergio mimo tradere*—"moreover, with Caesar ignorant since he was at Alexandria, Antonius was made 'master of the horse' through the kindness of [Caesar's] friends. At that point he decided it was his right to live with Hippias and give over to the actor Sergius profitable [?] horses" (*Phil.* 2.62). If Hippias is the *male mime* mentioned at Plut. *Ant.* 9.6 (though Shackleton Bailey questions Hippias' sex in his *Philippics* translation ad loc.), then Cicero jokes that Antonius' position as "master of the horse" (*magister equitum*) gives him the right (*suo iure*) to live with Hippias (from the Greek *hippos*, "horse") in a relationship in which Antonius presumably has the dominant role by dint of his office.

Active lovers can be derided for their excessive preoccupation with boys (although I know of no certain example from the late Republic). For the evidence, see MacMullen, esp. 488, 490 n. 21, 498; and Richlin 1992a, esp. 221–22, 224–25, 291, and index, s.v. "Pederasty." In this case, however, it seems to be not the sex of the partner that is faulted but the lover's enslavement to physical pleasure.

[54] See the discussion in Richlin 1981 and 1992a passim; Adams 124–30. Krenkel 1980: 77–80 provides a compendium of the various meanings of *irrumatio* throughout Roman life, concluding with a list of examples from the graffiti at Pompeii.

[55] The ancients generally—and in invective apparently always—perceived of male homoerotics as nonreciprocal: the beloved (*eromenos*) in a relationship would always play the passive role within that relationship and was portrayed as receiving little or no physical pleasure from the arrangement; cf. Dover 16, 100–109, passim, and more recently Halperin 30–38, who compares this polarization of sex roles to the larger social structure in Athens. On Rome, see Gonfroy, who traces links between sexual submission and servile status; Veyne 29–30, 33; Richlin 1992a, esp. 55–56; and Edwards 74–75, who discusses how "accusations of effeminacy may be seen as diluted threats of rape."

ter. For a Roman, subservience to a woman's desires implies sexual
passivity—and even ambiguity—in the male.

Accusations of womanlike behavior occur in a well-known passage
from Cicero's *Second Philippic*. In an earlier speech, Antonius, it seems,
claimed that Cicero had once been his teacher. Cicero replies that in fact
the young Antonius had never availed himself of the orator's instruction:

> ne tu, si id fecisses, melius famae, melius pudicitiae tuae consuluisses. sed
> neque fecisti nec, si cuperes, tibi id per C. Curionem facere licuisset. (*Phil.*
> 2.3)

> If you had in fact done that, you would have served your reputation and
> chastity better. But you didn't do it and, even if you wanted to, Gaius Curio
> wouldn't have let you.

Cicero implies that Antonius' role as Curio's beloved, a role he refers to
elsewhere in the speech (*Phil.* 2.44–45), explains in part his present moral
profligacy. Antonius' passive sexual position corresponds to an inability
to control his own moral upbringing. This formulation from 43 BCE explains the point of a joke dating from the previous century. Cornelia, the
mother of the Gracchi, had been slandered for having adulterous relations. Her son Gaius defended her from one attack as follows:

> ἐπεὶ δὲ διαβεβλημένος ἦν εἰς μαλακίαν ὁ λοιδορηθείς, [ὁ Γράγχος] "τίνα
> δὲ," εἶπεν, "ἔχων παρρησίαν συγκρίνεις Κορνηλίᾳ σεαυτόν; ἔτεκες γὰρ
> ὡς ἐκείνη; καὶ μὴν πάντες ἴσασι Ῥωμαῖοι πλείω χρόνον ἐκείνην ἀπ'
> ἀνδρὸς οὖσαν ἢ σὲ τὸν ἄνδρα." (Plut. *CG* 4.4)

> And when a man was hurling invective who was customarily accused of
> effeminacy, [Gracchus replied]: "What boldness of speech allows you to
> compare yourself with Cornelia? Did you give birth as she did? And besides,
> everyone in Rome knows that she spends more time in the absence of a man
> than you do, [although you are] a man."

Gracchus' barb implies that his unnamed opponent abandons features of
his masculinity by preferring to adopt the female role in his intercourse
with men. As a result of this denial of his true nature, he is less worthy of
respect than a woman. Other passages from the late Republic also show a
speaker relegating an opponent to a subservient status by alluding to his
submissive role in sexual situations.[56]

---

[56] These include a passage from Strabo's discussion of rhetorical wit in Cic. *De orat.*
2.265: *cum Sextus Titius se Cassandram esse diceret, "multos" inquit Antonius "possum tuos Aiaces
Oileos nominare"*—"When Sextus Titius kept calling himself a Cassandra, Antonius replied
'I can name a number of your Ajaxes.'" See also *Verr.* 2.3.159, 2.4.143, Plut. *Cic.* 7.7 =
Mor. 204f (all of Verres' son), and the remarks against Julius Caesar made by Calvus, Cic-
ero, and the triumphing soldiers (Suet. *Iul.* 49; similar accusations appear at *Aug.* 68, *Otho*

The invective against effeminacy strives to equate an opponent's status with that of a woman or even, as in the example just cited, with that of a failed woman. The abuse could go still further: humor often arises from depicting the opponent as threatening to become literally transformed into the opposite sex. For example, Cicero portrays the relationship between Antonius and Curio as a kind of marriage wherein Antonius rejects his maleness:

> sumpsisti virilem, quam statim muliebrem togam reddidisti. primo vulgare scortum; certa flagiti merces nec ea parva; sed cito Curio intervenit, qui te a meretricio quaestu abduxit et, tamquam stolam dedisset, in matrimonio stabili et certo collocavit. (*Phil.* 2.44)

> You donned the toga of an adult male, which you immediately turned into a woman's. At first [you were] a common whore; there was a fixed price for a trick—and not a small one; but Curio swiftly intervened and took you away from the prostitute's trade, settling you in a calm and stable marriage just as if he'd given you a wedding gown.

The ultimate degradation of the passive partner lies in equating not only his behavior but also his sex to that of a woman; later in the same speech, Curio is described as Antonius' husband (*vir*; *Phil.* 2.50). Other prominent Romans are described as women on account of their alleged intercourse with men: Bibulus publicly dubbed Julius Caesar the "Bithynian queen" for his relations with Nicomedes (Suet. *Iul.* 49), Cicero called Curio the younger "the little daughter of Curio" (*filiola Curionis*; *Att.* 1.14.5 = SB 14), and Clodius became "the people's female Appuleius" (*illa populi Appuleia*; *Att.* 4.11.2 = SB 86).

Public charges of effeminacy never, however, entirely negate the masculine vices of the accused: this type of invective often charges the opponent with the seemingly oxymoronic combination of passive, effeminate subservience and violent, male lust. The ambiguous halfway point between male and female provides the accuser with the unique opportunity of charging his opponent with the worst vices of both "sexes." In this case the danger is that the accused's physical makeup confuses distinctions that must remain clear. The effeminate male cannot recognize that the biological and social construction of maleness must coincide.

According to Suetonius, the elder Curio wished to show Caesar's reputation for both adultery and sodomy when he described Caesar in a

---

2.2). Occasionally—although not as often as is sometimes claimed—accusations of being a catamite do not seem to carry a literal force. See for example *Phil.* 2.77, where Cicero calls Antonius a *catamitus* in the middle of a narrative in which the orator tells of Antonius' secret visit to his wife. Even here, however, there occur references to Antonius' effeminate dress (*Phil.* 2.76).

public speech as "a man for all women and a woman for all men" (*omnium mulierum virum et omnium virorum mulierem*; Suet. *Iul.* 52.3). Cicero similarly scorns Verres as being a "man among women and a wanton little woman among men" (*vir inter mulieres, impura inter viros muliercula*; *Verr.* 2.2.192).[57] Parallel examples depict men engaging in both dominant and subservient sexual roles without any notion on the accuser's part that the charge seems to raise logical problems.[58] This realm of androgyny does not, however, simply indicate that there is "no consistency" on the part of the accuser.[59] Rather, the theoretical possibility that a man could lose his gender has opened up a legitimate space for invective. The "androgynous man" does not represent a breach of logic so much as a potential threat always inherent for the male.

It now remains to consider how the orator attempted to convey to his audience the truth behind these charges of effeminacy. We have repeatedly seen the need in invective for external, visible means of verification. And in fact, the extant texts from the Republic and other periods, including those writings outside oratory, reveal an awareness of a consistent set of features that were thought to characterize a dissipating masculinity.

[57] For the sarcastic use of *vir*, a word usually applied to Roman *nobiles*, and the word's stark contrast with *mulier*, normally reserved by Cicero for women of low social status, see Santoro L'Hoir, chaps. 1, 2. The same contrast occurs in *virilem . . . muliebrem* from *Phil.* 2.44, quoted in the text above.

[58] *Sest.* 20 (the effeminate Gabinius is a frequent adulterer), *Har. resp.* 42 (Clodius; cf. also *Pis.* 65, *Har. resp.* 59), *Phil.* 14.9; [Cic.] *Inv. in Sall.* 9 (Sallust cannot refrain from men; cf. 5.15, where all husbands are angry at Sallust's adultery); Catull. 57.1–2, 8–9; Liv. 39.15.9 (describing male celebrants at Bacchanalia); Sen. *Contr.* 1.praef.9; and, perhaps, the tantalizingly brief Lucilius 1048 (Warmington): *inberbi androgyni, barbati moechocinaedi.* Carson 154 n. 39 cites Greek texts where male adulterers are depicted as possessing effeminate traits. Sen. *Contr.* 2.1.6 offers an interesting possibility: young men act effeminate to attract women.

The notion of male/female flux may also explain a mysterious joke at *De orat.* 2.274: *"quid est tibi ista mulier?" "uxor." "similis me dius fidius"*—"Do you know that woman?" "[She's my] wife." "What a resemblance!" Wilkins ad loc. believes that "there is no need to find in [this remark] more than a joke *para prosdokian*: 'Ah, I thought she was some relation: she is so like you.'" The discussion in the text shows that the joke could be more barbed, implying effeminacy of the subject.

[59] The quoted phrase is from Richlin 1992a: 98, whose brief but well-documented account of rhetorical invective has been very helpful in shaping my own discussion, which I see as refining rather than substantially disagreeing with her observations. Edwards has proposed an alternative and intriguing explanation for this lustful man/woman: the effeminate male inherits all the negative qualities associated with women, including *incontinentia* (81–84). Hence he lusts after anything that will quench his desires. This hypothesis, however, seems to be contradicted by the passage from the elder Seneca with which Edwards opens her discussion, where the lust of the effeminate is described as a distinctly *male* trait ("in no way men except in lust"—*nusquam nisi in libidine viris*; *Contr.* 1.praef.10, quoted in text below).

The Category of the Effeminate Male

Effeminacy does not represent, as may first appear, a charge available at the whim of any accuser. Cicero's corpus contains no evidence that he himself was so charged, nor does the accusation enter the list of Vatinius' many vices.[60] In the case of Piso, it is applied only vaguely, chiefly through his affiliation with Gabinius. Yet in Cicero's treatise on humor in *On the Orator* book 2 the orator offers a mockery of effeminacy from the mid-second century BCE that at first sight appears to advise without reservation the use of such abuse:

> cum Q. Opimius consularis, qui adulescentulus male audisset, festivo homini Egilio, qui videretur mollior nec esset, dixisset "quid tu, Egilia mea? quando ad me venis cum tua colu et lana?" "non pol" inquit "audeo, nam me ad famosas vetuit mater accedere." (*De orat.* 2.277)

> The former consul Quintus Opimius, a man who'd had a bad reputation as a young boy, once had said to the witty Egilius—since he seemed rather effeminate (*mollior*) and [yet] was not—"What do you say, Egilia my girl? When are you coming over to my house with your distaff and wool?" Egilius replied, "I don't dare, by Pollux, since my mother has forbidden me to go near women with bad reputations."

Cicero relates this episode to demonstrate the attractions of wittily turning a charge back on an opponent (*est bellum illud quoque, ex quo is, qui dixit, inridetur in eo ipso genere, quo dixit*). It is significant, however, that the narrator has taken care to provide his reader with background on each of the participants in the anecdote. This background is essential for understanding the rhetorical advice being offered. The anecdote requires that the joke's audience know in advance about Opimius' notorious youth (*qui adulescentulus male audisset*). The hearers, then, must have some sensitivity to the truth of the charges being brought before them. Hence Opimius does not fail because his remark was not funny—this is not a relevant factor for Cicero's discussion. Rather, the humiliation of Opimius offers a clear warning to the potential orator that the substance of a charge must be verifiable. Opimius relied too much upon the signs of Egilius' effeminacy, signs that the joke's introduction reveals to be deceptive—Egilius only seemed effeminate (*qui videretur mollior nec esset*). Egilius, being accused by a speaker who lacks a proper regard for how to

---

[60] According to Plutarch, however, Verres accused Cicero of *malakia* (effeminacy) and implied that he was a passive homosexual (*Cic.* 7.7; *Mor.* 204f). Yet Cicero's reply to this charge seems to indicate that Verres did not address the orator by name.

use visible evidence, can then overcome the insult by referring to Opimius' infamous past.

Opimius cannot be faulted for thinking that Egilius' external appearance would incriminate him. In the late Republic, orators repeatedly appeal to specific external indicators—or groups of indicators—to demonstrate a male opponent's internal, effeminate character. For example, Cicero preserves the following "slight play on words" (*parva verbi immutatio*) that the elder Cato made in response to an anonymous opponent:

> si tu et adversus et aversus impudicus es. (*De orat.* 2.256)

> If both from the front and from behind you are a shamelessly effeminate male (*impudicus*).[61]

Cato mocks his opponent as a submissive homosexual with this charge of being "shameless from behind" (*aversus impudicus*). *Adversus* ("from the front"), in contrast, is usually taken to refer to the adversary's shameless way of speaking.[62] A passage from Gellius supplies a more satisfactory explanation:

> Plutarchus refert Arcesilaum philosophum vehementi verbo usum esse de quodam nimis delicato divite, qui incorruptus tamen et a stupro integer dicebatur, nam cum vocem eius infractam capillumque arte compositum et oculos ludibundos atque inlecebrae voluptatisque plenos videret: "nihil interest," inquit, "quibus membris cinaedi sitis, posterioribus an prioribus." (Gell. 3.5.1–2; cf. Plut. *Mor.* 126a, 705e)

> Plutarch relates that the philosopher Arcesilaus used strong language concerning a rich man [who was] exceedingly effeminate, but was said to be untainted and free from vice. For when [Arcesilaus] perceived his broken speech and artfully arranged hair and his playful eyes filled with charm and desire, he said, "It doesn't matter with what parts you're a submissive homosexual (*cinaedi*), those in back or those in front."

For Arcesilaus, the reputation of the rich man had no relevance; his exterior betrayed his true nature. The similarity between the witticisms of Cato and Arcesilaus may not be accidental; other passages from Cato's writings show the censor's familiarity with Greek aphorisms.[63] The "front parts" (*membra priora*) of the Arcesilaus episode and the "frontal

---

[61] As *OLD* notes s.v., *impudicus* (literally, "shameless") often refers explicitly to a passive homosexual (cf. *TLL* 7.1:711.37); that this is Cato's meaning here is clear from the parallel joke of Arcesilaus cited below in the text. Note that *impudicus* is also the word Seneca the younger uses of the pathic homosexual in *Epist.* 52.12 (quoted in the next paragraph of the text).

[62] So Monaco 1968 ad loc., following Turnebus.

[63] Astin 187–88.

shamelessness" (*adversus*) of Cato most likely refer, then, to the same
feature: the use of the mouth in fellatio. At the same time, however,
Cato, like Arcesilaus, must have found proof for these charges of effeminate behavior in his opponent's very appearance: the man's exterior indicates to an onlooker his hidden vice. The voice, hair, and eyes of the rich
man necessarily mark his effeminacy. This pair of anecdotes teaches an
important lesson. It does not matter how well immorality lies
concealed—one's true character will inevitably emerge in external signs.

A writer from the early Empire offers explicit testimony to a Roman
belief in the validity of external indicators. In one of Seneca's *Moral Epistles*, the philosopher teaches Lucilius how to distinguish unexamined ad-
ulation from true and considered praise. There is a difference, Seneca
affirms, between approval gained in the theater and at school. And how
does one determine the character of a critic? As in all areas of life, a clear
estimate of an individual's character arises from external factors:

> omnia rerum omnium, si observentur, indicia sunt, et argumentum morum
> ex minimis quoque licet capere: impudicum et incessus ostendit et manus
> mota et unum interdum responsum et relatus ad caput digitus et flexus ocu-
> lorum; improbum risus, insanum vultus habitusque demonstrat. illa enim in
> apertum per notas exeunt. (Sen. *Epist.* 52.12)

> There are all types of indicators for all things, provided they are attended to,
> and one may obtain evidence for character from even the smallest details:
> you can tell an effeminate man (*impudicus*) from his walk, from [the way] he
> moves his hands, from sometimes [even] a short reply, from [the way] he
> brings his finger up to his head, and from his eye movement. Laughter
> betrays the wicked man, expression and bearing the insane one. For those
> [qualities] come out into the open through signs.

When properly scrutinized, appearances do not deceive. Seneca seems
here to pass on a lesson he learned from his father, whose *Controversiae*—
collected in a handbook by the elder Seneca for his three sons—include a
diatribe against the youth of his day that shares all the same features of the
effeminate male, except for the reference to peculiar eye movement.[64]

---

[64] Eye movement is discussed by Cicero in his rhetorical works as an indicator of temporary, not permanent, character, and seems to be employed that way in his speeches (*Orat.*
60; *De orat.* 3.221–23).
I find the following links between the remarks of the two Senecas (the relationship
within these pairs will be elaborated in the text through parallels from the late Republic): (1)
incessus . . . et manus mota (*Epist.*) = *saltandi . . . studia* (*Contr.*), (2) *unum interdum responsum*
(*Epist.*) = *ad muliebres blanditias extenuare vocem* (*Contr.*), (3) *relatus ad caput digitus* (*Epist.*) =
capillum frangere and *immundissimis se excolere munditiis* (*Contr.*). I shall also discuss a fourth
element in the elder Seneca's text—depilation (*in istis vulsis atque expolitis*)—a practice that
the son, being concerned only with gesture and movement, does not include in his own list.

somnus languorque ac somno et languore turpior malarum rerum industria invasit animos: cantandi saltandique obscena studia effeminatos tenent, [et] capillum frangere et ad muliebres blanditias extenuare vocem, mollitia corporis certare cum feminis et immundissimis se excolere munditiis nostrorum adulescentum specimen est. quis aequalium vestrorum quid dicam satis ingeniosus satis studiosus, immo quis satis vir est? . . . ite nunc et in istis vulsis atque expolitis et nusquam nisi in libidine viris quaerite oratores. (Sen. *Contr.* 1.praef.8–9, 10)

Sleep and laziness and something more disgraceful than sleep and laziness— a passion for wicked deeds—have attacked their souls: obscene passion for singing and dancing has a hold on these effeminates. The model for our youths is in curling the hair, lightening the voice to the caressing sounds of a woman, competing with women in physical delicacy, and adorning themselves with unrefined finery. Which of your contemporaries is—how shall I say?—talented or studious enough? No; which is man enough? . . . Go on, look for orators among those [who are] depilated and smooth, in no way men except in lust.

This passage from the moralizing and conservative elder Seneca provides an important link between his son and the invective texts I have been considering. All the features that he describes as associated with effeminacy are found in representations of the late Republican banquet— singing, dancing, curled hair, womanly voices. As I proposed at the outset, late Republican invective against effeminacy tended to be conflated with fears of the immoderate feast.

I have argued that the effeminate banqueter is not simply a literary fiction, a composite figure patched together from the groundless anxieties of the orator's audience. Instead I presume that invective's efficacy requires at least some degree of correlation between the charges raised publicly and the realities of contemporary society. It is now time to consider the corollary to this claim: to what extent can the effeminate male be said to constitute a specific category of person?

During the past two decades scholars concerned with Greek antiquity have been attempting to clarify Greek attitudes toward male-to-male sexual conduct.[65] Recent debate has centered in particular on the distinctions

---

Quintilian (*Inst.* 5.9.14) also acknowledges the possibility of appealing to external signs of the effeminate male; he specifically mentions depilation (*corpus vulsum*), a mincing gait (*fractus incessus*), and feminine dress (*vestis muliebris*). In the anonymous Latin work *On Physiognomy*, the signs of the *effeminatus* correspond well with the categories mentioned by the younger Seneca (2.75–76 [Foerster]; cf. also 1.276, 1.415, 2.123; Aristotle *Phgn.* 808a12–16).

[65] Serious consideration of the subject began with Dover 1978. The wide-ranging survey of Boswell 1980 that followed has received much criticism for its contention that "gay people" have existed throughout the history of Western society; see the bibliography cited

between ancient and modern notions of homosexuality for, according to prominent researchers on sexuality, especially Michel Foucault, it is only since the late nineteenth century that male homoerotic behavior has played an integral role in the social definition of an individual. The societies of ancient Greece and Rome did not, they argue, attribute the same degree of importance to an individual's sexual orientation as does modern society. Preference for one type of erotic experience over another was "not a matter of typology involving the individual's very nature, the truth of his desire, or the natural legitimacy of his predilection."[66] Hence for the Greeks, at least, it is claimed that activity we in the twentieth century would label "homosexual" was simply a "set of acts" in which the sex of the person penetrated is irrelevant. Thus for them the sex of one's sexual partner did not occupy the same privileged position that it has in our culture in defining an individual's essence: "it is not immediately evident that differences in sexual preference are by their very nature more revealing about the temperament of individual human beings, more significant determinants of personal identification, than, for example, differences in dietary preference."[67] An individual's choice of sexual partner was not, according to this line of reasoning, considered an integral part of that person's character.

This Foucauldian model does not lack opponents. A careful reevaluation of legal evidence, biological writings, and social codes from classical Athens has cast considerable doubt on the notion that the Athenians viewed male–male sexual activity as both socially and morally equivalent to male–female intercourse.[68] Literary sources also provide obstacles to this claim. One central text is the speech of Aristophanes in Plato's *Symposium* (189c–193d), which purports to explain why human beings differ among each other in their choice of sexual partner—some men prefer men, some women prefer women, and the third group includes members of both sexes. In Aristophanes' speech, the desire of males for males represents not casual choice but "a whole way or tenor of life" that springs from sexuality.[69] Aristophanes clearly imagines male homoeroticism as a recognized part of a man's social identity. This debate over the

---

in Halperin 161 n. 32 and Boswell's own restatement of his views (1990). Patzer's study attempts to trace pederastic behavior to military ritual; see Halperin's critique (54–61).

[66] Foucault 1985: 190; see his entire discussion 187–203 and Halperin 15–40.

[67] Halperin 26, following Foucault; cf. Winkler 4. In a review of Halperin and Winkler, Thornton argues that their work has "seriously oversimplified Foucault's ideas" (182). Richlin 1993: 524–28 offers a detailed and convincing critique of the positions of Halperin and Winkler.

[68] Cohen 171–202; see esp. his assessment of legal attitudes toward pederasty in the context of the law of *hubris* (175–82).

[69] Thorp 58, who is responding to Halperin 18–21. Cf. Boswell 1990: 77; Golden 338; Cohen 190–92. Even Winkler admits that "*kinaidos* was a category of person, not just of acts," at least in so far as the *kinaidos* displayed deviant behavior (46).

ethical status of male homoerotic passion is by no means settled for
Greek antiquity. In the Roman Republic, however, I argue that a male's
choice of sexual partner was conceived of as an important component of
his social definition. Rhetorical invective from the period clearly demonstrates how public speakers used effeminate characteristics in their opponents to construct them as recognizable archetypes of a sexual "other."
There did exist a describable category of male, a person from whose
sexuality and sex-linked behavior the Roman orator strove to differenti-
ate himself.

Foucault did not treat the Roman Republic—and, arguably, hardly
treats Roman culture at all—in his survey of sexuality in the ancient
Mediterranean.[70] Certainly his assertion that, until recent centuries, the
"sodomite" was not defined by "a kind of interior androgyny, a her-
maphrodism of the soul," finds a clear refutation in the exegesis of the
younger Seneca quoted above, as well as in many of the texts I have cited
throughout this chapter.[71] For both Seneca's account and invective texts
from the late Republic are predicated on the notion that the signs by
which an observer may judge another person originate from the subject's
internal makeup—the identifiable traits, says Seneca, "come out into the
open" (*in apertum . . . exeunt*). This notion parallels the model for physical peculiarities discussed in chapter 1, by which external appearance
functions as a decipherable representation of internal morality.

A number of factors complicate the analysis of Roman sexual mores.
As I noted earlier, the influence of Greek prototypes is hard to disen-
tangle. Moreover, in contrast to those scholars who study the Greeks, the
cultural historian of Republican Rome must rely for evidence almost
solely on literary texts—no vase paintings or other modes of popular
expression exist in quantity sufficient to provide a meaningful counterpoint to the literary material.[72] There is, finally, the problem that compli-

[70] Cf. Richlin 1992a: xv–xvi on Foucault's neglect of Roman sources.

[71] Foucault 1980: 43; cf. 1985: 19, where, after discussing stereotypes of effeminacy in
the ancient world, Foucault asserts that it is "completely incorrect to interpret [these traits]
as a condemnation of . . . what we generally refer to as homosexual relations." Although
Foucault claims that he is only concerned with theoretical norms of behavior and not actual
practice (e.g., 1985: 12–13), statements such as these show him apparently violating his
own proscription.

Foucault's contention that the ancients had no conception of an "interior androgyny" is
also belied by Roman attitudes toward lesbians (a subject he neglects), to whom the extant
references "attribute male activities and apparatus" (Hallett 1989a: 221).

[72] For an exception, see Clarke, who analyzes male-male sexual acts depicted on Roman
drinking vessels of the early Empire. His observation that "all of the artists present the act
of lovemaking between males in a romantic, elevated manner" (284) certainly stands in
opposition to extant verbal descriptions that date to the Republic.

In a parallel example, Golden 332 notes how homoerotic acts are represented differently
on the Greek comic stage and in vase painting; cf. Halperin's addendum on how new

cates all studies of popular values in the ancient world: the bulk of the extant texts were produced by and for an elite minority. But careful analysis enables us to negotiate these apparent obstacles, as I have shown in my discussion of Cicero's attack on the peculiar physique of Gaius Fannius (chapter 1). In this passage, Cicero's appeal to his audience's predisposition against physical peculiarities revealed the importance Romans attached to physical appearance in determining an individual's moral character. In the case of invective against effeminacy it is also possible to recover at least in part the audience's presumed biases and predispositions. If a certain mode of life is represented publicly—even if only to be rejected—then the charges likely gain their force from some underlying reality.[73] One may argue to the contrary that since Latin apparently does not have a single word corresponding to our "homosexual," the speakers of Latin placed no importance on the role of male-to-male sexual encounters in a citizen's social definition—an interesting but by no means conclusive objection.[74] There may not have existed a particular word for such an individual, but he did possess a discrete set of signs. This set necessarily presupposes a specific category of men known for their pleasure, or at least complicity, in being sexually penetrated by other men. Although I willingly concede the Foucauldian point that this act may not constitute their sole defining moment as individuals, nevertheless their sexual role plays an integral part in their definition as responsible citizens.[75]

A recent study of the Roman construction of morality argues that since sexual invective was deployed for nonsexual ends—namely, the degradation of a prominent or potentially dangerous opponent—the group targeted by this type of abuse does not necessarily constitute a distinct, preexisting group of persons labeled as sexually deviant. The language of political abuse, it is claimed, is not what it appears: "in many cases to accuse a man of being susceptible to sexual penetration by other men was more a vivid metonymy for a generalised and pejorative claim that he

---

research into vase painting by Keith DeVries has forced him "to qualify or to moderate even further some of the already tentative general claims about the nature of Greek pederasty" (225).

[73] Beginning from passages in the praetor's edict on *infamia* (Ulp. *Dig.* 3.1.1), Richlin 1993 forcefully argues "first, that men identified as homosexuals really existed at Rome and, second, that their existence was marked both by homophobia within the culture and by social and civil restrictions" (530; see also 555–61). Thornton remarks on Foucault's neglect of the "problematic relationship between actual practice and public discourses" (183).

[74] For a critique of this line of argument see Boswell 1990: 69–70 and the remarks of D. Kennedy 29–30.

[75] Richlin 1993: 555–61 assesses whether, in the Republic, passive homosexuality could result in the curtailment of civil rights.

was effeminate rather than an accusation that could be directly related to the sexual preferences of the victim of the insult."[76] The assumption underlying this formulation is that it would be possible, had we more information, to distinguish between a set of Roman attitudes regarding "effeminacy" and a set regarding "sexual preference." Yet the gestures, movements, and dress of the effeminate male of late Republican invective cannot, as I have shown, be separated from an attendant sexuality. On the contrary, the male beloved is delimited by these very characteristics. Effeminacy connotes a specific sexuality. The precision with which the Romans defined the sexually passive male may best be shown by returning once again to the letter of Seneca quoted above. The polysyndeton of Seneca's formulation (*et . . . et . . . et . . . et . . . et*) makes it clear that he envisages all the different elements of his list as jointly characterizing the effeminate male (*impudicus*). Seneca provides a systematic formulation of the different features that cohere in the process of defining the passive male. It is surely no accident that these characteristics correspond to elements found in Ciceronian invective. Of course, it would be misguided to use these outward signs to define the precise nature of this group's sexuality. Yet our inability to supply such a definition does not thereby erase the group's existence.[77] Similarly, I do not wish to claim that frequent victims of this form of abuse, such as Marcus Antonius or Publius Clodius, were necessarily consciously aligned with a specific group of effeminate men. Yet the rhetorical power of the invective would seem to depend on the theoretical possibility that these people exist as a category of human beings. Once this is accepted, the next step, that there are actual persons who belong to this category, does not seem so difficult to take.

There is a point to be made before we return to primary texts from the Republic. As I have noted in previous chapters, standards of discretion and a desire for deniability affect the orator's choice of expression. If the orator uses too much detail in describing the sexual escapades of an opponent, he will risk losing his own respectability.[78] Hence there arose an alternative to the explicit description of homoerotic acts, an alternative that, as we have seen, was already widely accepted in the second century BCE: would anyone doubt but that a man displaying the typical characteristics "has done the same thing that pathics usually do" (Scipio Ae-

[76] Edwards 66–68. Edwards does, however, allow elsewhere for the reality of the sexual life of the accused: "This is not to say that there was no relationship between accusations of *mollitia* and certain sexual practices" (68); "sexual preference is taken to be the final test of whether or not [the hypocritical philosophers] are effeminate" (74).

[77] As assumed by Edwards 66: "There is little to suggest that Romans ever saw people with exclusively homosexual preferences as a distinct social group." She cites Veyne, MacMullen, and writings of Foucault in support of this assertion.

[78] See the discussion of Richlin 1992a: 13–26.

milianus in Gell. 6.12.5)? The speaker has access to a set of signs that allow him to raise specific charges, but to do so indirectly. Reference to these signs does not constitute mindless abuse; rather, the signs provide the audience with recognizable indications of immorality. The use of sexual discourse for political ends does not erase the fact that the discourse depends on physical and sexual relations.[79] We may never learn what precisely male-male sexual contact meant in Roman society; but unless, as was the case with physical peculiarities, we simply assume a gullible audience willing to be duped by a skillful orator, we must expect there to be some truth behind these constructions of effeminacy. I have consistently claimed that the Roman orator constructs beliefs not out of whole cloth but out of prejudices and biases already present in his society. A recognition of this process revives a reader's confidence in the relation between Roman beliefs and the orator's constructed reality, thereby increasing respect for the judgment of the Roman audience. In the remainder of my discussion, I shall concentrate on public invective texts—texts that refer to real persons—using others only to support my conclusions. In these oratorical passages the depictions of the effeminate male are meant to persuade. Are we to believe that an artistic construct entirely abstracted from reality could be so convincing?

Effeminate Signs

The indicators of effeminacy that the Roman orator employs fall into three basic categories: dress, adornment, and physical movement and gestures. These categories will of course overlap; as I observed in discussing banqueting themes, such fluid boundaries enable the orator to incriminate his opponent in seemingly different vices, while at the same time allowing deniability. Each individual item of visual evidence provides sufficient proof of deviance.

The mockery of effeminate dress at Rome has a heritage dating back to our earliest extant texts. In Plautus' *Menaechmi*, men who cross-dress change their sexual identity with their clothing. Menaechmus I, for example, identifies himself as Ganymede, Jupiter's boy lover, while wearing a woman's *palla* (*Men.* 143). Later in the same play, the parasite Peniculus accuses Menaechmus' twin of being the one who had sported woman's clothing. Menaechmus II responds threateningly:

> vae capiti tuo.
> omnis cinaedos esse censes, tu quia es?
> tun med indutum fuisse pallam praedicas?

(*Men.* 513–15)

---

[79] Foucault 1985: 12 encounters the same problem in his distinction between "discourses about sexuality" and "sexuality."

Watch what you say.
Do you think everyone is a passive homosexual (*cinaedos*) because you are?
Do you claim that I put on a woman's cloak?

The notion being mocked in this episode—that if a man puts on women's clothing it means he has feminine tendencies in sexual matters—has Greek precedents in both Old Comedy and oratory.[80] By the time of the late Republic, although this type of joke still occurs in the ridicule of effeminate men, it depends no longer upon a man wearing women's clothing per se but upon his wearing a type of clothing not normally worn by a Roman male. Long, flowing tunics, reaching to the ankles (*talaris tunica*) and wrists (*manicata tunica*), marked the effeminate male. In fact, the state of being "loosely belted" (*discinctus*) became the metaphorical equivalent to having an effeminate lifestyle.[81] As a result of these associations, Horace need merely describe a man as wearing "low-hanging tunics" for his reader to understand the implied sexual connotation.[82] In choice of dress, the orator found a readily available—and socially recognized—sign of deviance.

Such cumbersome garb must have hindered a person's normal range of movement. In the *Philippics*, Cicero couples the physical helplessness of a man in womanish clothing with the subservient role of a passive homosexual. The orator, after recounting the many Greek towns Gaius Antonius has succeeded in occupying, does not wish the senate to dwell too long on his enemy's prowess. Consequently, he adds the following disclaimer:

> quamquam miror tam diu morari Antonium; solet enim ipse accipere manicas nec diutius obsidionis metum sustinere. (*Phil*. 11.26)

> Yet I'm surprised that Antonius is waiting around for so long, since he usually welcomes wrist restraints (*manicas*) and does not endure for very long the fear of siege.

The double entendre refers ostensibly to Antonius' physical cowardice, to his normal willingness to accept handcuffs (*manica*) and to surrender when threatened with assault. At the same time, however, the phrase "to welcome wrist restraints" (*accipere manicas*) suggests Antonius' predilec-

---

[80] Aristophanes: Geffcken 83–84; oratory: Dover 75–76.

[81] *Discinctus* seems to have come to indicate loose morals by contrast to the "well-girt" soldier (*praecinctus*): see *TLL* 5.1:1316.59–66; Richlin 1992a: 92, 1993: 542 n. 45.

[82] Hor. *Sat*. 1.2.25 (*tunicis demissis*); see Rudd 143. Similarly, after describing Maecenas strolling through Rome "in loosened tunics" (*solutis tunicis*), Seneca remarks how the man's eunuchs are "more masculine than their master" (*magis tamen viri quam ipse*, Sen. *Epist*. 114.6; cf. 92.35). Quintilian explicitly states that a tunic worn below the knees is feminine (*Inst*. 11.3.138).

Bremmer 19 and n. 11 catalogues similar associations for the Greek world.

tion for the effeminate, wrist-length tunic (*tunica manicata*), while the siege metaphor describes his sexual subservience to other males.[83] The collocation of the mockery of clothing and sexual orientation recalls Scipio Aemilianus' critique of Galus, who as a young boy lay at banquets *cum amatore cum chiridota tunica*—"with a lover [and] a tunic reaching to the hands." Note that both features of Galus are described by a phrase that begins with the preposition *cum* and are emphasized by asyndeton; as in the *Philippics* passage, where infinitives are syntactically parallel (*accipere . . . nec . . . sustinere*), a grammatical construction reinforces the semantic connection: way of dress and its attendant sexual passivity call into question the legitimacy of Antonius' apparent military success.

The long tunic offered an indicator to which an orator could point when he wished to ridicule an opponent publicly. An opposite tendency—to gird up the toga, presumably to allow greater freedom of movement—also conveyed effeminacy. Although seemingly contradictory, these two restrictions in fact align upon the same axis of belief. Both extremes of dress indicate that no explicit comparison is intended either with feminine or with Greek or Eastern ways of dress. The manner of dress of the effeminate Roman draws its importance, rather, from what it is not: that is, its difference from standard and acceptable masculine appearance. For, according to Cicero, both a leisurely walk and hurried movement betray the same fault: a lack of firm resolution (*constantia*; *Off.* 1.131).

Cicero concludes his second oration against Catiline with a list of six different groups of people at Rome out of which the conspirator has composed his forces (*Catil.* 2.17–23). At the bottom of the orator's catalogue resides the lowest form of humanity:

> postremum autem genus est, non solum numero, verum etiam genere ipso atque vita; quod proprium est Catilinae, de eius dilectu, immo vero de complexu eius ac sinu; quos pexo capillo nitidos aut imberbis aut bene barbatos videtis, manicatis et talaribus tunicis, velis amictos, non togis; quorum omnis industria vitae et vigilandi labor in antelucanis cenis expromitur. (*Catil.* 2.22)

And finally there is the group [that is] last not only in my enumeration but also in its very character and way of life. It's Catiline's own group, coming

---

[83] Shackleton Bailey 1982: 225–26 interprets the siege metaphor as I do and cites possible parallels. He believes, however, that the connection of *manicae* with effeminacy "has no relevance here" because a parallel use at Verg. *Aen.* 9.616 refers to "sleeveless tunics" (225; he appears to follow Servius' interpretation here). It seems much more likely to me, however, that both the infinitive phrases following *solet* should have a double meaning; hence I understand, together with *OLD*, that *manicae* both here and in the *Aeneid* passage refer not to a kind of glove but to the "shackling" of the wrist by the long-sleeved tunic.

from his levy—or should I say from his close embrace. You see them, glis-
tening with their coifed hair, either without beards or with long ones, wearing ankle- and wrist-length tunics, and cloaked in sails, not togas. The entire drive of their life and sleepless labor is used up in predawn feasting.

The phrase "from his close embrace" (*de complexu eius ac sinu*), combined
with the mention of the long-flowing clothing, alludes to the effeminate
tendencies of this last group. These followers of Catiline hardly threaten
physical violence; it is their way of life that endangers the state.[84] The
description continues by delineating still further their androgynous
character—"in these packs roam all adulterers, all the unchaste and pathic. These boys, so sleek and delicate, have learned to love and to be
loved" (*in his gregibus . . . omnes adulteri, omnes impuri impudicique versan-
tur. hi pueri tam lepidi ac delicati . . . amare et amari . . . didicerunt; Catil.*
2.23)—and finally concludes with the previously cited joke about their
infatuation with dancing. The familiar amalgamation of feasting, as-
sorted sexual activity, and the dance resurfaces. Cicero points explicitly
to the visual cues of these vices with the direct address to the audience,
videtis ("you see"). Most prominent among these visual markers is
clothing. The conspirators wear clothes that can only be compared to
something not belonging to a proper wardrobe—a ship's sail; they do
not wear the proper mark of the Roman male, the toga.[85] External garb
betrays internal intention.

Distinction in dress also informs Cicero's ironic rebuttal to Clodius'
charge that the orator, being born in Arpinum, is a non-Roman:

> rusticos ei [Clodio] nos videri minus est mirandum, qui manicatam tunicam
> et mitram et purpureas fascias habere non possumus. (*In Clod.* 22)

> I shouldn't be surprised that I seem rustic to Clodius, since I can't wear a
> tunic that reaches to the wrist and a headband and purple garlands.

Cicero turns Clodius' accusation back upon his opponent. The orator
claims before the senate that Clodius thinks that to be Roman means to
sport exotic and effeminate clothing.[86] Through obvious irony, Cicero

---

[84] The description of Catiline's group by the historian Sallust contains the same elements
of censure. His group includes "whatever pathic, glutton, and gambler had destroyed his
patrimony with his hand, stomach, and penis" (*quicumque impudicus ganeo aleator manu ventre
pene bona patria laceraverat; Cat.* 14.2). May 51–58 examines how such descriptions contribute to Cicero's overall portrayal of the conspirators.

[85] For the loose toga as a mark of excessive refinement, see Smith ad Tibull. 1.6.40;
Tracy 60. For the converse case of the stern Roman in a scanty toga, see Hor. *Epist.* 1.18.30,
1.19.13.

[86] The wearing of purple occurs as an element of invective at *Clu.* 111, *Catil.* 2.5, and
Cael. 77 (where the prosecution apparently used this charge against Caelius). Tracy 60 lists
other disreputable colors.

implies that anyone with such a skewed notion of appearance represents a less acceptable Roman than a provincial such as himself.

Cicero's abuse of Clodius' clothing presents a special case on account of the Bona Dea affair of 62 BCE, in which the future tribune masqueraded as a woman to penetrate religious rites traditionally restricted to Roman matrons. The disguise allowed Cicero to call into doubt his opponent's masculinity on numerous later occasions: in the speech *On Behalf of His Home*, Cicero applies a familiar formulation to Clodius, calling him "contrary to what is right, often both a woman among men and a man among women" (*contra fas et inter viros saepe mulier et inter mulieres vir*; *Dom.* 139); he was murdered not because Milo had ambushed him but because "a woman had fallen upon men" (*mulier inciderat in viros*; *Mil.* 55). On this same occasion, Cicero jokes that Clodius was acquitted of impiety because the jury had decided a man (*vir*) had not witnessed the rites (*In Clod.* 4; cf. Schol. Bob. p. 86, 23–27 [Stangl]). By the time of Cicero's later invective, Clodius has become a male prostitute, pimping himself for the most prominent politicians of the day.[87] Effeminacy did not, however, prevent Clodius' still-male physique from practicing the worst manifestations of lust: Cicero's many jokes about Clodius' incestuous cravings for his sister are well-known, and the orator twice refers to a double vice of Clodius, who engages in sex with matrons at the Bona Dea rites while dressed as a woman (*Har. resp.* 8; *In Clod.* 23).[88] As I shall demonstrate in the next chapter when discussing Julius Caesar, Clodius' character exposes him to a twofold attack that reveals his double threat. A man's taking on effeminate dress can do more than provide an indication of sexual character; it can also, when the occasion demands, create that character.[89]

Closely allied to dress as an indicator of effeminacy is cosmetic adornment, which can include depilation, the wearing of perfumes, and fastidious concern for the hair.[90] All three features occur in both Scipio's abuse

---

[87] *Sest.* 39, 46, 48, 52; *Har. resp.* 1. Skinner 202–3 discusses these passages in the context of Catull. 79.

[88] Geffcken 82 discusses at greater length the significance of Clodius' apparel. Although her discussion primarily concentrates on the festive and comic elements of Cicero's technique, she also makes interesting observations on the connection between cross-dressing and homosexuality.

[89] Verres provides a notable exception; he is described as wearing feminine apparel while "leaning on a woman on the seashore" (*muliercula nixus in litore*; *Verr.* 2.5.86). Richlin 1992a: 101 remarks that Verres probably could escape charges of homosexuality because of "the notoriety of his excessive heterosexuality." As noted above, however, Cicero does at one point call Verres *impura muliercula* (*Verr.* 2.2.192). On legislation that curtails what clothes a Roman man might wear, see Manfredini 260–71; Dalla 18–23.

The notion that changing dress can alter sexual desire has been a common belief throughout the history of Western culture; see Garber passim.

[90] Colin 1955: 10–13 provides a long list of passages from the late Republic concerning perfumed men; for additional examples, see Griffin 93.

of Galus (*cotidie unguentatus, . . . supercilia radantur, . . . barba vulsa feminibusque subvulsis*) and Cicero's description of Catiline's "lowest class of humanity" (*pexo capillo, nitidos*). Similarly, the elder Seneca rebukes the tendency among the youth of his day "to primp themselves with unrefined finery" (*immundissimis se excolere munditiis*; *Contr.* 1.praef.9). The connections between such adornment and the feminization of the male are clear. In the *Third Philippic*, Cicero justifies Decimus Brutus' attack on the consul Antonius on the grounds that "one cannot tolerate serving an impure, unchaste, effeminate who is never, not even while afraid, sober" (*intolerabile est servire impuro, impudico, effeminato; numquam, ne in metu quidem, sobrio*; *Phil.* 3.12). The orator then begins his narration of the attempted crowning of Caesar at the Lupercal by describing Antonius holding a public assembly while "naked, perfumed, [and] drunk" (*nudus unctus ebrius*). The adjectives all recall the feast, together legitimating the earlier charge of effeminacy.

Adornment of the hair leads to effeminate gesture. The younger Seneca included among the indications of sexual submission "bringing the finger to the head" (*relatus ad caput digitus*; *Epist.* 52.12). Public figures in the late Republic also appeal to this mysterious sign in order to degrade an opponent. Pompeius provided an especially attractive target. Plutarch relates how in the year 56 BCE Pompeius neglected public affairs to spend time with his new, young wife. His eventual reappearance in the forum prompted Clodius to lead a group of supporters in the following taunt:

"τίς ἐστιν αὐτοκράτωρ ἀκόλαστος; τίς ἀνὴρ ἄνδρα ζητεῖ; τίς ἑνὶ δακτύλῳ κνᾶται τὴν κεφαλήν;" οἱ δὲ [πολλοὶ], ὥσπερ χορὸς εἰς ἀμοιβαῖα συγκεκροτημένος, ἐκείνου τὴν τήβεννον ἀνασείοντος ἐφ᾽ ἑκάστῳ μέγα βοῶντες ἀπεκρίναντο "Πομπήιος." (Plut. *Pomp.* 48.7)

"Who is the licentious general? What man is looking for a man? Who scratches his head with one finger?" As Clodius pulled up his toga and

---

The indicators I list in the text are those I have found employed in the extant works of Cicero and in other late Republican authors. The list is not, however, necessarily complete: Isidorus cites a passage from a speech of Gaius Gracchus to show that in the second century the wearing of more than one ring betokened effeminacy: *considerate, Quirites, sinistram eius; en, quouis auctoritatem sequimini, qui propter mulierum cupiditatem ut mulier est ornatus* ("Examine his left hand, citizens; do you see? This man whose authority you follow has, on account of his desire for women, adorned himself like a woman"; *ORF* 48.58). I know of no similar example from the late Republic of the use of this sign, but see Hor. *Sat.* 2.7.9; Quint. *Inst.* 11.3.142. The younger Seneca echoes Gracchus' concern when he laments a contemporary glut of effeminacy: *exornamus anulis digitos, in omni articulo gemma disponitur* ("We adorn our fingers with rings; on every joint a jewel is on display"; *Nat.* 7.31.2). This passage from Seneca also contains references to males employing depilation and feminine adornments: *levitate et politura corporum muliebres munditias antecessimus* ("In the smoothness and slickness of our bodies we've surpassed the finery of women").

shook it, the mob, just like a chorus well-trained in responsion, answered each time with a loud shout: "Pompeius!"

Clodius, it seems, prompts the crowd's response by improvising his own drag show: he pulls up his toga to match the stereotypic dress of the effeminate man (ἐκείνου τὴν τήβεννον ἀνασείοντος). The added conceit of scratching the head with one finger enjoyed wide popularity.[91] According to one functionalist interpretation of the gesture, the effeminate man scratches with a single finger so as not to disturb his carefully prepared hairstyle.[92] Other sources support this hypothesis. A letter of Cicero reveals that he too had concerns about Pompeius adopting a foppish demeanor, and contemporaneous images of the general show his desire to emulate the wind-blown hairstyle of Alexander the Great.[93] A remark by Cicero preserved in Plutarch further supports this connection between gesture and fastidious appearance: the orator once remarked that he had not thought Julius Caesar capable of overthrowing the Roman state, since he used to see Caesar "having such exquisitely arranged hair and scratching himself with one finger" (*Caes.* 4.9). The same collocation of an effeminate male's nice hairstyle and habit of head scratching occurs in Lucian (*Rhet. praec.* 11). This association of adorned hair and effeminacy also accords with an observation that has been made throughout these pages: the elements of feasting and effeminacy, with their shared unguents and adornment, continually intertwine as a topic for invective. A fastidious concern for the hair harmonizes well with the Roman stereotype of the effeminately adorned male.

The womanlike walk constitutes another physical affectation that invited ridicule in the late Republic. A joke of Cicero demonstrates that the Romans identified with each sex a certain style of stride:

Cicero . . . cum Piso gener eius mollius incederet, filia autem concitatius, ait filiae "ambula tamquam vir." (Macr. *Sat.* 2.3.16)

[91] For the application of this abuse to Pompeius, see also Calvus *FPL* 18 (Morel): *Magnus, quem metuunt omnes, digito caput uno / scalpit: quid credis hunc sibi velle? virum* ("Magnus, whom everybody fears, itches his head with one finger. What do you think he wants? A man"); Plut. *Mor.* 89e, 800e, *Pomp.* 48.7; Ammianus 17.11.4. A general reference to *pathici* using this gesture occurs at Iuv. 9.133.

[92] So Courtney, on Iuv. 9.133; cf. Suet. *Aug.* 68. Onians 138, on the other hand, attributes this belief to an ancient notion that the head contained "the generative soul," which had an "itching" whenever sex was desired. Onians's explanation, however, fails to account for why emphasis is placed in all our sources on the use of only *one* finger (Seneca does not specify "one," but does use the singular *digitus*), and why this gesture indicates only homosexual tendencies and not simply general sexual desire.

[93] *Att.* 2.3.1 (SB 23); Cicero does not mention specifically Pompeius' hairstyle. I discuss Pompeius' alleged effeminacy in more detail in chapter 5.

> Since his son-in-law Piso walked rather daintily, whereas his daughter walked with too much bustle, Cicero said to his daughter, "Walk like a man—*your* man."

Women were expected to walk slowly and softly, whereas men should move with quick determination.[94] The joke centers on the unexpected force of *vir*, "husband"; the word's normal meaning, "man," cannot apply to Piso's unvirile delicacy. Other Roman authors explicitly associate effeminate males with a specific manner of movement and carriage of the body that they describe with forms of the verb *incedere*. Juvenal, for example, notes of the *cinaedus* Peribomius that "he admits his perversity with his expression and his gait" (*vultu morbum incessuque fatetur*, 2.17), and Seneca includes *incessus* as one of the marks of the *impudicus* (*Epist.* 52.12; cf. *Nat.* 7.31.2: *tenero et molli ingressu suspendimus gradum; non ambulamus sed incedimus*—"we suspend our step in a dainty and soft stride; we don't walk, we glide"). In the case of this indicator, the long flowing tunics worn by the alleged effeminate may have forced him to affect a slow, swaying gait in the manner of a woman (see Hor. *Sat.* 1.2.25), but it is more likely that, as was the case with a person's physical appearance, a womanly stride supplied physiological evidence that a man was undergoing an internal transformation. This transformation, conversely, revealed itself in external traits.

In his speech *On Behalf of Sestius*, Cicero encourages his audience to observe an opponent's gait (*incessus*) in order to determine moral character. An exhortation to the jury finds Cicero commenting on the differing strides of the former consuls Piso and Gabinius:

> quorum, per deos immortales! si nondum scelera vulneraque inusta rei publicae vultis recordari, vultum atque incessum animis intuemini. (*Sest.* 17)

> By the immortal gods! if you don't want to recall so soon the crimes and wounds that they have branded on the state, then consider in your minds their expression and gait (*incessus*).

Other passages from his orations show that Cicero refers in the case of Piso to a stately stride, by which Piso allegedly impersonates a stern and noble Roman.[95] But for Gabinius, *incessus* surely refers to his notorious effeminacy, which Cicero immediately recalls in the portrait of the former consul that follows the quoted injunction to the jury (*Sest.* 18). In the passage cited, then, Cicero pretends to allay the pain of recollecting the

---

[94] Housman 163 believes there is a lacuna after *vir*, which he fills with *at genero "ambula tamquam femina"* ("But he said to his son-in-law, 'Walk like a woman—*your* woman'").

Gleason 1991: 392–93 describes perceptions of walking in later antiquity.

[95] I shall discuss Piso's hypocritical appearance in detail at the end of this chapter. For his feigned gait, see *Pis.* 24–25 and *Sest.* 19.

wrongs Piso and Gabinius have done the state by prefacing the account of
these wrongs with a portrait of the two men. This portrait will demonstrate how their evil natures could have been foreshadowed by, among
other things, the way they walked.

Another passage in which Cicero derides an opponent's walk brings us
back to the dance. After mocking Clodius' dress in the invective speech
Against Clodius and Curio (22, quoted above), Cicero continues his abuse
as follows:

> tu vero festivus, tu elegans, tu solus urbanus, quem decet muliebris ornatus,
> quem incessus psaltriae, qui effeminare vultum, attenuare vocem, laevare
> corpus potes. (*In Clod.* 22)

> But you alone are pleasant company, charming and witty. A woman's dress
> and a music girl's walk become you, a man who can adopt a womanish
> expression, speak in a high voice, and lightly lift the body.

Womanly garb fits Clodius, who puts on a new sex together with his
new clothing. The mention of the "music girl" (*psaltria*) and the phrase
"to lift lightly the body" (*laevare corpus*) recall dancing, which further
implicates the now effeminate Clodius in immorality by associating him
with the immoderate feast.[96] Gabinius participates in the same figural
banquet as Clodius. In the speech *Against Piso*, Cicero describes Piso as
emerging from a shadowy drinking hall with Gabinius, "that coifed
dancing girl" (*cum illa saltatrice tonsa*; *Pis.* 18).[97] I have already presented a
number of passages in which Cicero alerts his audience to Gabinius' passion for men; the reference to his love of dancing reaffirms this
characterization.

The charge also lay at hand for attacking an opposing speaker. Cicero
tells us how Sextus Titius, tribune of the plebs for 99 BCE, was a fine
orator, but his "gestures were so loose and delicate that a dance, the
'Titius,' was named after him" (*tam [erat] solutus et mollis in gestu, ut saltatio quaedam nasceretur, cui saltationi Titius nomen esset*; *Brut.* 225). It seems
likely that Cicero derives his information from a speech in which an opposing speaker derided Titius for his effeminacy and, in so doing, used
the tribune's external gestures as evidence for internal character. This
tactic was certainly used publicly against the orator Hortensius. Aulus
Gellius relates how this famous speaker often received abuse for his effeminate dress and gestures, reporting that Lucius Torquatus called him a
"female mime" and "addressed him as Dionysia, using the name of a

[96] Through references to passages from New Comedy, Geffcken 86 connects the *psaltria*
and the dance in Cicero's accusation here.

[97] Nisbet 1961 ad loc. thinks *tonsa* refers to Gabinius' fastidiously well-trimmed hair,
which is elsewhere described as being unusually long. As I have noted, such a concern for
hairstyle does indeed constitute the character of a Roman *effeminatus*.

notorious female dancer" (*gesticulariam Dionysiamque eum notissimae salta-
triculae nomine appellaret*, Gell. 1.5.2–3). Again an orator takes advantage
of external indicators in an attempt to reveal to his audience the "true
nature" of an adversary and to show that the testimony of his opponent, a
failed male, is not to be credited.[98]

The Roman orator could use a number of external indicators to implicate his opponent in effeminacy. Two signs listed by Seneca in his letter
to Lucilius remain: the pitch of the voice (*unum interdum responsum*) and
eye movement (*flexus oculorum*). Voice quality, a sign that betrays the
effeminate male in the physiognomic writers as well, is occasionally alluded to in the late Republic as a sign of effeminacy.[99] I have already
mentioned how Clodius' "metamorphosis" into a dancing girl includes
the thinning out of his voice (*In Clod*. 22). The orator Hortensius, in his
comeback to the slander of Torquatus just mentioned, alters the tone of
his voice as a way of impersonating an effeminate, dancing male (*voce
molli atque demissa*; Gell. 1.5.3). This form of mimesis seems to have been
a practice common among other public speakers of the period. Quintilian records how voice inflection played a role in *prosopopoeia*, a rhetorical technique in which the orator impersonates an absent or imaginary
speaker (*Inst*. 11.1.39). Orators undoubtedly employed still more vocal
tricks that are difficult, if not impossible, to detect in our written texts.
Eye movement, so far as I can discover, is not the subject of mockery in
our extant court speeches. Cicero does, however, frequently bid his audience to consider the eyes (*oculi*) of his opponent, but without specifying
what type of eyes signifies what type of character. For this information,
one can turn to the writers on physiognomy, whose findings often correspond with the categories of Ciceronian invective.[100]

The illicit banquets decried in Roman invective provide an effective
counterpoint to the activities of a proper Roman citizen. The verisimili-

---

[98] In Torquatus' case, it seems, his joke backfired. Gellius notes Hortensius' response:
*tum voce molli atque demissa Hortensius "Dionysia" inquit "Dionysia malo equidem esse quam quod
tu, Torquate,* ἄμουσος ἀναφρόδιτος ἀπροσδιόνυσος" ("Then Hortensius responded with a
soft and gentle voice, 'Dionysia? I much prefer to be a Dionysia than what you are,
Torquatus—without a muse, without Aphrodite, without Dionysus'").

[99] For the physiognomic treatises see 1.162.4, 2.135.3 (Foerster). Gleason 1995: 82–121
provides a full survey of the importance of the voice both in rhetorical treatises and in a
Roman's daily regime and self-presentation.

[100] For references to the eyes in Cicero's rhetorical works, see n. 64 above. The anonymous Latin compiler of physiognomy, following Polemo (for whom see Gleason 1995: 32),
spends twenty-four Teubner paragraphs discussing the meaning of various kinds of eyes,
calling it "the most important part of all physiognomical science" (*summa omnis physiog-
nomoniae*; 2.31 [Foerster]). Nevertheless, he still claims to have hardly exhausted the subject
(2.61). For other correspondences between the physiognomical treatises and Ciceronian
invective, see chapter 1, n. 37; above, nn. 46, 64; below, nn. 101, 102.

tude of these descriptions should not concern us any more than they did the Roman orator. In order not to implicate himself in the very vices he intends to attach to his opponent, the speaker must stand at a safe distance, certain of the banquet's corruption but unclear on any details that may betray personal involvement. This precarious position partly explains the rhetorical convergence of the effeminate male and convivial excess. The effeminate male displayed an easily defined appearance; his internal character emerged through his dress, adornment, and physical movement. By latching on to these available signs, the speaker conjured up an illicit world within which his opponent operated, a world of fluctuating gender and ambiguous sexuality. The realm of the banquet may escape precise description but its chief participant, under the scrutiny of a properly informed jury, stands ready to be exposed.

CODA: PISO TESTS THE RULES

And had I the scourging of sinners, I should deal
hardest with those who belie and betray the promises
that nature has planted on their brows.
—Montaigne, "On Physiognomy" 338

In the political sphere of the late Roman Republic, the external characteristics of an individual carried great representational meaning. Physical appearance, name, gestures, and dress could all contribute to an outsider's assessment of one's internal moral character. In these first four chapters I have shown how Roman political humor depended upon these constructed categories in maintaining social stability. By emphasizing an individual's projected persona, a Roman political figure could both exclude his opponents from society and at the same time display confidence in the workings of nature: if one can judge a person's moral character simply by visual scrutiny—and give proof of that character to others— then all bodes well for the state. For Cicero as orator, the stern figure of Lucius Calpurnius Piso, consul of 58 BCE, embodied a threat to this sense of security.

Piso presented Cicero's invective with a difficult rhetorical problem: in every aspect of Piso's outward appearance—in body, name, walk, and dress—he appeared to convey the qualities of a sincere, stern-faced Roman of old. As a result, the primary thrust of Cicero's attack on Piso is that his opponent's physical appearance in fact *belies* his true, morally repugnant nature. In devising this attack, the orator follows a familiar stratagem: the rhetorical handbooks advise that if an accuser faces an upright and morally sound defendant, he should claim that the accused has up until this point been hypocritically concealing his own faults.[101] Piso's political prominence allows Cicero to go even further: not only has his opponent concealed faults in order to avoid incurring guilt, but he has in fact hidden his very nature in order to secure personal political advancement to the detriment of the state. Yet Cicero's invective against Piso does not depend simply upon rhetoric for its persuasive power. Even if one recognizes a rhetorical debt in Cicero's presentation here, this does not mean that the orator does not appeal to ethical biases already present in his audience. Rather, one may best understand Cicero's attack on Piso in the context of Roman attitudes toward what constitutes a socially and politically correct male. In discussing Cicero's invective against Piso, I will follow the order of my first four chapters: physical peculiarities, name, movement and dress. Each aspect of Piso that the orator chooses to focus on represents the obverse of nearly every negative feature of Roman self-definition that I have analyzed. If one were to use the ethical criteria of Roman invective, Piso would appear unassailable.

Piso's physical appearance, writes Cicero, unjustly effected his political advancement—"your eyes, brows, forehead, in sum your entire expression (which is a kind of silent speech of the mind), *this* caused men to be deceived, *this* confused, beguiled, and misled those who were not familiar with you" (*oculi, supercilia, frons, voltus denique totus, qui sermo quidam tacitus mentis est, hic in fraudem homines impulit, hic eos quibus eras ignotus decepit, fefellit, induxit*; *Pis*. 1). Indeed, his stern eyebrows alone represented "a pledge to the state" (*pignus rei publicae*; *Sest*. 19).[102] Piso's appearance deceives almost everyone, from Greek philosophers (*Pis*. 68, 70) to the citizens of Capua, who, Cicero jests, actually *wanted* Piso to be an immoral magistrate (*Pis*. 24). The frequency with which Cicero employs this motif of Piso's physical hypocrisy attests to the seriousness of the charge.[103] Like Catullus' hirsute Egnatius, "whose dark beard makes him a good man" (*opaca quem bonum facit barba*; 37.19), Piso affects a stern physical appearance as camouflage for his morally corrupt character.

Names, too, helped Piso manipulate the expectations of the Roman populace. The noble connotations of the name *Piso* presaged its bearer's

---

[101] *Rhet. Her*. 2.5; cf. *Inv*. 2.34 and Sen. *Ben*. 5.15.1 ("whoever has one fault has them all").

The treatises on physiognomy also warn of individuals who are able to dissimulate through their dress, movement, and gesture; see Gleason 1991: 406–11.

[102] Piso's eyebrows also appear at *Pis*. 14, 20; *Prov*. 8 (Hughes argues that the description at *Pis*. 16 alludes to the mask worn by the stern father—*senex iratus*—in Roman comedy). The eyebrows were often considered an indicator of strong moral character in antiquity; see Plin. *Nat*. 11.138; Gell. 19.7.16; Quint. *Inst*. 11.3.74, 79; Sittl 92–94; Foerster's *index Latinus*, s.v.; and the metaphor *pone supercilium* (Richlin 1992a: 10–11).

[103] See also *Pis*. frag. 17 (= 18 Nisbet) and, apparently, frag. 6 (= 7 Nisbet) with Nisbet 1961 note; *P. red. in sen*. 15; *Sest*. 20, 22.

future glory, and its appeal to the people constituted a major source of his initial political success. Voters elected the *name* Piso, not the person.[104] Cicero claims that his opponent also used this name to connect himself to the Frugi branch of the clan. In this way, says Cicero, Piso could pretend "that 'frugality' seemed inherent to his family" (*ut ingenerata familiae frugalitas videretur*; *Sest.* 21).[105] Piso's character, however, belied the promise of his name: "you spurn your name through your character" (*moribus nomen [aspernaris]*; *Pis.* frag. 8). Cicero, in order to uncover for his audience this particular aspect of his opponent's hypocrisy, reveals Piso's "real" name, *Caesoninus Semiplacentinus Calventius*. Each element of this mock-glorious appellation pours scorn on Piso's provincial background; the new name thus provides a more accurate indication of the man's character than did the deceptive *Piso*.[106] Through the misuse of a noble name, Piso attempted to acquire a reputation that, according to Cicero, does not accord with his character.

Cicero alone of the Roman people and senate had the means of penetrating the former consul's false exterior. But only by chance—his close ties with other Pisones informed him that his opponent's ancestry did not place this Piso squarely within that distinguished family (*P. red. in sen.* 15). This admission on Cicero's part is significant: without independent information, the orator too would have been deceived by external appearance. And one would expect as much; after all, throughout his career the bulk of Cicero's invective against other opponents has been predicated upon a belief in the identification of external characteristics and internal character. Herein, then, lies Piso's greatest threat to the state: he provides an exception to the Roman bias that appearances should not deceive.

Piso misleads through his gestures and adornment as well. In his walk, the stern man occupied the opposite extreme of the effeminate *incessus*: an observer would think from his stride that he was viewing "one of the bearded men of old, an example of ancient rule, a vision of antiquity, a support to the republic" (*unum aliquem . . . ex barbatis illis, exemplum im-*

---

[104] *Pis.* 2: *nam tu cum quaestor es factus, etiam qui te numquam viderant, tamen illum honorem nomini mandabant tuo. aedilis es factus; Piso est a populo Romano factus, non iste Piso* ("For when you became quaestor, even those who had never seen you were entrusting the office to your name. You became aedile; a Piso was elected by the Roman people, [but] not the Piso who *you* are").

[105] Syme 1956: 21 doubts that this Piso had in fact any direct ties to the Frugi branch.

[106] *Pis.* 14 (cf. 53; *P. red. in sen.* 13; *Prov.* 7). As Nisbet 1961 suggests in his note on *Pis.* 14, the significance of *Caesoninus* seems to lie in the fact that Piso "may not have welcomed a reminder that his ancestors came into the Pisones by adoption." Calventius was Piso's maternal grandfather and a native of the Latin colony Placentia (hence *Semiplacentinus*). Along the same lines, Cicero portrays Piso in the early portions of *Against Piso* as an Insubrian (frag. 9) and Transalpine (frag. 11; cf. *P. red. in sen.* 15) Gaul.

peri veteris, imaginem antiquitatis, columen rei publicae; *Sest*. 19). His dress
too would never have hinted at his hidden, unbridled lust for pleasure
(*Sest*. 19; *P. red. in sen*. 13). The apparent frugality he displayed in his
banquets also seemed to accord with the best Roman tradition. Cicero
pretends to approve of this parsimony—"I'll praise an enemy" (*laudabo
inimicum*)—but his ironic description of Piso's table demonstrates that
this apparent virtue reflected in reality a mean and selfish nature (*Pis*. 67).
In these elements of his public persona as well, Piso reeks of hypocrisy.

Perhaps the most damning aspect of Piso's dual nature involves his
inability to discern the obvious signs of degeneracy in his consular colleague Gabinius. Cicero reproaches Piso for this oversight:

> non te illius [Gabini] unguentorum odor, non vini anhelitus, non frons ca-
> lamistri notata vestigiis in eam cogitationem adducebat ut, cum illius re sim-
> ilis fuisses, frontis tibi integimento ad occultanda tanta flagitia diutius non
> uti liceret? (*P. red. in sen*. 16)

> Didn't the smell of [Gabinius'] perfumes, the wine on his breath, and the
> forehead scarred with the traces of his curling iron lead you to think that,
> since you had in fact been just like him, you could no longer use the camou-
> flage of your forehead to conceal so many shameful actions?

Cicero's point is clear: any observer should have been able to recognize
the external signs of Gabinius' effeminacy. The perfumes and curled hair
anticipated an inner nature that would inevitably lead to disgraceful behavior (*flagitia*). As Cicero remarks in another context, Piso "does not
even know virtue [when he sees it] face-to-face" (*virtus, quam tu ne de facie
quidem nosti*; *Pis*. 81). Piso refuses to attend to clearly visible signs of
immorality. This failure reveals his unwillingness to heed normal Roman
conceptions of the relationship between exterior and interior. Not only
does his appearance provide the Roman audience with a forged text, but
Piso himself has not even learned how to read.

In chapter 1, I discussed the nature of invective in the orations *On Behalf
of Quintus Roscius* and *Against Vatinius*. Cicero's relationship with his audience in those two speeches embodies a kind of reading lesson, with the
orator as teacher. By pointing to the proper indicators exhibited on the
bodies of his opponents Fannius and Vatinius, Cicero provides the vocabulary that allows his audience to interpret properly the internal evil nature
of these two men. Cicero's lesson in regard to Piso is the opposite: in this
case he must teach his audience to see past the normal external signs of
immorality. "I am afraid," he says in his invective *Against Piso*, "that
there may be someone who does not yet discern this man's profound
evil, wrapped up in the layers of his brow" (*vereor ne qui sit qui istius*

insignem nequitiam frontis involutam integumentis nondum cernat; *Pis.* 12).
Cicero's mission, then, involves stripping away these layers of concealment in order that his audience can more easily make the requisite judgment.[107] Cicero has confidence that, eventually, Piso's success will betray
his inner character (*Pis.* 24). Once this has happened, all will be well with
Rome again. In his peroration to the speech *Against Piso*, Cicero represents Piso as a scapegoat for all the confusion he has caused:

> omnes memoriam consulatus tui, facta, mores, faciem denique ac nomen a
> re publica detestantur. (*Pis.* 96)

> Everyone is praying to cast out from the state any memory of your consul-
> ship, your deeds, your character, and, finally, your face and name.

The enumeration of what constitutes this particular Roman's career is
telling. Once Piso's face and name are out of sight, the proper determination of character can continue to operate as before, unhampered by
doubt.

---

[107] Cf. *Sest.* 22: *sed haec obstructio nec diuturna est neque obducta ita ut curiosis oculis perspici
non possit* ("But this covering is neither so long-lasting nor so thick that it cannot be penetrated by careful eyes").

Chapter 5

A POLITICAL HISTORY OF WIT

Nothing bothers me more in these troubled times
than not being able to laugh with you when there's
something to be laughed at. And there's a lot; I just
don't dare write about it.
—Cicero, June, 50 BCE (*Fam.* 2.12.1)

You ask me "Are you laughing in times like these?"
Well, what should I do? I'm tired of mourning.
—Cicero, June, 44 BCE (*Att.* 15.9.1)

Effective history, . . . if it chances upon lofty epochs,
it is with the suspicion—not vindictive but joyous—of
finding a barbarous and shameful confusion.
—Foucault, "Nietzsche, Genealogy, and History," 155

THE PRECEDING chapters have explored the most common types of humorous abuse practiced during the late Republic; malformed bodies, proper names, indecent mouths, and effeminate mannerisms were frequent objects of derision. For each of these particular categories, I assessed evidence from nonpolitical contexts—including religious, scientific, and philosophical treatises—to show that the efficacy of the abuse lay in specific biases circulating through all levels of Roman society. Humor, by constructing these biases into self-evident truths, has emerged as a powerful means of public denigration and social exclusion. To close this study, I step back from the systems and categories of wit previously discussed, placing my findings within a historical context as a way of exploring the explicitly political dimensions of humorous discourse during the late Republic. Cicero, whose wit purports to represent the prevailing values of his day—values that seek to isolate individuality as a threat to the state—clashes with two noteworthy individuals, Julius Caesar and Gnaeus Pompeius, whose own humor reveals an emphasis on individual worth. Such an emphasis rests uneasily with traditional—Ciceronian—categories of humorous abuse.

Reliquum est iocari

Cicero found little reason to joke in the final days of 50 BCE. Civil war loomed; Pompeius had sent word that he saw little hope for a reconciliation with Caesar (*Att.* 7.4.2 = SB 127). In this unfavorable climate Cicero composes a short, chatty letter to his friend Atticus (*Att.* 7.5 = SB 128). He inquires into the health of Atticus' family and of his own freedman Tiro, then turns, as often, to business matters (7.5.1–3). Political events receive short shrift, mentioned primarily in connection with the orator's fears for the future (7.5.4). Cicero then begins his closing remarks with a conventional sentiment; in an appended protasis, however, the current political situation breaks grimly through the convention:[1]

> iam plane mihi deest quod ad te scribam; nec enim de re publica, quod uterque nostrum scit eadem, et domestica nota sunt ambobus. reliquum est iocari, si hic sinat. (*Att.* 7.5.4 = SB 128)

> Now I really have nothing to write to you. [I can't write] about the republic, since we each know the same things, and our domestic affairs are known to us both. The only thing left is to joke—if *he* (*hic*) should allow it.

As war begins to threaten the state, Cicero envisions a situation in which free humorous expression could meet with disapproval.

Opinions differ concerning the referent of *hic*.[2] We need not enter into the controversy, for the obvious alternatives—Caesar and Pompeius—provide equally provocative backdrops for the following discussion. If *hic*

---

[1] Cicero discusses the different forms of letter writing at *Fam.* 2.4.1 (SB 48), where he distinguishes among the following three types: the informative (*ut certiores faceremus absentis*), the pleasant (*familiare et iocosum*), and the serious (*severum et grave*); see also *Att.* 5.5.1 (SB 98), 6.5.4 (SB 119). This threefold division appears to represent more a literary convention than a rigid system of epistolography; see H. Rabe, quoted by Shackleton Bailey ad loc.

[2] Tyrrell and Purser ad loc. (3:310) assert without argument that "*hic* is Pompey," while Shackleton Bailey ad loc. follows Manutius in glossing *si hic sinat* with *si per Caesarem liceat* ("if Caesar should allow it"), commenting only that "to take *hic* as Pompey spoils the point." Cicero's next sentence, however, seems to support Shackleton Bailey's conclusion—*nam ego is sum qui illi concedi putem utilius esse quod postulat quam signa conferri; sero enim resistimus ei quem per annos decem aluimus contra nos* ("For I am such that I think it's more useful to give in to his demands than to begin battle; for it's too late to resist the man whom we have spent ten years helping to prepare *against* us")—where *illi*, *ei*, and the subject of *postulat* must all refer to Caesar. If the *hic* in question did in fact refer to Pompeius, one would have expected Cicero at least to allude to him in what follows. The sequence *hic . . . illi . . . ei* does not argue against identification of all three pronouns with Caesar; Cicero is often imprecise in his use of demonstratives in the correspondence (*Att.* 7.4.2 = SB 127; see Shackleton Bailey on *Att.* 2.1.5 = SB 21).

represents Pompeius, then the general's "permission" presumably refers to his power to restore a political equilibrium in which jokes may once again be allowed. If one chooses Caesar as the referent, a similar, albeit darker, interpretation emerges: "Cicero affects to regard Caesar as already omnipotent."[3] Either reading produces the same conclusion. In Cicero's eyes, Pompeius/Julius Caesar regards the orator's humor as something to be controlled, as a potential threat to individual authority. And after the civil war and the death of Pompeius, the acquisition of this control will in fact constitute one of Caesar's great successes.

I have argued in the preceding chapters that many of the categories of abuse employed in Roman political humor arise from the rhetorical manipulation of social conventions. The dynamics of wit in relation to Pompeius and Caesar also rely on these conventions. The particular brand of humor of these two men and, conversely, the witty attacks that their behavior provokes alike attest to the most common characteristic of Roman humor: its stress on communal norms rather than individual needs. By analyzing separately the humor relating to Pompeius and Caesar, I shall show how the wit employed both by and against them contributes to the political tensions resulting in their ultimate clash. The conflict culminates, of course, in Caesar's victory. The fruits of this victory include the power to control Cicero's public display of wit.

POMPEIUS *IMPERATOR*

Plutarch records an anecdote from Pompeius' first consulship in 70 BCE that clearly establishes the character of Pompeius' pride in his own achievements. Upon completion of service in the army, it was customary for the members of the Roman cavalry (*equites*) to parade into the forum for an interrogation by the censors concerning how well they had performed their military duties. Pompeius, although serving as consul for the year, was still technically an *eques* following his recent victory over the Sertorians in Spain. The young general takes full advantage of this unusual situation. Descending into the forum "in full consular regalia" (τὰ . . . ἄλλα παράσημα τῆς ἀρχῆς ἔχων) and surrounded by a bodyguard of lictors, the former general presents himself before the censors:

εἶτα ὁ μὲν πρεσβύτερος [τιμητὴς] ἠρώτησε· "πυνθάνομαί σου, ὦ Πομπήιε Μάγνε, εἰ πάσας ἐστράτευσαι τὰς κατὰ νόμον στρατείας;" Πομπήιος δὲ μεγάλῃ φωνῇ, "πάσας," εἶπεν, "ἐστράτευμαι, καὶ πάσας ὑπ' ἐμαυτῷ αὐτοκράτορι." (Plut. *Pomp.* 22.6; cf. *Mor.* 204a)

---

[3] Shackleton Bailey ad loc.

Thereupon the senior censor asked: "Pompeius Magnus, I ask you: have you completed all your military duties in accordance with the law?" Pompeius responded in a loud voice: "I have completed them all, and all under myself as general."

The crowd shouted out approval—in spite of attempts by the authorities to control its enthusiasm (*Pomp.* 22.6). The pageantry of his entrance allows the general to accentuate the difference between himself and a normal *eques*, an emphasis that continues in his response to the censor's query. The set phrase κατὰ νόμον ("in accordance with the law"), added to ensure that the respondent has acted in accordance with Roman tradition, finds its syntactical partner in Pompeius' response ὑπ' ἐμαυτῷ αὐτοκράτορι ("under myself as general"). By this phrase Pompeius shows that his military service has been far from traditional; rather, it shared the features of his consulship by being, in both senses of the word, extraordinary.[4] The unsettling juxtaposition of traditional responsibility and individual prowess created by Pompeius' remark anticipates the contrasts that will dominate the general's later career as a statesman at Rome.

In the political sphere, Gnaeus Pompeius does not appear always to have succeeded admirably at public speaking. In 61 BCE, upon completion of his Eastern conquests, his first two addresses to the assembled people failed, according to Cicero, to please anyone. A subsequent appearance before the senate resulted in Crassus taking the opportunity to outspeak Pompeius in a contest to obtain Cicero's favor.[5] Five years later Crassus again demonstrated his superior rhetoric in a public assembly. When the consul Marcellinus asked in anger whether the rumors were true that Pompeius and Crassus intended to stand for the consulship of 55, the general replied, "Maybe"; Crassus, in his turn, gave the more politic response that he would do whatever he thought would benefit the republic.[6] Pompeius did not escape criticism for his noncommittal attitude. He retaliates with disdain:

ἐπιφυομένου δὲ Πομπηΐῳ Μαρκελλίνου καὶ σφοδρῶς λέγειν δοκοῦντος, ὁ Πομπήιος ἔφη πάντων ἀδικώτατον εἶναι τὸν Μαρκελλῖνον, ὃς χάριν οὐκ ἔχει λόγιος μὲν ἐξ ἀφώνου δι' αὐτόν, ἐμετικὸς δὲ ἐκ πεινατικοῦ γενόμενος. (Plut. *Pomp.* 51.6)

And when Marcellinus kept attacking Pompeius and seemed to be speaking forcefully, Pompeius remarked that Marcellinus was the most unjust of all

---

[4] Seager 26–27 sees this episode as intentionally staged by the censors, who "pandered to [Pompeius'] vanity."

[5] Both fact and interpretation depend on Cicero (*Att.* 1.14.1 = SB 14).

[6] Plut. *Pomp.* 51.6–7 (cf. *Crass.* 15.2, *Mor.* 204c; Dio 39.30.1–2).

men, since he was not grateful that on account of himself [i.e., Pompeius, δι' αὐτόν] he had become eloquent instead of speechless, and full to vomiting instead of starving.

Pompeius meets Marcellinus' attack with a double dose of sarcasm: Marcellinus should be thankful that Pompeius' military conquests have allowed him the freedom to express himself, and he should likewise be thankful that Pompeius' recent tenure as grain commissioner had lowered the price of food at Rome (the allusion to vomiting probably also refers to Marcellinus' vehement speaking style).[7] Although Pompeius follows traditional categories in inveighing against Marcellinus' oratorical techniques, a telling difference is marked by the phrase δι' αὐτόν ("on account of himself"). It is by the general's own actions, Pompeius asserts, that Marcellinus is enabled not only to speak but to subsist. The republic does not enter into the relationship, for it was Pompeius' actions as an extraordinary commissioner that relieved the food shortage at Rome.[8] This self-conception of Pompeius as an individual who transcends normal Roman practice can be traced back to his early career as a military commander.

These two anecdotes reveal a Pompeius who is concerned with using wit to underscore his own unique standing at Rome as both a military and a political leader. Pompeius' nontraditional status informs the humor—both favorable and unfavorable—directed *against* the general as well. As a young man, for example, Pompeius appears to have cultivated a resemblance to Alexander the Great, with the result that some detractors began to call him "Alexander" in derision (Plut. *Pomp.* 2.2).[9] Sim-

---

[7] I owe to Erich Gruen this explanation of Pompeius' first remark, which resembles Scipio Africanus' boast that his accusers have the freedom to speak only on account of his own actions (Polybius 23.14.3). Pompeius perhaps makes a similar claim here, in reference to his having saved Rome from the threat of Mithridates.

Marcus Antonius provided a frequent target for Cicero's jokes on a speaker's "vomitory" style—in part because Antonius had had the misfortune, on at least one occasion, of literally vomiting in public (*Phil.* 2.63; Plut. *Ant.* 9.6); see *Phil.* 5.20; *Fam.* 12.2.1 (SB 344), 12.25.4 (SB 373); cf. *Mil.* 78. For Pompeius' extraordinary tenure as grain commissioner, see *Dom.* 25 and Seager 110–12.

[8] I can think of no parallel for such bold assertions of power over another individual in the jokes of Cicero, a man commonly rebuked for boasting of his own achievements. It has been noted, however, that Cicero is most self-glorifying only at those moments when he must defend his actions in quelling the Catilinarian conspiracy (Allen, esp. 129–30; May 76, 86–87). Hence Cicero, unlike Pompeius, seems to take care always to have the salvation of the republic as a background to his boasts.

[9] Cf. also Plut. *Pomp.* 13.5; Sall. *Hist.* 3.88 (Maurenbrecher). The Alexandrian hairstyle mentioned by Plutarch (*anastolē*) is noted by Poulsen in coin depictions of Pompeius that were minted by his sons in Spain (18) and on Pompeius' bust in the Ny Carlsberg Glyptotek, which Poulsen dates to the Flavian era (42).

ilarly, when Lucius Marcius Philippus defended Pompeius on charges of extortion in 86 BCE, he said there was nothing unusual in a Philippus being an "Alexander lover"—Philip, of course, was the name of Alexander the Great's father (Plut. *Pomp*. 2.2 = *ORF* 70.13). At this stage in Pompeius' career, the humor appears harmless. As the young man continues to acquire military power, however, the ideas informing Philippus' joke come to represent more than admiration of Pompeius' abilities as a general.

In 77 BCE Rome needed to provide military intervention against the forces of the rebel Sertorius in Spain. When the consuls chose not to go, a motion was made in the senate to send Pompeius as proconsul.[10] Philippus, the "Alexander lover," took this opportunity to mock the unexpected refusal of the consuls: Pompeius should not be sent *pro consule* ("as a consul"), he explained, but *pro consulibus* ("instead of the consuls").[11] Although Philippus clearly approved of the choice, the point of his witticism does not appear to have been praise of Pompeius' ability, but denigration of the consuls.[12] The humor lies in replacing the familiar designation for the office of proconsul with the unfamiliar plural form. Philippus' invective, therefore, performs a function typical of Roman humor: the debasement of a political opponent.

A decade later, however, Pompeius' skills are needed for an even more untraditional appointment. Consequently, Philippus' play on words takes on new meaning. In 66 BCE Cicero pleads in the speech *On the Manilian Law* that Pompeius be granted an extraordinary military command over the eastern king Mithridates. In answer to Catulus' objections that nothing unprecedented (*novi nihil*; *Manil*. 60) should be given to Pompeius, Cicero argues forcefully, if not quite in response to Catulus' objection, that Pompeius has already been given a number of unprecedented responsibilities, each of which he has fulfilled successfully. Cicero includes in the list of Pompeius' successes his command against Ser-

[10] Seager 17 n. 34 cites, with relevant bibliography, the various theories concerning why the consuls chose not to go.

[11] The anecdote occurs at *Manil*. 62 (quoted in the text below); *Phil*. 11.18; Plut. *Pomp*. 17.4; and, elliptically, at *Vir. Ill*. 77.4.

[12] For this interpretation I rely on Plutarch's version, which does not seem to derive from Cicero's *On the Manilian Law*. The witticism has a familiar resonance with what Plutarch records L. Aemilius Paulus as saying after being chosen to his second consulship in 168 BCE, also as a result of the military incompetence of the consuls in office. According to Plutarch (*Mor*. 197f), Paulus had not sought the consulship, and so did not need to thank the people, "for he was not seeking the command as much as they were seeking a commander" (οὐ γὰρ αὐτὸς ἀρχῆς δεόμενος, ὡς ἐκείνων ἄρχοντος; if Plutarch translates a Latin original *consulatum* . . . *consulem*, then the similarity is so much the greater). On the historicity of this incident, see Gruen 1984: 212 n. 43.

torius, the occasion that a decade earlier had prompted Philippus' witticism about the consuls of 77. Cicero takes the opportunity to mention not only Pompeius' command at that time but the joke as well:

> quid tam inusitatum, quam ut, cum duo consules clarissimi fortissimique essent, eques Romanus ad bellum maximum formidolosissimumque pro consule mitteretur? missus est. quo quidem tempore, cum esset non nemo in senatu qui diceret "non oportere mitti hominem privatum pro consule," L. Philippus dixisse dicitur, "non se illum sua sententia pro consule, sed pro consulibus mittere." tanta in eo rei publicae bene gerendae spes constituebatur ut duorum consulum munus unius adulescentis virtuti committeretur. (*Manil.* 62)

> Is anything so strange as sending a Roman knight as proconsul to a very great and fearful war, when there are two most glorious and brave consuls? He was sent. And at that very time, when there were several senators who were saying it was improper to send a private citizen in place of a consul (*pro consule*), Lucius Philippus is said to have remarked that he voted for sending Pompeius not as a consul (*pro consule*), but instead of both consuls (*pro consulibus*). Such great hope rested in [Pompeius] for conducting the republic's affairs well that the duty of two consuls was entrusted to the bravery of one young man.

Cicero has changed the force of Philippus' joke. First, he does not mention the refusal of the consuls to be sent; instead he praises their abilities as "two most glorious and brave consuls" (*duo consules clarissimi fortissimique*). In this way the orator sets up the matter as a choice between Pompeius and the consuls, which does not seem to have been the case historically. By altering the historical context, he alters the purport of the witticism: it no longer simply derides the consuls but compares them with Pompeius. The implication follows that Philippus believed Pompeius' ability to be superior to the consuls'. In case Cicero's audience in 66 BCE has difficulty in drawing this conclusion from the newly revised anecdote, Cicero does it for them: "the duty of two consuls was entrusted to the bravery of one young man." The joke, originally spoken by Philippus as a wry commentary on the deterioration of consular authority, has been usurped to argue precedent for entrusting extraordinary commands to an individual.[13] Through this speech, Cicero helps obtain the extraordinary appointment of Pompeius. This will prove to have been an ill-advised move on the orator's part. By concentrating power in

---

[13] Schol. Gron. p. 322, 7–8 (Stangl) also recognizes Ciceronian rhetoric at work here: "Cicero has seized upon this as if Philippus said it in praise of Pompeius, not in scorn of the consuls" (*Cicero hoc rapuit, quasi [Philippus] hoc dixerit laude Pompei, non consulum vituperatione*).

an individual, Cicero helps create precisely those threats to the republic that both his own humor and the humor of others will later strive to combat.

These threats include kingship. In December 60, Pompeius sported military boots and white fillets (*caligae . . . et fasciae cretatae*), attire that portended to Cicero the trappings of a fop (*lascivus; Att.* 2.3.1 = SB 23). A tribune of the plebs for this year, Favonius, seizes the opportunity to criticize Pompeius for the associations suggested by his dress:[14]

> cui [i.e., Pompeio] candida fascia crus alligatum habenti Favonius: "non refert," inquit "qua in parte sit corporis diadema," exigui panni cavillatione regias ei vires exprobrans. (Val. Max. 6.2.7)

> When Pompeius had his shin bound with a white band, Favonius said to him: "It isn't important what part of the body wears the crown." He was reproaching him for his royal power by mocking his small cloth wrapping.

The white fillet marks a king (Suet. *Iul.* 79.1), whereas the boots are typical of the Roman soldier. Together the ensemble portends a desire for military conquest. Even in his attire Pompeius distinguishes himself from his fellow citizens; as an assertion of individuality, his appearance invites hostile wit.

Similar complaints regarding Pompeius' self-serving behavior emerge in the taunts of the populace in the following year. I have already discussed a different aspect of this joke, as it relates to names, in chapter 2. Cicero relates to Atticus the positive crowd reaction to some lines of Diphilus spoken at the Apollonian games of 59:

> Diphilus tragoedus in nostrum Pompeium petulanter invectus est: "nostra miseria tu es magnus" miliens coactus est dicere; "eandem virtutem istam veniet tempus cum graviter gemes" totius theatri clamore dixit, itemque cetera. (*Att.* 2.19.3 = SB 39; cf. Val. Max. 6.2.9)

> The tragedian Diphilus inveighed impudently against our friend Pompeius; he was compelled to say a thousand times, "You are great (*Magnus*) to our misery." He said to shouts of the whole theater, "The time will come when you'll lament gravely this same courage of yours," and other things as well.

The assembled people recognize the skewed values of Pompeius, who favors his own welfare over that of the state. The characteristic that Pompeius had presented as a virtue in his own witticisms—his ability to func-

---

[14] F. Münzer (*RE* 6:2074.52–59) puts Favonius' barb in the year 60 because of the passage cited from Cicero's correspondence with Atticus. Ammianus 17.11.4 also preserves the remark, without mentioning the name of the speaker, and says Pompeius wore the bandages to cover a wound.

tion successfully as an individual outside the arena of normal Republican practice—begins to be recognized as the vice that will cause his downfall.

The most telling criticism of Pompeius' omnipotent behavior, however, occurs four years later in 55 BCE, the time of his second consulship. During an examination of Lucius Scribonius Libo before the censors, the old man Helvius Mancia appears as a witness against the accused. Pompeius, speaking in Libo's defense, makes the witticism that the old man "was called back from the dead to make his accusations" (*ab inferis illum ad accusandum remissum*; Val. Max. 6.2.8). This reproach, a topic of humorous invective also found in Cicero, elicits a volatile response from Mancia:[15]

> non mentiris . . . Pompei: venio enim ab inferis; in L. Libonem accusator venio. sed, dum illic moror, vidi cruentum Cn. Domitium Ahenobarbum deflentem, quod summo genere natus, integerrimae vitae, amantissimus patriae, in ipso iuventae flore tuo iussu esset occisus. vidi pari claritate conspicuum M. Brutum ferro laceratum, querentem id sibi prius perfidia, deinde etiam crudelitate tua accidisse. vidi Cn. Carbonem acerrimum pueritiae tuae bonorumque patris tui defensorem in tertio consulatu catenis, quas tu ei inici iusseras, vinctum, obtestantem se adversus omne fas ac nefas, cum in summo esset imperio, a te equite Romano trucidatum. vidi eodem habitu et quiritatu praetorium virum Perpennam saevitiam tuam execrantem; omnesque eos una voce indignantes, quod indemnati sub te adulescentulo carnifice occidissent. (Val. Max. 6.2.8)

> You're not lying, Pompeius: I do come from the underworld; I come to accuse Lucius Libo. But while I was dallying down there, I saw Gnaeus Domitius Ahenobarbus, bloodied and weeping because, although born in the highest station, of untainted reputation, and most devoted to his fatherland, he was slain in the very flower of youth by your orders. I saw Marcus Brutus, conspicuous for comparable fame, torn by the sword and complaining that this had happened to him at first by your treachery, and then later by your cruelty. I saw a very bitter Gnaeus Carbo, the protector of your youth and of your father's property, bound by chains while serving his third consulship, chains that you yourself had ordered to be applied, and swearing before all that is good and evil that, while holding the highest office, he had been slain by you, a Roman knight. I saw with the same attire and cries of protest Perpenna, a man of praetor's rank, cursing your savagery; and all

---

[15] Cicero mocks the extreme old age of Lucius Gellius at Plut. *Cic.* 26.4. Mancia's reply, although not quite a joke, falls under the category of wit *in respondendo* (see chapter 1, n. 31).

Mancia must have been fairly old. He was old and important enough by 91 CE to be mentioned in Strabo's discussion of wit at *De orat.* 2.274 (where he tells a joke) and 2.266 (where he is the object of abuse).

these men were expressing their anger with one voice, because they had died uncondemned, at the hands of you, a prepubescent executioner.

Mancia uses Pompeius' witticism as an occasion to detail the consul's crimes against Rome. The dark irony of Mancia's description receives much of its power from being spontaneous, a rejoinder to Pompeius' feeble attempt at a joke. The "prepubescent executioner" (*adulescentulus carnifex*), a mere Roman *eques*, now serves as consul for the second time. Mancia's list becomes more tragic as he details how each of Pompeius' victims had served the state in his lifetime (*amantissimus patriae, . . . pari claritate conspicuum, . . . in tertio consulatu, . . . cum in summo esset imperio, . . . praetorium virum*). As the catalogue grows more full, the individual men merge into the larger notion of the Roman state. Pompeius has not only transgressed the bounds of justice in his treatment of Romans—they died uncondemned (*indemnati*)—but, equally important, he has slain, as a single man of the nonaristocratic class, recent benefactors to Rome. The individuality in which Pompeius takes pride has been turned against him. It now allows his enemies to find fault with him as one whose singular authority threatens the well-being of Rome and its people. For Mancia's rhetoric stresses that, before Pompeius, Rome and its best citizens constituted a unity.

POMPEIUS AND CIVIL WAR

The late months of 50 BCE brought uncertainty to many Roman political figures: should they assent to Julius Caesar's demands to run for consul in absentia or stand firm and support Pompeius in opposition to these demands? Cicero's correspondence often reflects wittily upon the uncertainty of the times. In a letter to Atticus of October 50, Cicero imagines himself being asked in the senate to give his opinion of Caesar's request:

"DIC, M. TULLI." quid dicam? "exspecta, amabo te, dum Atticum conveniam?" non est locus ad tergiversandum. (*Att.* 7.1.4 = SB 124)

"Your opinion, Marcus Tullius." What should I say?—"Wait a second please, until I meet with Atticus?" This is not the time for shilly-shallying.[16]

Pompeius too felt pressure to present publicly a definite decision in regard to Caesar. In October 51, when opposition from Caesar in Gaul was just beginning to be anticipated, Caelius records a remark Pompeius made during a discussion in the senate. The general has just affirmed that

---

[16] Cicero eventually settles this dilemma with another joke: *adsentior Cn. Pompeio, id est T. Pomponio*—"I agree with Pompeius (i.e., with Pomponius [Atticus])" (*Att.* 7.7.7 = SB 130). After the civil war has begun, jokes resume over the uncertainty of what to do; see, e.g., *Att.* 7.17.1 (SB 141).

if Caesar chooses to use a tribune to block senatorial proceedings on the distribution of provinces, then Pompeius will consider such actions as tantamount to direct disobedience of the senate. A question arises:

> "quid si" inquit alius "et consul esse et exercitum habere volet?" at ille [Pompeius] quam clementer: "quid si filius meus fustem mihi impingere volet?" his vocibus ut existimarent homines Pompeio cum Caesare esse negotium effecit. (*Fam.* 8.8.9 = SB 84)

> Another man asked, "What if [Caesar] wants both to become consul and to keep his army?" Look how calmly Pompeius [replied]: "What if my son wants to beat me with a club?" With these words he made sure men would think that Pompeius means business with Caesar.

As in his attack on Marcellinus' inept oratory, Pompeius again uses a traditional paradigm of humor to make his point. By employing the violent image of a son cudgeling a father, the speaker recalls the important Roman concept of *pietas*, the respect shown both toward the state and toward one's parents.[17] Regardless of what Pompeius was attempting to express directly through this harsh image, he does effectively cast Caesar's hypothetical demands as contrary to state values.[18] But this analogy has further connotations. Through the phrases "on account of myself" (δι' αὐτόν; Plut. *Pomp.* 51.6) and "under myself as general" (ὑπ' ἐμαυτῷ αὐτοκράτορι; Plut. *Pomp.* 22.6), Pompeius had foregrounded himself before the state as a prominent individual: he does the same here. In making Julius Caesar the son, Pompeius of necessity becomes the father. It is not, then, a matter of Caesar attacking the state through his demands, but attacking the "father," Pompeius. Once again Pompeius uses an image that recalls traditional values: violence to the state and violence to a parent constitute equally heinous offenses. Yet in expressing this image he points to his own status as a Roman who stands before all

---

[17] Parallels for a son threatening to hurt—and even kill—his father abound in the plays of Plautus, a writer who delights in the inversion of traditional Roman standards. Terence, by contrast, provides no such reference; see Segal 15–21.

In fact, Saller 151–65 argues that the punishment even of a son by a father was probably a rarity in Roman society. It certainly offered a topic of humiliation for the son when grown (Quint. *Inst.* 6.3.25, 48). This social reality would make Pompeius' inversion all the more striking to his audience.

[18] I can offer no original contribution to the debate over whether in Caelius' assessment of Pompeius' remark—*Pompeio cum Caesare esse negotium* ("Pompeius means business with Caesar")—*negotium* means "deal" or "quarrel." For the former position, see Stevens 178; Balsdon 1939: 176–77; W. Grant 10–11; and Gruen 1974: 460–70. The conclusions of these scholars, which arise primarily from historical arguments, seem to me to be challenged effectively by the grammatical parallels Shackleton Bailey adduces ad loc. for *negotium cum aliquo esse* meaning "have trouble with someone." My argument remains valid on either interpretation.

others—including Caesar. This imagined father/son relationship becomes all the more striking when one recognizes in it an inversion of reality: Pompeius had previously been Caesar's son-in-law.

Pompeius' tough language did not pass unnoticed. During a situation in the senate similar to that narrated by Caelius, concern arose over Pompeius' apparent lack of preparedness in the event that Caesar should march on Rome. Plutarch records the general's attempt to allay the senate's worries:

> [Πομπήιος] μειδιῶν τῷ προσώπῳ καὶ διακεχυμένος ἀμελεῖν ἐκέλευσεν· "ὅπου γὰρ ἄν," ἔφη, "τῆς Ἰταλίας ἐγὼ κρούσω τῷ ποδὶ τὴν γῆν, ἀναδύσονται καὶ πεζικαὶ καὶ ἱππικαὶ δυνάμεις." (Plut. Pomp. 57.5)

> With a smiling and calm expression [Pompeius] told them not to worry: "For," he said, "in whatever part of Italy I stamp the ground with my foot, there will rise up troops of infantry and cavalry."[19]

This image of Pompeius as a kind of mythical hero creating armies from the earth lingered in the minds of his audience. Favonius, the man who had mocked Pompeius' "royal garb" ten years earlier (Val. Max. 6.2.7), held the office of tribune of the plebs for 49. As Caesar's troops marched through Italy, Favonius derided the general's boast: "he ordered Pompeius to stamp his foot and summon the armies he had promised" (ἐκέλευε τὸν Πομπήιον τῷ ποδὶ τύπτειν τὴν γῆν, ἃς ὑπισχνεῖτο δυνάμεις ἀνακαλούμενον; Plut. Pomp. 60.4). The tribune calls Pompeius to account for posturing as the single savior of the Roman state.

This disappointment over Pompeius' inability to support his claims informs the many jokes Cicero makes in Pompeius' camp at Pharsalus, site of the final battles of the civil war. Marcus Antonius was later to condemn Cicero for his untimely wit on that occasion; Cicero attempts to defend himself in the Second Philippic:

> ne iocis quidem respondebo quibus me in castris usum esse dixisti: erant quidem illa castra plena curae; verum tamen homines, quamvis in turbidis rebus sint, tamen, si modo homines sunt, interdum animis relaxantur. (Phil. 2.39)

---

[19] Cf. Plut. Caes. 33.5; Appian BC 2.37. For the image of men being created from the earth, one can recall Deucalion and Pyrrha creating their children from stones or Jason sowing the dragon's teeth.

According to Manzo 119, Cicero depicts Pompeius as joking about his losses in early 49 as follows: "Cingulum" inquit "nos tenemus, Anconem amisimus" ("We have Cingulum/the belt, [but] we've lost Ancona/the elbow"; Att. 7.11.1 = SB 134). Shackleton Bailey ad loc., however, argues convincingly that the subject of inquit in this passage is most likely not Pompeius; the witticism is certainly not in keeping with Pompeius' humor as noted elsewhere.

I won't even respond about the jokes you said that I made in the camp. That
was indeed a camp filled with care. Yet even though people may be in a
troubled situation, nevertheless—provided they are human—their spirits
can on occasion be lifted.

Despite this eloquent defense, those jokes preserved by Plutarch and
Macrobius—if their authenticity can be trusted—reveal a humor far
from uplifting.[20] A witticism in Macrobius is typical of Cicero's cynical
tone at the time of Pharsalus:

> cum [Cicero] ad Pompeium venisset, dicentibus sero eum venisse respondit:
> "minime sero veni, nam nihil hic paratum video." (Macr. *Sat.* 2.3.7)

> When [Cicero] had arrived at Pompeius' camp, and some were saying that
> he had come late (*sero*), he replied, "I've hardly come too late (*sero*), since I
> don't see anything ready here."

The joke seems to depend in part on the double meaning of *sero* as both
"late" and "too late."[21] Another witticism echoes Favonius' frustration
that Pompeius claims absolute authority for himself and yet cannot de-
liver at the crucial moment. In contrast to that occasion, however, this
time Pompeius' promises have extended beyond the senate chambers:

> et cum donasset Pompeius transfugam civitate Romana, "o hominem bel-
> lum!" [Cicero] inquit, "Gallis civitatem promittit alienam, qui nobis nos-
> tram non potest reddere." (Macr. *Sat.* 2.3.8)

> And after Pompeius had given Roman citizenship to a deserter, [Cicero]
> said, "What a great guy! He promises the Gauls citizenship in a state that is
> not theirs when he can't restore our own to us."

I shall cite below a similar joke Cicero makes against Caesar (Macr. *Sat.*
2.3.12), where the historical situation completely transforms the intent
behind the witticism. In these two anecdotes from Pharsalus, Cicero
questions the validity of Pompeius' claims to individual authority. As we

---

[20] There are strong reasons to trust the evidence of Plutarch and Macrobius: there existed a collection of Cicero's jokes made by Tiro—or perhaps by Cicero or even someone
else—that is attested by Quintilian (*Inst.* 6.3.5), Schol. Bob. p. 140, 17 (Stangl), and Macrobius (*Sat.* 2.1.12). It does not seem unlikely that Plutarch also had access to this collection,
since three of his jokes are the same as Macrobius', who implies that Cicero's collection is
his source. In this particular instance of Cicero's jokes before Pharsalus, however, one cannot discount the possibility that jokes proliferated in the early Empire in order to create a
context for the *Phil.* 2 passage cited (Sen. *Suas.* 7 and Quint. *Inst.* 3.8.46 attest to the
popularity of declamations regarding the *Philippics* after Cicero's death).

[21] This is my effort to make the joke more witty than it may appear (Brugnola 33–34
thinks Cicero plays on the notion of arriving late for lunch). Compare the joke at Quint.
Inst. 6.3.49: after Milo's accuser repeatedly asked for the time when Clodius was killed,
Cicero replied "*sero*" (i.e., "late in the day" or "too late").

have seen, the orator earlier had helped raise Pompeius to an extraordinary command, in part by humorously equating the general's prowess
with that of the two Roman consuls. At Pharsalus the situation is reversed. Pompeius now stands as the target of a traditional Roman humor
that strives to isolate and mock his presumed individuality.

Plutarch preserves six more jokes from Pharsalus, which register a
blend of disdain and despair similar to the two from Macrobius just mentioned.[22] A witticism shared by both Plutarch and Macrobius is of particular interest, since it shows Pompeius once again drawing upon the parallel between filial and national loyalty to make his point:

> deinde interroganti Pompeio ubi gener eius Dolabella esset, [Cicero] re-
> spondit: "cum socero tuo." (Macr. *Sat.* 2.3.8)

> Then, when Pompeius asked [Cicero] where his son-in-law Dolabella was,
> [the orator] replied, "With your father-in-law."[23]

Pompeius' initial query represents an attempt to disarm Cicero by show-
ing that the orator does not command respect from his own "son." Cicero turns the paradigm around and consequently shows how cursorily
Pompeius has examined his own situation. Pompeius had earlier set himself up as father in opposition to the club-wielding son, Caesar. Cicero's
joke, however, shows that, as the former husband of Caesar's daughter
Julia, Pompeius too has ignored the summons of filial piety.[24] As the
Republic reaches its crisis, both men are unable to maintain one of the
foremost Roman values. Cicero's witticism highlights the effect civil war
has on family structure: the ties between Caesar and Pompeius, on the
one hand, and Cicero and Dolabella, on the other, have lost their symbolic value. The traditional conflation of loyalties to family and to state, a

---

[22] Plut. *Cic.* 38.3, 4, 5 (cf. *Mor.* 205d), 6, 7 (cf. *Mor.* 205e), 8.

[23] Plut. *Mor.* 205d gives Cicero's son-in-law as Piso, not Dolabella.

[24] The importance of sons-in-law in Roman society is attested by Catullus' claim to have
once loved his mistress Lesbia "as a father does his sons and sons-in-law" (*pater ut gnatos
diligit et generos*; 72.4).

The evidence of Suet. *Iul.* 83.1—*Q. Tubero tradit heredem ab eo [sc. Caesare] scribi solitum
ex consulatu ipsius primo usque ad initium civilis belli Cn. Pompeium, idque militibus pro contione
recitatum* ("Quintus Tubero relates that Pompeius was accustomed to be recorded as [Cae-
sar's] heir from the time of his first consulship to the beginning of the civil war, and that
this fact was read aloud to the soldiers at a public assembly")—shows that Caesar publicly
recognized Pompeius as an heir even after the death of Julia. This fact takes on special
importance since it appears that Pompeius would no longer have been legally considered
Caesar's son-in-law upon Julia's death (Pollux *Onom.* 3.6–7; cf. *Sest.* 6, *Clu.* 190). Perhaps
Caesar's change in his will, which Tubero dates to the beginning of the civil war, was
represented by Caesar as a renunciation of the man he had considered his son-in-law for the
previous decade. Tubero's contemporary account implies that Caesar made a public display
of removing Pompeius from his will; this would lend currency to Cicero's barb here.

conflation represented by the single word *pietas*, has become a vexed problem.

Pompeius seems to have had the final word in this exchange. As I have already noted, Cicero vacillated between Caesar and Pompeius both before and during the early days of the civil war. In February 49, a letter to Atticus finds Cicero expressing his despair at making a decision: "I have someone to flee, but no one to follow" (*ego vero quem fugiam habeo, quem sequar non habeo*; *Att.* 8.7.2 = SB 155). The epigram was to become very popular,[25] and it was to receive an ominous reply from Pompeius at Pharsalus. According to Quintilian and Macrobius, Pompeius did not handle well Cicero's humorous critique. The general, sensing in the orator's humor a lack of confidence in his own chances at success, turns to Cicero and says: "Go over to Caesar; [then] you'll fear me" (*transi ad Caesarem, me timebis*; Quint. *Inst.* 6.3.111).[26] Pompeius recognizes that Cicero will respect his military might only as an opponent in battle. For the orator refuses to surrender his right to free expression, a right that enables him to present his own views in the face of one more powerful and to do so without fear. As a result, Pompeius must use force to defend his preeminence, expelling the orator from his presence. Pompeius' remark recalls the fears voiced by Cicero in the letter quoted at the beginning of this chapter: when troubles beset the republic, the only thing remaining is to make jokes—provided it is allowed.

Early in Cicero's career, the depiction of Pompeius as a unique individual was meant to be construed as a positive marker of the young man's potential. As Pompeius' power consolidated, however, the threat inherent in this individuality emerges. As a result, he becomes open to humorous abuse from figures such as Favonius, Marcellinus, and eventually Cicero himself. Pompeius' own witticisms consistently foregrounded him before the state as a unique citizen, magistrate, and general; his critics employed humor to illustrate the negative aspects of this same position. This technique of abuse follows the same principles I have outlined in the previous chapters: the opponent notes and then attacks those elements that set his target apart from the remainder of society. Let's take

[25] Quint. *Inst.* 6.3.109, who cites as his source Domitius Marsus' work on *urbanitas*; cf. also Plut. *Cic.* 37.3, *Mor.* 205c; Macr. *Sat.* 3.3.7.

[26] Quintilian again cites Domitius Marsus as his source, and says this *would* be a joke, "if it had been uttered about a less important event or in another frame of mind, or even by somebody else" (*si de re minore aut alio animo, aut denique non ab ipso dictum fuisset*). It's too bad that Quintilian doesn't find Pompeius' most clever (and perhaps last) joke funny. Macrobius' version makes Pompeius' meaning clearer, and consequently less powerful: "I want Cicero to cross over to the enemy so that he'll be afraid of us" (*cupio ad hostes Cicero transeat, ut nos timeat*; *Sat.* 2.3.8). Gnaeus *filius* seems to have inherited his father's (lack of) humor; see Cassius at *Fam.* 15.19.4 (SB 216).

Pompeius' advice now and go over to Caesar, to see how the ultimate victor in the civil war finds his own means to cope with Cicero's wit. It will not involve simply expulsion.

JULIUS CAESAR, *RERUM SUARUM AUCTOR*

I analyze the humor relating to Julius Caesar in two stages. The first surveys Caesar's political and military career before the civil war. In the second section I examine public humor from approximately the time of the battles at Pharsalus until Caesar's assassination. Unlike the discussion of Pompeius and humor, here special caution must be used in interpreting those sources that are not contemporaneous with the first part of Caesar's biography, for there lurks a stronger danger that these sources project back upon Caesar's earlier career their own perception of him as dictator. As a way of controlling the discussion, then, I shall begin with the secure evidence provided by Caesar himself: his war commentaries on his campaigns in Gaul (*De bello Gallico*) and on the civil war (*De bello civili*).

As a military leader turned author, Caesar uses humor in a way that seems to contrast with Pompeius' early portrayals of himself as an individual to whom Rome exclusively owes its well-being. For Julius Caesar records in his writings not his own jokes but rather those of his common, nameless soldiers. This practice aligns well with his political platform to protect the rights of the people: the jokes reveal the good-natured confidence that his soldiers have in their own ability. Yet through his privileged position as an author who is presenting these jokes to a wide audience, Caesar necessarily separates himself from the people he celebrates. As a result, the humor present in the war commentaries reflects the paradox inherent in Caesar's own political position: being a representative of the people must entail standing both above and apart from the very people he represents.

A few passages from Caesar's *Gallic War* contain what appear to be jokes and puns that circulated around Caesar's camp and that presumably reflect common military parlance. It is significant that Caesar has chosen to include these witticisms in his narrative, for they reveal a military leader sensitive to the language and psychology of the common soldier. In Caesar's account of the capture of Alesia, for example, the narrator pauses in his description of the siege works to inform the reader of the nicknames the Roman soldiers have given the various military devices. One of the defense works used to prevent sallies from the town consists of a quincuncial system of trenches filled with stakes that have been cut to a point and camouflaged with tree branches. Caesar explains their function:

> quo qui intraverant se ipsi acutissimis vallis induebant. hos cippos appellabant. (*Gal.* 7.73.4)

> In this way, those who had fallen in impaled themselves on very sharp stakes. [The soldiers] called these stakes *cippi*.

Cippi were stone markers used to designate both property boundaries and burial sites.[27] The terminology of the soldiers (the presumed subject of *appellabant*) plays on both senses of the word. First, the designation toys with the notion of armed might marking property distinction (*cippi* as "boundary stones"). Alternatively, when construed as "tombstones," the *cippi* convey a self-fulfilling threat, marking the boundary between life and death. Caesar credits other witty appellations to his soldiers, in each case employing simply a verb in the unspecified third-person plural. A pit similar to the *cippi*, but containing only one stake, was called a "lily, from its resemblance to the flower" (*id ex similitudine floris lilium appellabant*; *Gal.* 7.73.8); stakes forced into the ground with hooked ends protruding receive the name "goads" (*stimulos nominabant*; *Gal.* 7.73.9). Each of the above three nicknames represents an ironic type of hostile humor that does not seem out of place in a siege. By crediting these names to his troops, Caesar reveals the relaxed attitude of his men and hence, by implication, his own success at building their confidence. Caesar seems aware of the power humor has in creating bonds among his soldiers.

Earlier in the *Gallic War*, however, Caesar records a similarly structured joke that his soldiers apply to more complex circumstances. A camp guarded by Quintus Cicero falls under the siege of the enemy. Cicero, under orders from Caesar, awaits his commander's arrival before putting up active resistance. Eventually, however, he must yield to his soldiers' demands to fight. Caesar portrays the soldiers' demands as a kind of joke:

> simul eorum [Cicero] permotus vocibus, qui illius patientiam paene obsessionem appellabant, siquidem ex castris egredi non liceret. (*Gal.* 6.36.2)

> [Cicero was] at the same time disturbed by the words of those who kept calling his decision to wait a kind of "siege" (*obsessio*), since they couldn't leave the camp.[28]

---

[27] Both meanings of *cippus* abound in inscriptions from boundary markers and gravestones, a fact that would support a multiple pun on the word by Caesar's soldiers (*TLL* 3:1078.6–29, 30–56). Heraeus 260–61 interprets *cippus* here as "foot shackles," a meaning found in a Latin-Greek glossary (2.100.53 [Goetz]: *cippus* . . . ποδοκακη). Heraeus cites other examples of military humor from sources besides Caesar.

[28] Seel notes in the *apparatus criticus* of his 1977 Teubner text that *siquidem* is a *hapax* in

Cicero eventually yields to this pressure, with disastrous consequences. I shall not conjecture here on the interesting question of why Caesar chose to represent a joke by the soldiers as Cicero's predominant motive for disobeying his orders. Rather, this brief overview shows how Caesar ascribes all the clearly indicated witticisms in his commentaries to the common soldiers and so creates a kind of social leveling in the narrative, as he allows voices other than his own to be heard. It would be difficult for readers of Caesar's text to picture this general proudly asserting, as Pompeius had, his military service "under himself as general." Other features of Caesar's style seem intended to further this impression that the general and his men are united in a common cause: his attribution to common soldiers of speeches quoted in direct statement, his plain style of narrative, as well as, perhaps, the avoidance of references to himself in the first person.[29]

At only one point in his commentaries does Caesar clearly identify an anecdote as a joke.[30] As in the previous examples, a common soldier receives credit for the witticism. In the first book of the *Gallic War*, Caesar prepares a bodyguard to accompany him to a colloquy with the German chief Ariovistus. Not wishing to entrust himself to the regular cavalry, which was composed entirely of non-Romans, he takes foot soldiers from his trustworthy Tenth Legion and mounts them on horses.

> quod cum fieret, non inridicule quidam ex militibus decimae legionis dixit plus quam pollicitus esset Caesarem ei facere: pollicitum se in cohortis praetoriae loco decimam legionem habiturum ad equum rescribere. (*Gal.* 1.42.6)

Caesar's corpus, but he defends it from deletion by Meusel and others with the attractive suggestion that Caesar intends the word to reflect camp parlance.

[29] Direct speech of common soldiers in *Gallic War*: *aquilifer* (4.25.3), *legatus* (5.30.2–3), *centurio* (5.44.3), *centurio* (7.50.4, 6); cf. also *captivus* (6.35.8) and *Haeduus* (7.38.2–3, 6–8). It has been argued that these examples of direct speech, all occurring in the later books, indicate that Caesar did not have time to complete revisions.

Plain style: Cic. *Brut.* 262; Hirtius *Gal.* 8.praef.6–9; cf. the remarks of Caesar himself as preserved at Gell. 1.10.4.

Third-person narrative: Caesar clearly follows a tradition in avoiding the use of the first person for himself (as does, for example, Thucydides, as well as Xenophon in *Anabasis*), but this does not mean that a leveling effect is still not created, and even intended, as a result (see also n. 28 above).

[30] There occur many instances of narrative irony that could be classified as humorous but that fall outside the scope of the present discussion. Most of these occur in the *Civil War*. For example, at *Civ.* 3.30.6 Caesar describes in detail Pompeius' careful preparations so that his forces will not be detected by the foe Antonius. The sentence following this description is *haec ad Antonium statim per Graecos deferuntur* ("this news was immediately reported to Antonius through some Greeks"); see also *Civ.* 3.31.1, with Malcovati's comments in *ORF* p. 455.

> After this happened, one of the soldiers from the Tenth Legion said rather wittily that Caesar was doing more for him than he had promised: for after promising that he would have the Tenth Legion as a general's bodyguard, he's now registering them among the *equites* (*ad equum rescribere*).

As in the other jokes from Caesar I have cited, the humor here depends upon simple wordplay. In this context, the phrase *ad equum rescribere* literally means "transfer to the cavalry"; but the phrase can also describe the technical process by which a censor transfers a citizen to the class of the *equites*, the highest census ranking for a Roman who does not belong to the political aristocracy. Apart from its singularity as the only wordplay labeled as a joke in the extant Caesarian corpus, the passage strikes the reader as even more curious because, by using the litotes *non inridicule* (literally "not unlaughably"), Caesar appears to apologize for introducing the joke into his historical narrative. The anecdote becomes even more significant when one recalls from Suetonius that, as a general, Caesar often showed off his wit.[31] Yet, as I have noted, Caesar has chosen in his commentaries not to attribute witticisms to himself.

There are two explanations, not necessarily mutually exclusive, for why Caesar relates this joke and chooses to attribute it to an anonymous soldier. The first has already received consideration. Just as other aspects of Caesar's narrative indicate a man concerned with leveling social boundaries, with presenting himself as a supporter of popular causes, so here too the anecdote humorously toys with the notion of a common foot soldier becoming an important figure in Roman society. This liberal stance has of course often been recognized as an important component of Caesar's popular image.[32] The joke of the soldier, then, depicts Caesar valorizing individual merit in opposition to the more traditional means of advancement in Rome, that is, through affiliation with prominent families. Cicero recognized Caesar's promotion of individual worth regardless of birth as an effective means for the general to gain popularity at the beginning of the civil war, as farmers and provincials rushed to join Caesar's troops (*Att.* 8.13 = SB 163). This foregrounding of individual merit recalls the discussion of Pompeius' wit. An important difference, however, should be noted: before the civil war at least, Caesar positions himself in the company of his equally deserving soldiers, not alone.

---

[31] For the humor of the general Caesar in Suetonius, see the epigrammatic statement at *Iul.* 34.2, the hyperbolic harangue to his troops at *Iul.* 66, and the means of avoiding bad omens described at *Iul.* 59 (one of which, the apotropaic remark *teneo te, Africa*, is praised for its strategy at Frontin. *Strat.* 1.12.2 and Dio 42.58.2–3). Polyaenus also records how Caesar used his wit to quell a potential revolt (8.23.15).

[32] See Yavetz *passim*. For mockery of Caesar's liberality by contemporaries, see Caelius' complicated puns at *Fam.* 8.1.4 (SB 77): *Plancus . . . magno congiario donatus a Caesare nec beatus nec bene instructus est* ("although Caesar has given Plancus a large bonus, Plancus hasn't become any better off [= better educated]").

Yet the joke reveals more about Caesar's self-conception: a second explanation of the humorous registration among the *equites* approaches the anecdote from the point of view not of the soldiers' change in status but of Caesar's. The joke's figural restructuring of society transforms the general into a *censor*, a magistrate who is empowered to make decisions over the status of Roman citizens. Here the parallel with the full significance of Pompeius' humor becomes apparent. For this joke, while presenting an apparently egalitarian Caesar, at the same time underscores his own prominence by portraying him as possessing the power to make unilateral decisions regarding citizenship. One can compare Pompeius' less subtle claim that it was through his own actions, and not those of the republic, that the consul Marcellinus had the power of free speech. The inclusion of the joke on Caesar the censor has disrupted the tone created by Caesar the narrator. The general who understands his common soldiers must at the same time have enough power to control them. This paradoxical but inevitable role of Julius Caesar, as a populist who towers over the people, was to provide a focus for the political invective directed against him as a statesman.

Julius Caesar As Statesman

Caesar's self-appointment as figural censor in the *Gallic War* was foreshadowed by the mockery of his actions as consul in 59. According to Suetonius' account of this year, Caesar instilled fear in the senate by forcibly expelling from the forum his consular colleague Bibulus (*Iul.* 20.1). As in the case of Pompeius, the thought of one-man rule spurs the Roman wit:

> unus ex eo tempore omnia in re publica et ad arbitrium administravit, ut nonnulli urbanorum, cum quid per iocum testandi gratia signarent, non Caesare et Bibulo, sed Iulio et Caesare consulibus actum scriberent bis eundem praeponentes nomine atque cognomine, utque vulgo mox ferrentur hi versus:
>
> > "non Bibulo quiddam nuper sed Caesare factum est:
> > nam Bibulo fieri consule nil memini."
> >
> > (Suet. *Iul.* 20.2)

From that moment on one man controlled all state affairs, and did so at his own discretion, so that there were several wits who, when sealing something as a witness, used to write out the date in jest not as taking place in the consulship of Bibulus and Caesar, but of Julius and Caesar (they were recording the same man twice, using his family name and cognomen). In addition, the following verses were soon widespread: "Not a thing hap-

pened recently in Bibulus' term, but in Caesar's. / For I don't remember
anything happening when Bibulus was consul."

Suetonius' introductory remarks on one-man rule indicate that he believed these lampoons to originate as much from fear of Caesar as from
mockery of Bibulus. Even if Suetonius' own comments derive from
hindsight, the anecdotes he cites clearly demonstrate popular recognition
that Caesar's acts were unusual, affecting, it is jokingly claimed, even the
way the Romans dated their business transactions. Such contrary behavior on Caesar's part did not begin with his consulship. An awareness of
Caesar's unique potential survives in the mockery of his behavior from
the earliest stages of his political career.

I have had many occasions to remark on how the Romans valued wit
spoken in defense against humorous abuse, a technique the rhetoricians
call humor *in respondendo*. Seneca notes that Vatinius did not condescend
to this technique, but rather, in the spirit of a true philosopher (*sapiens*),
accepted the abuse of his physical deformities and even directed such
abuse against himself.[33] Unfortunately, no contemporaneous example
survives illustrating how Vatinius followed this practice. However, some
exchanges from the early career of one of his principal political allies,
Julius Caesar, provide some notion of how this self-effacing rhetoric may
have operated. For when Caesar is confronted with abuse that follows the
traditional lines of Roman humor as I have outlined them in the preceding chapters, he does not attempt refutations *in respondendo*. Instead, he
embraces the charges levied.

The way a man chose to dress or adorn himself frequently affords a
political opponent the opportunity for verbal abuse.[34] The young Caesar
provided just such a target. His dress indicated to Sulla the danger he
would represent to the aristocratic class of the *optimates*:

> etiam cultu notabilem ferunt [Caesarem]: usum enim lato clavo ad manus
> fimbriato nec umquam aliter quam ut super eum cingeretur, et quidem flux-
> iore cinctura; unde emanasse Sullae dictum optimates saepius admonentis,
> ut male praecinctum puerum caverent. (Suet. *Iul*. 45.3; cf. Macr. *Sat*. 2.3.9)

> They say Caesar too was notable for his dress: for he wore a senatorial tunic
> that had fringes at the hands and was always belted so that it hung loosely.
> As a result came the anecdote that Sulla was continually warning the *opti-
> mates* to watch out for the poorly girded boy (*male praecinctum puerum*).

The third-century CE historian Dio Cassius adds that the looseness of
Caesar's dress drove Sulla to desire the young man's death (43.43.4). At

---

[33] Sen. *Dial*. 2.17.3, quoted in chapter 1.
[34] I discuss the coding of different forms of Roman male dress in chapter 4.

the end of Caesar's career, Cicero too noted the man's unusual style of clothing:[35]

> post victoriam Caesaris [Cicero] interrogatus cur in electione partis errasset: respondit "praecinctura me decepit." (Macr. *Sat.* 2.3.9)

> After Caesar's victory, Cicero, when asked why he had erred in his choice of sides, replied, "The strange girding (*praecinctura*) deceived me."

Cicero mocks the same type of dress with which Sulla earlier had found fault (*praecinctum, praecinctura*). Choice of clothing, it seems, had a correlation with political choice. Plutarch records that Cicero later admitted that he never thought a man who looked and acted as Caesar did could overthrow the republic (*Caes.* 4.9). Dio may be using the same source as Plutarch when he quotes Cicero, deceived by Caesar's dress, as saying he never would have suspected that one who girded himself so poorly could defeat Pompeius ("οὐκ ἄν ποτε προσεδόκησα τὸν κακῶς οὕτω ζων-νύμενον Πομπηίου κρατήσειν"; 43.43.5). According to these later sources, then, Julius Caesar consistently adopted an unusual way of dress, one that he retains from the days of Sulla up until at least the civil war. The fact that Sulla is said to have used Caesar's appearance to warn the *optimates* indicates that a mode of dress could be read as a statement of opposition to the aristocracy. It would not have been out of character for Caesar consciously to adopt an appearance that was so coded. His rhetorical and stylistic maneuvers in the war commentaries also serve to align him with the nonaristocratic element. Caesar used his dress to distinguish himself from the elite.

Caesar's own witticisms from the period can be used to test the hypothesis that his dress represents a statement of opposition to elite standards of appearance. In these jokes, Caesar questions more directly the traditional values propagated in Roman humorous abuse.

The previous chapter surveyed the mockery of Caesar's androgynous character: as a man for all women and a woman for all men (Suet. *Iul.* 52.3), he was open to charges of being Nicomedes' catamite (e.g., *Iul.* 49). At the same time—in an apparent paradox—he posed a threat to the chastity of Roman matrons (e.g., *Iul.* 51). The subject of Caesar's dual

---

[35] I assume that the word *victoriam* refers to a military, and not electoral, victory and hence the anecdote depicts Cicero's well-known hesitation in choosing sides at the beginning of the civil war.

There are three good reasons to believe that the anecdote given here by Macrobius represents an actual statement of Cicero: it is reported together with Sulla's similar remark, rendering it less likely that one has here simply a misattribution of speaker; the remark resembles the statement Plutarch ascribes to Cicero at *Caes.* 4.9 (mentioned below in the text); and, most important, Macrobius' apparent access to "Tiro's" edition of Cicero's jokes (see n. 20 above) makes it likely that Macrobius used this work as his source here.

sexuality reappears in Suetonius' account of an exchange in the senate in the year 59 BCE. Caesar has just acquired Gallia Cisalpina and Comata as his proconsular provinces.[36]

> quo gaudio elatus non temperavit, quin paucos post dies frequenti curia iactaret invitis et gementibus adversaris adeptum se quae concupisset, proinde ex eo insultaturum omnium capitibus; ac negante quodam per contumeliam facile hoc ulli feminae fore, responderit quasi adludens: in Suria quoque regnasse Sameramin magnamque Asiae partem Amazonas tenuisse quondam. (Suet. *Iul.* 22.2)

> Overjoyed by this, he didn't refrain from boasting in a crowded senate house a few days later that he had gotten what he wanted, in spite of unwilling and complaining opponents. As a result, [he said] he would pounce on all their heads (*insultaturum omnium capitibus*). When someone said in abuse that that would be a difficult thing for a woman to do, [Caesar] answered as if he were making an allusion: "In Syria too Semiramis was queen and the Amazons once held sway over a great part of Asia."

In reply to Caesar's taunt that he will force the entire senate to fellate him (*insultaturum omnium capitibus*),[37] one of those present alludes abusively to Caesar's reputation as a passive partner in sexual relations with men. This reputation had assuredly been strengthened by Caesar's refusal to alter the length of his notorious tunic. In replying to the accusation of effeminacy, Caesar adopts an uncommon stance. In the surviving examples of Republican abuse it is rare for the person under attack to accept openly, and then agree with, the criticism of an opponent.[38] Caesar embraces the charge of effeminacy by comparing himself to "other" famous women of great military prowess, including Semiramis, a queen who provides Cicero with an abusive appellation for the effeminate Gabinius (*Prov.* 9).

---

[36] Butler and Cary note cautiously on this passage that there is no valid reason to reject its historicity: "The story seems almost incredible. Truculence was not a characteristic of Caesar. But the account is explicit, and the incident is alleged to have taken place *frequenti senatu*, which tells against its being pure fiction." One might add that Caesar's "truculence" becomes considerably mitigated when it is noted that Suetonius implies with *invitis et gementibus adversaris* that Caesar's initial boast was a prompted response (i.e., of the valued type *in respondendo*).

[37] Richlin 1992a: 149–50; Adams 200. Compare the frequent threats of *irrumatio* ("oral rape") as an instrument of degradation in the invective poetry of Catullus, Martial, and the *corpus Priapeum* (Richlin 1992a passim).

[38] Vatinius, as already mentioned, seems to be an exceptional case (Sen. *Dial.* 2.17.3; cf. also the retort of Hortensius at Gell. 1.5.2–3, quoted in chapter 4). Conversely, there are many examples of an opponent accepting criticism and then somehow altering that criticism either into a traditional virtue (the Cicero/Clodius debate at *Att.* 1.16.10 = SB 16) or into a criticism of his opponent (Mancia's tirade against Pompeius). Caesar's reply here falls into neither category.

This anecdote from Suetonius exemplifies well how Caesar embodies a threat to the stability created and maintained by political invective. By embracing the charges that have been leveled against him, Caesar openly asserts his power over the traditional, elite standards that this type of humorous mockery supports.

A final example of Caesar's wit before Pharsalus concerns the use of perfumes, whose associations with excessive banqueting, dancing, and sexual activity were shown in chapter 4. After discussing Caesar's relative gentleness as a military commander, Suetonius adds the following note:

> ac nonnumquam post magnam pugnam atque victoriam remisso officiorum munere licentiam omnem passim lasciviendi permittebat, iactare solitus "milites suos etiam unguentatos bene pugnare posse." (Suet. *Iul.* 67.1)

> And often after a great military victory he relaxed the burden of [his soldiers'] duties and permitted everywhere every type of license. His customary boast was "My soldiers can fight well even when wearing perfume (*etiam unguentatos*)."

Caesar once again openly defies the common ethical standards of Roman humorous invective, in which perfumed banqueting never receives praise. This is not to say, of course, that Caesar would necessarily have allowed his men to fight while wearing perfume. Yet his remark points to an awareness of certain norms that Roman humor represented. Through his conscious opposition to these norms (as implied by *etiam*, "even"), the general acknowledges the value of his men as individuals capable of battling successfully, regardless of any presumed standards propagated in political invective.

This completes the survey of wit employed both by and against Caesar before the civil war. If the extant sources are reliable—one can certainly trust the passages from the *Gallic War* and there seems little reason not to trust Suetonius—then a provocative picture of Caesar emerges. The jokes related by Caesar the author indicate his concern to be seen as a sympathetic spokesman for the common soldier; yet in the one joke in which the general himself appears, Caesar figures himself as a prominent political magistrate, making unilateral decisions regarding the status of other citizens. This stance resembles his position as a statesman at Rome in the years preceding his proconsulship in Gaul. The wit directed against him at this time portrays Caesar as an individual standing in open opposition to traditional standards of Roman humorous abuse. Indeed, that portrayal is verified by the type of invective wielded by Caesar himself, who often chooses those traditional standards as his target. In dress and in speech, Caesar promotes an untraditional individuality. As was the case with Pompeius, humor reveals a preeminent individual presenting a distinct alternative to the norms of the traditional aristocracy. The situation does not change in the period following the civil war.

JULIUS CAESAR *DICTATOR*

For the post–civil war period the extant sources provide a greater amount of material from which to evaluate Caesar's own use of humor. In 47 BCE, Brutus was among those working to preserve the kingdom of the Galatian ruler Deiotarus. Caesar, upon hearing his vehement entreaties, remarked: "I don't know what this young man wants, but everything he wants he wants badly" (οὗτος ὁ νεανίας οὐκ οἶδα μὲν ὃ βούλεται, πᾶν δ' ὃ βούλεται σφόδρα βούλεται; Plut. *Brut.* 6.4). Caesar follows the same tradition Pompeius had when he mocked Marcellinus' excessively passionate delivery.[39] Yet Caesar's seemingly innocent joke takes on sinister overtones if one considers the historical context of Brutus' speech. Brutus does not, as would have been the case in the prewar Republic, plead for Deiotarus before the senate, but before the single authority of Caesar as dictator. Cicero remarks in his own speech on behalf of Deiotarus how this situation calls for a new type of oratory (*Deiot.* 40; cf. *Lig.* 30, quoted below). It is no longer necessary to voice appeals to pity, Cicero argues, since Caesar's famous "clemency" (*misericordia*) arises spontaneously and does not require rhetorical arguments for its employment. Brutus' unclear appeals, then, may reflect not an inept speaking method but an uncertainty of how his plea will be understood by the dictator, now the sole dispenser of justice.

It appears that others were mocked by Caesar as well for their uncertainty about how to behave before him. Cicero notes that Atticus was kidded by Julius Caesar for excessive use of "please" (*quaeso*) in a letter Atticus wrote to ask the dictator for a favor (*Att.* 12.6a.2 = SB 243). A letter of Cicero to Caesar from 54 also points to Caesar's dislike of excessive deference. Cicero records how he was "justly mocked" by Caesar (*iure lusisti*) for a breach of impropriety—perhaps a joke (*Fam.* 7.5.3 = SB 26). These three examples—from Brutus, Atticus, and Cicero—point to a Caesar whose unique position of superiority befuddles those who are attempting to address him.

---

[39] Compare, for example, the jokes on the vehement speaking style of Curio *pater* at *Brut.* 216–17 (cf. Quint. *Inst.* 11.3.129) and Val. Max. 9.14.5. Cf. also *Brut.* 225 (Sextus Titius); Quint. *Inst.* 11.3.126.

For other examples of Caesar employing jokes that accord with "traditional" categories, see Plut. *Caes.* 62.5 (where he mocks the effeminate appearance of Dolabella and Antonius), 52.9 (mocking a soldier's cowardice, for which one can compare *De orat.* 2.272 [Africanus]); Quint. *Inst.* 6.3.75 [Caesar Strabo]).

Turning now to Caesar's witticisms in a more public context, one finds that, like Pompeius' or Caesar's own prewar jokes, the humorous *ad hominem* attacks Caesar employs do not emerge from the traditional Roman values propounded in humor. Rather, as the above remarks to Brutus, Atticus, and Cicero demonstrate—although there the witticisms are less barbed—Caesar's public invective springs from the dictator's feelings of superiority and condescension.

Suetonius devotes a section of Caesar's biography to explaining the unpopularity that led to the dictator's assassination. First he cites Caesar's failure to rise when approached by a deputation of senators bearing him honors (*Iul.* 78.1). The second explanation advanced by the biographer, dating from October 45, conveys Caesar's sense of humor:

> idque factum eius tanto intolerabilius est visum, quod ipse triumphanti et subsellia tribunicia praetervehenti sibi unum e collegio Pontium Aquilam non assurrexisse adeo indignatus sit, ut proclamaverit: "repete ergo a me, Aquila, rem publicam tribunus!" (Suet. *Iul.* 78.2)

> And this action of his seemed all the more intolerable because he had himself become angry when Pontius Aquila, a member of his own augural college, did not rise when Caesar was passing in triumph by the seats of the tribunes. As a result [the general] shouted out: "Go ahead, Aquila, take back the republic from me—Mr. Tribune!"

The meaning is clear. In his final triumph of the civil war, Caesar represents the state as his own personal possession. The attack does not represent simply disdain for Aquila. Through the scornful word *tribunus*, placed emphatically in final position to heighten the irony between his own power and Aquila's relative impotence, Caesar underscores his lack of concern for the powers of the important office of the tribunate. According to Suetonius, Caesar's ironic abuse of Aquila's actions did not stop here:

> et nec destiterit per continuos dies quicquam cuiquam nisi sub exceptione polliceri: "si tamen per Pontium Aquilam licuerit." (Suet. *Iul.* 78.2)

> And over the course of the days that followed he did not refrain from promising anything to anyone without adding the following proviso: "Only with the permission of Pontius Aquila."

Again Caesar's barb emerges from the point of view of one secure in his own unique position of power, a position gained at the expense of other traditional Republican offices. Aquila, however, did eventually withhold his permission. History next finds his name in a list of the assassins on the Ides of March (Appian *BC* 2.113; cf. Dio 46.38.3).

In the beginning of 44, controversy reigned in Rome over whether

Caesar was planning a kingship for himself. According to Plutarch's account, in the days following an attempted coronation of the dictator at the festival of the Lupercalia, statues of Caesar were found with crowns on their heads. Two tribunes of that year, Flavius and Marullus, immediately removed the crowns and arrested those suspected of wanting Caesar to become king (Plut. *Caes.* 61.8).[40] As a result of the tribunes' actions, the people gave these two men the nickname *Brutus*, in reference to the legendary regicide who ended the kingship in 509 BCE. Caesar did not, according to Plutarch, welcome this praise:

ἐπὶ τούτῳ Καῖσαρ παροξυνθεὶς τὴν μὲν ἀρχὴν ἀφείλετο τῶν περὶ τὸν Μάρυλλον, ἐν δὲ τῷ κατηγορεῖν αὐτῶν ἅμα καὶ τὸν δῆμον ἐφυβρίζων πολλάκις Βρούτους τε καὶ Κυμαίους ἀπεκάλει τοὺς ἄνδρας. (Plut. *Caes.* 61.10)

And Caesar, angered at this, deposed from office Marullus and his henchman, and in his accusations of them he upbraided the people as well, by repeatedly referring to the tribunes as "Brutes" and "Cumaeans."

Part of the humor here derives from a pun on the literal meaning of *Brutus* ("dull witted"): Caesar mocks the tribunes for their stupidity. But when one considers Caesar's role in the joke, the remark becomes a self-fulfilling statement, much as had his "censor" joke in the *Gallic War*. As Caesar ridicules the people for using the name *Brutus* by himself punning upon its validity, the very power the dictator wields in allowing him to depose these tribunes attests to his own role as a kind of authoritarian king. Even if it is true, as the historians Appian (*BC* 2.108) and Nicolaus (frag. 130.69) suggest, that Marullus and Flavius engineered this entire affair—including the crowning of the statues—in order to discredit Caesar, this conclusion still remains valid. By this account, Caesar's reaction to the ruse—his immediate dismissal of the men from their rightful office—confirms the very point that the tribunes were attempting to express through their alleged deception.

The epithet "Cumaeans" (Κυμαῖοι) may also be revealing of Caesar's character. The adjective is usually explained by referring to a passage in which the geographer Strabo comments on the proverbial stupidity of the inhabitants of Cumae (13.622). Commentators, however, have noted that such an explanation does not yield a double sense—as the name Brutus does—in any reference to kingship.[41] That Plutarch does not gloss the pun suggests that a clue can be found in his text. Such a clue occurs in the previous chapter of Caesar's biography (*Caes.* 60.1). There

---

[40] The incident also appears in Liv. *Perioch.* 116; Plut. *Caes.* 60.2–3; Dio 44.9–10; Appian *BC* 2.108.

[41] See, for example, Garzetti ad loc.

Plutarch recounts that those who wished Caesar to become king had spread an oracle from the Sibylline books prophesying that the Romans could conquer Parthia only under the aegis of a king. Legend had it that Tarquin received the original Sibylline books from Cumae. With the epithet "Cumaeans," then, Caesar mocks the tribunes as "Sibyls" because they have referred to this prophecy of the Sibylline books as proof that Caesar plans to make himself king.[42] Such mockery of the trappings of Roman religion characterizes other witticisms told by the dictator.[43] On this reading, Caesar's wit has dual force: Marullus and Flavius become "stupid regicides" who have arrived from Cumae spreading unbelievable prophesies.

In the case of humor directed *against* the dictator, one finds a general awareness of how improper it was felt to invest one figure with control over the various powers of the Republic that had formerly belonged to the senate and people. Since many of the jokes concerning Caesar's manipulation of political institutions are familiar and require little exegesis, I shall pass through them quickly; they clearly portray Caesar as a prominent and dangerous individual.

In May 49, Cicero reports to Caelius the recent political advancement of two Roman *equites*, Oppius and Curtius, at the hands of Caesar:

> togam praetextam texi Oppio puto te audisse; nam Curtius noster dibaphum cogitat, sed eum infector moratur. hoc aspersi ut scires me tamen in stomacho solere ridere. (*Fam.* 2.16.7 = SB 154)

[42] The extant sources for the Sibylline prophesy are all late (although see *Div.* 2.110, with Pease's [1963] note), and speak of it as a rumor that circulated in the days prior to Caesar's assassination (Suet. *Iul.* 79.3: *varia fama percrebuit*; Plut. *Caes.* 60.2: λόγον τινὰ κατέσπειραν; Appian *BC* 2.110: λόγος . . . ἐφοίτα; Dio 44.15.3: λόγου . . . τινος . . . διελθόντος). The language of the sources renders it possible that this rumor had currency in early 44, when the tribunes were deposed.

On Caesar's plans for a campaign against Parthia, see Gelzer 322.

[43] I have already had occasion to mention two other instances of Caesar's mockery of religious practice, namely Suetonius' record of Caesar's attempts to avert omens (*Iul.* 59 in n. 31). Suetonius also records Caesar's remark upon finding a sacrificial victim without a heart—"*nec pro ostento ducendum si pecudi cor defuisset*"—"it should not be considered a portent if a cow doesn't have a *cor*" (*Iul.* 77; *cor* means both "heart" and "brain" or "sense"). The biographer interprets the remark as indicative of Caesar's arrogance in desiring one-man rule. Cicero, however, also mocks this type of divination at *Div.* 2.37 and was skeptical that the Sibylline books contained anything other than vague riddles (*Div.* 2.110–11). Polyaenus (8.23.33) records a similar incident concerning Caesar and says his quick wit encouraged the soldiers. It is difficult to evaluate the historicity of such anecdotes. Lucan's epic attests to a tradition that regarded Caesar as impious (cf. his violation of a sacred grove at 3.399–439; on the debt Caesar's depiction has here to previous literature, see Phillips). These and other complexities surrounding the politics of Roman religion at this period, together with Caesar's silence about gods, omens, or divination in his writings, make it virtually impossible to assess these jokes with any confidence.

I think you've heard that a bordered priest's toga is being woven for Oppius; our friend Curtius is planning on a double-dyed one [as worn by the augurs], but the dyer is making him wait. I've sprinkled this in so you'll know that—although I'm upset—I can nevertheless usually laugh.[44]

The humor of Cicero's remarks derives from the unusual situation of *equites* adopting priestly roles, a situation recalling the common soldiers who were "transferred to the cavalry" in the only joke of the *Gallic War*. Additional humor comes from Cicero making the bestowal of these offices into a simple matter of providing the appropriate garb—only a slow dyer keeps Curtius from practicing augury.[45] Behind all this lurks the puppet master Julius Caesar, who is made conspicuous by his absence; the lack of an agent to whom the political gifts can be attributed only underscores the arbitrary nature of their bestowal.

The abuse Caesar received for enlisting non-Roman elements into the senate is well-known. Again the jokes derive their humor from the unprecedented and therefore shocking nature of Caesar's actions. Suetonius records a pair of popular lampoons current during the last two years of Caesar's life:

peregrinis in senatum allectis libellus propositus est: "Bonum factum: ne quis senatori novo curiam monstrare velit." et illa vulgo canebantur:

> "Gallos Caesar in triumphum ducit, idem in curiam:
> Galli bracas deposuerunt, latum clavum sumpserunt."

(Suet. Iul. 80.2)

When foreigners were admitted into the senate a placard was put up reading "Good deed:[46] may no one wish to show a new senator the way to the senate house." The following too was commonly sung: "Caesar leads the Gauls in triumph—and likewise into the senate house: / the Gauls have pulled down their trousers, and put on the senator's purple stripe."

Macrobius preserves two jokes in which Cicero complains of the size of the senate:

ait Cicero praetereunti Laberio et sedile quaerenti: "recepissem te nisi anguste sederem." (Macr. *Sat.* 2.3.10; cf. Sen. *Contr.* 7.3.9)

---

[44] For *praetexta* as a priest's robe, see Shackleton Bailey ad loc.

[45] See Tyrrell and Purser ad loc. for an interesting interpretation of the *infector* as Julius Caesar. Manzo 127 asserts without argument that *infector* refers "without a doubt [to] Caesar."

[46] *Bonum factum [sit]* was apparently a formula used to provide an auspicious beginning to an edict; cf. Suet. *Vitellius* 14.4, Plaut. *Poen.* 16. The second lampoon resembles Cicero's joke at *Phil.* 13.28.

Cicero said to Laberius as he was passing by [in the theater] in search of his seat: "I'd have made room for you if the seating [in the senatorial section] weren't so tight."[47]

[Cicero] cum ab hospite suo P. Mallio rogaretur ut decurionatum privigno eius expediret adsistente frequentia dixit: "Romae, si vis, habebit; Pompeis difficile est." (Macr. *Sat.* 2.3.11)

When Cicero was asked by his friend Publius Mallius to secure a provincial office for his step-son, because of excessive crowding [in the Roman senate Cicero] replied: "He'll get one at Rome, if you want; at Pompeii it's difficult."

Suetonius records Caesar's reaction to criticism of this type: "if he had secured the help of vagabonds and assassins in safeguarding his reputation, these men too would have received the same sort of thanks" as the new senators (*si grassatorum et sicariorum ope in tuenda sua dignitate usus esset, talibus quoque se parem gratiam relaturum*; *Iul.* 72). The remark recalls Caesar's witticisms before Pharsalus. For Caesar now, after having gained a position of great power, continues to mock the conventional methods for facilitating political advancement: the loyal service of even the lowest members of society, Caesar implies, would take precedence over traditional qualities such as birth and wealth. The barbs against foreign senators also recall Sulla's warning to the *optimates* about the young Caesar's strange choice of clothing: beware the man who does not follow tradition.

Caesar also met with scorn for taking steps to control the electoral sphere. In late 46, Cicero remarks to Atticus that the dictator has the power to select candidates for Rome's magistracies while still in Spain. The orator's witticism demonstrates his feelings that the elections were becoming meaningless.

scribe, quaeso, quid referat Celer egisse Caesarem cum candidatis, utrum ipse in Fenicularium an in Martium campum cogitet. et scire sane velim numquid necesse sit comitiis esse Romae. (*Att.* 12.8 = SB 245)

Please write [to tell me] what Celer says Caesar has done in regard to the candidates, and whether he himself plans [to enter] the Campus Martius or

[47] Shaw ad loc., following Schwartz 265–66, interprets this joke as referring specifically to the foreign elements that have been admitted into the senate. The argument runs as follows: if this anecdote dates to the games of 47, then Laberius had just been playing a Syrian slave on stage (Macr. *Sat.* 2.7.4) and is passing through the senatorial seating to his own place among the *equites*. Josephus says that Caesar had permitted certain Syrians to sit in senatorial sections at the games (*Jewish Antiquities* 14.210). Hence Cicero's jest includes a reference to there being no room among the senators for another "Syrian."

the Fenicularian field [in Spain]. I should very much like to know whether I
have to be in Rome for the elections.

While a military leader in Gaul, Caesar had figurally usurped the powers
of censor. In a similar fashion Cicero envisions the commander in Spain
allowing the current field of battle (*Fenicularius . . . campus*) to take precedence over the traditional field of elections, the *Campus Martius*.

Finally there are the many jokes about Caesar appointing men late in
the year to fill consular vacancies. The short tenure of these
appointments—Vatinius was consul for only a few days, while Caninius
Rebilus held office for only one—resulted in criticisms that the dictator
was denigrating the most important office of the free Republic (for example, *Fam.* 7.30.1 = SB 265; Suet. *Iul.* 76.2–3). Cicero's jokes on these
occasions rank among his most clever. After Vatinius' short tenure the
orator remarks on how his consular term marked a great portent—for
during Vatinius' consulship there was neither winter, spring, summer,
nor autumn (Macr. *Sat.* 2.3.5); when Vatinius upbraids Cicero for not
visiting him while sick, the orator responds: "I wanted to come during
your consulship, but nightfall prevented me" (Macr. *Sat.* 2.3.5). Caninius Rebilus' term was even more remarkable, says Cicero, for at that
time no one ate lunch; no crimes were committed either, for the consul
was so vigilant that during his entire term he did not sleep (*Fam.* 7.30.1 =
SB 265). Many similar jokes survive.[48] They are of particular interest
here because of their emphasis upon the irregular nature of these events,
an irregularity that, as Cicero points out, is really only laughable at a
distance; to one who is present, the incongruity portends the end of
something. After setting down his jokes about Caninius in a letter to
Curius, Cicero remarks, "You think these things are funny—that's because you're not here. If you were able to see this, you wouldn't hold
back your tears" (*haec tibi ridicula videntur; non enim ades. quae si videres,
lacrimas non teneres; Fam.* 7.30.2 = SB 265).

Caesar's detractors easily make the transition from joking about the
dictator's absolute control over the consulship to attacking his alleged
desire to become king. Aquila's refusal to stand as Caesar passed in triumph prompted a response from the conquering general that seems to
figure the republic as his own hard-earned possession. In a triumph from
the previous year, the mocking song of the soldiers anticipates Caesar's
formulation:

---

[48] Macr. *Sat.* 2.3.6 (Caninius as a "hypothetical" consul; the riddle over in what consulship Caninius was consul—*quaereretur quibus consulibus consul fuerit*; another version of Caninius as the consul who did not sleep, for which see also Dio 43.46.4, Macr. *Sat.* 7.3.10);
Macr. *Sat.* 2.2.13 (cf. 7.3.10: in addition to *flamines diales*, there are now *consules diales*);
Macr. *Sat.* 7.3.10 and Plut. *Caes.* 58.3 (Cicero planned to visit Rebilus when consul, but
night overtook him; the same joke is quoted in the text about Vatinius).

ἀθρόοι ἀναβοήσαντες εἶπον ὅτι, ἂν μὲν καλῶς ποιήσῃς, κολασθήσῃ, ἂν
δὲ κακῶς, βασιλεύσεις. (Dio 43.20.3)

Shouting out altogether they said, "If you behave well, you will be pun-
ished; if you behave badly, you will be king."[49]

The soldiers mock Caesar's desire to become king as well as the means
by which he intends to accomplish this desire—"by behaving badly."
Their chant in fact parodies a line from a child's song—"whoever behaves correctly will be king; whoever doesn't, won't" (*rex erit qui recte
faciet; qui non faciet non erit*: Porphyrio on Hor. *Epist.* 1.1.62; cf. Otto n.
1537). The world has turned upside down. A proverb—a repository for a
culture's values, as well as a common touchstone for Romans of this
period mocking their opponents—no longer has any validity in the politics of Caesar's dictatorship.[50]

The soldiers mock... Humor could also turn to hyperbolic mockery when it portrayed Caesar conceiving of himself not merely as a king but as something more
than human. Cicero remarks to Atticus in July 45 of Caesar's plans to
enlarge the city:

o rem indignam! gentilis tuus urbem auget quam hoc biennio primum vidit,
et ei parum magna visa est quae etiam ipsum capere potuerit. (*Att.* 13.35.1
= SB 334)

A shocking affair! Your namesake [an architect] is increasing a city that he
saw for the first time only in the past couple of years, and [Caesar] thought it
wasn't big enough—even though it could hold *him*.[51]

The hyperbole follows the pattern of a similar barb against Scipio Africanus' ambitions that Cicero had recorded in *On the Orator*.[52] Caesar's

[49] A joke preserved at Quint. *Inst.* 6.3.61 seems to date from this same event. After
witnessing the wooden towns carried in Fabius Maximus' triumph, followed by the ivory
ones in Caesar's, a certain Chrysippus remarked that Fabius' trappings were simply "boxes
for holding Caesar's towns" (*thecas esse oppidorum Caesaris dixit*; cf. Dio 43.42.1).

[50] I know of no example of a speaker humorously inverting a proverb for his own advantage. But for the converse—a speaker appealing to the "universal truth" of a proverb in
order to support his condemnation of an opponent—see *De orat.* 2.258, 261.

[51] Tyrrell and Purser believe ad loc. that Cicero here playfully uses *gentilis* ("namesake")
to inform Atticus that the architect is an Athenian. Shackleton Bailey ad loc. disagrees,
arguing that *gentilis tuus* means the architect was named Caecilius or Pomponius (Atticus'
two nomina), since he maintains that *gentilis* cannot refer to the cognomen *Atticus*. But cf.
Varro *Rust.* 3.6.1, where Fircellius Pavo is imagined to object to an improper discussion of
the peafowl (*pavo*) for the sake of his *gens* (*gentilitatis causa*).

I agree with Shackleton Bailey ad loc. that *ei* refers to Caesar, and not to the architect
(*pace* Tyrrell and Purser).

[52] *De orat.* 2.250: "When the elder Africanus kept trying to fit a garland to his head at a
banquet, but it kept breaking, Publius Licinius Varus remarked, 'Don't be surprised that it
doesn't fit—he has a swelled head'" (*Africano illi superiori coronam sibi in convivio ad caput*

plans for himself have grown so great that the city of Rome no longer has
room for his ambitions. As a result, Caesar must change Rome so that it
can accommodate him. Cicero finds similar evidence for Caesar's mega-
lomania in his attempts at calendar reform:[53]

> Κικέρων γοῦν ὁ ῥήτωρ, ὡς ἔοικε, φήσαντός τινος αὔριον ἐπιτέλλειν
> Λύραν· "ναί," εἶπεν, "ἐκ διατάγματος." ὡς καὶ τοῦτο πρὸς ἀνάγκην τῶν
> ἀνθρώπων δεχομένων. (Plut. Caes. 59.6)

> When someone happened to say that the constellation Lyra was rising the
> next day, the orator Cicero remarked, "Yes it is; by decree," as if men were
> being forced to accept even this.

In both these jokes, Caesar's introductions of innovation are figured as
unwelcome aspects of his power: a new architect changes the shape of the
city, new regulations are changing the shape of the sky.

Another event allows Cicero to mock Caesar's pretensions to equal
status with the divine. After Caesar's return from the fighting in Spain,
the senate honored the commander by installing in the temple of Quirinus a statue of Caesar inscribed "to the unconquered god" (Dio 43.45.3).
Atticus owned property nearby. The coincidence prompts Cicero to
remark:

> domum tuam pluris video futuram vicino Caesare. (Att. 12.48.1 = SB 289)

> I see that your home will be worth more now that Caesar is your neighbor.

Cicero recalls the witticism in the next letter to his friend. This time the
joke has more chilling overtones:

> de Caesare vicino scripseram ad te, quia cognoram ex tuis litteris. eum σύν-
> ναον Quirino malo quam Saluti. (Att. 12.45.2 = SB 290)

> I wrote to you about your neighbor Caesar because I learned about it from
> your letter. I prefer him to be a temple-mate with Quirinus than with Well-
> Being (Salus).

Some scholars believe that Cicero alludes here to a hope that Caesar will
share the fate of Quirinus (Romulus): according to one version of the
myth, Rome's founder had been murdered by the senate and cut to
pieces.[54] But another interpretation—one not necessarily uncomplemen-

---

accommodanti, cum ea saepius rumperetur, P. Licinius Varus "noli mirari," inquit "si non convenit,
caput enim magnum est"). Strabo presents the joke as having only positive connotations ("it is
on a head of vast capacity"); but compare the joke on "Memmius the Great" (magnus Memmius) at De orat. 2.267.

[53] For the possible political implications of this reform, see Yavetz 111–14.

[54] Liv. 1.16.4; DH 2.56.4; Val. Max. 5.3.1; Plut. Rom. 27.5. This interpretation, adopted
by Tyrrell and Purser, is doubted by Shackleton Bailey ad loc. Manzo 131 offers yet another
possibility: Cicero alludes to the fire that destroyed the temple of Quirinus in 49.

tary with the first—is both less allusive and more in keeping with the discussion thus far. All the jokes that have been discussed throughout this chapter have been based on criticizing a person who makes himself an individual of prominence in the state. Through Cicero's witticism, the danger symbolized by such individuality becomes concrete. Julius Caesar, by his proximity to the divinity *Salus*, would have posed a threat to the very well-being (*salus*) of the state. He will do less harm sharing his quarters with Quirinus.

At about the same time Cicero was writing these letters to Atticus, he expressed more directly the repercussions of Caesar's supposed omnipotence:

> quippe ab Androne quodam Laodiceno salutatus [Cicero], cum causam adventus requisisset comperissetque—nam ille se legatum de libertate patriae ad Caesarem venisse respondit—ita expressit publicam servitutem: "ἐὰν ἐπιτύχῃς καὶ περὶ ἡμῶν πρέσβευσον." (Macr. *Sat.* 2.3.12)

> And in fact, after having been greeted by a certain Andron from Laodicea, [Cicero] inquired of his reasons for coming [to Rome]. When he found out—for Andron answered that he had come as an ambassador to Caesar concerning the freedom of his homeland—Cicero represented the public servitude as follows: "If you succeed, send an embassy for us too."

The irony is clear—the only person who can directly grant the Romans freedom is, in Cicero's mind, the very instrument of the loss of that freedom.

Other Romans had a different solution. Some sources that narrate the deposition of the tribunes Marullus and Flavius allege that the affair of Caesar's crowned statues was arranged by his enemies in order to discredit the dictator. In discussing the incident earlier in this chapter, I chose to suspend judgment on its historicity, preferring rather to focus on Caesar's reaction and how it sheds light on the man's self-conception. There does exist independent evidence, however, that Caesar's opponents latched on to the rumors of kingship to underscore the threat Caesar posed to the free Republic.

In the days preceding the Ides of March, placards appeared on the statues of Caesar and of the tyrannicide Lucius Brutus.[55] Suetonius includes among them the following couplet, affixed to Caesar's statue:

> Brutus, quia reges eiecit, consul primus factus est:
> hic, quia consules eiecit, rex postremo factus est.
>
> (*Iul.* 80.3)

> Brutus, because he drove out the kings, became the first consul:
> this man, because he drove out the consuls, has finally become king.

[55] Suet. *Iul.* 80.3; Plut. *Brut.* 9.5–7, *Caes.* 62.7; Appian *BC* 2.112; Dio 44.12.3.

The similar rhythm of the two halves of the inscription underscores the inevitability of their contents. Caesar's opponents represent kingship as the natural historical consequence of the dictator's actions. After eliminating the consulship, kingship must be the culmination (*postremo*) of Caesar's plans.

In the days following Caesar's assassination, Cicero uses a discussion of divination to criticize Caesar's desire for power:

> tu vero quid habes quare putes, si paulo ante cor fuerit in tauro opimo, subito id in ipsa immolatione interisse? an quod aspexit vestitu purpureo excordem Caesarem ipse corde privatus est? (Cic. *Div.* 2.37)

> But what reason do you have for thinking that, if there were a heart (*cor*) in a choice bull only a moment before, it would have suddenly disappeared in the act of sacrifice? Or was [the animal] deprived of the seat of its senses (*cor*) upon looking at Caesar, senseless (*excors*) in his purple robes?

The pun depends upon the conception that the heart (*cor*) is the center of reason.[56] The notion that an animal can spontaneously lose an organ is matched in its absurdity by the ambitions of Caesar, ambitions recognizable from the royal coloring of his clothing. Cicero finds in the phenomenal world potential justification for Caesar's murder—his appearance, which is his character, does not accord with the natural workings of Roman politics.

The abusive humor directed against Caesar defines him as an individual who attempts to stand alongside the gods and in opposition to the senate, the elected officials, and eventually the entire tradition and well-being of the Roman state. These modes of alienation used against Caesar, which operate along lines similar to those examined in earlier chapters, describe an elite-centered ethos that Caesar opposes not only with his wit but with his very appearance. This open defiance met with constant resistance. Caesar's opponents responded to his confrontational stance with a propagandist campaign to discredit the dictator, a campaign that included humorous invective and culminated in Caesar's assassination. The success of Caesar's detractors is confirmed by confusion in the ancient sources as well as by centuries of scholarly debate over what precisely Caesar's political future would have included.[57] In closing, I shall

---

[56] For the pun, cf. Suet. *Iul.* 77 (quoted in n. 43 above) and Plaut. *Cist.* 63–66. For the date of composition of *On Divination*, see the commentary of Pease (1963: 13–15), who cites this anecdote as evidence that the work was not published until after Caesar's assassination.

[57] For the uncertainty over Caesar's plans in the extant ancient sources, see most recently Yavetz 185–213; he discusses modern scholarly judgments of Caesar in his first chapter, "Caesar and Caesarism in the Historical Writing of the Nineteenth and Twentieth Centuries" (10–57).

attempt to lend perspective to this debate by demonstrating not only that Caesar could employ humor as a powerful political weapon, but also that he took steps during his lifetime to control its use by others.

CICERO'S STOMACH

In the middle of the year 45, Atticus informs Cicero that Marcus Brutus, a former Pompeian (and future assassin), has decided to reconcile with Caesar. Brutus justifies his actions, Atticus reports, by insisting that Caesar now supports the more traditional members of the state, the *boni* (literally, "the good men"). Cicero's response betrays little sympathy:

> itane? nuntiat Brutus illum ad bonos viros? εὐαγγέλια. sed ubi eos? nisi forte se suspendit. (*Att.* 13.40.1 = SB 343)

> Is that so? Brutus proclaims that Caesar [has gone over] to the *boni*? Great news. But where [will he find] them? Perhaps he's hung himself.

Cicero clearly implies that Caesar's alleged change of heart has occurred too late. All the most prominent Romans have died in the civil war and its aftermath, and the only way to effect a reconciliation is to follow them beyond death.[58] Cicero leaves open the question of how he has himself survived. For this one must turn to a letter he sent in response to Caerellia's query of why he endured Caesar's rule so submissively. Cicero replies with what Quintilian calls "sort of a joke" (*aliquid ioco simile*): "these affairs must be endured either with Cato's spirit or Cicero's stomach" (*haec aut animo Catonis ferenda sunt aut Ciceronis stomacho*; Quint. *Inst.* 6.3.112). Cato, like all good *boni*, committed suicide. Cicero relies on his *stomachus*.

The Latin *stomachus* reacts in two different ways when it has swallowed something disagreeable: it can either rise up in annoyance ("he raged with anger and stomach"; *Verr.* 2.2.48) or accept with forbearance ("to have a good stomach"; Martial 12.praef.). Julius Caesar helps gloss what Cicero means by the word in this letter to Caerellia. Soon after the Ides of March, Cicero learned of a remark that Caesar once made on an occasion when the orator had been waiting to be invited into Caesar's presence. In a letter to Atticus, Cicero relays the dictator's words in direct speech:

> ego dubitem quin summo in odio sim, cum M. Cicero sedeat, nec suo commodo me convenire possit? atqui si quisquam est facilis, hic est. tamen non dubito, quin me male oderit. (*Att.* 14.1.2 = SB 355)

[58] The joke perhaps contains an additional note of irony in a pun on the word *boni*: the only way Caesar can become a "good man" is by performing the good deed of suicide (Sen. *Dial.* 5.23.2 has a similar joke about Philippus, the father of Alexander). Cicero also puns on the literal meaning of *boni* (and the related *optimates*) at *Att.* 2.5.1 (SB 25), 14.10.1 (SB 364); *Fam.* 4.3.2 (SB 202).

Can I doubt I am most greatly despised, when Marcus Cicero sits [waiting]
and he cannot meet with me at his own convenience? And yet if anyone is
easygoing (*facilis*), it is he. Still, I don't doubt that he despises me.[59]

This ability to "wait" constitutes the greater part of Cicero's *stomachus*.
When one turns to Cicero's orations from this period, it is possible to
discern another aspect of this *stomachus*: Cicero refrains from his normally sharp humor.

This should occasion no surprise. In the three orations Cicero ad-
dresses to the dictator Caesar in order to obtain pardon for his friends—
On Behalf of Marcellus, *On Behalf of Ligarius*, and *On Behalf of King
Deiotarus*—the one person who could possibly qualify for Cicero's normal brand of abuse is Caesar and, to use Caesar's generous assessment,
Cicero was too "easygoing" for that.[60] In one of these speeches, in fact,
Cicero admits that humorous invective no longer has a place in public
oratory. I have already mentioned, in the context of Brutus' own speech
for Deiotarus, the passage from Cicero's *On Behalf of King Deiotarus* in
which the orator describes the new style of speaking one must employ
before the new audience—the one man, Caesar (*Deiot.* 40). In his speech
On Behalf of Ligarius, he clarifies what this new rhetoric entails:

> causas, Caesar, egi multas equidem tecum, dum te in foro tenuit ratio hon-
> orum tuorum, certe numquam hoc modo: "ignoscite, iudices; erravit,
> lapsus est, non putavit; si umquam posthac." ad parentem sic agi solet. (*Lig.*
> 30)

> I have for my part pleaded many cases with you, Caesar, while the demands
> of your public positions kept you in the forum, but certainly never like this:
> "Forgive [my client], gentlemen of the jury; he made a mistake, he slipped
> up, he wasn't thinking; if ever again . . ." That's how one pleads before a
> parent.

It is difficult not to see bitter humor behind Cicero's words. Having lost
his "reign in the forum" (*amisso regno forensi*; *Fam.* 9.18.1 = SB 191), the
orator no longer needs to persuade an audience, but to plead with a single
autocrat. Cicero has in fact cast Caesar in the very role in which the
traditional humorous attacks on the dictator have tried to portray him—

---

[59] In a later letter to Atticus (*Att.* 14.2.2 = SB 356), Cicero phrases Caesar's words
somewhat differently: *ego nunc tam sim stultus ut hunc ipsum facilem hominem putem mihi esse
amicum, cum tamdiu sedens meum commodum expectet?* ("Could I be so stupid as to think this
easygoing [*facilis*] man is friendly to me after he's been sitting around so long waiting at my
convenience?").

[60] Cicero does, however, have sly ways of inserting criticism of the dictator; see the
unnecessarily detailed critique of Caesar as a tyrant (*tyrannus*) that the orator puts in the
mouth of Blesamius at *Deiot.* 33–34.

in the role of a parent deciding whether to punish a child. Through the self-irony of this passage from *On Behalf of Ligarius*, the orator tries to register a complaint that can hardly be heard.

His private remarks from this period echo this bitterness more loudly. Upon learning that his nephew Quintus had warned Caesar about the orator's potential danger to the dictator, Cicero tells Atticus: "This would be frightening if I didn't see that the king knows I have no spirit" (φοβερὸν ἂν ἦν *nisi viderem scire regem me animi nihil habere*; *Att.* 13.37.2 = SB 346). Cicero accepts his spiritless situation a little more cheerfully in a letter to Fabius Gallus from September 45. During this period a fad seems to have developed among anti-Caesarians, including Cicero, for writing encomia of Cato, who had preferred suicide to continuing his life under Caesar's rule.[61] Cicero had asked Gallus to send off a copy of his own *Cato* for the orator's perusal (*Fam.* 7.24.2 = SB 260). In Cicero's next letter, Caesar, himself the author of a treatise with the self-descriptive title *Anticato*, suddenly intrudes upon the correspondence:

> sed heus tu, manum de tabula! magister adest citius quam putaramus; vereor ne in catomum Catonianos. (*Fam.* 7.25.1 = SB 261)

> Watch out! take your hand from your writing tablet! Teacher is here sooner than we'd thought. I'm afraid he'll give us Catonians a flogging (*in catomum*).

Catomum derives from the Greek phrase κατ᾽ ὦμον ("over the shoulder") and here describes the position of a flogged man supported over the shoulders of another as he is beaten. Caesar's opponents are schoolboys cowering in constant fear of punishment. This portrayal recalls Cicero's description of Caesar as a parent before whom one begs forgiveness. Fear of repression by Caesar has threatened Cicero's ability to speak—and joke—freely.[62] For Cicero knew from experience how quickly these fears could be realized. The imaginary scenario of Caesar suddenly entering the room to silence the orator has ominous parallels with Cicero's situation during the previous year.

[61] Cicero mentions his *Cato* (and the problems of writing it without offending Caesar) at *Orat.* 35; *Att.* 12.4.2 (SB 240), 12.5.2 (SB 242), 12.40.1 (SB 281), 12.44.1 (SB 285), 13.27.1 (SB 298), 13.46.2 (SB 338). For Caesar's *Anticato*, see *Att.* 12.41.4 (SB 283), 13.50.1 (SB 348), 13.51.1 (SB 349); Suet. *Iul.* 56.5; Tac. *Ann.* 4.34.7; Iuv. 6.338; Plut. *Cic.* 39.6, *Cat. Mi.* 36.3; Appian *BC* 2.99.

[62] Cicero's fears would seem vindicated by the fact that Oppius and Balbus felt the need to censor the orator's philosophic "Letter of Advice" to the ruler Caesar (see especially *Att.* 13.27.1 = SB 298, 13.28.2 = SB 299; also *Att.* 12.40.2 = SB 281, 12.51.2 = SB 293, 12.52.2 = SB 294, 13.1.3 = SB 296, 13.26.2 = SB 286, 13.31.3 = SB 302, and cf. 13.19.2 = SB 326). In the summer of 46 Cicero complains to Paetus that Caesar is signing the orator's name to senatorial decrees that Cicero has never even seen, much less approved (*Fam.* 9.15.4 = SB 196).

In the summer of 46, Lucius Papirius Paetus sent his friend Cicero two letters expressing concern over the orator's safety.[63] It seems that Caesar had received a report of some statements, allegedly made by Cicero, that Paetus feared might arouse Caesar's displeasure. Cicero's response— *Epistula ad familiares* 9.16—represents an attempt to allay Paetus' fears. There is no need to worry about Caesar hearing statements that have been falsely ascribed to me, the orator writes, for Caesar receives information about everything I say.

Cicero begins his letter by reassuring Paetus of his own good standing among Caesar's friends. Their open respect for him must represent actual feelings, he argues, since their superior position gives them no reason to present a false front.[64] He then proceeds to explain his relationship with Caesar himself; their stable converse stems from the easygoing attitude (*facilitas*) that characterized Cicero's dealings with Caesar between 46 and 44 BCE:

> de illo autem quem penes est omnis potestas, nihil video quod timeam, nisi quod omnia sunt incerta cum a iure discessum est nec praestari quicquam potest quale futurum sit quod positum est in alterius voluntate, ne dicam libidine. sed tamen eius ipsius nulla re a me offensus est animus; est enim adhibita in ea re ipsa summa a nobis moderatio. ut enim olim arbitrabar esse meum libere loqui, cuius opera esset in civitate libertas, sic ea nunc amissa nihil loqui quod offendat aut illius aut eorum qui ab illo diliguntur voluntatem. (*Fam.* 9.16.3 = SB 190)

> As for the man in whose hands all power resides—I see no reason to be afraid, unless [we consider] that nothing is certain when right no longer prevails, and that nothing in the future can be guaranteed when it has been placed at another's will, much less whim. And yet his own feelings have not been hurt by any act of mine, since I have employed in this very area the greatest amount of moderation (*summa . . . moderatio*). For just as once I considered it my task to speak freely (*libere loqui*) (since by my help there was freedom in the state), in the same way, now that freedom is lost, [my task is] to say nothing that might offend either his will or the will of those whose friendship he values.

In order for Cicero to keep his easygoing demeanor—which he calls here *summa . . . moderatio*—the orator must make sacrifices. He must give up his position as spokesman for the state; he can no longer speak as a free

[63] I follow Demmel's (33–35) reconstruction of these two lost letters, which derives almost entirely from the text of the surviving *Fam.* 9.16.

[64] *Fam.* 9.16.2 (SB 190): *ego uno utor argumento quam ob rem me ex animo vereque arbitrer diligi, quia et nostra fortuna ea est et illorum ut simulandi causa non sit* ("I have one indication why I think they really and truly like me; because both their fortune and mine are such [*ea*] that there's no reason to pretend"). I follow Shackleton Bailey's interpretation of *ea*: "for I am down in the world and they are up."

citizen (*libere loqui*). The preceding chapters have examined at length how Cicero's role as a spokesman for Roman values and free speech includes his use of humor. It is not surprising, then, to see him turn next in this letter to his reputation as a wit:

> effugere autem si velim non nullorum acute aut facete dictorum opinionem, fama ingeni mihi est abicienda; quod, si id possem, non recusarem. (*Fam.* 9.16.3 = SB 190)

> Moreover, if I were to refuse credit for the many sharp and witty remarks I have made, I should have to reject my reputation as a wit (*fama ingeni*): I would not refrain from doing so, if it were possible [to refuse credit].[65]

The price of Cicero's subservience to Caesar, of his outward *facilitas*, is the loss of his reputation as a wit. With the end of freedom (*[libertate] nunc amissa*) comes the end of Cicero's unrestricted employment of humor.

Cicero cannot, however, shed his reputation quite so readily. Throughout his career he has confronted the problem of other people who would make humorous remarks and attribute them to his own authority.[66] If such false attribution were to continue now, it would mark a clear threat to Cicero's safety, which is precisely Paetus' concern. A solution is offered for securing Cicero's protection—by Caesar. Just as the learned scholar Servius Claudius could distinguish a true verse of Plautus from a forged one on account of his close study of the playwright's works, so too has Caesar, himself a compiler of other people's jokes, trained his ear to discern Cicero's true witticisms from those falsely attributed to him (*Fam.* 9.16.4 = SB 190).[67] The problem appears almost to be solved. If Cicero can trust Caesar's abilities, then he can rest assured that Caesar will not unjustly be angered at something Cicero did not actually say.

Cicero's entire explanation depends upon the underlying assumption that he will not, in fact, attempt to criticize Caesar.[68] If Caesar hears

---

[65] So Shackleton Bailey ad loc., following Tyrrell and Purser: *quod = famam abicere, id = effugere opinionem.*

[66] In 54 BCE Cicero complains about jokes being attributed to him that he has not in fact made (*Planc.* 35). The complaint recurs in 50 in a letter to Volumnius Eutrapelus (*Fam.* 7.32.1 = SB 113).

In 58 BCE the opposite phenomenon occurred. Cicero wrote to Atticus urging him to pass off his invective speech *Against Clodius and Curio* as a forgery (*Att.* 3.12.2 = SB 57; I cannot agree with Haury 1989: 137 n. 2, who thinks the remark a joke). I shall discuss below a particular case where a joke ascribed to Cicero creates considerable problems for its alleged author (*Fam.* 11.20.1 = SB 401).

[67] Suetonius praises the learning of Claudius at *Gramm.* 3.1.

[68] Cicero clearly recognizes the difficulties with this assumption, but appears to subscribe to it in order not to worry Paetus. For in 50 BCE, the orator uses remarkably similar language about the verity of his own words in an obvious jest with Appius Claudius.

criticism, Cicero assures Paetus, then the dictator's discerning ear will be
sure to conclude that it did not come from the orator. Caesar, however,
does not appear to have shared these assumptions, as the next part of
Cicero's letter indicates. The dictator will take steps to guarantee the
orator's cooperation in the control of subversive remarks. The situation
Cicero depicts here displays Caesar's power at its most insidious:

> audio Caesarem . . . si quod adferatur ad eum pro meo quod meum non sit
> reicere solere. quod eo nunc magis facit quia vivunt mecum fere cottidie
> illius familiares; incidunt autem in sermone vario multa quae fortasse illis,
> cum dixi, nec inlitterata nec insulsa esse videantur. haec ad illum cum reli-
> quis actis perferuntur; ita enim ipse mandavit. sic fit ut, si quid praeterea de
> me audiat, non audiendum putet. (*Fam.* 9.16.4 = SB 190)

> I hear that . . . if anything is brought to Caesar that is claimed to be mine
> but is not, he usually rejects it: he does this now all the more because I have
> living with me almost every day his companions. In our various conversa-
> tions many remarks drop that may appear, when I have said them, to lack
> neither learning nor wit in their eyes. These remarks are delivered to Caesar
> along with the rest of the day's news: those are his own orders. In this way it
> happens that if he hears anything about me other than these things, he
> thinks he should not heed them.

According to Cicero, Caesar places the orator's opinion on a par with the
daily events of the city and senate.[69] To show the sincerity behind this
flattery, the dictator sends men to write down any remarks of Cicero that
might seem the least bit intelligent or humorous. In doing so, Caesar
wields the ultimate control over Cicero's humor. In a move that Cicero
represents to Paetus as Caesar's attempt to protect the orator—"I am so
respected, so watched over by all those whom Caesar loves that I think I
am loved by them" (*sic enim color, sic observor ab omnibus iis qui a Caesare
diliguntur ut ab iis me amari putem*; *Fam.* 9.16.2)—the dictator in fact stifles

---

Appius had taken offense with something Cicero had written him; the orator replied ironically: *si, ut scribis, eae litterae non fuerunt disertae, scito meas non fuisse; ut enim Aristarchus
Homeri versum negat quem non probat, sic tu (libet enim mihi iocari), quod disertum non erit, ne
putaris meum* ("If, as you write, this letter was not well-expressed, then consider that it was
not mine; for just as Aristarchus denies to Homer a verse he does not like, so should you—I
like to make jokes—consider anything that is not well-expressed not to be mine": *Fam.*
3.11.5 = SB 74; cf. *Fam* 7.32.2 = SB 113).

[69] For this meaning of *acta*, see Tyrrell and Purser ad loc. Demmel 43 regards this claim
as characteristic of Cicero's bravado. This may be true in part, although Cicero seems
uncharacteristically self-effacing in this letter (an exception occurs in section 3, *cuius [sc.
mea] opera esset in civitate libertas*, an apparent reference to his consulship; but see n. 8 above).
In any event, if Demmel is right, such hyperbole would not invalidate the facts of Cicero's
letter: namely, that Caesar's friends meet with the orator daily to report back what he says.

any further opportunity for free humorous expression.[70] Despite Cicero's apparent trust in Caesar's intentions behind this "espionage"—a trust he perhaps adopts so as not to worry the already troubled Paetus—the writer soon slips back into doubting the true intent both of his visitors and of their friend Caesar: he concludes that the wise thing to do is to say nothing stupid or rash; "as for the rest, I can't guarantee what anyone might claim I have said, or how Caesar will take it, or how trustworthy are these live-in companions who continually come and watch over me" (*cetera vero, quid quisque me dixisse dicat aut quo modo ille accipiat aut qua fide mecum vivant ii qui me adsidue colunt et observant, praestare non possum*; *Fam.* 9.16.5). Cicero has been effectively silenced; but even in this state he cannot be assured of his *dignitas*—or even his safety (*Fam.* 9.16.6). The power of political humor to defend the traditions of the state has been repressed and, as a result, its importance to freedom at Rome receives the ultimate proof. The situation imagined in the letter to Atticus with which this chapter opened has now been realized. "The only thing left is to joke—if *he* should let us." Caesar has withdrawn his permission.

EPILOGUE: CICERO AFTER THE IDES

After the death of Caesar, Cicero no longer recognizes a need to maintain his easygoing demeanor. In a letter to Atticus from April 44, he remarks that the new political climate makes his own former tolerance unnecessary (*Att.* 14.12.2 = SB 366). Subsequently, in late 43, Cicero published the *Second Philippic*, a scathing indictment of the political career of Marcus Antonius, Caesar's political heir. This speech, filled with humorous abuse redolent of the period before the civil war, attests to Cicero's attempts to reestablish himself as a public representative of traditional Republican values. His bitter private jests about Antonius not being slain on the Ides resemble earlier jokes in which he desires the death of a political foe.[71]

One of the final jests recorded in Cicero's letters dates to November 44 and bears on the reception of his *Second Philippic*. The writer fears that

[70] I wonder if similar motives of intimidation lie behind the visit of Caesar and his army to Cicero's villa at Puteoli (*Att.* 13.52 = SB 353). Cicero deflates the tension in this letter with a joke: *quid multa? homines visi sumus. hospes tamen non is cui diceres "amabo te, eodem ad me cum revertere." semel satis est* ("Need I go on? We acted like human beings. But he's not the kind of guest to whom you'd say, 'If you're in the neighborhood again, please stop by.' Once is enough"; *Att.* 13.52.2). And what about the reputed "reconciliation dinner" the general had with Catullus after the poet's scandalous poems about Mamurra (Suet. *Iul.* 73)?

[71] Jokes on overlooking the assassination of Antonius: *Fam.* 10.28.1 (SB 364), 12.4.1 (SB 363; cf. Macr. *Sat.* 2.3.13); *Att.* 14.12.1 (SB 366); *Phil.* 2.34. For jokes before the civil war expressing desire for an opponent's death, see Caelius in *Fam.* 8.15.2 (SB 149); Quint. *Inst.* 6.3.49, 68, 84; and Plut. *Cic.* 26.3, 4.

certain passages of the speech may offend his friend Sicca. Cicero follows up this expression of concern with an obscure joke in which either he or Atticus seems to allude to the freedom to publish slanderous orations that existed when Rome was under the sway of the triumvirs.[72] Whatever the meaning of the joke, it excited Cicero's admiration. He exclaims *moriar nisi facete!* ("May I die if that wasn't funny!"). This wish was to become darkly ironic. Antonius eventually gave Cicero's *Philippics* as the reason for proscribing the orator and nailing his head and hands to the speaker's rostrum in the forum.[73] By dropping his *facilitas*, Cicero hastens his own death.

A few months after this letter on the *Second Philippic*, Cicero's jests bring him into conflict with another prominent figure in Rome. Ironically, the fears Cicero had attempted to allay in his letter to Paetus appear to have been realized, for the controversy arises over a joke that Cicero himself may not even have uttered. According to Decimus Brutus a certain Labeo Segulius, an apparent enemy of the orator, attributed the remark to Cicero in order to arouse displeasure against him (*Fam.* 11.20.1 = SB 401).[74] Brutus informs Cicero that this joke constitutes the only complaint about Cicero that has been registered by the young Octavian—the future Augustus:

> quod pro me non facio, id pro te facere amor meus in te tuaque officia cogunt, ut timeam. . . . Labeo Segulius, homo sui simillimus, narrat mihi apud Caesarem se fuisse multumque sermonem de te habitum esse; ipsum Caesarem nihil sane de te questum nisi dictum quod diceret te dixisse, laudandum adulescentem, ornandum, tollendum; se non esse commissurum ut tolli possit. (*Fam.* 11.20.1 = SB 401)

> My love for you and your good favors toward me compel me to do for you what I do not do for myself: I am afraid. . . . Labeo Segulius, a man always true to his nature, tells me that he was with Caesar [Octavian] and that there was much discussion about you. Caesar himself had no complaints at all about you except for the remark that he says you said, that "the young man

---

[72] *Sed illo tempore opus est quod fuit illis triumviris* ("But we need the time that there was when *they* were triumvirs"; *Att.* 16.11.1 = SB 420). See Shackleton Bailey ad loc. for possible explanations, together with Frank 275, which he cites.

[73] Liv. *Perioch.* 120; Sen. *Suas.* 6.17, 19, 21; Plut. *Ant.* 20.3–4, *Cic.* 48.6; Appian *BC* 4.20; Dio 47.8.3–4.

[74] Velleius 2.62.6 credits Cicero with the witticism; Suet. *Aug.* 12.1 only cites anonymous *alii.* On the question of whether *tollendum* contains a pun on the meanings "elevate [to the skies]" and "eliminate," I believe that Velleius' belief that a pun does exist (*cum aliud diceret, aliud intellegi vellet*) should take precedence over Tyrrell and Purser's objections and Shackleton Bailey's doubts. Bell's discussion of *tollo* (246–49), cited with approval by Woodman in his commentary on Velleius ad loc., does not, so far as I can tell, contribute in any way to resolving this problem.

must be praised, honored, and lifted up—and away (*tollendum*)." He said he would not allow himself to be "lifted up and away."

Suetonius lists this remark as one of the reasons Octavian eventually abandoned the aristocratic cause supported by Cicero and allied himself with Marcus Antonius.[75] The proscriptions that resulted in Cicero's death were soon to follow. If Suetonius can be trusted, he provides convincing evidence for the close relationship between the free Roman state and Ciceronian wit. In what were to be the final days of the Republic, a joke eventually cost the orator his life.

[75] Suet. *Aug.* 12.1. A possible reason to doubt Suetonius' testimony occurs in Brutus' next letter to Cicero: *quae tibi superioribus litteris mea manu scripsi terrendi tui causa homines loquuntur* ("As for what I wrote to you with my own hand in my previous letter, people are saying these things to frighten you"; *Fam.* 11.23.2 = SB 402).

WORKS CITED

PRIMARY TEXTS

The following lists contain all abbreviations of all ancient authors and texts I cite; citations of Greek and Roman texts follow the guidelines of either Liddell and Scott's *Greek-English Lexicon* (LSJ) or the *Thesaurus linguae Latinae* (*TLL*), except in certain cases where I have diverged for the sake of greater clarity. In my text and notes, Cicero should be presumed to be the author where none is indicated. Translations are mine unless indicated otherwise.

Works of Cicero

ORATIONS
Arch. (*On Behalf of Archias*)
Balb. (*On Behalf of Balbus*)
Caecin. (*On Behalf of Caecina*)
Cael. (*On Behalf of Caelius*)
Catil. (*Against Catiline*)
Clu. (*On Behalf of Cluentius*)
Deiot. (*On Behalf of King Deiotarus*)
Div. in Caec. (*Interrogation of Caecilius*)
Dom. (*On Behalf of His Home*)
Flacc. (*On Behalf of Flaccus*)
Font. (*On Behalf of Fonteius*)
Har. resp. (*On the Response of the Soothsayers*)
In Clod. (*Invective against Clodius and Curio*)
Inv. in Sall. (*Invective against Sallust*; spurious)
Leg. agr. (*On the Agrarian Law*)
Lig. (*On Behalf of Ligarius*)
Manil. (*On the Manilian Law*)
Mil. (*On Behalf of Milo*)
Mur. (*On Behalf of Murena*)
P. red. in sen. (*To the Senate on His Return from Exile*)
Phil. (*Philippics against Marcus Antonius*)
Pis. (*Against Piso*)
Planc. (*On Behalf of Plancius*)
Prov. (*On the Consular Provinces*)
Q. Rosc. (*On Behalf of Quintus Roscius*)
Quinct. (*On Behalf of Quinctius*)
Rab. perd. (*On Behalf of Gaius Rabirius on a Charge of Treason*)
Rab. post. (*On Behalf of Gaius Rabirius Postumus*)
S. Rosc. (*On Behalf of Sextus Roscius*)
Scaur. (*On Behalf of Scaurus*)

Sest. (*On Behalf of Sestius*)
Sull. (*On Behalf of Sulla*)
Vat. (*Against Vatinius*)
Verr. (*Against Verres*)

OTHER PROSE WORKS
Ac. (*Academics*)
Ad Brut. (*Letters to Brutus*)
Ad Q. fr. (*Letters to His Brother Quintus*)
Att. (*Letters to Atticus*)
Brut. (*Brutus*)
De orat. (*On the Orator*)
Div. (*On Divination*)
Epist. fr. (*Fragments* from letters)
Fam. (*Letters to His Friends*)
Fat. (*On Fate*)
Fin. (*On the Limits of Good and Evil*)
Fr. or. inc. (*Fragments* from uncertain orations)
Inv. (*On Rhetorical Invention*)
Leg. (*On the Laws*)
Nat. deor. (*On the Nature of the Gods*)
Off. (*On Moral Duties*)
Orat. (*The Orator*)
Part. (*On the Classification of Oratory*)
Rep. (*On the Republic*)
Tusc. (*Tusculan Disputations*)

COMMENTARIES
(cited in text or notes by modern author's name only)
Austin, R. 1960. *M. Tulli Ciceronis Pro M. Caelio oratio.* Oxford.
Cavarzere, A. 1983. *Lettere [Cic. Fam. 8]: Marco Celio Rufo.* Brescia.
Davisius, J., et al. 1824. *M. Tulli Ciceronis De legibus libri tres.* Frankfurt.
Denniston, J. 1926. *M. Tulli Ciceronis In M. Antonium orationes Philippicae prima et secunda.* Oxford.
Fausset, W. 1887. *M. Tullii Ciceronis Pro A. Cluentio Oratio.* London.
Haury, A. 1969. *Orationes in Catilinam.* Paris.
Holden, H. 1903. *M. Tulli Ciceronis Pro Publio Sestio oratio ad iudices.* London.
Kenter, L. 1971. *M. Tullius Cicero, De Legibus: A Commentary on Book I.* Amsterdam.
Kinsey, T. E. 1971. *Pro P. Quinctio oratio.* Sydney.
Landgraf, G. 1882. *Ciceros Rede für Sex. Roscius aus Ameria.* Erlangen.
Long, G. 1851–58. *Orationes.* London. 4 vols.
Mitchell, T. 1986. *Verrines II.1.* Warminster, England.
Nisbet, R. G. 1939. *M. Tulli Ciceronis De domo sua ad pontifices oratio.* Oxford.
Nisbet, R. G. M. 1961. *In L. Calpurnium Pisonem oratio.* Oxford.
Pease, A. 1955. *De natura deorum.* 2 vols. Cambridge, Mass.
———. 1963. *M. Tulli Ciceronis De divinatione: Libri duo.* Darmstadt.

Pocock, L. 1926. *A Commentary on Cicero in Vatinium*. London.

Rabbie, E. 1989. In *M. Tullius Cicero, De oratore Libri III*, ed. A. Leeman, H Pinkster, and E. Rabbie. 3 vols. Heidelberg.

Sandys, J. 1885. *Ad Marcum Brutum Orator*. Cambridge.

Shackleton Bailey, D. R. 1965–1970. *Cicero's Letters to Atticus*. 7 vols. Cambridge.

———. 1977. *Cicero, Epistulae ad Familiares*. 2 vols. Cambridge.

———. 1980. *Cicero, Epistulae ad Quintum fratrem et M. Brutum*. Cambridge. [All three works on the letters cited as "Shackleton Bailey"]

Tyrrell, R., and L. Purser. 1904. *The Correspondence of M. Tullius Cicero*. 7 vols. Dublin.

Wilkins, A. 1892. *M. Tulli Ciceronis De oratore libri tres*. Oxford.

Zumpt, C. 1831. *M. Tulli Ciceronis Verrinarum libri septem*. Berlin.

Other Greek and Roman Texts

Appian: *BC* (*Civil Wars*), *Reg.* (*Concerning the Kings*)

Aristotle: *EN* (*Nicomachean Ethics*), *GA* (*On the Generation of Animals*), *Phgn.* (*On Physiognomy*), *Pol.* (*Politics*), *Rhet.* (*Rhetoric*), *Rh. Al.* (*Rhetoric to Alexander*)

Caes. (Julius Caesar): *Civ.* (*Civil War*), *Gal.* (*Gallic War*)

Carm. de fig. (*Carmen de figuris vel schematibus*)

Catull.: Catullus (*Poetry*)

DH: Dionysius of Halicarnassus (*Roman Antiquities*)

Dio: Dio Cassius (*Roman History*)

Fest.: Sextus Pompeius Festus (*De verborum significatu*)

Frontin. (Frontinus): *Strat.* (*Strategemata*)

Fronto: Marcus Cornelius Fronto (*Correspondence*)

Gell.: Aulus Gellius (*Attic Nights*)

Hirtius: *Gal.* (*Gallic War* [book 8 only])

Hist. Aug.: *Historia Augusta*

Hor. (Horace): *Carm.* (*Odes*), *Epist.* (*Epistles*), *Sat.* (*Satires*)

Isid. (Isidore of Seville): *Diff.* (*Differentiae*), *Orig.* (*Origines*)

Iust. (Justinian): *Cod.* (*Codex*), *Dig.* (*Digest*)

Iuv.: Juvenal (*Satires*)

Justin: *Epitome of the Philippic History of Pompeius Trogus*

Liv.: Livy (*History of Rome*); *Perioch.* (*Epitomes*)

Lucian: *Rhet. praec.* (*A Professor of Public Speaking*)

Macr. (Macrobius): *Sat.* (*Saturnalia*)

Marcell. (Marcellus Empericus): *Med.* (*De Medicamentis*)

Nepos: *Epam.* (*Epaminondas*)

Ov. (Ovid): *Am.* (*Amores*), *Ars* (*The Art of Love*), *Epist.* (*Letters from Pontus*)

Paul. (Julius Paulus): *Dig.* (Fragments in Justinian's *Digest*)

Plato: *Phil.* (*Philebus*), *Rep.* (*Republic*)

Plaut. (Plautus): *Amph.* (*Amphitruo*), *Asin.* (*Asinaria*), *Aul.* (*Aulularia*), *Bacch.* (*Bacchides*), *Cas.* (*Casina*), *Cist.* (*Cistellaria*), *Men.* (*Menaechmi*), *Mil.* (*Miles gloriosus*), *Poen.* (*Poenulus*), *Pseud.* (*Pseudolus*), *Stich.* (*Stichus*), *Trin.* (*Trinummus*)

Plin. (Pliny the Elder): *Nat.* (*Natural History*)

Plut. (Plutarch): *Mor.* (*Moralia*) and the following *Lives*: *Ant.* (*Marcus Antonius*),
  Brut. (*Brutus*), *CG* (*Gaius Gracchus*), *Caes.* (*Julius Caesar*), *Cat. Ma.* (*Cato the
  Elder*), *Cat. Mi.* (*Cato the Younger*), *Cic.* (*Cicero*), *Cor.* (*Coriolanus*), *Crass.*
  (*Crassus*), *Publ.* (*Publicola*), *Pomp.* (*Gnaeus Pompeius*), *Rom.* (*Romulus*), *Sull.*
  (*Sulla*)
Pollux: *Onom.* (*Onomasticon*)
Priscianus: *Gramm.* (*Institutiones Grammaticae*)
Quint. (Quintilian): *Inst.* (*On the Training of the Orator*)
Rhet. Her.: *Rhetorica ad Herennium* (*Rhetoric to Gaius Herennius*)
Sall. (Sallust): *Cat.* (*On the Conspiracy of Catiline*), *Hist.* (*Histories*)
Sen. (Seneca the Elder): *Contr.* (*Controversiae*), *Suas.* (*Suasoriae*)
Sen. (Seneca the Younger): *Ben.* (*On Benefits*), *Dial.* (*Dialogues*), *Epist.* (*Moral
  Epistles*), *Nat.* (*Natural Questions*)
Serv. (Servius): commentary on Vergil's *Aeneid*
Suet. (Suetonius): I cite the following biographical works: *Aug.* (*Augustus*),
  Gramm. (*Grammarians*), *Iul.* (*Julius Caesar*), *Rhet.* (*Rhetoricians*), *Tib.* (*Tiberius*)
Tac. (Tacitus): *Ann.* (*Annals*), *Dial.* (*Dialogue on Orators*), *Hist.* (*Histories*)
Ter. (Terence): *Ad.* (*The Brothers*), *Hau.* (*The Self-Tormentor*), *Hec.* (*The Mother-
  in-Law*)
Tertullian: *Apol.* (*Apologeticus*)
Ulp. (Ulpian): *Dig.* (Fragments in Justinian's *Digest*)
Val. Max.: Valerius Maximus (*Facta et dicta memorabilia*)
Varro: *Ling.* (*On the Latin Language*), *Rust.* (*On Agriculture*)
Vell.: Velleius Paterculus
Verg. (Vergil): *Ecl.* (*Eclogues*)
Vir. Ill.: Anonymous biography *De Viris Illustribus* (*Of Famous Men*)

OTHER WORKS CITED

Adams, J. N. 1982. *The Latin Sexual Vocabulary*. Baltimore.
Ahl, F. 1985. *Metaformations*. Ithaca.
Albini, U. 1959. "L'orazione contro Vatinio." *Parola del passato* 14: 172–84.
Alföldi, A. 1966. "Les *cognomina* des magistrats de la République romaine." In
  Mélanges d'archéologie et d'histoire offerts à André Piganiol, 2:709–22. Paris.
Alford, R. 1988. *Naming and Identity: A Cross-Cultural Study of Personal Naming
  Practices*. New Haven.
Allen, W. 1954. "Cicero's Conceit." *Transactions and Proceedings of the American
  Philological Association* 85: 121–44.
Althusser, L. 1990. "Theory, Theoretical Practice and Theoretical Formation:
  Ideology and Ideological Struggle." In *Philosophy and the Spontaneous Philoso-
  phy of the Scientists and Other Essays*, ed. G. Elliot, 1–42. London and New
  York.
Appel, G. 1909. *De Romanorum precationibus*. Giessen.
Arkins, B. 1982. *Sexuality in Catullus*. Altertumswissenschaftliche Texte und
  Studien 8. Hildesheim.
Arndt, E. 1904. "De ridiculi doctrina rhetorica." Diss., Kirchain.

Astin, A. 1978. *Cato the Censor*. Oxford.

Audollent, A. 1904. *Defixionum tabellae*. Paris.

Austin, J. C. 1923. *The Significant Name in Terence*. Illinois Studies in Language and Literature 7.4. Urbana, Ill.

Bächtold-Stäubli, H., ed. 1934–35. *Handwörterbuch des deutschen Aberglaubens*. 10 vols. Handwörterbücher zur deutschen Volkskunde Abt. 1. Berlin and Leipzig.

Badian, E. 1988. "The Clever and the Wise: Two Roman *Cognomina* in Context." In *Vir Bonus Discendi Peritus: Studies in Celebration of Otto Skutsch's Eightieth Birthday*, ed. N. Horsfall. 6–12. *Bulletin of the Institute of Classical Studies*, suppl. 51. London.

Balsdon, J. 1939. "Consular Provinces under the Late Republic: II. Caesar's Gallic Command." *Journal of Roman Studies* 29: 167–83.

———. 1979. *Romans and Aliens*. London.

Barton, C. 1993. *The Sorrows of the Ancient Romans*. Princeton.

Basanoff, V. 1947. *Evocatio*. Paris.

Becker, H. 1963. *The Outsiders*. Glencoe, N.J.

Bell, A. J. 1923. *The Latin Dual and Poetic Diction*. Oxford.

Bentz, M. 1992. "Zum Porträt des Pompeius." *Mitteilungen des Deutschen Archäologischen Instituts, Römische Abteilung* 99: 229–46.

Bergson, H. 1956. "Laughter." In *Comedy*, ed. W. Sypher, 59–190. Garden City, N.Y.

Bieber, M. 1961. *The History of the Greek and Roman Theater*. Princeton.

Billows, R. 1982. "The Last of the Scipios." *American Journal of Ancient History* 7: 53–68.

Blayney, J. 1986. "Theories of Conception in the Ancient Roman World." In *The Family in Ancient Rome: New Perspectives*, ed. B. Rawson, 230–36. Ithaca.

Bloom, A. 1994. "The Body Lies." *New Yorker*, 18 July, 38–49.

Boswell, J. 1980. *Christianity, Social Tolerance, and Homosexuality*. Chicago.

———. 1990. "Concepts, Experience, and Sexuality." *differences* 2.1: 67–87.

Bourdieu, P. 1984. *Distinction: A Social Critique of the Judgement of Taste*, trans. R. Nice. Cambridge, Mass.

———. 1990. *The Logic of Practice*, trans. R. Nice. Stanford.

———. 1991. "The Economy of Linguistic Exchanges." In his *Language and Symbolic Power*, ed. J. B. Thompson, trans. G. Raymond and M. Adamson, 37–89. Cambridge, Mass.

Bremmer, J. 1992. "Walking, Standing, and Sitting in Ancient Greek Culture." In *A Cultural History of Gesture*, ed. J. Bremmer and H. Roodenburg, 15–35. Ithaca.

Broughton, T. R. S. 1951. *Magistrates of the Roman Republic*. 3 vols. Cleveland.

Brown, P. 1988. *The Body and Society*. New York.

Brown, R. 1987. *Lucretius on Love and Sex*. New York.

Brugnola, V. 1896. *Le facezie di Cicerone*. Castello.

Butler, H., and M. Cary, eds. 1927. *C. Suetoni Tranquilli Divus Iulius*. Oxford.

Cantarella, E. 1992. *Bisexuality in the Ancient World*, trans. C. ó Cuillenáin. New Haven.

Caplan, H., trans. 1954. *Rhetorica ad Herennium*. LCL. Cambridge, Mass.

Carandini, A. 1986. *"Domus e insulae sulla pendice settentrionale del Palatino."* *Bullettino della Commissione Archeologica Communale in Roma* 91: 263–65.

Carson, A. "Putting Her in Her Place: Woman, Dirt, and Desire." In D. Halperin, J. Winkler, and F. Zeitlin 135–69.

Cèbe, J.-P. 1967. "Catulle et la physiognomonie." *Annales de la Faculté des Lettres d'Aix* 43: 174–78.

Chase, G. 1897. "The Origin of Roman *Praenomina*." *Harvard Studies in Classical Philology* 8: 103–84.

Clarke, John R. 1993. "The Warren Cup and the Contexts for Representations of Male-to-Male Lovemaking in Augustan and Early Julio-Claudian Art." *Art Bulletin* 75: 275–94.

Coarelli, F. 1980. *Roma*. Rome.

Cohen, David. 1991. *Law, Sexuality, and Society: The Enforcement of Morals in Classical Athens*. Cambridge.

Colin, J. 1952–53. "Juvénal, les baladins et les rétiaires d'après le MS d'Oxford." *Atti dell'Accademia delle Scienze di Torino* 87–88: 315–86.

———. 1955. "Luxe oriental et parfums masculins dans la Rome alexandrine." *Revue belge de philologie et d'histoire* 33: 5–19.

Collier, G., and V. Bricker. 1970. "Nicknames and Social Structure in Zinacantan." *American Anthropologist* 72: 289–302.

Cornish, F., et al., trans. 1912. *Catullus, Tibullus, and Pervigilium Veneris*. LCL. Cambridge, Mass.

Courtney, E. 1980. *A Commentary on the Satires of Juvenal*. London.

Crawford, J. 1984. *M. Tullius Cicero: The Lost and Unpublished Orations*. Hypomnemata 80. Göttingen.

Crook, J. 1967. "A Study in Decoction." *Latomus* 26: 363–76.

Cugusi, M. S. 1982. *Marci Porci Catonis orationum reliquiae*. Turin.

Dalla, D. 1987. *"Ubi Venus mutatur": Omosessualità e diritto nel mondo Romano*. Milan.

D'Arms, J. 1981. *Commerce and Social Standing in Ancient Rome*. Cambridge, Mass.

David, J.-M. 1980. "*Eloquentia popularis* et conduites symboliques des orateurs de la fin de la République: problèmes d'efficacité." *Quaderni di storia* 12: 171–211.

———. 1983. "Les orateurs des municipes à Rome: intégration, réticences et snobismes." In *Les "bourgeoisies" municipales italiennes aux II*ᵉ *et I*ʳ *siècles av. J.-C.*, 309–23. Paris and Naples.

Demmel, M. 1962. "Cicero und Paetus." Diss., Köln.

Dessau, H. 1906. *Inscriptiones Latinae selectae*. Berlin.

Douglas, A. 1958. "Roman Cognomina." *Greece and Rome* 27: 62–66.

Dover, K. 1978. *Greek Homosexuality*. New York.

Dumézil, G. 1970. *Archaic Roman Religion*, trans. P. Krapp. Chicago.

———. 1943. *Servius et la fortune*. Paris.

Dupont, F. 1985. *L'Acteur-roi, ou, Le Theatre dans la Rome antique*. Paris.

Earl, D. 1967. *The Moral and Political Tradition of Rome*. Ithaca.

Edwards, C. 1993. *The Politics of Immorality in Ancient Rome*. Cambridge.

Elliott, R. 1960. *The Power of Satire: Magic, Ritual, Art.* Princeton.

Erbse, H. 1957. "Textkritische Beiträge zu den Biographien Plutarchs." *Rheinisches Museum*, 3rd ser., 100: 271–94.

Evans, E. 1935. "Roman Descriptions of Personal Appearance in History and Biography." *Harvard Studies in Classical Philology* 46: 43–84.

——. 1969. *Physiognomics in the Ancient World. Transactions of the American Philosophical Society* 59.5. Philadelphia.

Feher, M., et al., eds. 1989. *Fragments for a History of the Human Body.* 3 vols. *Zone* 3–5. New York and Cambridge, Mass.

Finley, M. 1985. *The Ancient Economy.* London.

Flambard, J.-M. 1978. "Nouvel examen d'un dossier prosopographique: le cas de Sex. Clodius/Cloelius." *Mélanges d'Archéologie et d'Histoire de l'École Française de Rome, Antiquité* 90: 235–45.

Fordyce, C. 1961. *Catullus: A Commentary.* Oxford.

Foucault, M. 1977. "Nietzsche, Genealogy, and History." In his *Language, Counter-Memory, Practice: Selected Essays and Interviews*, ed. D. Bouchard, trans. D. Bouchard and S. Simon, 139–64. Ithaca.

——. 1980. *The History of Sexuality*, trans. R. Hurley. New York.

——. 1985. *The Use of Pleasure*, trans. R. Hurley. New York.

Fraenkel, E. 1925. Review of F. Beckmann, "Zauberei und Recht in Roms Frühzeit" (diss., Münster 1923). *Gnomon* 1: 186–200.

——. 1961. "Two Poems of Catullus." *Journal of Roman Studies* 51: 46–53.

Frank, T. 1920. "*Tulliana.*" *American Journal of Philology* 41: 275–82.

Frazer, J. 1911. *The Golden Bough.* 3rd ed. 12 vols. London.

Freese, J., trans. 1926. *Aristotle: The "Art" of Rhetoric.* LCL. Cambridge, Mass.

Freud, S. 1960. *Jokes and Their Relation to the Unconscious*, trans. J. Strachey. In vol. 8 of *The Complete Psychological Works of Sigmund Freud*, ed. J. Strachey. London.

Frye, N. 1957. *Anatomy of Criticism.* Princeton.

Fuss, D. 1989. *Essentially Speaking: Feminism, Nature, and Difference.* New York and London.

Garber, M. 1991. *Vested Interests: Cross-dressing and Cultural Anxiety.* New York.

Garton, C. 1972. *Personal Aspects of the Roman Theatre.* Toronto.

Garzetti, A. 1954. *Plutarchi vita Caesaris.* Florence.

Geertz, C. 1984. "Anti Anti-Relativism." *American Anthropologist* 86: 263–78.

Geffcken, K. 1973. *Comedy in the "pro Caelio."* *Mnemosyne*, suppl. 30. Leiden.

Gelzer, M. 1968. *Caesar: Politician and Statesman*, trans. P. Needham. Cambridge, Mass.

Gilmore, D. 1987. *Aggression and Community: Paradoxes of Andalusian Culture.* New Haven.

Gleason, M. 1991. "The Semiotics of Gender: Physiognomy and Self-Fashioning in the Second Century CE." In D. Halperin, J. Winkler, and F. Zeitlin 389–415. Incorporated into Gleason 1995, chap. 3.

——. 1995. *Making Men: Sophists and Self-Presentation in Ancient Rome.* Princeton.

Goetz, G. 1888–1923. *Corpus glossariorum latinorum.* 5 vols. Leipzig.

Golden, M. 1991. "Thirteen Years of Homosexuality (and Other Recent Works on Sex, Gender, and the Body in Ancient Greece)." *Échos du monde classique* 35: 327–40.

Gombrich, E. 1982. "The Mask and the Face." In *The Image and the Eye: Further Studies in the Psychology of Pictorial Representation*, 105–36. Oxford.

Gonfroy, F. 1978. "Homosexualité et idéologie esclavagiste chez Cicéron." *Dialogues d'histoire ancienne* 4: 219–62.

Graf, F. 1991. "Prayer in Magic and Religious Ritual." In *Magika Hiera*, ed. C. Faraone and D. Obbink, 188–213. Oxford.

———. 1992. "Gestures and Conventions: The Gestures of Roman Actors and Orators." In *A Cultural History of Gesture*, ed. J. Bremmer and H. Roodenburg, 36–58. Ithaca.

Grant, M. 1924. *The Ancient Rhetorical Theories of the Laughable*. University of Wisconsin Studies in Language and Literature 21. Madison, Wisc.

Grant, W. 1947. "Cicero, *ad Fam.* viii.8.9." *Classical Review* 61: 10–11.

Grassmann, V. 1966. *Die erotischen Epoden des Horaz*. Zetemata 39. Munich.

Greenblatt, S. 1987. "Capitalist Culture and the Circulatory System." In *The Aims of Representation*, ed. M. Krieger, 257–73. New York.

Greenidge, A. H. J. 1901. *The Legal Procedure of Cicero's Time*. Oxford.

Griffin, J. 1976. "Augustan Poetry and the Life of Luxury." *Journal of Roman Studies* 66: 87–105.

Groot, J. de. 1910. *The Religious System of China*. 6 vols. Leyden.

Gruen, E. 1974. *The Last Generation of the Roman Republic*. Berkeley.

———. 1984. *The Hellenistic World and the Coming of Rome*. Berkeley.

Haines, C., trans. 1957. *The Correspondence of Marcus Cornelius Fronto*. 2 vols. LCL. Cambridge, Mass.

Hallett, J. 1977. "*Perusinae glandes* and the Changing Image of Augustus." *American Journal of Ancient History* 2: 151–71.

———. 1978. "*Morigerari*: Suet. *Tib.* 44." *Antiquité classique* 47: 196–200.

———. 1984. *Fathers and Daughters in Roman Society: Women and the Elite Family*. Princeton.

———. 1989a. "Female Homoeroticism and the Denial of Roman Reality in Latin Literature." *Yale Journal of Criticism* 3: 209–27.

———. 1989b. "Woman as *Same* and *Other* in the Classical Roman Elite." *Helios* 16: 59–78.

Halperin, D. 1990. *One Hundred Years of Homosexuality*. New York.

Halperin, D., J. Winkler, and F. Zeitlin, eds. 1991. *Before Sexuality*. Princeton.

Hands, A. 1962. "Humour and Vanity in Cicero." In *Collana di Studi Ciceroniani*, ed. E. Paratore, 2:115–25. Rome.

Haury, A. 1955. *L'ironie et l'humour chez Cicéron*. Leiden.

Henderson, J. 1991. *The Maculate Muse*. Rev. ed. New York.

Heraeus, W. 1902. "Die römische Soldatensprache." *Archiv für lateinische Lexikographie und Grammatik* 12: 255–80.

Héritier-Augé, F. 1989. "Semen and Blood: Some Ancient Theories concerning their Genesis and Relationship." In M. Feher et al. 3:158–75.

Herter, H. 1927. Review of M. Grant, *The Ancient Rhetorical Theories of the Laughable* (Madison, Wisc., 1924). *Gnomon* 3: 721–27.

Hijmans, B. 1978. "Significant Names and Their Function in Apuleius' *Metamorphoses*." In *Aspects of Apuleius' "Golden Ass,"* ed. B. Hijmans and R. van der Paardt, 107–22. Groningen.

Hirzel, R. 1962. *Der Name: Ein Beitrag zu seiner Geschichte im Altertum und besonders bei den Griechen.* Amsterdam. Originally published as *Abhandlungen der Sächsischen Akademie der Wissenschaften. Philologisch-historischen Klasse* 36 (1927).

Hofmann, J. B. 1951. *Lateinische Umgangssprache.* Heidelberg.

Holst, H. 1925. *Die Wortspiele in Ciceros Reden.* Symbolae Osloenses 1. Oslo.

Hopkins, K. 1983. *Death and Renewal.* Cambridge.

Housman, A. E. 1918. "Jests of Plautus, Cicero, and Trimalchio." *Classical Review* 32: 162–64.

Hubbell, H., ed. and trans. 1949. *Cicero: De inventione.* LCL. Cambridge, Mass.

Hughes, Joseph J. 1992. "Piso's Eyebrows." *Mnemosyne* 45: 234–37.

Jacobelli, L. 1995. *Le pitture erotiche delle Terme Suburbane di Pompei.* Rome.

Janko, R. 1984. *Aristotle on Comedy.* London.

Jerome, Thomas. 1923. *Aspects of the Study of Roman History.* New York and London.

Jones, D. 1970. Review of I. Kajanto, *The Latin Cognomina* (Helsinki, 1965). *Classical Review* 84: 208.

Jordan, H. 1860 *M. Catonis praeter librum de re rustica quae exstant.* Stuttgart.

Kajanto, I. 1965. *The Latin Cognomina.* Helsinki.

Kelly, J. M. 1966. *Roman Litigation.* Oxford.

————. 1976. *Studies in the Civil Judicature of the Roman Republic.* Oxford.

Kennedy, D. 1993. *The Arts of Love: Five Studies in the Discourse of Roman Love Elegy.* Cambridge.

Kennedy, G. 1972. *The Art of Rhetoric in the Roman World.* Princeton.

Kent, R., trans. 1938. *Varro: De Lingua Latina.* 2 vols. LCL. Cambridge, Mass.

Keyes, C., trans. 1928. *Cicero: De Re Publica, De Legibus.* LCL. Cambridge, Mass.

Kiefer, O. 1934. *Sexual Life in Ancient Rome,* trans. G. and H. Highet. London.

Kirk, G. 1985. *The Iliad: A Commentary.* Vol. 1, *Books 1–4.* Cambridge.

Koch, H. 1861. "Zu Cicero's Rede *pro Sestio.*" *Sokrates* 15: 384.

Krenkel, W. 1980. "*Fellatio* and *irrumatio*." *Wissenschaftliche Zeitschrift der Wilhelm-Pieck-Universität, Rostock* 29: 77–88.

————. 1981. "Tonguing." *Wissenschaftliche Zeitschrift der Wilhelm-Pieck-Universität, Rostock* 30: 37–54.

Laqueur, T. 1990. *Making Sex: Body and Gender from the Greeks to Freud.* Cambridge, Mass.

Latte, K. 1960. *Römische Religionsgeschichte.* Munich.

Leeman, A. D. 1982. "The Technique of Persuasion in Cicero's *pro Murena*." In *Éloquence et rhétorique chez Cicéron,* ed. W. Stroh and W. Ludwig, 193–236. Entretiens sur l'antiquité classique 28. Vandoeuveres-Geneve.

Lesky, E. 1950. *Die Zeugungs- und Vererbungslehren der Antike und ihr Nachwirken.* Abhandlungen der Akademie der Wissenschaften und der Literatur, Mainz. Geistes- und sozialwissenschaftliche Klasse 19. Wiesbaden.

Lilja, S. 1965. *Terms of Abuse in Roman Comedy.* Helsinki.

Lind, L. R. 1976. "Primitivity and Roman Ideas: The Survivals." *Latomus* 35: 245–68.

Linderski, J. 1986. "The Augural Law." *Aufstieg und Niedergang der römischen Welt* II 16.3: 2146–312.

Loposzko, T. 1989. "Sextus Clodius Damio?" *Historia* 38: 498–503.

Luck, G. 1982. "Love Elegy." In *The Cambridge History of Classical Literature*. Vol. 2, *Latin Literature*, ed. E. J. Kenney, 405–19. Cambridge.

MacMullen, R. 1982. "Roman Attitudes to Greek Love." *Historia* 31: 484–502.

Magli, P. 1989. "The Face and the Soul," trans. U. Lubin. In M. Feher et al. 2:87–127.

Magnino, D. 1963. *Plutarchi vita Ciceronis*. Florence.

Malcovati, E. 1976. *Oratorum Romanorum fragmenta*. Turin.

Manfredini, A. 1985. "Qui commutant cum feminis vestem." *Revue internationale des droits de l'Antiquité* 32: 257–71.

Manzo, A. 1969. *Facete dicta Tulliana*. Biblioteca della Rivista di Studi Classici, Saggi Vari 5. Turin.

Marache, R. 1978. *Aulu-Gelle: Les Nuits Attiques*. Vol. 2. Paris.

Marcus, M. 1976. "Power of a Name." *Psychology Today*, October, 75–80.

Marrou, H. 1956. *A History of Education in Antiquity*, trans. G. Lamb. London.

Marx, F. 1904–5. *C. Lucilii carminum reliquiae*. 2 vols. Leipzig.

Maslakov, G. 1984. "Valerius Maximus and Roman Historiography: A Study in the *exempla* Tradition." *Aufstieg und Niedergang der römischen Welt* II 32.1: 437–96.

May, J. M. 1988. *Trials of Character: The Eloquence of Ciceronian Ethos*. Chapel Hill, N.C.

McCartney, E. 1918–19. "Puns and Plays on Proper Names." *Classical Journal* 14: 343–58.

Merguet, H. 1962. *Lexikon zu den Reden des Cicero*. Hildesheim.

Meusel, H., F. Kramer, and W. Dittenberger, eds. 1968. *C. Iulii Caesaris commentarii de bello Gallico*. Dublin.

Mommsen, T. 1864. *Römische Forschungen*. Berlin.

———. 1887–88. *Römisches Staatsrecht*. 3 vols. Leipzig.

Monaco, G. 1968. *Cicerone: L'excursus "de ridiculis."* Palumbo.

———. 1970. *Quintiliano: Il capitolo "de risu."* Palumbo.

Montaigne, M. de. 1958. *Essays*, trans. J. M. Cohen. New York.

Monteil, P. 1964. *Beau et laid en Latin*. Paris.

Neudling, C. 1955. *A Prosopography to Catullus*. Oxford.

Nicholas, B. 1962. *An Introduction to Roman Law*. Oxford.

Nicolet, C. 1980. *The World of the Citizen in Republican Rome*, trans. P. Falla. Berkeley.

Nietzsche, F. 1956. *The Genealogy of Morals*, trans. F. Golffing. Garden City, N.Y.

Nisbet, R. G. M. 1958. "The *invectiva in Ciceronem* and *epistula secunda* of Pseudo-Sallust." *Journal of Roman Studies* 48: 30–32.

Ogilvie, R. 1965. *Commentary on Livy 1–5*. Oxford.

Onians, R. 1951. *The Origins of European Thought*. Cambridge.

Opelt, I. 1965. *Die lateinischen Schimpfwörter und verwandte sprachliche Erscheinungen*. Heidelberg.

Otto, A. 1890. *Die Sprichwörter und sprichwörtlichen Redensarten der Römer.* Leipzig.

Pack, R. 1938. "Errors as Subjects of Comic Mirth." *Classical Philology* 33: 405–10.

Paoli, U. 1963. *Rome: Its People, Life, and Customs*, trans. R. Macnaghten. New York.

Patzer, H. 1982. *Die griechische Knabenliebe.* Wiesbaden.

Peradotto, J. 1990. *Man in the Middle Voice: Name and Narration in the "Odyssey."* Princeton.

Perl, G. 1982. "Der Redner Helvius Mancia und der *pictus Gallus*: Cic. *de orat.* 2.266." *Philologus* 126: 59–67.

Perrin, B., trans. 1919. *Plutarch: The Parallel Lives.* 11 vols. LCL. Cambridge, Mass.

Peter, H. 1897. "Die Litteratur der Witzworte in Rom und die geflügelten Worte im Munde Caesars." *Neue Jahrbücher für Philologie und Paedagogik* 155: 853–60.

Phillips, O. 1968. "Lucan's Grove." *Classical Philology* 63: 296–300.

Plass, P. 1988. *Wit and the Writing of History.* Madison, Wisc.

Potter, D. 1986. *The Singing Detective.* London and Boston.

Poulsen, F. 1936. "Les portraits de Pompeius Magnus." *Revue archéologique*, 6th ser., 7: 16–52.

Rackham, H., trans. 1931. *Cicero: De finibus bonorum et malorum.* LCL. Cambridge, Mass.

———, trans. 1944. *Aristotle: Politics.* LCL. Cambridge, Mass.

Ramage, E. 1973. *"Urbanitas": Ancient Sophistication and Refinement.* Norman, Okla.

Rawson, B. 1968. Review of I. Kajanto, *The Latin Cognomina* (Helsinki, 1965). *Classical Philology* 63: 154.

Rawson, E. 1975. "Caesar's Heritage: Hellenistic Kings and Their Roman Equals." *Journal of Roman Studies* 65: 148–59.

Richlin, A. 1981. "The Meaning of *irrumare* in Catullus and Martial." *Classical Philology* 76: 40–46.

———. 1988. "Systems of Food Imagery in Catullus." *Classical World* 81: 355–63.

———. 1992a. *The Garden of Priapus.* Rev. ed. Oxford.

———. 1992b. "Roman Oratory, Pornography, and the Silencing of Anita Hill." *Southern California Law Review* 65: 1321–32.

———. 1993. "Not before Homosexuality." *Journal of the History of Sexuality* 3: 523–73.

Ritti, T. 1977. "Immagini onomastiche sui monumenti sepolcrali di età imperiale." *Memorie della Classe di Scienze morali e storiche dell'Accademia dei Lincei* 21: 257–397.

Rogin, M. 1987. *"Ronald Reagan," the Movie: And Other Episodes in Political Demonology.* Berkeley.

Rose, H. J. 1926. *Primitive Culture in Italy.* London.

Rossi, O. 1924. "De M. Catonis dictis et apophthegmatis." *Athenaeum*, n.s., 2: 174–82.

Rudd, N. 1966. *The Satires of Horace.* London.

Saint-Denis, E. 1965. *Essais sur le rire et le sourire des Latins.* Publications de l'université de Dijon 32. Paris.

Saller, R. 1991. "Corporal Punishment, Authority, and Obedience in the Roman Household." In *Marriage, Divorce, and Children in Ancient Rome*, ed. B. Rawson, 144–65. Oxford.

Salmon, E. T. 1982. *The Making of Roman Italy*. London.

Santoro L'Hoir, F. 1992. *The Rhetoric of Gender Terms*. Mnemosyne, suppl. 120. Leiden.

Scarborough, J. 1969. *Roman Medicine*. Ithaca.

Schrader, G. 1989. "Der unschuldige Verbrecher. Zur Geschichte der Kriminalanthropologie." In *Natur nach Mass: Physiognomik zwischen Wissenschaft und Ästhetik*, ed. R. Fischer, 59–75. Marburg.

Schulze, W. 1966. *Zur Geschichte lateinischer Eigennamen*. Berlin. Originally published as *Abhandlungen der königlich Geschichte der Wissenschaften zu Göttingen. Philosophisch-historische Klasse*, Neue Folge V, 5 (Berlin 1933).

Schur, E. 1971. *Labeling Deviant Behavior: Its Sociological Implications*. New York.

Schwartz, J. 1948. "Sur quelques anecdotes concernant César et Cicéron." *Revue des études anciennes* 50: 264–71.

Seager, R. 1976. *Pompey: A Political Biography*. Oxford.

Segal, E. 1968. *Roman Laughter*. New York.

Shackleton Bailey, D. R. 1956. *Propertiana*. Cambridge.

————. 1960. "Sex. Clodius—Sex. Cloelius." *Classical Quarterly* 54: 41–42.

————. 1981. "*Ecce iterum Cloelius*." *Historia* 30: 383.

————. 1982. "Notes on Cicero's *Philippics*." *Philologus* 126: 217–26.

————, trans. 1988a. *Cicero: Philippics*. Chapel Hill, N.C.

————. 1988b. *Onomasticon to Cicero's Speeches*. Norman, Okla.

Shaw, A. 1955. "A Historical Commentary on the Second Book of Macrobius' Saturnalia." Diss., Pennsylvania.

Sickinger, J. 1883. "De linguae Latinae apud Plutarchum et reliquiis et vestigiis." Diss., Heidelberg.

Sittl, C. 1890. *Die Gebärden der Griechen und Römer*. Leipzig.

Skinner, M. 1982. "Pretty Lesbius." *Transactions and Proceedings of the American Philological Association* 112: 197–208.

Smith, K. 1913. *The Elegies of Albius Tibullus*. New York.

Stanley, K. 1963. "Rome, *eros*, and the *versus Romae*." *Greek, Roman and Byzantine Studies* 4: 237–49.

Stevens, C. 1938. "The Terminal Date of Caesar's Command." *American Journal of Philology* 59: 169–208.

Stroh, W. 1975. *Taxis und Taktik*. Stuttgart.

Süss, W. 1910. *Ethos*. Leipzig and Berlin.

Syme, R. 1939. *The Roman Revolution*. Oxford.

————. 1956. "Some Pisones in Tacitus." *Journal of Roman Studies* 46: 17–21.

————. 1979. *Roman Papers*. Vol. 1. Oxford.

Tarrant, R. 1976. *Seneca: Agamemnon*. Cambridge.

Thalmann, W. 1988. "Thersites: Comedy, Scapegoats, and Heroic Ideology in the *Iliad*." *Transactions and Proceedings of the American Philological Association* 118: 1–28.

Thornton, B. 1991. "Constructionism and Ancient Greek Sex." *Helios* 18: 181–93.

Thorp, J. 1992. "The Social Construction of Homosexuality." *Phoenix* 46: 54–61.

Thylander, H. 1952. *Étude sur l'épigraphie latine*. Lund.

Tracy, V. 1976. "Roman Dandies and Transvestites." *Échos du monde classique* 20: 60–63.

Treggiari, S. 1969. *Roman Freedmen during the Late Republic*. Oxford.

Usener, H. 1901. "Italische Volksjustiz." *Rheinisches Museum* 56: 1–28.

Vasaly, A. 1993. *Representations: Images of the World in Ciceronian Oratory*. Berkeley.

Veyne, P. 1985. "Homosexuality in Ancient Rome." In *Western Sexuality: Practice and Precept in Past and Present Times*, ed. P. Ariès and A. Béjin, trans. A. Forster, 26–35. Oxford.

Versnel, H. 1970. *Triumphus: An Inquiry into the Origin, Development, and Meaning of the Roman Triumph*. Leiden.

Wagenvoort, H. 1947. *Roman Dynamism*. Oxford.

Warmington, E., trans. 1979. *Remains of Old Latin*. 4 vols. LCL. Cambridge, Mass.

Weeks, J. 1981. "Discourse, Desire, and Sexual Deviance: Some Problems in a History of Homosexuality." In *The Making of the Modern Homosexual*, ed. R. Plummer, 76–111. London.

Weinstock, S. 1971. *Divus Iulius*. Oxford.

Wessner, P., ed. 1931. *Scholia in Juvenalem vetustiora*. Leipzig.

Williams, G. 1962. "Poetry in the Moral Climate of Augustan Rome." *Journal of Roman Studies* 52: 28–46.

———. 1978. *Change and Decline: Roman Literature in the Early Empire*. Berkeley.

Winkler, J. 1990. *The Constraints of Desire: The Anthropology of Sex and Gender in Ancient Greece*. New York.

Wiseman, T. P. 1971. *New Men in the Roman Senate, 139 B.C.–A.D. 14*. London.

Wissowa, G. 1912. *Religion und Kultus der Römer*. Munich.

Woodman, A. J. 1983. *Velleius Paterculus: The Caesarian and Augustan Narrative (2.41–93)*. Cambridge.

Yavetz, Z. 1983. *Julius Caesar and His Public Image*. Ithaca.

INDEX LOCORUM ET IOCORUM

This index includes all passages from ancient authors cited in the text or notes. Page numbers in italics mark passages I think would have provoked laughter in the Roman audience. The listing hardly claims to be definitive but represents the range of Republican invective, from gentle irony to simple wordplay to savage abuse.

GENERAL INDEX

Roman names are listed either under the form in general use or by the name that occurs in the ancient texts I cite. For a listing of Greek and Latin passages cited, see the *Index Locorum et Iocorum*.

About the Author

ANTHONY CORBEILL is Assistant Professor of Classics at the University of Kansas.